THE PARTITION OF BENGAL AND ASSAM, 1932–1947

The fragmentation of Bengal and Assam in 1947 was a crucial moment in India's socio-political history as a nation state. Both British Indian provinces were divided as much through the actions of the Muslim League as through those of Congress and the British colonial power. Attributing partition largely to Hindu communalists is, therefore, historically inaccurate and factually misleading.

The Partition of Bengal and Assam, 1932–1947 provides a review of constitutional and party politics as well as of popular attitudes and perceptions. The primary aim of this book is to unravel the intricate socio-economic and political processes that led up to partition, as Hindus and Muslims competed ferociously for the new power and privileges to be conferred on them with independence. As shown in the book, well before they divorced at a political level, Hindus and Muslims had been cleft apart by their socio-economic differences. Partition was probably inevitable.

Bidyut Chakrabarty is Professor and Chair of Political Science at the University of Delhi, India.

THE PARTITION OF BENGAL AND ASSAM, 1932–1947

Contour of freedom

Bidyut Chakrabarty

LONDON AND NEW YORK

First published 2004 by RoutledgeCurzon

This edition published 2016 by Routledge
2 Park Square, Milton Park, Abingdon, Oxfordshire OX14 4RN
711 Third Avenue, New York, NY 10017

First issued in paperback 2016

Routledge is an imprint of the Taylor and Francis Group, an informa business

© 2004 Bidyut Chakrabarty

Typeset in Times by Wearset Ltd, Boldon, Tyne and Wear

All rights reserved. No part of this book may be reprinted or reproduced or utilised in any form or by any electronic, mechanical, or other means, now known or hereafter invented, including photocopying and recording, or in any information storage or retrieval system, without permission in writing from the publishers.

British Library Cataloguing in Publication Data
A catalogue record for this book is available from the British Library

Library of Congress Cataloging in Publication Data
A catalog record for this book has been requested

ISBN 13: 978-1-138-86224-1 (pbk)
ISBN 13: 978-0-415-32889-0 (hbk)

DEDICATED TO PABLO, BARBIE AND
TUTUN FOR THEIR CRITICAL
APPRECIATION OF MY CREATIVITY

CONTENTS

List of tables		viii
Acknowledgements		ix
Abbreviations		x
	Introduction	1
1	The Hindu–Muslim differences: the socio-economic and cultural dimensions	36
2	Divide and rule: the Communal Award and its implications in Bengal	55
3	Politics of accommodation and confrontation: the second partition of Bengal	85
4	An alternative to partition: the united Bengal scheme	132
5	Redefining borders: the Boundary Commission and the partition of Bengal	154
6	Construction and consolidation of identities: the Sylhet referendum and partition	176
7	History of partition or partition of history? The fractured and wounded voice of the people	209
	Conclusion	239
	Glossary	251
	Bibliographical essay	253
	Bibliography	262
	Index	273

TABLES

1.1	Categories of agricultural workers as a percentage of the total agricultural workforce in British Bengal, 1911–31	37
1.2	Percentage of total population and rent-receivers in majority Muslim divisions, 1911	38
1.3	Changes in cultivated areas in the moribund and active delta regions	39
1.4	Collection of rents in some east Bengal districts, 1928–41	40
1.5	The increase in voters between 1920 and 1937	50
2.1	Elected members of the District Boards in Bengal, 1928	58
2.2	Increase in Muslim seats in the Bengal and Punjab legislatures	60
2.3	The Communal Award: distribution of seats	63
2.4	Election results, 1937	78
3.1	Numbers of abducted women, dead and injured in the riots in Tippera and Noakhali	106
3.2	Distribution of the 30 000 Armed Forces	110
4.1	Percentage of Muslims and non-Muslims by district according to the Census of India 1941	148
5.1	Breakdown of population according to the Census of India, 1941	158
5.2	Voting pattern in referendum held on 6–7 July 1947	159
5.3	District of Murshidabad: proportions of Muslims and non-Muslims, 1941	166
5.4	Demographic composition of each police station in the district of Nadia	166
5.5	Subdivisions of Barasat and Bashirhat: proportions of Muslims and non-Muslims, 1941	167
5.6	Demographic composition of police stations in Malda, 1941	167
6.1	Subdivisions of Sylhet	177
6.2	Demographic composition of Sylhet	179
6.3	Labourers from outside Sylhet	180
6.4	Results of the Sylhet Referendum, 6–7 July 1947	188
6.5	Percentage of Hindus voting for remaining in Assam	194

ACKNOWLEDGEMENTS

I have thought about and written parts of this book over the last couple of years, but put it together in a draft form during my Cambridge sojourn in 2003. Without the support of Dr Gordon Johnson, the President of Wolfson College, Cambridge, it would not have been possible. I am thankful to Professor Partha Chatterjee for having supported the project since it was mooted. Despite his teaching and other commitments at Harvard, Sugato was always very helpful during the preparation of this book. My children – Urna and Pablo – always provided emotional resources by shifting my attention away when I was stuck while articulating my thoughts. By descending at regular intervals, my best critic made me realise the importance of a family ambience in creativity. It would not be improper to record my appreciation for my mother, who managed the children when I was struggling to meet the dateline. I am grateful to Rajinder, who was always available when needed. I remember Bhuwan, who was equally helpful. I appreciate Prakash for his support. My gratitude goes to Ashok and Minu for their help in making my campus life most interesting and memorable. I am indebted to Mamatadi and Piklu for having made my stay in London during the preparation of this book most comfortable and exciting.

Some of the ideas in this book were presented in seminars in different parts of the globe. I am thankful to those who helped in streamlining my arguments and thoughts on such a complex subject as the formation of nation in a transitional society. I gratefully acknowledge the support given by the publishers of my articles on related themes in *Modern Asian Studies* (Cambridge 23, 3, 1998), *Indian Economic and Social History Review* (Sage 39, 4, 2003) and *South Asia* (South Asian Studies, Australia 26, 2, 2003).

Bidyut Chakrabarty
Delhi, India

ABBREVIATIONS

ABP	*Amrita Bazar Patrika*
AICC	All India Congress Committee
BLC	Bengal Legislative Council
BPC	Bengal Provincial Congress
BPCC	Bengal Provincial Congress Committee
CPI	Communist Party of India
CSASC	Centre for South Asian Studies, Cambridge
IAR	Indian Annual Register
IESHR	*Indian Economic and Social History Review*
IOR	India Office Records
IS	*Indian Struggle*
JAS	*Journal of Asian Studies*
JNP	Jawaharlal Nehru Papers
JNSW	Jawaharlal Nehru Selected Works
JPS	*Journal of Peasant Studies*
KPP	Krishak Praja Party
MAS	*Modern Asian Studies*
ML	Muslim League
NAI	National Archives of India
NMML	Nehru Memorial Museum and Library
PCC	Provincial Congress Committee
WBSA	West Bengal State Archives

INTRODUCTION

The 1947 Great Divide is the most significant signpost in the evolution of South Asia as a socio-political unit.[1] After having drawn the boundaries of two independent states, India and Pakistan, the British had finally withdrawn. If there was cause to rejoice at the end of colonialism, the celebrations were undoubtedly marred by a tragic partition along religious lines which took an unacceptable toll in human life and suffering. The process of decolonisation was, on the one hand, a clear failure of the nationalist leadership who strove hard to sustain India's political unity since Pakistan was born on the basis of two-nation theory. On the other hand, for those supporting the demand for a separate Muslim state, colonialism came to an end with a clear positive note. Partition is therefore centrally constitutive of nationhood. Not only was India redefined; Pakistan was also articulated in socio-political terms in the wake of the struggle, and spearheaded by the Muslim League, linking Muslims irrespective of socio-economic status to form a sovereign Muslim state. Partition is a moment of contest as well. Both the Hindus and Muslims redefined their identities through a process of contestation of vision, contestation of beliefs and contestation of history. The period between 1932 and 1947 sharply shows the mutation in the formation of Hindus and Muslims as communities opposed to each other in the political arena. What was distinctive about this period was the growth of the communities as political units in a permanent adversarial relationship. This was further consolidated following the introduction of the communal electorate in the 1937 provincial elections. With the acceptance of the principle of majority, Muslims automatically became the most powerful community in Bengal and Punjab by their sheer demographic strength. In other words, religious identity as a demographic category became probably the single most crucial criterion in determining the distribution of governmental power in these Muslim-majority provinces. Yet it would be entirely wrong to gloss over the internal differences among the Muslims that rallied around the campaign for Pakistan as a bloc. So, the questions that need to be asked are how and why did the idea of Pakistan cause such excitement? How could so many disparate groups attain the goal of Pakistan? How could a highly stratified community, united only by religious ties, act in unison to fight for Pakistan? What were the factors that bridged the regional, class and sectional chasms to develop overriding interests in a separate Muslim state? In other words, how and why did the two-nation theory strike roots undermining the syncretistic tradition? Answers to these questions may not be easily available, although, drawing upon empirical materials from Bengal and Assam, an attempt will be made here to tackle some of them. Undoubtedly, the political history of the partitioned provinces provides significant clues to grasp the processes that finally led to partition, which Jinnah described as 'a surgical operation' to cut India into two halves.[2]

The respective nations of India and Pakistan began their journeys as soon as the transfer of power was formally executed following the acceptance of India's bifurcation by even the Gandhian Congress, which always held views challenging Jinnah's two-nation theory. What this signifies is the immense importance of partition, which is usually conceptualised in contrasting ways. For the Congress, partition was but a decisive milestone in the growth of a nation state that failed to negotiate a satisfactory solution to the problem of religious difference. To the Muslim League and its supporters, partition was associated with victory and liberation from both the British rule and possible Hindu domination in future India. So what was 'nationalism' to the League was 'sectarianism' to the Congress. In grasping these binary opposite ideological configurations, the Great Divide seems to be equally significant. Partition was therefore not merely an imperial device, it was also the culmination of a process that began unfolding with the consolidation of Muslims as a distinct socio-political community.

Notwithstanding the definite role of the *divide-et-impera*,[3] the acceptance of the League as the true representatives of the Muslims in the Muslim-majority provinces of Bengal and Punjab clearly indicates a radical change in India's political landscape. It had become clear by 1940 that Bengal and Punjab 'will significantly count in a settlement of Moslem problems ... [and] if these two provinces withdraw support, Jinnah's position might rapidly be undermined'.[4] By associating the Congress with the Hindus, the largest section of India's Muslim population articulated their vision of freedom in terms of Jinnah's two-nation theory. Thus the future of India was decided not only by those who remained decisive in 'high politics', but also by those actors at the grassroots who translated the idioms of 'divisive' politics in terms of concrete plans and programmes. In other words, though the *Quaid-i-Azam* was the architect of the two-nation theory, his role as the founder of a separate Muslim nation state was largely supplemented by those League volunteers who genuinely believed, due to a complex web of events and happenings in the 1940s, in Pakistan as the fulfilment of their aspired goal. In espousing the cause of Pakistan, what figured prominently were communal sentiments directed against the Hindus for their alleged conspiracy with the British to defeat the League campaign.[5] In fact, the 1945 Direct Action resolution was adopted by the Muslim League to 'protest against the "letting down" of the Muslim League by the Viceroy and Cabinet delegation, "under pressure" from the Congress and against the evident desire of the Congress to dominate the Muslims and other minorities in India'.[6]

The 1947 Great Divide

Partition is 'the moment of the constitutional establishment of two dominions with accompanying bloodbath'.[7] Pressing for a separate Muslim state, the 1940 Lahore resolution was the first official pronouncement of Pakistan or partition by the Muslim League. Though the term 'Pakistan' was nowhere mentioned, by demanding an independent state/states for the Muslims, the resolution translated the goal of a sovereign Muslim state in concrete terms.[8] Seeking to organise Indian Muslims around the Pakistan demand, the resolution was remarkable for at least two important reasons; first, that the resolution was proposed by Fazlul Haq, the most popular Muslim leader in Bengal, suggests the growing dominance of the League in the Muslim-majority provinces; and secondly, for the first time an unequivocal demand was formally articulated insisting that the areas in India in which Muslims constituted a majority should be made into an independent state containing autonomous and sovereign units.[9] Furthermore, it argued that Indian Muslims constituted a majority-nation in the north-west and east of India, and ought to be treated at par with the Hindu majority in all future constitutional negotiations.

The idea contained in the resolution was not novel. Since it was proposed formally in an annual session of the League, which 'had, by then, the backing of the Moslem population of India', it was, as Khaliquzzamman reminisced, 'an avalanche which uprooted all the old fossilised structure of the political shibboleths which had kept the minds of Indian Muslims engaged for about a century, and paved the way for a direct march towards a definite goal'.[10] Writing on this resolution, Edward Benthall insisted that 'it would be dangerous to brush Pakistan lightly aside because there is no doubt that the scheme has fired the imagination of millions of Moslems throughout India'.[11] On another occasion, he further reiterated that 'the Moslems are not prepared to subject themselves to the majority community which encircles them, and assertions are openly made that civil war will follow any settlement that places the Moslems into the hands of the Hindu majority'.[12] This is what guided the official assessment of the situation. Wavell, responding to the Bengal Governor, Casey, wrote, 'I do not believe that Pakistan will work. It creates new minority problems quite as bad as those we have now and the Pakistan state or states would be economically unsound ... but for the mass of Muslims, it is a real possibility and has very strong sentimental appeal. [Hence] we cannot openly denounce Pakistan until we have something to offer in its place'.[13]

Despite doubts regarding Pakistan's viability, the colonial power became increasingly sensitive to the claims advanced by the Muslim League. By 1945, not only did the League insist on 'the division of India as the only solution of the complex constitutional problem of India'[14], its election campaign was also based on the issue of Pakistan. If the Muslims voted in favour of the League in the 1946 elections, 'the League will be entitled to ask for Pakistan without any further investigation or plebiscite'.[15] During the election campaign, Jinnah also identified the areas constituting Pakistan. According to him, those provinces with a clear Muslim majority naturally belonged to Pakistan and hence Sind, Baluchistan, the North West Frontier Province and Punjab in the north-west of India, and Bengal and Assam in the north-east, were provinces earmarked for Pakistan. The forthcoming elections, he declared, 'will decide the matter once for all and when they are over, Pakistan will become an immediate reality'.[16] In Punjab, Jinnah and his League colleagues were reported to have drawn on the religious sentiments of the Muslim voters by underlining that 'the question a voter is called on to answer is – are you a true believer, or an infidel and a traitor?'.[17] As the poll outcome revealed, the 1946 election was a referendum for the League.[18] While in the first provincial poll, in 1937, the League failed to make an impact even in the Muslim majority provinces by 1946 it became the only representative of the Muslims by polling in most (if not all) cases close to its maximum natural strength. This was a remarkable achievement in terms of both leadership and organisation.

An unambiguous verdict in favour of the Muslim League in the Muslim-majority provinces in the 1946 elections radically altered India's political landscape, in which the League emerged as a stronger party in its negotiations with the British in the last phase of the transfer of power. The idea that Muslims were more than a political minority and were in fact a significant political entity gained momentum following the resignation of the Congress ministries and their refusal to co-operate with the war effort. In that particular context, the League's strength rose in its bargaining with the British for 'a parity' with the Congress in future constitutional negotiations. Furthermore, it was also easier for the League to justify its claim as the only organisation to speak on behalf of Indian Muslims following the 1946 poll outcome. Immediately after the results were announced, the League, in its April session, therefore modified the Lahore resolution so that instead of demanding 'independent states' it now argued for 'a sovereign independent Muslim state,'[19] presumably to secure the consolidation of a single Muslim constitutional entity. After all, the League demand for parity 'rested on the claim that it represented a cohesive entity known as the Muslim nation'. By demanding 'independent states', the Pakistan resolution 'threatened to undermine the idea of Muslim solidarity and, with it, the basis of the League's political ideology'.[20]

In the penultimate year of the transfer of power the League secured parity with the Congress, and in the 1946 Shimla conference the League and Congress representation was equated.[21] What originated in the form of the Lahore resolution became feasible, and Jinnah's appeal to 'unsettle the settled notions ... of Muslims being a minority [that] had been around for so long'[22] was finally translated into reality. Thus, not only did the *Quaid-i-Azam* succeed in dramatically altering the role of the Muslims in the overall constitutional settlement on the eve of the Great Divide, he also transformed the Muslim community into a nation[23] by ascertaining 'territorial sovereignty to a heterogeneous community turned homogeneous nation'.[24] The Muslim community for Jinnah was, therefore, not 'an abstract historical–political entity ... but a separate nation with distinct interests [which] could not be treated only as a minority'.[25]

That Muslims constituted a self-determining political community was always emphasised, to completely dissociate from the Hindus seeking to establish 'a Hindu Raj'.[26] The Hindu–Muslim schism was not merely based on religious differences but also on certain fundamental principles guiding their respective lives. As Muslims drew upon completely different sociocultural values, it was unthinkable that they could live as 'a mere minority in a Hindu-dominated India'. While explaining the Hindu–Muslim chasm in colonial India, Ambedkar thus argued that the Hindu–Muslim 'antagonism ... is formed by causes which take their origin in historical, religious, cultural and social antipathy of which political antipathy is only a reflection. These form', he further elaborated, 'one deep river of discontent which, being regularly fed by these sources, keeps on mounting to a head and overflowing its ordinary channels'.[27] Hence Ambedkar held the Hindus equally responsible for the rise of Muslim separatism that was finally resolved in the emergence of Pakistan as a nation.[28]

Although Islam was not the only driving force behind the Great Divide, it had undoubtedly fed 'the religiously based communalism'[29] that grew in importance in a conducive political environment during the war and its aftermath. The League strategy appears to have been guided by two well-defined considerations. On the one hand, by demanding favour as the League co-operated with the war efforts, its leadership resorted continuously to pressure tactics.[30] On the other, the League was engaged in virulent propaganda seeking to mobilise the Muslims along communal lines, as the following appeal from *The Star of India* clearly illustrates:

> The time has come to the little rats to know that the lion is not dead, only sleeping; the challenge is to be accepted; the enemy is

5

to be met on its own ground; Mussalman cannot resort meanness and traceries which characterise their political enemies; the Hindus will see to whom Bengal belongs; they shall be taught the lesson they need.[31]

The consolidation of Muslim communal forces was matched, if not surpassed, by the rising tide of Hindu communalism.[32] Especially in the aftermath of the Calcutta riot, Hindu communalism grew at an alarming rate, resorting to intimidation, coercion and terror. Meetings were organised by the Hindu Mahasabha to defuse the drive for Pakistan,[33] and its leader, B. S. Moonjee launched a campaign supporting violence, if necessary, to protect the Hindus from communal attack.[34] Probably its worse form was articulated in the 1946 Bihar riot, where the organised Hindu bands wiped out the Muslim villages in the Patna, Gaya and Monghyr districts. Apart from the Hindu Mahasabha, which had a direct role, the Congress workers were also reported to have incited riots in many cases.[35] The Bihar riot made the Hindus vulnerable in Bengal and part of Assam, where they constituted a minority. What strengthened the movement for partition in Bengal was certainly the feeling that 'Hindus were not safe in the League-ruled Bengal'.[36] The Congress leadership gradually realised that however undesirable the partition of Bengal (and Punjab), there was really no alternative to it. Its reluctance officially to endorse the Mahasabha-sponsored 'communal' campaign for partition alienated a large number of Hindus in rural Bengal. The Congress was identified 'as being incapable of dealing with the Muslim challenge and safeguarding Hindu lives'.[37] It became increasingly clear that 'the claim that the Congress represents India is less and less true since it cannot now claim to represent all the Hindus, apart altogether from its claim to represent the Moslems and other minorities'.[38] This certainly projected the Hindu Mahasabha as the sole representative, and its leader, Shyama Prasad Mookherjee, as the sole spokesman (sic) of the Hindus.

B. R. Ambedkar, in his book *Pakistan or the Partition of India*,[39] endorsed the claim for Pakistan in terms of realist politics. According to him, partition was possibly the best solution to resolve the constitutional impasse in India, for two reasons. First, given the hostility of the Muslims to the idea of a single central government, inevitably dominated by the Hindu majority, it was certain that if there was no partition, the animosity and suspicion between the communities would remain: 'burying Pakistan is not the same thing as burying the ghost of Pakistan'.[40] Furthermore, given the demographic composition of what was proposed as Pakistan, there was no doubt that it would be a homogeneous state and hence free from communal bickering and mutual distrust. Secondly, Ambedkar felt that in united India, where more than a third of the population was Muslim, 'Hindu dominance could be a serious threat to the very existence of the polity'. In such a state, Muslims apprehending the tyranny of the Hindu majority were likely to organise themselves into 'a theocratic party', provoking in turn the rise of Hindu fundamentalist forces seeking to establish 'a Hindu raj'. Partition would radically alter the situation where Muslims in Hindustan would be 'a small and widely scattered minority' joining different political parties in accordance with what they consider 'as most protective' of their socio-economic and political interests. As a result, a party like Hindu Mahasabha that drew on the principle of 'a Hindu raj' would gradually disappear. Persuaded by the logic of his argument, Ambedkar suggested that the lower castes of Hindu society should join hands with the Muslim minority to fight the Hindu high castes for their rights of citizenship and social dignity.[41]

It would not be irrelevant to refer to Iqbal's arguments defending the demand for Pakistan. Conceptualising Pakistan in two-nation theory format, Iqbal offered a map of the redistribution of territory forming a Muslim state comprising the north-west part of India and Bengal.[42] His blueprint for Pakistan was based on language, race, history, religion and economic interests within the federal system, with maximum autonomy for the provinces. In order to protect Muslim identity and form a strong political unit, he suggested the idea of bringing together the north-western states of Punjab, Frontier, Sind and Baluchistan under one state, of which Bengal would invariably be a part given the Muslim preponderance in its demography. Such a state would cement the bond among the Muslims by creating 'a sense of responsibility and patriotism'. Unlike Ambedkar, who had a realistic aim of proper administration of the subcontinent in the aftermath of the British rule, Iqbal had a wider spiritual agenda of creating 'an Islam' capable of containing 'the influence of Arab imperialism [that] had shackled its civilization, culture, *shariat* and education for centuries'.[43]

There is one final point. The 'high politics of India's partition'[44] also epitomise the role of the last Viceroy, Louis Mountbatten. Despite his expressed desire to sustain India's unity following the Cabinet Mission plan, he soon realised after reaching Delhi that 'the Cabinet Mission plan and a unitary government were no longer feasible propositions and it was quite plain that a truncated Pakistan offered the only prospect of an agreed settlement'.[45] Once it had been decided, the Viceroy was keen to transfer power at an earlier date than June 1948. In his perception, an early withdrawal would certainly be advantageous to the British interests, and the substantial gains were as follows:

> (a) the terrific world-wide enhancement of British prestige and the enhancement of the prestige of the present government; (b) the completion of the framework of world strategy from the point of view of Empire defence; (c) the early termination of present responsibilities especially in the field of law and order; (d) a

further strengthening of Indo-British relations which have enormously improved since the statement of 20 February, 1947.⁴⁶

Although India became free earlier than had been decided, due to Mountbatten's insistence, he was also criticised on two counts: first, in 'a true Machiavellian style',⁴⁷ the last Viceroy took the advantage of the lack of consensus among the Congress, Sikh and League politicians and imposed his own 'solution' on the Indian question. Second, his plan to transfer power almost a year in advance plunged both the new-born dominions into serious administrative and political crisis. Owing to the suddenness of the event, the government failed to take adequate steps to prevent the human massacre during the transfer of population in Punjab. On the basis of his own experience as 'an insider', W. H. Morris Jones, however, exonerated Mountbatten for his responsibility, underlining that 'a slower process would probably have produced not less but more of both slaughtering and suffering'.⁴⁸ Similarly, Mountbatten was also absolved of the charge that, due to the rivalry among the Indian representatives, the Viceroy had easily made his way in so far as the actual transfer of power was concerned. As Nicholas Mansergh argued, the partition emerged from a triangular situation involving the British, the Congress and the League which itself limited the freedom of manoeuvre that even the most purposeful or enlightened of leaders enjoyed. It was therefore difficult for a single man to change the course of action in circumstances where the British government, though a key player, gradually became peripheral once the announcement of the final withdrawal had been made. The divided landscape of the two independent dominions that finally emerged was, therefore, the outcome of a peculiar unfolding of events in which those who participated 'were in a measure, not always fully realised, the prisoners of a pattern of politics which always pressed in upon their liberty of action'.⁴⁹

The 1946 Calcutta riot and afterwards

There is no doubt that the killing and looting that began in Calcutta in August and then spread to Noakhali, Bihar and other parts of India played a decisive role in bringing about partition. What was conspicuous about these riots was the growing communalisation of Hindus and Muslims, who participated in the mayhem as antagonistic competing blocs. As Krishnan wrote:

> The Great Calcutta Killing of August 1946 was a turning point in Indian history. ... It was like a civil war in which the provincial government [of the Muslim League] had become partisan. ... The British Government found itself unable to maintain law and

order. ... It was also now evident to Indian leaders that it would be more prudent to accept Pakistan than to let the country to slip into civil war and chaos.

Starting in August 1946 India suffered an unprecedented communal violence for nearly a year. ... The process started with the Calcutta outbreak of 16 August 1946, was continued in Bihar and Noakhali, and ended in the Punjab carnage of March 1947. These riots convinced the overwhelming majority of Hindus and Muslims that the partition of the subcontinent was inevitable.[50]

This is not, however, to argue that the 1946 riots were solely responsible for partition. What resulted in the vivisection was certainly the well-grounded Hindu–Muslim chasm, nurtured historically by a process in which not only had these communities played significant roles, but the contribution of the British Government was equally significant. By 1944, as the official reports show, 'the demands of Hindus and Muslims have crystallised into irreconcilability'.[51] The 1946 partition riots seem to have accelerated the pace of the constitutional negotiations that finally culminated in the Great Divide. Thus Suhrawardy, who was alleged to have played a decisive role in the Calcutta riot, wrote: 'Jinnah's Direct Action strategy, bathed in the blood of the Muslims of Calcutta, won him a great political victory and made Pakistan inevitable'.[52] Partition became inevitable because the tension, argued Parcival Spear, 'could no longer be restrained within peaceful bounds, and to the bloody August riots in Calcutta (where Hindus were the sufferers) was added the communal outbreak in Bihar (where Muslims were the victims)'.[53]

As the history of the subcontinent unfolded, Jinnah's idea of Pakistan that was 'a thing of laugh at five years ago ... [became] the slogan and watchword of the Muslim masses'.[54] The Muslims gradually became so powerful that 'a Moslem movement would be a spontaneous movement needing no political agitation to stir it up if their rights were in jeopardy'.[55] In August 1947, Jinnah achieved Pakistan but did not get what he wanted.[56] What finally emerged as Pakistan was 'but two spaces of map, without a natural frontier along the new dividing lines, without a ready capital, without the apparatus of national government or much trained skill to exercise it, a weak and feeble infant, a dry-mouthed end to a romantic dream'.[57] India also paid a heavy price for freedom – the communal forces were neither defeated, nor was unity totally achieved. The story of the decolonisation of India is not only about the emergence of the Muslim League, with its demand for a sovereign Muslim state from March 1940 and its mobilisation of Muslim provincial support, but also about British and Congress tactics which contributed to the rise of the League and the solidification of its communal support. Also, the circumstances of 'a declining empire may have continued as much to Muslim political unification as the League's appeal to the nationalism' supposedly inherent in Muslim religious communalism.[58] The Raj came to its end 'amidst convulsions in which not only Hindus and Muslims, but also Sikhs and Muslims slaughtered one another, a holocaust unprecedented'[59] in India's recent history. If the British, argued Penderel Moon, 'had been bold enough and uninfluenced by the glamour of empire, wise enough to launch India as a Dominion some fifteen to twenty years earlier, much bitterness and feeling of frustration, perhaps the tragedy of partition, would have been avoided'.[60]

Partition and memory

Partition is a living memory; its story is still unfolding more than fifty years after the subcontinent was divided. Today the overwhelming memory of 1947 for people across the whole of north India and Bengal remains that of *batwara* or *vibhajan* (partition), and not *azadi* or *swadhinata* (independence). There were diametrically opposite views on the nation that appeared following partition. The construction of nationhood meant the dislocation and violent displacement of those identified as 'aliens' overnight.[61] The divergent 'voices' that emerge are articulated in the contemporary literature through contested visions of independence, national identity and citizenship.[62]

What this study is (not) about[63]

Partition was a defining moment in South Asian history.[64] Communities were constituted, deconstituted and reconstituted.[65] Nations were born. Thus partition was the terminal point of a political negotiation in which the communal schism between Hindus and Muslims appears to have been decisive in demarcating the boundaries of the newly emerged nations. It is now well established that the colonial power, for obvious reasons, clung to divisive policies to sustain its rule. Partition was not forced upon the subcontinent, but it emerged as the best possible alternative at a particular historical conjuncture. Even the Congress that never accepted the two-nation theory was forced to swallow its outcome, possibly to avoid a further bloodbath in the name of protecting communal pride and interests. On a simplistic reading of historical processes, this may perhaps be attributed to the failure of the nationalism that the Gandhi-led Congress nurtured and refined over decades. What is missing is the growing complexity of the socio-economic and political milieu in which the 'nationalist' agenda had also undergone dramatic changes. In other words, since nationalism everywhere has been the product of particular/or distinctive histories, its articulation is certain to vary substantially in accordance with specific historical circumstances. In the history of India's freedom struggle, partition is therefore a remarkable sequence in the formation of competing and jostling communities with a specific political agenda.

Another important point to make before placing this study in relation to the available literature is the significant role of religion in cementing the communal bond. What counted more and more in the context of partition were 'believer and non-believers, Hindus and Muslims and Sikhs'.[66] As is evident, the campaign for partition – whether spearheaded by the Hindus or Muslims or Sikhs – gained momentum even in the villages in the name of 'a service to religion'. Colonialism separated Hindus and Muslims by its divide and rule strategy. What accounted for the gradual consolidation of these two rival blocs was probably the logic internal to these communities, which, of course, had its root in the larger socio-economic and political environment. For instance, the rise and consolidation of Hindu blocs in the 1920s in Bengal drew largely upon 'communal common sense of dying Hindu'. The Hindu demographic strength was certain to decline, as the argument runs, in view of the proliferation of Muslims due to reasons connected with their social system. The fear of being outnumbered by Muslims appeared to be an effective instrument for those 'engaged in the mobilization for an exclusive Hindu constituency'.[67] Equally important was the process that led to the construction of a Muslim bloc and consequently the 'othering' of the Hindus. With their economic prosperity at the grassroots through jute cultivation, Muslims gradually emerged as key players in 'high politics', and demands were placed for reservations of seats for the community in educational institutions and government employment. Since the progress of a people is evidenced 'by the increase of wealth and knowledge',[68] several leading Muslim intellectuals of various districts constantly emphasised the necessity of material improvement for their community. Islam had a role to play, and thus Usman, the model farmer in *Adarsha Krishak*, 'calls out the *azan* when he goes to work in his fields',[69] indicating the commitment to community imperatives along with dedication to profession.

It is now evident that, whatever the approach and howsoever diverse interpretations, 'the fact is that Hindu-Muslim partnerships exploded in the 1940s, and the weakness of the secular ideology – the emblem of the desire to create a world beyond religious divisions – became all too clear to that generation'.[70] Although religion played a crucial role in the formation of Pakistan, the Congress failure to assess the minority problem in the proper perspective was equally responsible for the alienation of the Muslims from the Gandhi-led nationalist movement. Notwithstanding the Congress negotiations with a handful of elite Muslims in the wake of the 1916 Lucknow Pact and the 1922–23 Congress–Khilafat merger, the chasm between the Hindus and Muslims was always exploited to advance the cause of the respective communities. How was this possible? In his article

'The Muslim Mass Contact Campaign: analysis of a strategy of political mobilization',[71] Mushirul Hasan argued that the elite-level pacts appeared futile in view of the genuine socio-economic differences between the Hindus and Muslims. In this thoroughly researched piece, he also underlined that the 1937 Mass Contact Campaign, probably the last serious Congress attempt to attract Muslim support, 'ran into serious trouble within two years of its launching, not so much due to Muslim League's opposition or the lack of Muslim support but because of Congress' own reluctance to pursue it with any vigour or sense of purpose'. The Congress decision to abandon the struggle of mass contact for ministry 'allowed Jinnah perhaps involuntarily to take advantage of deteriorating communal relations and rally his community around the divisive symbol of a separate Muslim homeland'. The scenario appears complete in view of the carefully devised scheme of political representation of the British and Jinnah's success in reaping the benefit in his favour. Farzana Shaikh has shown that, in the formation of Pakistan, what was crucial was the institutionalisation of politics on the basis that Congress could not represent Indian Muslims.[72] Similarly, the argument put forward by R. J. Moore that Pakistan 'would not have emerged without [Jinnah]' shows the extent to which Quaid-i-Azam intelligently manipulated the otherwise conducive socio-economic and political reality towards the attainment of Pakistan.[73] Supporting Moore's assessment of Jinnah, Akbar Ahmed attributed the success of the campaign for Pakistan to Jinnah by asserting that 'when a leader who commands respect in the Muslim community appears and can focus on a cause, Muslims are capable of moving mountains'.[74] True, Jinnah spearheaded the campaign for Pakistan; his success, however, was attributed to a society ravaged by the communal disharmony, imperial exploitation and other divisive tendencies so obvious in a colonial set-up. At the ground level, particularly in Bengal, the Hindu–Muslim hiatus, at least in socio-economic terms, was exploited by those supporting the Muslims (including the Muslim League) to highlight the economic tinge of communal schism; at the level of organised politics, the Congress' reluctance to come to terms with the Muslim leadership immediately after the first provincial elections in 1937 institutionalised a sense of persecution in Muslims. Thus emerged, as Moore argues, 'the essential link between Jinnah's leadership and the emergence of Muslim national consciousness', because Jinnah 'personified the Muslim sense of persecution by Congress denial of their achieved status'.[75]

A landmark in the history of partition was the remarkable success of the Muslim League in mobilising Muslim support, irrespective of class, for a separate Muslim homeland in Bengal and Punjab, when it had had no significant support base before 1940. Both David Gilmartin and Ian Talbot attribute the success of the Pakistan campaign in Punjab to a prevalent religious leadership that shifted its loyalty from the Unionist Party to the

INTRODUCTION

Muslim League. Politically, it was probably the most conclusive step towards the creation of a separate Muslim homeland. An argument highlighting the growing influence of the Muslim religious leadership in mobilisation seems plausible, especially in the light of a sudden eclipse of the national-secular forces in the province, which Jinnah called, 'the cornerstone of Pakistan'. In order to delineate the background of the religious support for the Pakistan movement in Punjab, Gilmartin[76] looks into the connections between the structure of religious leadership and the structure of Muslim politics in twentieth century Punjab. By analysing the role of the revivalist Sajjada Nashins in garnering support for Pakistan, Gilmartin demonstrates the extent to which religion and religious symbols acted as crucial variables in the 1947 Great Divide. In his view, the support of Sajjada Nashins to the Muslim League largely accounted for latter's triumph in the elections in 1946. The victory, to quote Gilmartin, 'was a sweeping religious mandate for Pakistan and marked the most important step on the road to Pakistan formation'.

Talbot's formulation, couched more or less in a similar fashion, is a further elaboration of Gilmartin's thesis. By concentrating on the growth of the Muslim League in the Punjab, he has shown the overarching importance of traditional social and religious networks in mobilising political support. According to his findings, the League was able to create and sustain its strong political base by relying on 'the *sufi* and kinship networks'. It was mainly through these and through the linking of the Pakistan scheme to the solution of the villagers' wartime economic difficulties that 'League politics were able to reach down and embrace the rural voters who held the key to the successful creation of a new Muslim nation-state'. A thorough study of the Punjab situation therefore reveals the complex interplay of religion and politics in the rise of Pakistan. It also shows the extent to which Pir's *fatwas* and landlords' economic influence and their leading position in the kinship networks acted favourably in the process that led to the vivisection of the subcontinent of India.[77]

While conceptualising the communal identity of both Hindus and Muslims in the context of the freedom struggle, religion has rightly been emphasised as a significant ingredient. Partha Chatterjee's article 'Bengal politics and the Muslim masses, 1920–47'[78] is an attempt to articulate theoretically the process in which Islam played a crucial role in organising the Muslim peasants against the Hindu zamindars. Since in Bengal peasants were largely Muslims and landlords Hindus, the Hindu–Muslim chasm had acquired a class dimension.[79] Hence, riots and other skirmishes involving Hindus and Muslims always had a class tinge. For instance, as Chatterjee argues, a study of riots in east and north Bengal in the 1920s and 1930s shows that 'the ideology which shaped and gave meaning to the collective acts of the peasantry was fundamentally religious'. He further adds that religion in such a community 'provides an ontology, an epistemology as well as a practical code of ethics including political ethics'. When this community acts politically, the symbolic meaning of particular acts – their signification – must be found in religious terms'.[80] In the case of Bengal (and also Assam), it was Islam which provided the peasantry with a readymade organising principle for a specific type of politics. Moreover, given the social composition of peasants and zamindars, a continued climate of peasant agitation regarding zamindari oppression was 'translated in the Muslim-dominated areas into ideological terms that were pronouncedly anti-Hindu'.[81] In such a context, the Congress support to the zamindars, the majority of whom were Hindus, strengthens further the characterisation of the Congress as a communal organisation – and thus the alienation between the Congress and the Muslims appeared unbridgeable. In his analysis of the Bengal agrarian class conflict, Sugata Bose reiterated the point by underlining that the consolidation of Hindu–Muslim communal identity owed largely to the changes in the key elements of the Bengal agrarian social structure. According to him, with the rupture of rural credit relations in the aftermath of the Great Depression of the 1930s 'the unequal and symbiotic social networks in east Bengal were torn apart'.[82] Since the talukdar-mahajans and trader-mahajans no longer played the role of guaranteeing the peasants subsistence, 'the old deference disappeared [and] in the small peasant economy of east Bengal, they had ceased to perform any useful function. Once a political challenge came within the realm of possibility, the strength of a religious identity was exploited as a readily available and, for the privileged co-religionists, a safe ideology'.[83] Religion, described as an integral component of communal consciousness, imparted, concludes Bose, 'a sense of collectivity and ideological legitimation in a specific historical conjuncture when the balance of class power in the countryside has already changed'.[84]

While Partha Chatterjee and Sugata Bose draw upon the socio-economic and political processes at the grassroots to grasp the growth of communal consciousness that was articulated in the movements, by both the Hindus and Muslims, demanding partition, Leonard Gordon looks at the institutional politics to gauge the importance of religion and the cultural distinctiveness of Bengal in the so-called separatist politics. In his 'Divided Bengal: problems of nationalism and identity in the 1947 partition',[85] Gordon explains partition in terms of an intelligent handling of the demand for a separate Muslim homeland by the provincial leadership following the Muslim League's rise to prominence. When the Pakistan resolution was adopted in 1940, the League was confident that a sovereign Muslim state was to be formed in those areas where Muslims constituted a majority. As is evident, the Pakistan formula was presented to the Muslims in Bengal as the only device to escape Hindu domination. Two distinct voices were recorded by Gordon to substantiate his point. Abul Hashim, the General Secretary of the League, argued for a multinational

INTRODUCTION

state drawing its sustenance from the laws of Shariat. In his words, 'it is not in the contemplation of the Muslims to reserve any advantage for themselves, except their right to govern their own society according to the laws of Shariat'.[86] The other voice was that of Abul Mansur Ahmad, a former Congress member who joined the League in 1940. For Ahmad, Pakistan meant 'cultural autonomy'. By culture, he meant Bengali culture and literature, developed, to some extent, by the Hindus as well. While characterising the Bengali culture, Ahmad was quite emphatic that 'it was to be Bengali culture freed from Hindu linguistic and religious shackles; it was to be Muslim but distinctive from [that] of West Pakistanis. So it was to be Bengali and Muslim, but divergent from the culture of Bengalis [of West Bengal] and other Muslims'.[87] Gordon thus inferred that 'religious and cultural factors and interests' played a crucial role in rallying the Muslims around the demand for Pakistan despite differences among themselves in class terms. Simultaneously with Muslim consolidation as a community, a process that helped to crystallise Hindu communal identity loomed large. Undoubtedly, the Shyama Prasad Mookherjee-led Hindu Mahasabha had a significant role in popularising the demand for partition at the grassroots. What made Mahasabha acceptable to the Hindus in rural Bengal was certainly the extreme communalism of the Suhrawardy ministry, which was held responsible for 'the 1946 August bloodbath in Calcutta and Noakhali'. Hindus pledged to 'fight for partition ... to avoid Muslim rule, in free Pakistan, or in united independent Bengal, or in free federated India'.[88]

Partition was made possible because of an environment in which the Hindu–Muslim relationship was articulated in antagonistic terms. Several factors were at work. The growing social distance between Hindus and Muslim in quotidian life, intense competition for jobs and education, the politicisation of religion and the use of religious symbols were factors that further aggravated the situation. Nationalism – whether of the Congress or League variety – was nurtured in peculiar circumstances where the religiously informed cultural identity of both the Hindus and the Muslims figured prominently in the final negotiation for power with the British. Since the Hindu–Muslim cultural identity was constantly redefined in the light of historical needs and future aspirations, it would be theoretically misleading and factually wrong to 'essentialise' communal identities in terms of fixed socio-cultural characteristics. It is true that religion provided the necessary bond to construct a community at a particular historical juncture, but its effectiveness in consolidating the bond by placing one community against another depended a great deal on the circumstances in which the role of the colonial state was no less significant. In other words, apart from the centrality of the colonial state in this process, Hindu–Muslim identities were not just products of colonial institutions and economic changes, but were created by the communities on the strength of inherited cultural resources as well as invented traditions.[89] It is also important, in grasping the processes that led to partition, to underline that overemphasis on 'the cultural roots of Indian nationalism leaves unexamined the myriad subaltern contestations of an emerging mainstream nationalism which like its adversary, colonialism, may well have only achieved dominance without hegemony ... Continued privileging of religious distinctions thwarted many well-meaning attempts at accommodating differences within a broad framework of Indian nationalism'.[90]

There is no denying that the explanation of partition in terms of binary opposition between secular nationalism and religious communalism is too simplistic to capture the complex unfolding of processes preceding the Great Divide. While dwelling on the structural contour of politics, based on the above binary opposition, Ayesha Jalal has brought out the multi-layered Muslim identity that can hardly be subsumed by a blanket category like 'religious communalism'. In her words, '[e]xploding communalism to uncover the manifold and contradictory interests driving the politics of Muslim identity in South Asia might enable a better appreciation of difference as a lived cultural experience, one that is forever changing in response to broader historical dynamics, rather than an abstract, sterile and essentialised category awaiting a fresh round of scholarly bandaging'.[91] In a recent work, Jalal reiterates the argument by underlining that 'the strategic essentialising of religious community is deemed more important than its utility as a point of reference for the assertion of cultural difference'. She therefore concludes that overemphasis on the Islamic dimensions of the discourse of Muslim identity, as if these are unproblematically singular in meaning, 'ignores the spatial and temporal aspects of historical change that shaped the emerging contradictions and contestations within the community of Islam in India'.[92] In the entire configurations, the role of the colonial government was no less insignificant. Colonialism had invested religion, argues Jalal, with greater significance through its peculiar configuration of the domain of the 'public' and the 'private'.[93] It played havoc because the growing sense of cultural differences was translated into a politics of identity devoid of considerations, other than that of the religious community through well-crafted constitutional devices, adopted during the course of twentieth century.

Undoubtedly, identity – whether Hindu or Muslim – is constructed through a complex process of contestation. It is also acknowledged that exclusive identity does not develop in a vacuum and derives sustenance, if not inspiration, from the perception of the other. What is, however, clearly visible is the significant role of religion in this process. Religion provided the idiom, vocabulary and symbols for support mobilisation. Muslims were, informs Tazeen M. Murshid, recruited in the name of Islam that defined 'community or the *millat*'. The Muslim League, seen 'as the house of Islam came to be equated with Islam and all those Muslims who supported parties other than the League were labeled as traitors to Muslims and to Islam'.[94] It was therefore not surprising that Kazi Nazrul Islam, despite being a Muslim, failed to be elected and even lost his deposit simply because 'not only was he believed to an atheist because of his communist sympathies, but he was also considered to a *kafir*, because of the nature of his literary output and his lifestyle including his marriage to a Hindu woman'.[95]

The role of the colonial state was formidable in the consolidation of political interests around the communally divided Hindus and Muslims. 'By treating the Muslims as a separate group, [the colonial state] had', argues David Page, 'divided them from other Indians. By granting them separate electorates, it institutionalized that division'.[96] For Gilmartin, the role of the British electoral system in shaping the meaning of Muslim community cannot be understated.[97] The introduction of separate electorates drew upon the principles that had long helped to defend and consolidate the organisation of the colonial state. In this sense, Muslim identity became an identity defined less by ideology than by 'common heritage and common descent'. For the British, the importance of a such a definition of Muslim community 'lay in the fact that it allowed them to appropriate the concept to strengthen their own political system while underscoring the illegitimacy of appeals to religious symbols as defining elements for the state system'.[98] Communally compartmentalised electorates, Jalal points out, 'had helped transform the case of Muslim distinctiveness into an assertion of nationhood at the level of all-India political discourse'.[99] The resort to Islam was the single most important mobilisational device to generate support for a movement seeking a separate Muslim homeland. In Bengal and Assam, as will be shown below, the League's strategy was to draw upon the Hindu hatred for Muslims that was always equated with 'Islam in danger'. The well-publicised Pirpur report, prepared by the League and presented before the All Indian Muslim League session in 1940, articulated the Muslim fear of being submerged by Hindu domination if a sovereign Muslim state was not formed. The Congress campaign for Ramrajya, the endeavour to impose Bande Mataram in the legislature and its preference for Hindi as a compulsory language in the Congress-ruled provinces were issues that alienated the Muslims from the Congress that was, by 1940, identified with the Hindus.[100] In consequence, a space was created which the League filled by a consistent organisational effort by its able leadership. As a contemporary report suggests, by the middle of 1944 the League membership had increased dramatically by enrolling about 550 000 members from rural Bengal.[101]

The League gained in an atmosphere where the two-nation theory inspired the imagination of Muslims in rural Bengal and Assam as being the best possible means to avoid the Hindu Raj. For them, Pakistan promised protection from 'the possible atrocities of a Hindu-headed polity'.[102] Perhaps the essential appeal of Pakistan was the hope it held of freedom from Hindu domination. M. A. Ispahani, a business magnate from Bengal, articulated the feeling by saying that there was 'an almost fanatical determination among Muslims not to be dominated by Hindus [for] it was impossible for the Muslims to achieve economic emancipation at the hands of the Hindus'.[103]

In its campaign for Pakistan, the League had succeeded in bringing to the forefront the *mullahs*, *moulvis* and other religious men who had a readymade support base among the rural Muslims.[104] It would not be an exaggeration to say that without their contribution in gradually expanding the Muslim League support base, the Pakistan campaign would have lost much of its vigour. Rafiuddin Ahmed has shown how itinerant mullahs or religious preachers prompted the masses to look beyond the borders of Bengal in search of their supposed Bengali Islamic past and attach 'greater importance to their being Muslim as opposed to their local or regional identity'. This new emphasis proved crucial to 'the subsequent emergence of a measure of social cohesion in a diversified and even culturally polarized community'.[105] The preachers seeking to Islamise the masses emerged as powerful agents in the political mobilisation of the rural Muslims. Given the uncritical acceptance by the people at the grassroots, not only did they play significant roles in shaping the attitudes of the ordinary Muslims, they also provided the required link between the upper classes and poorer peasantry. In the growth and consolidation of a Muslim communal identity especially in the 1940s,[106] the first victim was certainly the syncretistic tradition in Bengal, so assiduously nurtured in the nineteenth century, to evolve an alternative Bengali identity, as Asim Roy so brilliantly demonstrated.[107]

Despite the absence of coherent political ideology and differences, internal to the Muslims as a community, in 1946 the Bengal Muslims voted for the Muslim League and hence for the creation of Pakistan almost unanimously. The League secured by far the largest percentage of Muslim votes in Bengal, as compared to the other provinces.[108] If the results of the 1946 elections alone are taken as the basis, Jinnah appears, comments Jalal, to have 'gone some way towards vindicating his claim to be the spokesman of the Indian Muslim'.[109] The Pakistan demand, despite being vague and imprecise, had brought the Muslims together under the League banner.[110] The idea as projected, informs Tazeen Murshid, allowed people to conjure up whatever meanings or attributes took their fancy. It offered the hope of a separate state for the Muslims to realise more fully their distinct religious and cultural identity. For the bulk of the Muslim peasantry, Pakistan 'became the dream of a promised land, a utopia, or a return to the age of *Khulafa-i-Rashidin*. It had a millennial appeal which, for a while, covered up the deep divisions within the Muslim community'.[111]

Varying interests had been brought together under a single banner in the process of political mobilisation in which the differences with the Hindus 'other' invariably figured. Similarly, among the educated Muslims, the Hindu 'other' acted as a cementing factor in garnering support for Pakistan. For instance, Abul Mansur Ahmad, a former Congress member, saw in Pakistan 'an appropriate arrangement to pursue a distinct way of life in opposition to Hindu chauvinism'. He refused to acknowledge the works of Rabindranath Tagore, Vidyasagar and Bankimchandra as representing Bengali culture because they, in their literary creations, neither depicted the Bengali Muslim life nor accorded respect to their language by simply ignoring Mussalmani Bangla in disdain.[112]

The scene was similar in Uttar Pradesh, Sind, Punjab, the Central Provinces and Berar, Bombay and Madras.[113] The most glaring description of the growing popularity of the demand for Pakistan as being the only way of ensuring the Muslim well-being is certainly the one provided by R. W. Sorensen, who reminisced:

> Therefore Moslem Leaguers are in earnest when they believe that Pakistan is the inviolable prelude to their communal well-being and prosperity. They may or may not be deluded in this, other elements may adulterate their zeal, but in the emotional fervour of the two thousand or so students who greeted us with green flags chanting Pakistan in unison at Lahore; in the frenzied cries that met Jinnah when he spoke to thousands in the same town when we were there; in the long elaborate exposition I heard at a Moslem tea gathering at Allahabad; in the somewhat confused utterances of three opulent and corpulent Moslem spokesmen at Peshwar; in the presence of those who pursued me at the last Indian gathering; and in score of other instances, I perceived that Pakistan had caught on with large number of Moslems and had become an intense political–religious faith.[114]

Out of the discussion, two basic points have emerged which are useful in grappling with the gradual acceptance of Pakistan by both the Hindus and Muslims in the tumultuous phase of India's struggle for independence. First, the success of the Pakistan demand was due to a large extent to the consolidation of Muslims as a community in opposition to the Hindu other.[115] Similarly, Hindus in Bengal emerged as a counterweight as the zeal to protect their communal interests drew heavily upon the constructed Muslim other.[116] There are examples where Hindus and Muslims devised arrangements for united platforms against the British that appeared ephemeral due to internal weaknesses in elite-based solutions.[117] Secondly, what decisively shaped the future of South Asia was largely the well-publicised Hindu–Muslim schism, which acquired a completely

INTRODUCTION

different meaning in the context of colonialism. By assiduously following a strategy to permanently isolate the principal communities from one another, the British consolidated the chasm for its own imperial design.

What does this book propose to do? Given the vast scope of the subject, far being a complete account of the event and its outcome, the book is merely an attempt to understand partition in terms of the complex unfolding of socio-economic and political processes in the context of a declining colonial order. The questions that need to be asked are, why and how did the two nation theory gain salience in the 1940s, and why and how did the Hindus and Muslims emerge as competing and jostling blocs in the aftermath of the introduction of the 1932 Communal Award, glossing over clear internal division in socio-economic terms? So, in the formation of 'separate' blocs, the role of the colonial government was decisive, and the growing separation between the principal communities was but 'an emerging pattern of pragmatic engagement with the prevalent social, political and economic processes'.[118] The exercise is therefore a matter-of-fact narration of those forces that promote or impede this process in an imperial context that had undergone changes following 'the determination [of the British government] to warp the Indian question towards electoral politics'[119] once the separate electorate was constitutionally conceded to the Muslims.

The book draws upon Bengal and Assam, where new boundaries were demarcated in the wake of the 1947 transfer of power. Literature on Assam is scanty, and hence the present exercise is unique in laying a foundation for further work on the subject. Bengal continues to remain as important an area of research as it was before. Hence, it would not be appropriate to comment on the major trends in contemporary scholarship on Bengal partition. The basic question that appears to have influenced the search is centred on the processes that manifested in the construction of distinctly separate, if not 'antagonistic', communities during the period preceding the Great Divide. While dwelling on communal riots in Bengal in the twentieth century,[120] Suranjan Das draws out the changing complexion of Hindu–Muslim antagonism. Whereas in the earlier period riots in Bengal were relatively unorganised, less connected with institutional politics, and had a strong class orientation, the latter communal outbreaks were characterised by two distinct features: (1) a merger of class and communal identities and (2) a convergence of elite and popular communalism. The outcome was a clear horizontal polarisation of virtually the entire population into two competing blocs with support from the respective political elites. Given the emphasis, Das seems to be interested more in the description of specific riots and less in the processes that unfolded differently in different periods of Bengal's history. The story, far from being complete, is indicative of the political trends that loomed large as partition emerged as the best possible solution under those circumstances. Tazeen

Murshid provides a rather sophisticated version of this thesis by underlining the importance of the growing complexity of the socio-economic and political processes in Bengal in the construction of 'an apparently exclusionist' Muslim identity in which Islam was but one, if an important, factor. While explaining the rising incidence of communalism, she argues that 'the growing self-assertion of Bengal Muslims, the increasing popularity of the Pakistan idea and the accompanying communal conflict led to the association of religiosity and communalism'.[121] Couching her arguments in the black and white binary opposition between secularism and communalism, Murshid seems to have outlined the process of community formation in a rather unproblematic manner. As a result, her intervention in the debate is reduced to an affirmation, if not confirmation, of who became more communal in what was a struggle against colonialism for freedom. This is most explicit in her attempt to exonerate Suhrawardy of his responsibility in effecting the famous 1946 Calcutta killings.[122]

In her endeavour to grapple with the transformation of the Bengali bhadralok from being nationalist to communal, Joya Chatterjee provides an interesting twist to the entire literature on partition. With the introduction of the principle of majority following the implementation of the 1932 Communal Award, the Bengali bhadralok lost their hegemony in provincial politics. According to Chatterjee, Hindu communal identity was constructed in Bengal from the 1930s onwards, initially as an alliance of the educated and the well-to-do landed and professional classes with the lower middle class, but increasingly to mobilise the sanskritising aspirations of low caste groups and having as its main political objective the refusal to accept the rule of the Muslim majority.[123] She argues, 'the communalism of the bhadralok was directed against the fellow Bengalis.... It was the celebration of British rule as an age of liberation from the despotism of Muslims. Its key political objective was to prevent this "despotism" from returning when the British left India, and to deny that Muslims could be Bengalis, and by extension Indians'.[124] There is denying that Hindu communalism became a force in the 1930s and 1940s in Bengal. What is not true is that 'the organized Hindu opinion became less anti-British'.[125] Indeed, the allegation that the British bureaucracy in connivance with the League government was promoting only the Muslim interests further consolidated the anti-British feelings of the Hindus. In her zeal to attribute partition only to communal Hindu bhadralok, Joya Chatterjee actually misses, perhaps to corroborate the early Cambridge cynicism, the equally important role of Muslim communalism. In other words, in what finally became partition, the role of the Muslim communal forces was nonetheless significant in creating an atmosphere where the division of Bengal along religious lines emerged as the best possible solution.

The thesis, trapped within the old binary opposition between secular nationalism and religious communalism, fails to make any distinction between religious sensibility and religious bigotry. Hence it would be difficult to 'disentangle the many different roots of [partition], running along different levels of determination and with very different temporalities'.[126] It is empirically inadequate and theoretically misleading to assume that since Hindu–Muslim fraternity broke down in the 1920s (as manifested in frequent riots) and the Congress took a narrowly defined position for protecting the Hindu rentier interests, there was 'a transformation in the long duration of ideological construction from "nationalism" to "communalism". This is not to deny the growing importance of communalism in provincial political configurations. What is obvious is that anti-colonial nationalism of Hindus and Muslims alike had always been influenced by their religiously informed cultural identities, embroidered with an array of religious symbols and empowered by religion as faith'.[127]

The question that needs to be asked is, how did the communally argued two nation theory strike roots in Bengal, which was a glaring example of co-existence in the everyday life of Muslim peasants of numerous Islamic and non-Islamic practices, and of periodic attempts to 'purify' Islam'.[128] The story of this metamorphosis must be pieced together among political strategies adopted for much shorter duration in institutional arenas that involve only a small number of people. What is crucial in narrating this story is to focus on the imperial design and the 'nationalist' response. The nature of response varied. For instance, the opposition to the 1932 Communal Award was largely confined to Calcutta and its vicinity, and it was mainly the upper caste bhadralok who spearheaded the campaign. There was not a very strong counter Muslim response, apart from presenting written memorandum supporting the British initiative. The political scene was radically transformed following the assumption of power by the Muslim League and its partners from 1937 onwards. By the 1940s, the challenge to Muslim authority had been crystallised and was expressed unambiguously both within the legislature and outside. This is not, however, to suggest that partition was the result of elite manipulation. Instead, there exists a huge body of evidence indicating large-scale mass participation in partition-related movement.[129] Simply to gloss over this dimension and attribute partition to 'a large number of telegrams received by the All India Congress Committee from Bengal'[130] is not only inaccurate but is also a clear distortion of the historiography of partition. What is therefore relevant is to piece together the stories scattered around various levels of political activity, including the level of high politics, to draw out the significance of the socio-political processes that finally culminated in partition. However, it is important to be careful not to lose the importance of the way in which Muslim majoritarian politics unfolded in Bengal. The strategy that C. R. Das adopted to bring together local Muslim leadership seemed to have been shelved, and there was hardly 'any serious hegemonic attempt to mobilize the consent of the Hindu minority for Muslim leadership over Bengali society'.[131] The attempts that were made were foiled by the Hindu or Muslim High Commands or by the British. For instance, the desire of the Bengal Congress to form a coalition with the Krishak Praja Party in the aftermath of the 1937 elections was thwarted by the 'obstructive' attitude of the All India Congress Committee, and later by the well-devised British policy against any inter-communal political alliance to prevent Congress from coming to power. On the Muslim side, the gradual decline of Fazlul Haq as an effective mass leader drawing upon cross-communal alliances was certainly a significant development in Bengal politics in which 'the religiously-informed Muslim communal identity' figured prominently in political mobilisation. It was therefore relatively easier for Suhrawardy and Abul Hashim to 'promote their own version of mass contact campaign, based on a particular Islamic populism'.[132] Their campaign resulted not only in expanding the constituency of League; it also 'enabled the League to put its mantle over the *krishak*[133] movement for which Haq had once been the charismatic spokesman'.

How can the gradual but steady rise of Islamic populism be explained, especially in the context well-entrenched syncretistic tradition in Bengal? According to Asim Roy, who wrote extensively on the Islamic syncretistic tradition in Bengal, by the early 1920s 'a growing Islamic consciousness steadily challenged aspects of syncretistic tradition as reflected most clearly in the progressive decline, both in quantity and quality, of the rich and time-honoured syncretistic literary output'. A new variety of 'Islamic punthi, using rather contrived concoctions of Urdu–Bengali dictions', proliferated.[134] The contribution of mullahs and pirs was nonetheless crucial in the entire process. While the former catered to 'the religious, ritualistic and liturgical needs of the believers, the latter provided for more spiritual, esoteric, mystical and emotional needs'. In view of their role, 'the rural Muslims were forced ... out of their fragmented social life to become increasingly interactive with other Muslim groups and localities'. The emphasis on sharpening the Islamic consciousness helped to achieve two objectives – social integration of the Muslim community, and greater differentiation of Muslims from non-Muslims. These developments had 'the effect of leavening the ground for the subsequent penetration of urban religious and political influences into the rural areas, successfully trying to impose a broad frame of religious unity on the community for the ultimate objective of its political mobilization'.[135] In the growth of Bengali Muslims as an exclusive political community, it is important not to miss the immensely significant role the British government had in selectively distributing economic and political favours and patronage to sustain, if not strengthen, its rule. There is a point when Peter Van der Veer argues that 'religious identities [though] produced in religious configurations are related more to other more comprehensive configurations, such as state'.[136]

INTRODUCTION

Under these circumstances, the peasant–populist consolidation in Bengal, with its powerful use of Islam 'as a religion of agrarian solidarity and justice',[137] virtually became an instrument in a communal campaign for Pakistan at the cost of other religious minorities.

The Great Divide was both an event and a process. What happened on 15 August 1947 through a formal transfer of power was also an outcome of processes that had roots in the complex unfolding of South Asian history since the introduction of the British rule. These were processes in which the roles of the individuals and communities were structured around colonialism, which had its own dynamics linked with the hegemonic British Empire. Thus the 1947 transfer of power is not merely a division of the subcontinent of India; it is probably a unique description of the growth and consolidation of Hindus and Muslims as communities with different political goals. Striving to link different levels of political articulation in the context of British rule, the study seeks to map out the processes that finally led to the vivisection following the devolution of power to the two independent nations.[138]

Bengal and Assam were divided following the announcement of Louis Mountbatten on 3 June, though the principle that determined the divisions was different. While Bengal was partitioned following largely the demographic composition of the areas – namely, the Muslim-majority areas constituted the new province of Pakistan while the Hindu-majority districts formed west Bengal – Assam was separated as a result of a referendum in which Hindus and Muslims participated to create a new nation.

By dwelling on Bengal and Assam, this study has sought to capture the processes of fission and fusion that seem to have worked in the formation of the Hindus and Muslim as communities. This is a story of fission, because members of both communities were united as separate entities during the campaign for partition. What brought them together irrespective of the obvious socio-economic schism among themselves was perhaps a well-nurtured feeling of hatred and intolerance for those outside the communal boundary. Thus the fissure between the Hindus and Muslims appeared, at least during the period preceding partition, to be permanent and real. This is also a story of fusion since Hindus and Muslims rose as distinct communities bypassing the well-entrenched class differences segregating one group of people within the same community from another. Thus despite being divided internally, Hindus and Muslims emerged as competing blocs highlighting their exclusive identity, fed by intolerance for those belonging to the 'other' community.

The period from 1932 to 1947 is extremely important for two reasons. First, during these fifteen years Muslims became stronger in the institutional arena of politics, particularly in Bengal largely due to their demographic preponderance. In the consolidation of political interests along communal lines, the role of the imperial ruler was also decisive. By recognising Muslims as a separate group it divided them from the rest, and by granting them separate electorates it institutionalised that division. Secondly, the rise of Muslims as a strong contender for power in the final phase of the transfer of power dramatically altered the political arithmetic in both Assam and Bengal. By effectively mobilising Muslims in Assam since the introduction of 'the Line system', indigenous Muslim leadership, particularly *Mollahs* and *Ulemas*, made the task of the League easier because its organisation was not as well-entrenched as in Bengal, especially after 1943. The League's success in the referendum owed largely to Maulana Bhasani, the self-styled religious leader who swayed the Muslims in Sylhet in favour of Pakistan presumably because of his overwhelming popularity among them. While the League was in favour of division in Assam, in Bengal its opposition to partition provoked mass movements, spearheaded by the Hindu Mahasbaha with tacit Congress support, demanding integration with India to escape Muslim atrocities. By dealing separately with Bengal and Sylhet of Assam, this study seeks to lay out the processes that finally led to the rise of two independent dominions following the Great Divide. The Hindu–Muslim chasm was not merely political, as is generally assumed; it also had roots in the colonial socio-economic and cultural milieu. Underlining the distinctive socio-economic and cultural characteristics of Bengal, it is argued in Chapter 1 that differences between the two communities in the public sphere had their roots in the quotidian life of Hindus and Muslims at the grassroots, apart from the obvious feelings of hatred of the Muslim peasants against the Hindu landlords.

Already divided, Hindus and Muslims were further alienated by the introduction of MacDonald's Communal Award in 1932, which radically altered the balance of power in favour of the Muslims in Bengal by constitutionally endorsing the demographic strength as a source of power. The Hindu representation was further slashed by Gandhi's insistence on sharing seats with the Scheduled Castes. As a result of the Gandhi–Ambedkar Poona Pact and the Communal Award, Bengal faced a situation in which, as shown in Chapter 2, Hindus permanently lost their significant presence in the legislative arena. Chapter 3 is a further elaboration of the processes that began unfolding with the 1932 Award. By selectively analysing those legislative acts that exacerbated communal tension, this chapter shows that the Muslim ministry adopted these discriminatory laws to accrue benefits to the hitherto underprivileged Muslims. In a communally charged environment, these laws, despite being humanitarian, further aggravated the Hindu–Muslim rivalry which had its worse form in the 1946 Calcutta riot, followed by the Noakhali carnage. It has been shown that these communal outbreaks in quick succession left no option for the Hindus in east Bengal but to press for partition due largely to the communalisation of Muslims in the wake of these riots. Chapter 4 constitutes another significant milestone in the Great Divide. Even after the announcement of the 3 June plan, some of the prominent Congressmen sought to save the division of the province in collaboration with the provincial Muslim League leadership. For the League, it was a ploy to avoid bifurcation of the province in the interest possibly of a greater Pakistan. Though the campaign had the potential it did not take off, presumably because of the hidden agenda of the League which gradually became clear. Chapter 5, which focuses on the Radcliffe Commission, examines the arguments and counter-arguments of the Muslim and Hindu representatives defending their scheme of partition. As there was hardly any unanimity among the Indian representatives, the Cyril Radcliffe-authored imperial design of the future provinces ultimately prevailed.

Chapter 6 deals with the Sylhet Referendum. Sylhet in Assam was the only district where Muslims constituted a majority, largely due to migration of Bengali Muslims to Assam for jobs in the tea gardens and cultivable *char* land. This radically transformed Sylhet's political economy. Not only did the Muslims gradually become the majority; they also emerged as a significant partner in provincial politics. As the chapter demonstrates, the Muslim's leadership of the provincial Congress was substantially marginalised by the overwhelming presence of the Bengali Muslim leaders, who became the natural choice for the Bengali Muslims. The Muslims in Sylhet were mobilised with the decision to follow strictly 'the Line system' in 1946. What brought the Muslims together was the obvious apprehension of losing their livelihood if they were forcibly evicted from the district. Apart from this survival instinct, what cemented the bond among the affected Muslims, like their counterparts in Bengal, was Islam, which united them irrespective of class, clan and creed. Thus religion created not only a sense of community but also a national bond among the Muslims that was translated in votes during the referendum. The relatively unknown story of Sylhet therefore provides a sub-text to the Great Divide, which tends to be defined mostly in terms of the partition of Bengal and Punjab.

The final chapter is an attempt to recreate the story of partition from literary inputs. Seeking to capture the history of a fragmented and wounded society, this chapter is an entry point to grapple with the diverse 'voices' of the people who confronted a situation which was just thrashed upon them. What is glaringly clear is that the story of partition cannot be conceptualised in a straitjacket formula, couched in the binary opposition between religious communalism and secular nationalism, as is generally done. The stories – whether from Bengal or Punjab – clearly suggest that the day-to-day interaction between Hindus and Muslims at the ordinary and local levels was so interwoven as to have formed well-entrenched cultural notes and practices. In other words, though located in completely different geographical areas, the creative writings on partition provide the resources to construct the story of the final days of the British withdrawal and its impact on communal relations in conjunction with activities at the level of 'high' politics involving the three major actors – the Congress, the Muslim League and the British.

The principal argument the book seeks to articulate is concerned with the complexity of events and processes that eventually culminated in the vivisection of the sub-continent of India in 1947. Rather than explaining partition in terms of the old and simplistic binary opposition between secular nationalism and religious communalism, the aim of the book is underline the importance of the political processes that projected the Muslim League as a true representative of the Muslims in Bengal and Assam, and Jinnah as their sole spokesman. An assessment of this conundrum in the context of a declining empire will hopefully shed light on why and how different forms, identities and consciousness were articulated into a powerful campaign for a separate Muslim state in these two British Indian provinces just on the eve of the so-called 'surgical operation'.

Notes

1 While explaining the significance of the Great Divide, H. V. Hodson thus argues, 'The Great Divide, which by separating Britain from India undid two centuries of imperialism and by separating India and Pakistan imposed a draconian solution to a still more ancient problem of Hindu–Muslim rivalry for power'. (See Hodson 1969: 542–3.)

2 Mansergh *et al.*, Vol. IX, 1980. Jinnah's statement was quoted in the Viceroy's personal report no. 3 of 17 April 1947, pp. 390–1. There is close correspondence with Jinnah's views in the newsmagazine *Millat* (Nation), which accused the Congress and the Hindu Mahasabha of performing the role of Parashuram as they 'together raised a sharpened pickaxe to slice "Mother" into two' *Millat*, 28 Chaitra, 1353, 2 April 1947, quoted in Bose and Jalal (1997: 51).

3 In his Ramgarh presidential address, Abul Kalam Azad thus argues that: [f]or a hundred and fifty years, the British imperialism has pursued the policy of divide and rule, and by emphasising internal differences, sought to use various groups for the consolidation of its own power. That was the inevitable result of India's political subjection, and its folly for us to complain and grow bitter. A foreign government can never encourage internal unity in the subject country, for disunity is the surest guarantee for the continuance of its own domination' (Azad's 1940 presidential address at Ramgarh, in Zaidi and Zaidi 1981: 356).

4 Centre for South Asian Studies, Cambridge (CSASC), Benthall Papers, Box No. XIX, Benthall's diary notes of the political situation in 1940.

5 By 1946, with the failure of the constitutional negotiations between the Congress and Jinnah, it was clear that the Muslims had no option but to go for direct action since the British appeared to have coalesced with the Congress to strike at the foundation of a separate Muslim state following the withdrawal of the British. The Direct Action resolution was adopted in July 1946 at the annual session of the Muslim League (see India Office Records (IOR), London R/3/1/135, The Direct Action Resolution of the Muslim League).

6 IOR, John Tyson Papers, Eur. E 341/40, John Tyson's note, 17 August 1946. (John Tyson was the private secretary to the Bengal Governor, 1945–47.)

INTRODUCTION

7 Pandey 1994: 215
8 As the Lahore resolution goes, 'that the areas in which the Muslims are numerically in a majority in the North-Western and Eastern Zones of India should be grouped to constitute "independent states" in which the constituent unit shall be autonomous and sovereign'. (See the resolution, adopted by the twenty-seventh session of the Muslim League on 23 March 1940, in Pirzada (undated), *Foundations of Pakistan: All India Muslim League documents*, Vol. II: 337.)
9 Even the Viceroy, in his appreciation of the political situation, underlined the importance of the Lahore resolution. According to him: 'though the scheme for a vivisection of India has been bitterly denounced by Hindus of all parties, ... there is a growing consciousness of the strength of Moslem opinion behind the League; and even the Congress would like, if they could, to appease Moslem suspicion of majority rule' (see IOR, L/PJ/8/787, Telegram, the Viceroy to the Secretary of State, 19 April 1940).
10 Khaliquzzaman 1961.
11 CSASC, Benthall Papers, Box No. XVII, Edward Benthall's note on the constitutional reform in India, 1940, p. 8. Drawing attention to the mass consternation regarding the Viceroy's remark that the proposed scheme of Pakistan was nothing but 'a counsel of despair', Benthall warned the government of adverse consequences not only in India but elsewhere if the Muslims were alienated.
12 CSASC, Benthall Papers, Box No. XIV, Edward Benthall's diary note of 9 May 1940.
13 IOR, R/3/1/105, Wavell to Casey, 1 January 1945.
14 Jinnah's statement in the *Dawn*, 21 September 1945. According to Jinnah, 'no attempt will succeed except on the basis of Pakistan and that is the major issue to decided by all those who are well-wishers of India and who are really in earnest to achieve real freedom and independence of India, and the sooner it is fully realised, the better'.
15 IOR, R/3/1/105, V. P. Menon to Even Jenkins, the Governor of Punjab, 20 October 1945.
16 IOR, R/3/1/105, Wavell to Pethick-Lawrence, 25 October 1945. Reporting on Jinnah's election campaign to the Secretary of State, Pethick-Lawrence, Wavell expressed his 'uneasiness' about the confidence the Muslims were showing in securing Pakistan in the aftermath of the 1946 elections.
17 IOR, R/3/1/105, the Governor of Punjab to Wavell, 16 August 1945. Jenkin, the Punjab Governor, was 'perturbed about the situation because there is a very serious danger of the elections being fought, so far as Muslims are concerned, on an entirely false issue. Crude Pakistan may be quite illogical, undefinable and ruinous to India and in particular to Muslims, but this does not detract from its potency as a political slogan'.
18 Only a privileged 12.5 per cent of the total population and a mere 11 per cent of Muslims had the actual right of political choice (see Jalal 1985: 149).
19 The Delhi resolution was accepted by the convention of Muslim League legislators on 9 April 1946 (see Pirzada (undated), *Foundations of Pakistan*, Vol. II: 512–13).
20 Shaikh 1986: 547–8.
21 The Congress dismissed Jinnah's demand for parity because 'in numerical terms this meant the equation of minority with majority, which was both absurd and politically impossible'. To this Jinnah retorted that 'the debate was not about numbers nor even about communities but about Nations. Nations

were equal irrespective of the size'. For details of Jinnah's argument, see Mansergh (1999: 227–30).
22 Jinnah's Presidential address in the 1940 Lahore session of the All India Muslim League (see Pirzada (undated), *Foundations of Pakistan*, Vol. II: 337).
23 Jinnah always insisted that 'there are two major nations in India. This is the root cause and essence of our troubles. When there are two major nations how can you talk of democracy which means that one nation majority will decide everything for the other nation although it may unanimous in its opposition ... these two nations cannot be judged by western democracy. But they should be treated as equals and attempts should be made to solve the difficulties by acknowledging this fact'. Jinnah's press statement, *Dawn*, 1 August 1946.
24 Jalal 1998: 2185.
25 Brass 1991: 94.
26 *The Star of India*, 24 March 1940.
27 Ambedkar 'Thoughts on Pakistan', in Hasan 2000: 48.
28 Francis Robinson, however, does not subscribe to the view that Muslims in India constituted 'a nation'. His study of the Uttar Pradesh Muslims suggests that by most of the standards applied to modern European nations, they were not a nation. Being Muslim, of course, argues Robinson, 'did not make them a nation' (Robinson 1974: 345). Robinson's argument does not appear to be tenable, since 'nation is always imagined into existence and never derivative'. In the context of colonialism, the Muslim 'nation' was constructed through a complex process of contestation involving the British, the Hindus and a particular type of imperial rule that unfolded with the partial devolution of power to the Indians in the beginning of the twentieth century.
29 Jalal 1996: 101.
30 IOR, R/3/1/129, Burrows to Wavell, 8 January 1947. As Burrows reported, Nazimuddin insisted that 'the Muslims needed to be favoured in exchange of the services rendered to the British during the war'. As early as 1940, Edward Benthall warned the Government of an embarrassment 'if the Muslim demands are coupled with loyal assistance in the war' (see CSASC, Benthall Papers, Box No. XIX, Benthall's diary notes on the political situation in 1940).
31 *The Star of India*, 4 March 1941.
32 IOR, L/I/1/777, confidential appreciation of the political situation, October 1946. According to this official report, 'under Hindu Mahasabha and Arya Samaj, communal bitterness [against the Muslims] has reached an alarming height. The Mahasabha expressed misgivings that by working on the nerves of the Viceroy and Nehru, Jinnah would succeed in securing the compulsory grouping of provinces which, in Hindu opinion, means Pakistan in another form. The Working Committee of the Mahasabha urged the Government to declare the League illegal if it continued to pursue unconstitutional methods'.
33 IOR, L/I/1/777, confidential appreciation of the political situation, October 1946.
34 NMML, B. S. Moonjee Papers, Subject File No. 30 (Communal riots in Bengal), speech at the All India Hindus Mahajati Sammelan, Delhi, 19 August 1946.
35 The Bihar riots had shown the dangerous face of Hindu communalism. Attributing the killings in Bihar to the lower rung of the Provincial Congress, the Viceroy wrote: 'they were undoubtedly organised and organised very thoroughly, by the supporters of the Congress'. Viceroy to the Secretary of State, 22 November 1947 (see Mansergh *et al.*, Vol. IX, 1980: 139–40).
36 In his press statement of 7 May 1947, Shyama Prasad Mookherjee thus

argued, 'we Hindus of Bengal ... have suffered for a long time. We have allowed ourselves to be subjected to the tyranny of majority oppression. But we are not going to tolerate this any longer ... throughout the length and breadth of this province, a new movement is rising which will make the interests of the Hindus felt. If we cannot get justice by legitimate means, it will be our natural duty to resort to every possible form of obstruction and agitation for the purpose of safeguarding our interests and privileges' (see *Amrita Bazar Patrika*, 7 May 1947).

37 NMML, B. S. Moonjee Papers, Subject File No. 74 (Communal riots in Bengal), Ashutosh Lahiri, the General Secretary, All India Hindu Mahasabha, to Moonjee, 8 November 1946.
38 IOR, L/PJ/8/655, Burrows to Mountbatten, 21 January 1947.
39 B. R. Ambedkar, *Pakistan or the Partition of India*, (pamphlet), Bombay, 1945 (2nd edn).
40 B. R. Ambedkar, *Pakistan or the Partition of India*, (pamphlet), Bombay, 1945 (2nd edn), p. vii.
41 B. R. Ambedkar, *Pakistan or the Partition of India*, (pamphlet), Bombay, 1945: 352–8. For a detailed analytical discussion of Ambedkar's argument in favour of the claim for Pakistan, see Chatterjee 2001: 414–15.
42 Datta 2002: 5037.
43 Puri 2003: 491.
44 The expression is borrowed from Asim Roy (1990).
45 Moon 1989: 1170. Endorsing the views of Penderel Moon, Nicholas Mansergh, in his account of the transfer of power, argues that (a) Mountbatten's recommendation to bring forward the date of transfer without the League's acceptance of a united India left the British government with no alternative other than to hand over to more than one authority and (b) the early date had the great advantage of ridding Britain of responsibility for an unruly country, putting more pressure on the Indian politicians, and implying a successful conclusion to the extensive negotiations (see Mansergh 1999: 234).
46 IOR, R/3/1/158, Viceroy to Ismay, the Secretary of State, 11 May 1947.
47 Sherwani 1986.
48 Morris Jones 1982: 30.
49 Mansergh 1999: 234.
50 Krisnan 1983: 22.
51 IOR, R/3/1/105, Casey, the Bengal Governor to Wavell, 6 November 1944.
52 *Memoirs of Huseyn Shaheed Suhrawardy* 1987: 26.
53 Spear 1965: 387.
54 IOR, Tyson Papers, Eur. E 341/41, John Tyson's note, 17 November 1946.
55 IOR, L/PJ/8/655, Burrows to Mountbatten, 11 April 1947.
56 To the Congress demand that the British should quit, Jinnah responded with the demand that they should divide and quit. He was, however, only partly successful because what he asked for was not the division that followed the transfer of power. The full demand was for an independent state of Pakistan comprising two areas, one in the north-west (consisting of Sind, Baluchistan, North West Frontier Province and Punjab), the other in the north-east (consisting of Bengal and Assam). His demand rested on community, and that 'every argument that could be used in favour of Pakistan can equally be used in favour of the exclusion of the non-Muslim areas from Pakistan'. So, following the partition of Bengal and Punjab, Jinnah was left with what he had once dismissed as 'a mutilated, a moth-eaten and truncated Pakistan' (see Mansergh 1999: 230).

INTRODUCTION

57 Hodson 1969: 402.
58 Singh 1987: 237.
59 Jalal 1985: 1.
60 Moon further added that 'by 1947, the British Raj was outmoded and its end some years overdue. Mountbatten rang down the curtain on 15th August, not a moment too soon' (Moon 1989: 1171).
61 Alan Campbell-Johnson, (1951: 356) who was with Mountbatten during the last phase of the transfer of power reminisced: 'there had been many communal migrations before, but never of this magnitude.'
62 For a competent and thorough review of literature on the 1947 Great Divide, see Mahajan 2000: 17–35, and Tai Yong Tan and Kudaisya 2000: 7–30.
63 I owe this to Atul Kohli (1987: 12–14). Gyanendra Pandey also articulated the scope of his recently published work on partition in this way (Pandey 2001: 17).
64 Partition has been an important theme in recent scholarly writings. It is impossible to list all of them, so only the major works have been referred to. There are both macro- and micro-studies; while the former revolve mainly around the all India scene, the latter focus on Bengal and Punjab and other British-Indian provinces to draw out the impact of partition. Of the major macro-studies, the following are very useful: Jalal 1985; Page 1987; Singh 1987; Hasan 1993, 1997, 2000, 2001a; Menon 1993; Ahmed 1997; French 1997; Butalia 1998; Moon 1998; Mahajar 2000; Prasad 2000; Kaul 2001; Pandey 2001. For micro-analysis, the following titles have forwarded arguments which are useful to grapple with local situations. Brass 1974; Robinson 1974; Sen 1976; Rashid 1987; Gilmartin 1988; Talbot; Das 1991; Low 1991; Chatterji 1995; Murshid 1995; Low and Brasted 1998; Singh 1999; Bandyopadhyay 2001.
65 Communal identity is a constructed category because communities constantly recreate themselves. However, its extent is limited. The fluidity of communal identities is not completely free-floating, but relates to conceptions of time and space, and the relationships between histories, cultures and biographies. That communal identity is open to change also confirms that identity is no more than a relatively stable construction in an ongoing process of social activity. The act of re-definition is not a matter of accident. By highlighting some aspects of their distinctive character, setting themselves new goals and redefining themselves in certain ways, communities articulate themselves differently. Yet, a re-definition of communal identity that they can effect is constrained by the past they inherit. In other words, the process of self-creation does not occur in a historical vacuum. A community's identity is therefore 'neither unalterable and fixed, nor a voluntarist project to be executed as it pleases, but a matter of slow self-recreation within the limits set by its past'. For a detailed exploration of this argument, see, Chakrabarty 2003.
66 Pandey 2001: 198.
67 Datta 1999: 22.
68 Datta 1999: 71.
69 Datta 1999: 73.
70 Hasan 2001b: 2.
71 The article first appeared in Sission and Wolpert (1998); it was later reproduced in Hasan 1993.
72 Shaikh, 1986, reproduced in Hasan 1993.
73 Moore 1983, also reproduced in Hasan 1993.
74 Ahmed 1997: xxi.
75 Moore 1993: 165.

INTRODUCTION

76 Gilmartin 1988.
77 Ian Talbot developed this argument fully (see Talbot 1988).
78 Chatterjee 1982a, reproduced in Hasan 1993.
79 Persuaded by the logic of the argument, M. Mujeev thus sharply comments, 'the needs which found political expression were not the needs of the community as a whole but those of a class, which consisted of big and small landlords and the lawyers, doctors, government servants who belonged to the families of these landlords' Mujeev 1970: 410.
80 Chatterjee 1982a, reproduced in Hasan 1993: 264.
81 Chatterjee 1982a, reproduced in Hasan 1993: 272.
82 Bose 1986: 181.
83 Bose 1986: 231.
84 Bose 1986: 28.
85 Gordon 1978, reproduced in Hasan 1993.
86 Gordon 1978, reproduced in Hasan 1993: 298.
87 Abul Mansur Ahmad, 'End of a betrayal and restoration of Lahore resolution', Dacca, 1975, quoted in 1993: 300.
88 This is what Leonard Gordon has drawn from interviews with those who underwent the trauma of partition. What is fascinating is the argument that very few of those Hindus who suffered 'had thought that there would be partition until the middle of 1940s'. After that event, they said, 'Hindus and Muslims could not trust each other [and] would not live together. They also felt this terrible bloodbath [of 1946] had been inspired by and was the responsibility of the Muslim League Government in Bengal and would never agree to live under a Muslim League Government'. Gordon 1978, reproduced in Hasan 1993: 304.
89 This is not peculiar to Bengal, as contemporary researches on the community formation elsewhere have shown that almost the same processes appear to have unfolded. For instance, the works of Oberoi (1994), Gupta (1996) and Datta (1999) are persuasive articulations of this process in the context of colonialism.
90 Jalal 1998: 2183.
91 Ayesha Jalal, in Bose and Jalal 1997: 103.
92 Jalal 2001: 57.
93 Jalal 2000: 101.
94 Murshid 1995: 204.
95 Murshid 1995: 203.
96 Page 1987: 260. Anita Inder Singh pursues the point further, and argues that the privileging of one community as against another continued to remain the basic thrust of the imperial rule till the transfer of power. In the process, neither the British nor the Congress gained: 'the Muslim League was the only party to achieve what it wanted' (Singh 1987: 242).
97 Corroborating the argument, D. A. Low (1991: 7) argues that, in the light of the available research, 'it then seems more and not less important to allow for the considerable assistance which Muslim leaders in pre-independence India secured in pursuing their objectives from their imperial British Masters [sic]. Whether it was Viceroy Willingdon in the 1930s, or Viceroy Linlithgow in the 1940s, the evidence is now palpable that they constantly acted to bolster India's principal Muslim politicians as a counterweight to the Congress and that as a consequence these Muslim leaders enjoyed a quite extraordinary degree of influence upon events. Both Fazli Husain in the 1930s and Mohammad Ali Jinnah in the 1940s used their leverage to that effect: Husain in

INTRODUCTION

influencing the delegation of power to the provinces under the Government of India Act of 1935; Jinnah in insisting not only that he should be treated as the leader of India's Muslim on par with Gandhi from the Congress but also as Muslim India's "sole spokesman", superior to the Muslim Chief Ministers of India's Muslim majority Provinces, Sikander Hyat Khan and Fazlul Haq more especially'.

98 David Gilmartin, in Low 1991: 110.
99 Ayesha Jalal, in Bose and Jalal 1997: 93.
100 The Congress leadership seemed to be aware of the consequences. Rajendra Prasad, for instance, wrote to Vallabhbhai Patel that opposition to the hoisting of the national flag and the singing of *Bande Mataram* was gaining strength because of the 'thoughtlessness and inopportune action of our workers and sympathizers at certain places'. Patel in his reply expressed disappointment, and clearly stated that he regarded this 'as an unseemly demonstration of our intolerance'. National Archives, New Delhi, Rajendra Prasad Papers, File II/1937, Prasad to Patel, 28 September 1937, and Patel to Prasad, 2 October 1937.
101 *Amrita Bazar Patrika*, 9 September 1944. The trend was similar throughout India. Even in Sind, where political activity had been sporadic even during the Khilafat enthusiasm, the League 'set up 450 branches, comprising at least in theory 126,484 members' (Hasan 1995: 17).
102 Moore 1983.
103 The Bengal Governor, Casey's diary note, 2 January 1946, in Mansergh *et al.*, Vol. VI, 1970: 732.
104 Undoubtedly, these *mullahs* and *pirs* had contributed to the League's success at the 1946 polls. Their increasing presence in the campaign for Pakistan, especially in the aftermath of the 1946 elections, caused 'a peculiar tension in the Muslim League hierarchy since 'the men of religion were hardly the disciplined cadres of a League command – whether at the centre or in the provinces' (Jalal 1985: 172).
105 Ahmed 1981: 184. Interestingly, what was evident in Bengal had parallels elsewhere. Ernest Gellner (1969) has shown in his study of Morocco that the saints acted as intermediaries among several tribes to create a religious unity that encompasses the distinctive tribal identities as well.
106 The role of these religious preachers have also been acknowledged elsewhere. Ernest Gellner, for instance, has shown in his study of Morocco that the saints can act as intermediaries among several tribes and thus create a religious unity that encompasses tribal diversity (Gellner 1969).
107 Roy 1973, 1977. Roy later developed his argument in *The Islamic Syncretistic Tradition in Bengal* (Roy 1983).
108 The Muslim League won 83.6 per cent of the Muslim votes in Bengal, while in Punjab its share was 65.1 per cent (IOR, R/3/1/128, Wavell to Nehru, 8 May 1946). Furthermore, the League captured all the Muslim seats in the elections to the central legislative assembly. More importantly, the League secured nearly 75 per cent of the total Muslim vote cast in the elections to provincial assemblies throughout India – a remarkable improvement on the abysmal 4.4 per cent it had registered in the 1936–37 elections (Jalal 1985, pp. 171–2).
109 Jalal 1985: 171.
110 The 1946 election was remarkable in the sense that its outcome marked, as Sucheta Mahajan has lyrically put, 'the cleavage between the two stories of nationalism and communalism. The Congress sweep of the general seats strengthened its position at the head of the nationalist firmament. But equally

INTRODUCTION

emphatic was the victory of the Muslim League in the Muslim seats, a flagrant challenge to the Congress' claim to be the voice of all the Indian people. There was a new dimension too. The Muslim League was increasingly inclined to speak in a voice that rang out distinct from the Congress and the British. It was no longer content to provide the orchestrated cacophony desired by the British when the monotone of the nationalist forces seemed dangerously hypnotic. The League's call was "Pakistan", a Muslim nation that had gained freedom from Britian and from "Hindu" India'. (Mahajan 2000: 384–5).

111 Murshid, in Low 1991: 159. According to Murshid, the unity that was forged as political expedient was ephemeral and the possibility of forging a deeper unity among the Muslims was never explored. As a result, once Pakistan emerged as an independent state there was demand for clarity as to what it stood for. As Hindus were no longer to fight against, other forms of conflict and competition within Muslim society surfaced in a big way.

112 Ahmad 1988: 201. While being critical of the 'Hindu literary figures', Ahmad also strongly defended, in his 1944 address to the Rennaissance Society, a clearly distinct identity of the Bengali Muslims by undermining the differences with their counterparts in what later became West Pakistan. For a brief description of this speech, see Ahmad 1988: 200–2.

113 Hasan 1995: 16–19.

114 Sorenson 1946, quoted in Hasan 1995: 16.

115 The most explicit description of the growth of the Muslims as a community in opposition to the Hindu other is certainly the one provided by Rahi Masoom Reza in his novel *Aadha Gaon* (Half-a-village). In one context, Reza clearly articulated the feeling through a dilagoue the Aligarh students had with the villagers. The students declared, 'you must be aware that at the present time, throughout the country, the Muslims are engaged in a life and death struggle for existence. We live in a country where our position is no more than equivalent to that of salt in dal [lentils]. Once the protective shadow of the British is removed, these Hindus will devour us. That is the reason that Indian Muslims require a place where they will be able to live with honour'. Reza 1994, quoted in Hasan 1997: 117.

116 Chatterji 1995: 149–90.

117 Examples include: C. R. Das' 1923–24 Bengal Pact; the desire to forge a Congress–Krishak Praja Party coalition ministry led by Fazlul Haq in 1937; the 1940 anti-Holwell monument movement; the idea behind the formation of the Progressive Coalition ministry in 1941; and finally the 1947 United Bengal scheme (see Bandyopadhyay 2001: 293).

118 Hasan 1997: 21.

119 Gallagher, 1973: 615.

120 Das 1991.

121 Murshid 1995: 205–6.

122 Murshid 1995: 177–81 and 213–14.

123 This section draws upon Chatterjee 1997: 32–3.

124 Chatterji 1995: 268. While dwelling on the diminishing importance of Bengali Hindu bhadralok, Chatterji reiterates the argument by stating that 'Partition was a last throw of the dice by bhadralok Bengalis in an attempt to win back a lost pre-eminence' (see Bandyopadhyay 2001: 312).

125 Chatterjee 1997: 35.

126 Chatterjee 1997: 33.

127 I owe this point to Sugata Bose, who developed it further in his essay

INTRODUCTION

'Between monolith and fragment: a note on the historiography of nationalism in Bengal', in Bandyopadhyay 2001: 283–96.
128 This aspect has been brilliantly brought out by Richard M. Eaton, in his *The Rise of Islam and Bengal Frontier, 1204–1760*, Oxford University Press, Delhi, 1994.
129 Bandyopadhyay, in Hasan and Nakazato 2001: 151–96. According to Bandyaypadhyay, 'the Partition movement in Bengal in 1947 was by no means just a bhadralok affair, although the initiative came evidently from them. ... [The] dalit brethren in Bengal had identified themselves with the Hindus and were prepared to cooperate with their co-religionists across class and caste lines against what at that moment appeared to be their projected "Other", the Muslims. This meant their crossing the boundary, at least for the moment, and leaping onto the domain of the India, predominantly Hindu nation, as represented by the Congress-[Hindu] Mahasabaha combine in those critical days of colonial rule in India' (Hasan and Nakazato 2001: 191, 194).
130 Chatterji 1995: 251–4.
131 Chatterjee 1997: 36.
132 Hashim 1974. This campaign has received an elaborate academic treatment by Taz-ul-Hashmi 1992.
133 Joya Chatterji, in Bandyopadhyay 2001: 309.
134 Asim Roy, in Bandyopadhyay 2001: 209–10.
135 Asim Roy, in Bandyopadhyay 2001: 211.
136 van der Veer 1996: 30.
137 Chatterjee 1997: 37.
138 David Page argues that 'the final act of devolution [of power] was also a final act of division' (Page 1987: 265).

1
THE HINDU–MUSLIM DIFFERENCES
The socio-economic and cultural dimensions

The nature of agrarian relations and their impact on political development in the pre-1947 Bengal had a decisive influence on the complexion and articulation of institutional politics. The Hindu–Muslim differences in both socio-political and cultural terms laid the foundation of communal political groups. Capitalising on the disproportionate economic development between the two communities, the Muslim political forces strengthened their claims for a separate state. Among the Hindus, the rise of the lower castes and their challenge to the domination of the upper castes also had a noticeable impact on provincial political arithmetic. The aim of this chapter is to elucidate this socio-economic background, since this was both the source and context of political articulation in Bengal. Ecological and demographic influences brought about variations in the political economy of the province. By concentrating on these influences, an attempt will be made to show how they caused differential development in the rapidly changing economy of pre-partition Bengal.

The political economy of Hindu–Muslim relations

Bengal's socio-economic configurations provided a crucial structural condition in which the Hindu–Muslim relations were articulated. The fact that the peasantry in east Bengal was predominantly Muslim and landlords largely Hindu remained important in organising one community against another. In view of a well-defined borderline between the two communities, the clash of economic interests between the Muslim peasantry and their oppressors, the high caste landlords and moneylenders with whom the entire Hindu community came to be identified in the Muslim mind, seemed to be inevitable. In other words, '[a]lthough the conflicts were basically economic, the prevailing ideological atmosphere of grievance of the Muslim peasantry soon acquired a communal colour'.[1] The Muslim vested interests who had grievances against the Hindu landlords and moneylenders undertook a well-planned campaign to draw mileage out of this. The combination of religious appeal with economic interests created 'a politically volatile situation highly susceptible to communalist propaganda'.[2] Those who organised the Muslim peasantry under these peculiar circumstances continued to emphasise this dimension, underplaying, if not ignoring, the exploitative role of the Muslim landlords. According to the available evidence, the rent-receiving classes expanded rapidly between 1921 and 1931 (see Table 1.1). The religious composition of these rent-receiving classes, however, in Table 1.2, challenges the established hypothesis that communalism owed its growth predominantly (if not exclusively) to a disproportionate economic development between the two communities. In view of a specific pattern of crowd behaviour in the communal riots – some were agrarian conflicts – it is easy to discern the role of communalism in uniting one community against another.

Table 1.2 clearly demonstrates that in these Muslim-majority divisions, the number of Muslim rent-receivers was no less significant than anywhere else in Bengal. The fact that the Muslim anti-zamindari movement in these areas was directed predominantly against the Hindu zamindars and talukdars confirms the role of communalism in consolidating one community against another.

The situation deteriorated especially after the Great Depression of the 1930s, which brought a decisive change in the balance of class power in rural Bengal. As the recent work of Sugata Bose has shown, the rupture in the system of rural credit relations deprived Hindu talukdars and traders of their dominance. With their reluctance to provide credit to the peasants as *mahajans* (money lenders and lenders of food grain during the lean period), they lost social credibility in the Muslim-dominated small peasant economy of east Bengal in particular. As Bose argues, the rentier and trading classes 'ceased to perform any useful function. Once a political challenge came within the realm of possibility, the strength of a religious identity was exploited in a readily available and, for the privileged co-religionist, a safe ideology'.[3] So at a critical juncture of Bengal's history,

Table 1.1 Categories of agricultural workers as a percentage of the total agricultural workforce in British Bengal, 1911–31

	1911	1921	1931
Rent-receivers	4.13	4.02	7.90
Owner-cultivators	85.76	83.74	52.63
Tenants	—	—	8.81
Agricultural labourers	10.10	12.23	30.76*

Source: Mukherji 1982: 231.

Note
*At the all-India level, the increase in agricultural labourers was massive. According to a study by Karunamoy Mukherjee, between 1882 and 1931, the increase was from 7.5 to 33 million – an increase of 78.78 per cent (Mukherjee 1957: 114).

Table 1.2 Percentage of total population and rent-receivers in majority Muslim divisions, 1911

Districts	Muslims (percentage of total population)	Muslims (percentage of rent-receivers)	Hindus (percentage of total population)	Upper caste Hindus[1] (percentage of rent-receivers)	Others (percentage of rent-receivers)
Rajshahi	60.93	37.22	35.53	20.04	42.74[2]
Dhaka	68.55	33.44	30.80	38.50	28.06
Chittagong	71.37	49.13	24.73	30.74	20.13

Sources: *The Census of India*, 1911, Vol. V, Part II, p. 299, Appendix to Table XVI (Part II): distribution of actual workers in certain groups (by caste for Hindus, by race for Christians and by religion for members of other religions). Also, Chatterjee, 1982: 11.

Notes
1 Upper caste Hindus are *Brahman, Baidya* and *Kayastha.*
2 In the Rajshahi division, Rajbangshi constituted 8.34 per cent of the total rent-receivers.

religious–communal identity did impart a sense of collectivity and an ideological legitimation once the balance of class power had undergone a decisive shift. Since they no longer played any useful role, they were considered parasites and hence, Bose has argued, Muslims were easily convinced of their exploitative role. The control of the state machinery by the KPP–Muslim League alliance after the 1937 elections changed 'organised politics' significantly. Once the political division at the institutional level of politics came to correspond to a religious cleavage, and religion in the countryside came to provide an ideology uniting Muslims with different political commitments under the same banner, the communal schism was unbridgeable.[4]

The discussion pursued so far has drawn attention to a gradual deterioration in the income of the Bengali agrarian population. Until 1929, Bengal agriculture accommodated rapidly growing demographic pressure without any substantial change in its structure. This was due to the extension of the cultivated area,[5] and the growth of high-value cash crops like rice and jute. It has been well demonstrated in various works on the Bengal agrarian economy how jute strengthened 'the small peasant economy' and how the sudden decline of price as a result of the Depression affected it adversely. According to B. B. Chaudhuri, by the turn of the twentieth century there was very little cultivable land in Bengal that was not fully employed.[6] It has also been shown how developments within the Bengal agrarian economy contributed to the rise of a *rentier* class, the basic root of which lay perhaps in the size of the gap between the fixed rent payable to the government and the total rent extracted from the actual tiller. According to a 1918–19 estimate, 'proprietors and tenure-holders intercepted as much as 76.7 percentage of the gross rent of Rs. 12.85 Crores, only Rs. 2.99 Crores being collected as land revenue'.[7]

The gap between rent and revenue along with income from other sources, like trade and commerce or incomes from professional activity, constituted the financial basis of the *madhyabitta sreni* (middle class) as they were identified in the contemporary literature.[8] Since there was no grave dislocation within the agrarian economy until the Great Depression, this class continued to thrive, but their income from rent began decreasing from the mid-nineteenth century with the proliferation of estates and tenures. With the exception of two districts in north Bengal, by the end of the nineteenth century the zamindari property became increasingly characterised by extensive fragmentation due to inheritance customs. The position was particularly bad in west and central Bengal because the limit to the natural expansion of land had virtually been reached by the second half of the nineteenth century. The situation in east Bengal was not as gloomy as it was elsewhere because land was more fertile and the process of natural expansion of land continued almost until 1932 (see Table 1.3).

Moreover, the fact that jute was a high-value crop for the world market and grown in east Bengal, enabled the peasants to meet the rent demands of an expanding class of *rentiers*. However, there was a limit as well. Since the demand for jute in the world market was a determining factor, the peasants themselves could not expand jute cultivation. The demand for jute in the international market increased by 35 percent between 1922 and

Table 1.3 Changes in cultivated areas in the moribund and active delta regions (in acres)

West Bengal	Normal cultivated area at the end of the nineteenth century	Cultivated area, 1931–32	Percentage increase or decrease
Burdwan	1 248 300	742 100	−40.6
Nadia	990 400	913 200	−7.8
Murshidabad	1 106 600	946 500	−14.5
Jessore	1 303 600	887 300	−31.9
Hooghly	541 400	293 900	−45.7
East Bengal			
Dhaka	1 086 169	1 709 000	+57.3
Bakerganj	1 660 000	2 015 000	+21.4
Mymensingh	3 076 800	3 674 500	+19.4
Faridpur	1 295 800	1 470 300	+13.5
Tippera	1 315 900	1 472 800	+11.9
Noakhali	169 087	192 600	+6.4 [sic]

Source: Evidence of the British India Association in the Bengal Land Revenue Commission, *The Report of the Land Revenue Commission*, 1940, Vol. III: 284.

1929,[9] but the Depression affected its market adversely. Thus with the sudden decline of its demand in the world market during the depression, the fragility of 'the small peasant production' was exposed in east Bengal. Everybody associated with land was hard-hit. As Table 1.4 shows, between 1928–29 and 1940–41, the fall in the collection of rent was alarming in the major jute-growing districts.

It is evident that rental incomes declined drastically between 1929 and 1941. The rent-receiving classes and small landlords adopted 'the certificate procedure' to realise the arrears of rent but, given peasants' inability to pay because there was little/less money for jute, the certificate procedure never became effective. Even the old device of 'selling the defaulters' holdings'[10] did not work because there was little money available for the purchase. The situation took an alarming turn in view of the growing 'no rent mentality' of the late 1930s in the jute-growing areas of east Bengal which, according to the Dhaka Divisional Commissioner, posed 'a serious threat to the zamindari system itself'.[11]

The Great Slump brought about drastic changes in the Bengal political economy. As a result of a sudden decrease of income from land, the moneyed class (with whatever money they had), in large numbers, started investing in houses in cities, in shares and in other securities rather than in land.[12] The sudden fall in the demand for jute in the world market adversely affected the jute-cultivators; in the absence of an alternative source of livelihood, their economic conditions were more precarious than ever. Thus the Congress was identified as 'anti-peasant'[13] because of its opposition to the 1928 Bengal Tenancy (Amendment) Act, which benefited at least a section of the agricultural population by proposing to withdraw the right of pre-emption for the zamindars and the transfer fee payable to the zamindars.[14] Not only did it strengthen anti-Congress propaganda in rural Bengal; it also consolidated the position of those Muslims opposed to the Congress under the *Nikhil Banga Praja Samiti*, which became in 1936 the Krishak Praja Party.[15] Since its inception, the *Praja Samiti* had strengthened its support base by organising the rural masses on

Table 1.4 Collection of rents in some east Bengal districts, 1928–41 (shown as percentages)

	Dhaka	Mymensingh	Rangpur	Dinajpur	Tippera
1928–29	54.09	40.82	29.75	62.94	56.44
1940–41	26.91	15.90	15.76	29.17	30.19

Source: Chaudhuri 1984: 7.

Note
Figures for 1940–41 were not truly representative of the changes in the post-Depression period because of the war crisis.

agrarian issues. It had a remarkable success in east Bengal, where Congress always backed zamindars against the prajas.[16] Although the Praja movement strove to reach beyond the landlords by championing the intermediary landed interests, it was equally opposed to the idea of extending occupancy rights to the bargadars.[17] Despite the limitation of the Praja movement, it was nonetheless radical because (1) it challenged the foundations of the age-old zamindari domination; (2) it provided the relatively under-privileged agricultural classes with an opportunity to organise themselves for an effective resistance to the landed gentry; and (3) as a result not only did it raise popular consciousness, but it also initiated a novel process of mass mobilisation on socio-economic and cultural grounds.

The quotidian life of Hindus and Muslims in Bengal

The schism between Hindus and Muslims was articulated not only in the public sphere but also in the social and cultural transactions in people's quotidian life that divided the Hindus and Muslims more effectively than resolutions of the League, speeches in the Congress sessions or political pacts.[18] 'Socially', as Tamijuddin remarks, 'Muslims were in most respects untouchables to the Hindus ... and if therefore a Muslim somehow happened to enter the cook-shed of a Hindu, even if he did not touch food or utensils, all cooked food stored in the house along with the earthen pots were considered polluted and thrown away'.[19] In addition to this, the perception that because the landlords were Hindus they exploited the Muslim tenants[20] exacerbated the situation, given the composition of zamindars and cultivators in east Bengal. Moreover, the humiliating treatment of Muslim tenants by Hindu landlords did not escape notice. As Tamijuddin narrated:

> Muslim tenants, most of whom were cultivators, while visiting the landlords' office were to squat on the gunny clothes spread on the floor or planks or on *piris* [low stools not higher than an inch or two] placed on their floor, while Hindu peasants of similar status were allowed to sit on the raised *farash* [knee-high platform covered with shatranj or sheets] on which the officers of the landlords used to be seated. Muslims, not allowed to smoke from the same hookas [smoking pipe] as the Hindus, were to smoke from the inferior *hookas* meant for them or from the *chhilims* [cone-shaped earthen containers of tobacco prepared from smoking placed on the perpendicular cylinder of a *hooka*] with the help of their fingers and folded palms.[21]

The socio-economic segregation of the two communities was so pronounced that they felt that they were 'two distinct communities in spite of fraternization in certain fields of activity'.²² An anecdote recounted in the reminiscences of Mrinal Sen, the famous film maker, also confirms that even the educated middle class families in east Bengal were not free from prejudice against Muslims. A regular member of the house, Jasimuddin, the noted Bengali poet, was, as Sen informs us, never integrated with the family as a Hindu would have been. The poet perhaps realised this and one day Jasimuddin, as Sen further mentions, 'said to my mother, Mother, if it is true that I am one of your sons, why do you feed me seating me outside? Why is it that you never let me sit with your sons to eat from the same plate'?²³ This is one side of the story showing perhaps the dilemma of an otherwise enlightened Bengal family in completely breaking the age-old socio-cultural barrier. What is revealing is the response of Sen's mother, who found herself in difficulty:

> What Jasim said was not untrue after all. But mother was helpless. She explained to him that she had no objection to having him sit inside while feeding but the servants of the household would not accept this arrangement. She also mentions that it is she who washes up the plates, used by Jasimuddin'.²⁴

Sen's illustration confirms the cultural segregation of Hindus and Muslims even in Faridpur, which was relatively free from communal troubles during the pre-partition days, and also the dilemma of these families, otherwise free from anti-Muslim prejudices, that had simultaneously accepted and transgressed the communal differences. Not willing to attribute the Hindu–Muslim discord to British rule, Nirad Chaudhuri thus argued that it was implicit in 'the very unfolding of our history and could hardly be avoided'. According to him, there were 'four distinct aspects in our attitude towards [the Muslims]' as it was shaped by tradition.

> In the *first* place, we felt a retrospective hostility toward the Muslims for their one-time domination of us, the Hindus; *secondly*, on the plane of thought we were utterly indifferent to the Muslims as an element in contemporary society; *thirdly*, we had friendliness for the Muslims of our own economic and social status with whom we came into personal contact; our *fourth* feeling was mixed concern and contempt for the Muslim peasant, whom we saw in the same light as we saw our low-caste Hindu tenants, or in other words, as our livestock.²⁵

In the public arena too, the Muslims were often bypassed on very flimsy grounds. For instance, what had caused massive consternation among the Muslims was the Hindu refusal to accept the vocabulary commonly used by them as part of the Bengali language. This was a phenomenon which persisted from the time of the Non Co-operation Movement until long after the formation of the KPP–Muslim League coalition ministry in Bengal. In 1938, the education department had refused 'a school text book, written by Abul Mansur Ahmad, [because] it contained no glossary of words of foreign, meaning Arabic or Persian, origin'.[26] With the adoption of the 1932 Communal Award,[27] the Muslims realized, as Abul Mansur Ahmad, an erstwhile Congress member, noted, 'where mere number counts, they must necessarily be a power'.[28] The Muslims began to 'feel that their language, culture and religion would be swamped, [and] they also had the natural fears of a minority and kept demanding safeguards so as to preserve their own way of life and combat their impotence [sic]'.[29] Given the polarisation between the Hindus and Muslims at the grassroots, religion provided the basis of 'a national bond ... and became the rallying cry of a political organisation demanding the creation of a separate Muslim homeland'.[30] The so-called two-nation theory was, as Nirad Chaudhuri pointed out, 'formulated long before Mr. Jinnah or the Muslim League: in truth, it was not a theory at all; it was a fact of history [which] everybody knew as early as the turn of the [twentieth] century'.[31]

The Mussalmani Bangla

In the construction and consolidation of Muslim identity as distinct from the Hindus, the role of the Mussalmani Bangla was immensely important. Although the doctrinal differences between the two principal communities were wide and varied, historically these differences were not of such importance as to divide them in blocs antagonistic to one another. In fact, any unprejudiced consideration of historical Islam would suggest that 'the basic doctrinal principles had very little to do with the political confrontation between the Muslims and the Hindus'.[32] It was only through skilful manipulation of certain religious symbols and constant ideological propaganda that these differences were articulated and utilised in strengthening the claim for a separate homeland for the Muslims. A well-designed scheme in this direction was the Mussalmani Bangla, a curious hybrid which made indiscriminate use of Arabic, Persian and Urdu words.

The story began in the late nineteenth century,[33] but the most significant step was undoubtedly the formation of the Islam Mission Samity in 1904 at the behest of Maniruzzaman Islamabadi, a self-styled preacher of repute seeking to undertake a programme of revivalism and reform in Bengal.[34] In its inaugural meeting, the Samity pledged to pursue the following plan of action to popularise Islam among the Bengali Muslims who were apparently 'ignorant of their cultural roots':[35]

> (a) publication of booklets in simple Bengali on religion and to arrange their free distribution; (b) publication of a magazine

(*Islam Darshan* or *Muslim Dharma*) as a mouthpiece of the mission for free distribution; (c) appointment of salaried missionaries, who would undertake preaching in different parts of Bengal; (d) sending of preachers and missionaries to the remote corners of Bengal where the rays of Islam had not penetrated; (e) translation of religious book on Islam into Bengali; (f) establishment of contacts with Anjumans and such other bodies in different part of Bengal and (g) setting up of a national library for the benefit of preachers, speakers and missionaries.[36]

The basic objective was two-fold: first, the fact that Islam was a cementing force was recognised and its role in both constructing and consolidating a powerful Muslim bloc was, therefore, immensely significant. Secondly, in order to establish the Muslims as a pre-eminent political group in the public arena, the Samity suggested specific programmes involving not only the salaried missionaries but also those 'interested in safeguarding the interests of Muslims in Bengal'.[37] It is true that the Samity never became as effective as was anticipated, but it had certainly contributed to a process that loomed large in the course of time. The Muslim intellectuals realised the importance of creating a space for them not only for survival but also for strengthening their claim for power and privileges in the new environment, created in the aftermath of political and institutional changes, introduced by the colonial administration.

What was initiated by the Islam Mission Samity in 1904 blossomed fully with the formation of *Bangiya Mussalman Sahitya Samity* in 1911 in Calcutta, in which renowned Muslim intellectuals – Moniruzzaman Islamabadi, Mohammad Shahidullah, Mozammel Haq, Eyakub Ali and Hatem Ali Khan – participated. Its principal aim was to bring about 'a national awakening of the Bengal Muslims through the creation of an exclusively Muslim literature or national literature', which was absolutely necessary 'to develop the community as strongly as the Hindus'. Drawing on Islam, the Samity also articulated its objectives in such a way as to consolidate the Islamic identity in opposition to the Hindus. The major aims are, for instance,

(a) translation into Bengali of the scriptures and works of history, written in Arabic, Persian and Urdu; (b) preservation of old Muslim Bengali literature; (c) collection and immediate publication of biographies of *pirs* and *walis* in different part of Bengal; (d) writing of a national history of the Bengali Muslims underlining the importance of ancient Muslim aristocratic families of Bengal; (e) circulation of monthlies, weeklies and other magazines among Muslims and (f) encouraging the Bengali Muslim authors to produce good books on the history of Islam.[38]

HINDU–MUSLIM DIFFERENCES

It is now clear that an attempt was constantly made to culturally separate the Bengali Muslims from their Hindu counterparts. These efforts are also illustrative of the rise of the Muslim middle class in the public arena. Despite its apparent popularity among the educated Muslims, the Samity's activities were primarily confined to holding annual conferences and drafting resolutions until the arrival of Akram Khan[39] on the scene. He was already known for his campaign for the Mussalmani Bangla in the columns of *Ahl-e-Hadis*. An erstwhile Congress member, Khan also opposed the first partition – since it aimed 'at weakening the emerging Bengali nation [it] should be resisted'.[40] Supporting the Mussalmani Bangla as viable, Akram Khan, in his presidential address to the third conference of the Bangiya Mussalman Sahitya Samity, declared,

> Bengali has to be enriched with Arabic and Persian words ... [I]n the current style of written Bengali, the idolatry of the Hindus is so apparent and the Mussalman loses his way in this. First we need publication of our religious texts and our national history in Bengali. Muslim nationalism is completely religious [and] to its great peril the Muslims can forget that their national language is Arabic. ... Urdu is neither our mother tongue nor our national tongue. However, for the protection and nourishment of Muslim nationalism we need Urdu.[41]

Not only did Akram Khan lay down the foundation of the Mussalmani Bangla; he also set the agenda for those involved in the development of Bengali as a completely different language with roots only in Islamic tradition. Whilst justifying the inclusion of Arabic and Persian words, he was, however, guarded in articulating his views on Urdu. Critical of the languages endorsing Hindu idolatry, he argued in favour of Urdu probably because of its importance as a binding factor among the Muslims other than the Bengali Muslims.

Taking cues from Akram Khan, S. Wajed Ali prepared a new set of Bengali alphabets, heavily influenced by Urdu phonetics. While presenting them in the 1924 annual conference of the Bangiya Mussalmand Sahitya Samity, he justified the change 'to facilitate proper pronunciation of Islamic words in the vernacular'.[42] According to him, the present form of Bengali was not equipped to accommodate the Arabic and Persian words. Hence not only were they often misspelt, but they also conveyed a different meaning on occasions presumably due to the absence of the grammar supporting Arabic and Persian. The recommended changes, he was confident, 'will provide a new literary model by appropriately modifying the philological foundation and phonetical style of the Bengali language'.[43] Wajed Ali's suggestion created dissent among the leading Muslim intellectuals. Critical of the blind acceptance of Arabic and Persian language,

Habibur Rahman of the Samity, for instance, argued that the Muslims should familiarise themselves with the language of the Bengali Hindus, although it should be 'ornamented with judicious use of Islamic words'.[44] Challenging Wajed Ali, he further pointed out that the haphazard and unsystematic use of Arabic and Urdu words in the Bengali language, as some over-enthusiasts had already indulged, would cause irreparable damage to the Bengali language and its rich literature. He thus recommended that in order to 'gain parity with the Hindus in the literary field, the Muslim writers should write in the accepted and familiar form [with a constant endeavour to] introduce the Islamic spirit in the language'.[45] Unlike Ali, he was even comfortable with the word *Ishwar* as a synonym of *Allah* because they convey the same meaning while words like *janmajanmantar* or *mangolghat* were simply unacceptable because of the inherent Hindu religious sense.[46] The views expressed by Habibur Rahman were endorsed by a group of leading Muslim intellectuals.[47] Admitting that Islamisation of the language was a prerequisite for a cultural revival, they did, however, recommend 'a careful import of Islamic words into Bengali [without] seriously affecting the existing shape of the language'.[48]

The trend was therefore for the inclusion of words endorsing the Islamic spirit. The primary goal was to change the structure of the language by introducing appropriate modifications in the style of writing. Islamisation of Bengali was necessary because it was felt that the 'Bengali of the Muslims was weak than that of the Hindus ... because the Bengali language had not been adequately Islamised and the Bengali Muslims were yet to become *pucca* Muslims'.[49] This was conveyed in a memorandum presented to the University of Calcutta. Appreciating the adoption of Bengali as a medium of instruction in the Matriculation examination, it was insisted that the university authority should 'create an environment for the development of [Mussalmani Bangla], the language of the majority in Bengal'. In response to a Calcutta University notification[50] underlining the difficulty in supporting the language, which was not only adequately developed but also divisive, the Samity appeared to have lost a cause. A movement was therefore planned to force the university to adopt a policy according official sanction to those Arabic and Persian words 'which have found place in Bengali language for proper and spontaneous expression of different thought and culture and which will be absolutely necessary [for] the vitality of Bengali language'.[51] No movement was launched, and those championing the Mussalmani Bangla appeared to have toned-down their protest. Insisting that 'in order to introduce Muslim thought and ideas and also for creating an Islamic atmosphere in the realm of Bengali prose, poetry and fiction', Abul Mansur Ahmad, one of the leading member of the group endorsing the demand, argued, 'we are in favour of using Arabic and Persian words'.[52] Even the noted writers – like Rabindranath Tagore, Satyendranath Dutta, Mohitlal Mojumdar and Nazrul Islam – borrowed

Arabic and Persian words while expressing their thoughts. Thus the aim of the Mussalmani Bangla was not to create a language of patchwork character by indiscriminately borrowing words of foreign origin, [but] to strengthen the language [by] carefully selecting those useful words which are not simply replaceable.[53]

The campaign for the Mussalmani Bangla seemed to have gained considerably probably because of the demand of another group of Muslim writers in favour of developing 'the Bengali national literature by drawing upon the mediaeval *Punthis*'.[54] For those seeking to defend the distinctive identity of the Bengali Muslims, the *Punthi* literature of the seventeenth and eighteenth centuries had laid the foundation of the national literature. Articulated in the language of the subalterns, most of these tracts deal with the heroic deeds of both real and fictitious Muslim characters in suppressing the *kafirs* or the infidels, though there are romantic stories as well. Not only are they Islamic thematically; the language of the *Punthis* is also Islamic due to the abundance of Arabic and Persian words. A staunch supporter of the Mussalmani Bangla, Abdul Karim insisted on popularising the *Punthis* as probably the only link between the educated Muslims and the plebeian masses. Since the language of the *Punthis*, written in the past, was outdated, the aim of the contemporary Muslim writers was, as Karim argued, 'to develop and refurbish them in such a way as to make them meaningful in contemporary Bengal'. They were also useful models 'to show how Islamic words can be used properly and appropriately'.[55]

Despite their appeal in rural areas, *Punthis* were hardly taken seriously by those, engaged in developing the Mussalmani Bangla. Critical of the indifference of the Muslim intellectuals, Abdul Majid, in an article in the *Saogat*, held the view that the absorption of the *Punthis* was probably 'the most appropriate, if not the only, step to help develop a national literature to the satisfaction of both the common masses and educated minority.'[56] The story was, however, different as soon as Akram Khan began writing in the Mohammadi group of papers supporting the *Punthis* as 'necessary for strengthening the edifice of the Muslim national literature'.[57] During the 1930s, both Akram Khan and his colleague Shahidullah selectively published the adapted versions of several *Punthis* in the Bangiya Mussalman Sahitya Patrika, presumably to strengthen Mussalmani Bangla, which had by then became a marker of the Bengali Muslims especially in urban Bengal.[59]

What had drawn the attention of the ideologues of the Mussalmani Bangla was not the language of the *Punthis*, but the thematic and ideological characteristics of the stories which were invariably Islamic in spirit and tone. The details of these stories may not always have corresponded with reality, but generally evolved around the places renowned in the history of Islam – Istahmbul, Baghdad, Samarkand and Bukhara – and the central figures were invariably Muslims.[59] By linking with the tradition of the rural Muslim masses, the Mussalmani Bangla sought to attain a basic goal of isolating the majority of Muslims from their Hindu counterparts. The mentality of the Muslim was cast in a mould sharply distinct from the expanding world of educated high-caste bhadralok in Bengal. This cleavage in consciousness had explosive long-term implications in the politics of twentieth century Bengal.[60] Thus the effort of creating a distinct language for the Bengali Muslims was strategically appropriate in a context when Muslims were politically most powerful due to changes in the institutional arena following the acceptance of a demographic majority as a possible source of power and privileges.

Muslim identity institutionalised

The newly formed Praja Samiti represented the interests of certain emerging socio-economic groups – *jotedar* (landowner), *sampanna praja* (cultivator) and professional – in Muslim society.[61] At a conference in Dhaka in April, 1936, over which Fazlul Haq presided, the Praja Samiti became the Krishak Praja Party (KPP), which strove to unite the activities of the samitis throughout the province.[62] The east Bengal Muslim landlords reacted instantly, and in May formed a United Muslim Party under the presidentship of Nawab Habibullah of Dhaka in alliance with the New Muslim *Mazlis*, a Calcutta-based political group of Muslim business interests.[63] Referring to the composition of the Muslim Party, Fazlul Haq sarcastically remarked that any Muslim unity forged in 'Nawab's *ahsan manzil* and not *krishak*'s hut would never last long'.[64] Haq's popularity as a leader and non-Bengali dominance in the Muslim League and its elite character were the reasons why the Muslim League did not penetrate the areas where the KPP had strongholds.[65]

Although in August 1936 Jinnah attempted to bring all Muslim political forces under the Muslim League Parliamentary Board, his move was abortive and the Bengali Muslims went to the first provincial polls deeply divided. The election results showed that the KPP had won forty and the Muslim League thirty-nine of Muslim constituencies and the KPP polled 11 per cent more votes than the Muslim League.[66] Soon after the elections, the KPP initiated negotiations with the Congress over the formation of a coalition or a Congress-backed KPP ministry. However, the Congress High Command's decision not to accept office and a disagreement between the Congress and the KPP on economic and political programmes provided the League with an opportunity to share power with the KPP.[67] On being offered the chief ministership, Haq agreed to form a coalition with the Muslim League, compromising on fundamental issues. For instance, all the major promises made in the KPP election manifesto regarding the abolition of zamindari without compensation, free primary education and the release of political prisoners[68] were put aside. In an eleven-member ministry, Haq accommodated eight zamindars, and was in a minority within the ministry because of the eleven ministers, four were Muslim Leaguers, three non-Congress caste Hindus and two non-Congress scheduled caste nominees.[69]

Haq's failure to comply with the election pledges caused dissension within the KPP. At one stage, in March 1938, a majority of the KPP members of the Legislative Assembly sat with the opposition in order to strengthen the anti-coalition bloc.[70] The internal schism within the KPP appeared irredeemable when a dissident KPP group led by Nausher Ali broke away in protest against Haq's consent to the idea of issuing certificates to the defaulters to realise the rents due to the government.[71] The Haq faction thus became a minority within the coalition and his position became untenable, caught, as he was, between two strong and formidable forces – the Muslim League within the coalition, and the combined opposition of the Congress and the KPP in the legislature. These currents and cross-currents presumably influenced Haq's decision to join the Muslim League at its 1937 annual session in Lucknow.

The period between 1937 and 1940 saw Haq attempting to champion the Muslim cause. In 1939, he declared that he was 'a Muslim first and Bengali afterwards.'[72] To establish himself as a genuine Muslim leader he also agreed to introduce the famous Lahore resolution demanding a separate homeland for Muslims. According to a recent work on the KPP, Haq did not endorse Jinnah's two-nation theory, yet he supported the resolution as the only alternative to safeguard Muslim interests.[73] This indicates how calculating he was as a politician. Whatever Haq felt, the fact remains that the outcome of his involvement with the All India Muslim League helped Jinnah favourably in two ways: (1) the task of mobilising the Bengali Muslims was made easier as they found that their leader, Haq, was a supporter of a separate homeland for the Muslims; (2) in order to shape his stipulated Muslim homeland, Jinnah brought the powerful Muslim leaders from both Bengal and Punjab within the fold of the League. This was a significant step in the formation of a separate state in 1947, as it ensured a merger of national and regional Muslim power bases – a merger consolidating the organisational strength of Muslims in India. The 1940 Lahore session was thus a grand success for Jinnah: he succeeded in projecting the demands of Muslims through the leader of a Muslim majority province.

The above summary dealing with the emergence of Muslims not merely as a community but also as a political force in the wider struggle for independence demonstrates that Muslim separatism owed its growth to the realisation, initially of the aristocratic Muslims and later of an English-educated Muslim middle class, of their insignificant role in the power structure. The situation was further complicated with the extension of franchise (Table 1.5), the penetration of formal government institutions

Table 1.5 The increase in voters between 1920 and 1937

Year of election	Council		Assembly	
	No. of voters	Percentage of Muslims	No. of voters	Percentage of Muslims
1920	465 127	1.8	53 935	0.2
1923	463 386	1.8	45 401	0.2
1926	529 995	2.0	63 320	0.2
1936–37	19 610	0.07	3 462 767	12.6

Source: Computed from the tables in the report of the *Indian Statutory Commission*, Vol. III, p. 131, and also the *Report of the Reforms Office*, Bengal, 1932–37, pp. 289–90.

into rural areas, and the opening up of governmental appointments to a relatively larger section of people. With the arrival of new Muslim groups on the political scene, there developed simultaneously a strong pro-Haq support base in the 'unorganised' world. Despite his association with the zamindar-dominated League, Haq pressed hard for the adoption of a series of executive and legislative measures (Bengal Tenancy Amendment Act 1938; the work of the Debt Settlement Boards; the Money Lenders Act) which increased Haq's popularity among the Muslim peasants. In east Bengal, any effort to bring down the Haq ministry was interpreted as a betrayal not only of 'the Muslim cause' but also of 'the peasant cause'.[74] Furthermore, the fact that the chief minister was a Muslim led them to think that they should not be afraid of the police.[75] The interaction between the 'organised' and 'unorganised' worlds of politics[76], based obviously on different perceptions of the actors involved, illustrates a general ideological change among the Muslims.

Concluding observations

Setting the scene, this chapter brings out the complexity and perhaps the impossibility of reconciliation of Hindu–Muslim rivalry. It is evident that the socio-economic schism laid the foundation of communal division. What radically altered the circumstances was a far greater awareness among the newly emerged Muslim leadership of the importance of an organisation to pursue the socio-economic and political goals of the demographically preponderant community. The formation of the Krishak Praja Party in 1936 was certainly a dramatic development for two important reasons: first, Muslims were now organised both as Muslims and as Bengalis to further their cause in opposition to the Hindu counterparts; and secondly, in its consolidation as a powerful community following the adoption of the 1932 Communal Award, the importance of Islam was tremendous – especially in glossing over the obvious differences among the Bengali Muslims. It would probably not be wrong to suggest that the growing strength of the Muslims was largely due to religion, which cemented the bond by drawing upon the communal differences with the Hindus.

Similarly, the construction of the Mussalmani Bangla and the continuous support of the educated Muslim middle class appeared to have been derived from a well-planned design to champion one community against another. By insisting on the inclusion of Arabic and Persian words in Bengali, the Muslim intellectuals were clearly in favour of a language that was not only different but also de-linked from the Hindu intellectual roots. It was also possible for the Mussalmani Bangla to strike roots presumably because of the government patronage. In a communally charged environment, the Mussalmani Bangla became merely a communal instrument despite its obvious literary flavour and strength.

Notes

1 Ahmed 1981: 186.
2 Ahmed 1981: 187.
3 Bose 1986: 231.
4 See Chakrabarty 1985.
5 A common method was to farm out jungle land and other cultivable wastes on tenurial leases to enterprising men who were to clear the land and settle the *raiyats*. Another way, common to east Bengal, was the sudden emergence of *char* (alluvial plain) as a result of a river's change of track.
6 Chaudhuri 1967.
7 Mukherjee 1933, cited in Chatterjee 9.
8 Bhavanicharan Bandyopadhyay, *Kalikata Kamalalaya* (Bengali), Calcutta 1343 (Bengali Shakabda): 8–13.
9 Bagchi 1972: 280.
10 Chaudhuri 1984: 108.
11 WBSA, 51/6/1939, Report of the Dhaka Divisional Commissioner on the no-rent situation, 25 September 1939.
12 Chaudhuri 1984: 108–9.
13 Ahmad 1968: 53.
14 Chatterjee, P. Agrarian Relations and Politics in Bengal: some considerations in the making of the Tenancy (Amendment) Act, 1928, Occasional Paper No. 30, Centre for Studies in Social Sciences, Calcutta, 1980.
15 Jatindra Nath De, 'The history of the Krishak Praja Party: a study of changes in classes and inter-community relations in agrarian Bengal, 1937–47, unpublished PhD thesis, University of Delhi, 1980.
16 Ahmad 1968: 60–1.
17 Ahmad 1968: 151.
18 Sabyasachi Bhattacharya puts this point to argue that the roots of partition lay not in the public sphere but in the quotidian experience of the Hindus and Muslims in the villages. According to him, the communal division was consolidated in 'the manner in which members of different communities related or did not relate with one another' (e.g. commensality, social entertainment and associative patterns), the tropes which were part of conventional language embedding prejudices not consciously thought of (e.g. *nayray* for Muslims, *chanral* for

Namushudras), the communal signature in language (i.e., Mussalmani *Bangla*), the modes of address (e.g. *tui* for low caste Muslims and *atraf* Muslims), intolerance regarding forbidden food (e.g. Muslim prejudice against pork eaten by some Hindu lower castes and tribes, and of course Hindu prejudice regarding beef), community-wise and caste-wise clustering of residence and settlements in villages and sometimes in towns, the separation of low-caste and high-caste Hindu and Muslim hostels in schools and colleges (not only in Calcutta and Dhaka but also in mofussil towns) and the day-to-day face-to-face interaction. See his 'The logic of fission: Bengal or Bengals' (unpublished paper), p. 2.
19 Tamijuddin Khan, *Memoirs*, p. 35 (unpublished).
20 Ahmed 1970: 86.
21 Tamijuddin Khan, *Memoirs*, p. 37 (unpublished).
22 Ibid., p. 39.
23 Sen 1987: 11.
24 Sen 1987: 12.
25 Chaudhuri 1968: 225. Chaudhuri further explained that of these four modes of feeling, 'the first was very positive and well-organised intellectually; the rest were mere habits, not possessing very deep roots'.
26 Ahmad 1978: 272–6. Abul Mansur Ahmad's communalism, as Tazeen M. Murshed wrote, 'was largely a reaction to Hindu chauvinism which amounted what may be called "Hindu separatism". In 1944, he refused to acknowledge the works of Rabindranath Tagore, Vidyasagar and Bankimchandra as representing East Bengali culture, because they did not depict the life of Bengali Muslims nor used their language' (Murshid 1995: 173).
27 For details of the 1932 Communal Award, see Chapter 2.
28 Ahmad 1968: 61.
29 Nawaz 1995: 21.
30 Bose 1986: 232.
31 Chaudhuri 1968: 227.
32 Ahmed 1981: 183.
33 For a detailed study of the genesis of the growth of the Mussalmani Bangla, see De 1998: 47–77; Sarkar 1991: 189–200.
34 Born in Chittagong in 1875, Maniruzzaman Islamabadi wandered through the land. His wanderings took him to Rangpur, Calcutta, Rangoon, Lahore and different parts of Orissa and Assam. He was sometimes a school teacher, reporter or a peasant leader, and often a preacher of Islam. Educated in Hooghly Imambara, Islamabadi was one of the founders of the Bangiya Musalman Sahitya Samiti (later on Bangiya Musalman Sahitya Parishad) in 1911, and was by now well-known as a publicist on such issues as the Hindu–Muslim problem, discrimination against Muslims, the quality of education, colonialism, Islam, the destiny of Islamic civilisation, the nature of imperial power (particularly in Turkey) and the state of the Bengali language. The biographical details of Maniruzzaman Islamabadi draw upon Samaddar 2000: 448–9.
35 *Islam Pracharak*, 23 March 1904.
36 *Islam Pracharak*, 23 March 1904.
37 *Islam Pracharak*, 28 March 1904.
38 *Bangiya Mussalman Sahitya Patriaka*, 1, 1, 1325 [1911], p. 1, cited in Anisuzzaman 1969: 103.
39 Akram Khan was born in the 24 Parganas in 1868. His father, Maulana Bari Khan, was a scholar in Arabic and Persian, a follower of the *ahl-e-hadis*. After completing his school education in Calcutta Madrasa, he began his 70-year long career in writing and activism. He worked in several newspapers and journals

in editorial and other capacities till 1910, when he was able to publish his own newspaper, the *Saptahik Mohammadi*. Other publications too commenced under his guidance: *Dainik Jamana* (1920), *Saptahik O Dainik Sebak* (1921), *Dainik Mohammadi* (1922), *Masik Mohammadi* (1927), *Dainik Azad* (1936) and *Saptahik Comrade* (1946). Although he was politically baptised by the Congress in the wake of the 1905–08 Swadeshi Movement, in 1936 he joined the Muslim League. As the President of the Bengal Muslim League from 1941 to 1947 he became the most determined and consistent advocate of Pakistan, and even after partition he remained a loyal champion of the League. This biography draws upon Samaddar 2000: 452–3.
40 *Barshik Mohammadi*, Vol 1(1), 1334, cited in Anisuzzaman 1969: 162.
41 Akram Khan's presidential speech in the conference of the Bangiya Mussalman Sahitya Samity, 1919, reproduced in Anisuzzaman 1969: 216.
42 *Sahityik*, 1, 9, Sravana, 1334 (Bengali Shakabda).
43 Ibid.
44 *Islam Darshan*, 2, 8, Agrahayan, 1328 (Bengali Shakabda).
45 *Sahityik*, 1, 9, Sravana, 1334 (Bengali Shakabda).
46 Habibur Rahaman on the Mussalmani Bengali, *Islam Darshan*, 2, 8, Agrahayan, 1328 (Bengali Shakabda).
47 Such as Syed Nawab Ali Chowdhury, Shahidulla, Akram Khan, Lutfar Rahman, Abdur Razzaq, Anwar Hussain, Muztaba Ali, Abul Mazid, Abul Hakim, Rezaul Karim, Abul Kalam Shamsuddin. Most of these authors expressed their views in support of Habibur Rahman in their individual writings, published in the *Masik Mohmmadi* or *Saogat* or *Islam Darshan*.
48 Abul Kalam Shamsuddin, 'Sahitye Sampradayikata', *Islam Darshan*, 3, 1, Aswin, 1329 (Bengali Shakabda).
49 *The Star of India*, 5 August 1926, and *The Mussalman*, 7 August 1926.
50 *Amrita Bazar Patrika*, 2 August 1926.
51 *The Mussalman*, 23 October 1932.
52 *The Star of India*, 6 February 1936.
53 *The Star of India*, 6 February 1926.
54 Anisuzzaman 1969: 110.
55 Abul Karim's presidential address to the reception committee of the Bangiya Mussalman Samity in *Bangiya Mussalman Sahitya Patrika*, 1, 1, Baisakh, 1325 (Bengali Shakabda).
56 *The Saogat*, 4, 2, Sravana, 1353 (Bengali Shakabda).
57 *Bangiya Mussalman Sahitya Patrika*, 1, 4, Magh, 1325 (Bengali Shakabda).
58 Critical of the efforts of these Muslim writers, the top Bengali intellectuals like Rabindranath Tagore, Ramesh Chandra Bandyopadhya (in *Probashi*) and Sajani Kanto Das (in *Sanibarer Chhithi*) warned of the adverse consequences if Mussalmani Bangla was allowed to strike roots. Although Tagore was not in favour of rejecting altogether the Arabic and Persian words in Bengali, he was however very disturbed by the design of these Moulvi Sahebs who 'by seeking to flaunt their communal identity [would] not only in the long run spell disaster for the Bengali language and literature but also drive a wedge between Hindu–Muslim communal harmony'. *Probashi*, 32, 5, Bhadra, 1339, p. 602.
59 For details of different stories that figured prominently in the writings of these Muslim writers, see De 1998: 111–19.
60 As Rajat Ray argues, 'Bengali bhadralok, claiming superior knowledge and intellect, were contemptuous of the *Mussalmani Bangla* which both in language and ideas ... were a world apart from ... the reformed modern prose of Bengal' (Ray 1995: 13–14).

61 Jatindra Nath De, The history of the Krishak Praja Party: a study of changes in classes and inter-community relations in agrarian Bengal, 1937–47, unpublished PhD thesis, University of Delhi, 1980, p. 226.
62 Ahmad 1968: 98–9.
63 Momen 1972: 46–7.
64 WBSA, 56/1936, report from the Chittagong Commissioner to the Chief Secretary, Government of Bengal, 7 August 1936.
65 Haroon Rashid, The Bengal Provincial Muslim League, 1906–47, unpublished PhD thesis, University of London, 1983, p. 11.
66 IOR, R/3/2/2, John Anderson, Bengal Governor to Linlithgow, 8 February 1937.
67 See Chapter 2.
68 The KPP election Manifesto, published in *The Star of India*, 12 September 1936.
69 IOR, R/3/2/2, John Anderson, Bengal Governor to Linlithgow, 9 March 1937.
70 Sen 1976: 118–19.
71 Chatterjee 1982: 14.
72 IOR, R/3/2/64, Bengal Governor to the Governor General of India, 5 November 1939.
73 De 1974.
74 WBSA, Home-Poll 242/1939, report from the Chittagong Commissioner to the Chief Secretary, Government of Bengal, 4 May 1939.
75 Ibid.
76 Articulated in the legislative arena, the organised world of politics revolves around the established democratic norms of the western variety. With tremendous influence in the political articulation, the unorganised world of politics was invariably structured around idioms and styles which are clearly outside the accepted notions of politics and political mobilisation.

2

DIVIDE AND RULE

The Communal Award and its implications in Bengal

The debate over the separate and joint electorates as rival modes of election to the various representative institutions by the British began with the Simla deputation of 1906 and remained controversial till 1947. Not only was the issue controversial in the pre-Independent India, it also raises debates among contemporary historians and political scientists. For John Gallagher, the Communal Award was nothing but 'a sign of [the] determination [of the British Government] to warp the Indian question towards electoral politics'.[1] While looking into the operational aspect of the Award, Anil Seal also affirmed that 'by extending the electorate, the imperial croupier had summoned more players to his table'.[2] Looking at the Award from the British point of view, both of them thus arrived at the same conclusions: (1) the Award introduced the native politicians to the sophisticated world of parliamentary politics; and (2) as a result of the new arrangement, as stipulated in the 1935 Act, politics now percolated down to the localities. The available evidence, however, does reveal that the Award and the constitutional rights guaranteed to the Indians under the Act were the price the British paid for the continuity of the Indian Empire. What thus appears to be a calculated generous gesture was very much a political expedient. The surrender of power to Indian hands, though at the regional levels, was not welcomed by some senior officers, who saw an eclipse of British authority in this endeavour.[3]

Bengal was a special case because (firstly) the representatives of the British power were divided on the question of the share of the two principal religious communities, Hindus and Muslims; and (secondly) the Award shook the foundations of Hindu domination.

This chapter thus deals with the complex question of how the Award was made and the reactions of the Bengali politicians, regardless of their religion, once the electoral arrangement of the Communal Award was a settled fact.

The Communal or Macdonald Award of 1932, according to the note circulated to the Commissioners and Collectors 'by the British Government at the request of the Indians themselves',[4] was an institutional arrangement to split the Indian electorate primarily on grounds of religion. Ramsay Macdonald, the British Prime Minister, felt that in view of the failure of the communities to frame a constitution acceptable to all, 'the government would have to settle the question of representation for the Indians as well as the checks and balances the constitution should contain to protect the minorities from an unrestricted and tyrannical use of the democratic principle expressing itself through majority power'.[5] In his press statement, he defended the government decision by referring to the fact that 'the contrast between these intermingled population[s] extends far beyond a difference in religious faith: differences of race and of history, a different system of law, widely opposed social observances and absence of intermarriage, set up barriers which have no analogy in the distinctions that may exist between religious denominations in any other existing state. It is not therefore altogether surprising that ... separate representation, namely, the grouping of a particular category of voters in territorial constituencies by themselves, so as to assure to them an adequate number of members of their own faith and race has been favoured'.[6]

Separate representation, wrote Macdonald, on the official notification of the Award, 'is primarily designed to secure adequate protection for the minorities; it is bound to continue in some form or other until minorities are disposed to trust to majority rule, and until a political accommodation between Moslems and Hindus is reached'.[7] In real terms, it meant distribution of central as well as provincial legislative seats in accordance with the principle of weightage to the religious minorities. The Hindus were demographically preponderant in all the provinces except Bengal and Punjab, where Muslims constituted a majority of the population. The Communal Award therefore turned the Hindu fear of losing political domination to near certainty.

This type of electoral arrangement was not new. John Lothian, chairman of the *Franchise Committee, 1932*, justified the idea of separate electorate by referring to the past.

> He wrote to the Viceroy: it [separate representation] dates back at least to 1892 when in a Despatch on the New Council's Bill which was brought before the Parliament, the government of India wrote as follows: Indian society ... is essentially a congeries of widely separated classes, races and communities with divergences of interests and hereditary sentiment which for ages have precluded common action or local unanimity. Representation of such a community upon such a scale as the Act permits can only be secured by providing that each important class shall have at least the opportunity of making its views known in the council by the mouth of some members specially acquainted with them ... The Morely–Minto Reforms of 1909 and the Montague–Chelmsford

Reform of 1919 were based on the same principle. [Not only that], the Lucknow Pact of 1916, the result of an agreement between the Indian National congress and the All India Muslim League, was designed to provide the basis of responsible government through a communal settlement.[8]

The Muslim leadership voiced their demand for 'separate electorates' as convincingly as they could. A. K. Ghuznavi, a Bengali Muslim leader, emphasised in his memorandum to the Simon Commission, 1927, that as the Muslim community was educationally, economically and politically behind the Hindus of the province, 'further extensions of parliamentary institutions without proper and definite safeguards would place the Muslims permanently in a position subservient to the Hindus'.[9] Jinnah's *14 Points* were the formulations of the above in concrete terms. These points, *inter alia*, demanded that 'all legislatures in the country and other elected bodies should be reconstituted on the definite principal [principle] of adequate and effective representation of minorities in every province without reducing the majority of any province to a minority ... the representation of communal groups should continue to be by means of separate electorate'.[10] The Aga Khan, who attended the Round Table Conference on behalf of the Muslim League, pressed for communal electorate for two reasons: (1) this would put a brake on the possible rate of political advance along Hindu nationalistic lines; and (2) this would enable the Muslims to counter Hindu domination everywhere.[11]

The Muslim demand for a separate electorate in the Muslim majority areas of Bengal and Punjab appears at first to have been derived from communal jealousy. By referring to the 1927–28 District Board elections in Bengal, the Congress High Command at the All Parties Conference, 1928, emphasised that economic and educational superiority did not help the Hindus at the above elections and there was a clean sweep in favour of the Muslims in Chittagong and Mymensingh. Table 2.1 illustrates the trends.

In terms of the distribution of seats, Muslims, forming 54 per cent of the population (according to the 1931 Census), shared only 45 per cent of the district board seats. The Hindus, constituting 43.3 per cent of the total (1931 Census), were, though they had no seats in Mymensingh and Chittagong, well ahead of the Muslims with 54 per cent of the seats.

The results are certainly indicative of an electoral swing in favour of the Muslims, especially in those districts where they constituted a majority. However, to conceive that the Muslims could, on their demographic strength, replace the Hindus would equally be misleading because the right to franchise was still based on 'property qualification'. As long as this was the case, the Muslims, deprived of their rights to suffrage on property grounds, could not fully benefit from a 'joint electorate'.

The election outcome distressed the Bengal Congress leadership. Subhas

Table 2.1 Elected members of the District Boards in Bengal, 1928

	District	Total no. of seats	No. of Hindu members	No. of Muslim members
1.	24 Parganas	20	16 (64.2)	4 (34.6)
2.	Bogra	15	4 (16.6)	11 (82.5)
3.	Bakargunj	20	4 (28.7)[1]	15 (70.6)
4.	Midnapore	22	21 (88.2)	1 (6.8)
5.	Rajshahi	18	7 (21.3)	11 (76.6)
6.	Rangpur	18	7 (31.5)	11 (68.1)
7.	Khulna	16	11 (50.0)	5 (49.8)
8.	Hooghly	20	17 (81.9)	3 (16.0)
9.	Darjeeling	20	18 (71.0)	2 (3.2)
10.	Mymensingh	22	0 (24.3)	22 (74.9)
11.	Pabna	16	3 (24.1)	13 (75.8)
12.	Noakhali	16	6 (22.3)	10 (77.6)
13.	Jalpaiguri	16	14 (55.0)	2 (24.8)
14.	Tippera	19	13 (25.8)[2]	6 (74.1)[3]
15.	Nadia	20	15 (39.1)	5 (60.2)
16.	Burdwan	16	14 (78.0)	2 (18.5)
17.	Murshidabad	15	7 (45.0)	8 (53.6)
18.	Faridpur	20	8 (36.3)	12 (635)
19.	Malda	15[4]	8 (40.6)	7 (51.6)
20.	Howrah	12	10 (79.3)	2 (20.3)
21.	Birbhum	16	15 (68.1)	1 (25.1)
22.	Bankura	10	9 (86.3)	1 (4.6)
23.	Jessore	16	1 (38.2)	15 (61.7)
24.	Dacca	22	16 (34.2)	6 (65.4)
25.	Chittagong	20	0 (22.6)	20 (72.8)
26.	Dinajpur	18	4 (44.1)	14 (49.1)
	Total	458	248 (54.14%)	209 (45.63%)

Source: All Parties Conference 1928, *Report of the Committee appointed by the Conference to determine the Principles of the Constitution of India*, pp. 154–5.

Notes
1 one Christian.
2 no election in Chandpur and therefore three nominated.
3 two nominated.
4 election failed, all nominated.
The figures in parentheses indicate the proportion of the total population.

Chandra Bose, in his letter to Motilal Nehru, attributed the success of the Muslim candidates to communal awakening.[12] This gave a boost to the Muslim leaders, like Maulvi Nausher Ali, MLC and Maulvi Abdur Rauf, MLC, who were reported to have changed their views on the question of a 'separate electorate'.[13] There was, on the other hand, a group of Muslims, led by Azizul Haque who refused to accept these district board election results as the fair index of Muslim strength. In his book *A Plea for Separate Electorates in Bengal*,[14] Haque argued that the outcome was due to the bitter communal dissension within the localities of east Bengal – the communal excitement followed by the communal riot in 1926 – and the constant communal bickering on the issues of constitutional concessions since the Montague–Chelmsford Reforms, 1919. Secondly, the Congress, politicians and Hindu leaders did not show as much interest as they might have in the Council elections, which had the power and authority to frame policies and programmes affecting the communities. In these elections, he continued, party and propaganda machinery played a determining role, and since the Muslims were economically backward, they could not afford to spend as much money as the Hindus and therefore in no way would the outcome be different.[15] Thirdly, he argued that as long as the franchise qualification was based on property, Muslims could not compete with Hindus. Haque referred to the 1919 Montague–Chelmsford Reforms, which fixed the franchise qualification at the payment of municipal taxes of not less than one rupee and a half, or road and public works cess of not less than one rupee, or chawkidari tax or union rate of not less than one rupee, or chawkidari tax or union rate of not less than two rupees or one rupee in cess, in order to demonstrate that though the Muslims constituted a majority (25 million), there were only 522 000 Muslim voters compared to 591 000 Hindu voters.

Finally, having concentrated on the details of the results on which the Congress High Command defended their plea, namely overwhelming Muslim support in Chittagong, Mymensingh and Jessore, Haque exposed the logical flaws in the interpretation. According to him, the demographic preponderance of the Muslims and the fact that the majority of them were voters ensured Muslim victory in Mymensingh (Muslims formed 75 per cent of the population and secured 75 per cent of the seats), and Chittagong (67 per cent of the population and secured 38 per cent of the seats). In contrast to these figures, he argued that Muslims in Nadia, making up 60.2 per cent of the population, had 25 per cent of the district board seats in 1927–28; Dhaka, with over 65 per cent of the population Muslims, obtained only 27 per cent of the seats and in Tippera, where the Muslims formed 74 per cent of the population, they won only 31 per cent of the seats.[16]

Thus the Congress assertion that the Muslims needed no constitutional protection by 'separate electorate', as expressed in the 1928 All Parties Conference,[17] was, according to Haque, based on over-simplification and misrepresentation of the election results.[18]

The Muslims' electoral victory could therefore never be a reason to support 'joint electorate'. However, A. H. Ghuznavi and H. S. Suhrawardy saw in it the basis of the rise of Muslim power in Bengal. Having looked at the results of the local and district board elections in which the Muslims performed well, particularly in the Muslim majority districts of east Bengal, they were convinced that 'joint electorate with reservation of seats would not harm the Muslim interests'. Accordingly, Ghuznavi and Suhrawardy worked out a pact type arrangement with B. C. Chatterjee, a

Hindu Mahasabha leader. The Ghuznavi–Chatterjee Pact agreed to the continuance of the distribution of seats in the Bengal legislature under the Communal Award for ten years. Thereafter, the two communities would get an equal number of legislative seats under a joint electorate scheme. This principle, equal share of seats, was to be followed in the appointment of ministers and in the field of public employment.[19]

The agreement remained on paper, and neither the Muslim leaders nor their Hindu Mahasabha counterparts endeavoured seriously to work it out. Not only that; the all India Hindu Mahasabha leadership did not approve the agreement in view of its plan to organise a nationwide campaign for the repeal of the Communal Award.[20] The Hindu Mahasabha position is perfectly logical because, had they acquiesced in the pact in Bengal in which the Hindus were more adversely affected than anywhere else, the anti-Award agitation would perhaps have received no attention.

By strictly following the demographic strength of the two principal communities, the Communal Award suggested that of 250 seats in the Bengal Legislature, Hindus be given 80 and the Muslims 119; in the Punjab, of 175 seats Hindus be given 43 and Muslims 86.[21] There had been, as Table 2.2 shows, a gradual increase in Muslim seats in the legislature since the Morley–Minto Reforms of 1909.

The situation was particularly harmful for Hindus in Bengal, especially after the acceptance of the Poona Pact by the All India Congress, for this had further reduced the proportion of legislative seats for the Hindus. This Pact was preceded by the Government declaration of its intention to establish special constituencies for the depressed classes for a period of twenty years.[22] However, Gandhi's vehement objection to 'statutory separation' of the depressed classes even in a limited form, from the Hindu fold[23] led to 'the inclusion of the depressed classes into the general or Hindu constituencies',[24] and, according to the Pact, depressed classes secured thirty seats in Bengal and eight in the Punjab.[25]

Table 2.2 Increase in Muslim seats in the Bengal and Punjab legislatures

Legislative councils	% of Muslim members to total elected members			
	Morley–Minto Reforms, 1909	Montague–Chelmsford Reforms, 1919	Lucknow* Pact, 1916 Act	1935
Bengal	18	40.5	50	47
Punjab	19	48.5	40	48

Source: J. Gallagher, 'From Civil disobedience to communalism', Paper presented to Postgraduate Seminar, Institute of Commonwealth Studies, University of London, 1964, p. 4.

Note
*Page 1982: 34.

The arrangement finally arrived at illustrated a conflict of opinion between the Governor of Bengal and Lord Willingdon, the Viceroy, over the question of Hindu-Muslim representation in Bengal under the Communal Award. Samuel Hoare, the Secretary of State, recommended the distribution of seats between the communities in proportion to their respective demographic strength, and accordingly 41.4 per cent (of the seats) were reserved for the Muslims and 40.4 per cent for the Hindus. The balance of power was to be held by the Europeans.[26] The Bengal Governor, John Anderson, accepted the scheme on the ground that 'it will not give the Muhammadans that permanent and absolute majority ... Nor will it give them a numerical superiority comparable to their superiority on a population basis. But it will make them the largest communal group in the Legislative Council and will do away with the present inadequate and to my mind unfair representation. On the other hand, it will give the Hindu community the weightage to which they are entitled in view of their wealth and prominence in all ranks of life.'

He insisted that care must be taken 'not to diminish the importance of the Hindu group by giving too large a proportion of the seats ... to the depressed classes [out of the Hindu share]. For it is quite possible that in the not too distant future, there may be a combination between the Muhammadans and the depressed classes against the Zamindars and moneyed classes who are mainly caste Hindus and care must be taken not to reduce the representatives of the latter to impotency in matters affecting their own interests'.[27]

Anderson therefore recommended that the Muslims should have 44.4 per cent and the Hindus 42.8 per cent.[28] This was in conformity with Hoare's recommendation, merely taking into account the number of seats given by the Europeans in the Minorities Pact. However, this was not received favourably by Lord Willingdon, who, as David Page has shown, 'considered it unsatisfactory from the all India point of view because if the Bengali Muslims did not get their majority, there was a danger that they would go over to the Congress.'[29] Accordingly, Willingdon proposed that the Muslims should get 48.4 per cent and the Hindus only 39.2 per cent of the seats,[30] on the ground that the Muslims who, on the whole 'have generally supported the government ... will non-cooperate too if ... you give them less ... than ... [what] I propose for Bengal'.[31] Anderson did not agree with the Viceroy because he felt that 'the ultimate success of the reforms in this province will depend on securing friendly cooperation of Hindus, Muslims and [Europeans]'.[32] However, the proposed plan, as he found, had the appearance of putting Hindus 'permanently in the position of hopeless inferiority'.[33] The inevitable danger was, according to the Governor, that 'the plan will enrage the Hindus [who would think that] it is obviously designed to hold them down in the hope that Moslems may eventually gain a sufficient proportion of special constituencies to give them a permanent statutory majority.'[34] On the other hand, by granting only a few seats to the Muslims, which fell short of giving them an absolute majority, the scheme could not win Muslim support either. The Governor's own preference was, however, for a distribution favourable to the Hindus.[35] The Prime Minister himself seems to have agreed with Anderson in principle, because he realised that the idea of winning the support of a particular community by granting special privileges 'keeps the trouble going and the price [is] paid not only today but through a long time.'[36]

There was also the question of European representation. At the beginning of 1931, Edward Benthall of the Bird Company did not like the idea of a settlement purely on a population basis because it would be unfair to the Hindus and also to the Europeans, 'as it would give a permanent majority to mere numbers regardless of educational, financial and economic factors'.[37] Since in the past the Europeans had held the balance between the two communities, they, he emphasised, should not be treated on a population basis. Accordingly, he proposed that the Europeans should be given 13.3 per cent of the seats.[38] In offering the above to the Europeans in his proposed scheme,[39] Samuel Hoare thus seems to have been influenced by Benthall's suggestion. Though the Bengal Governor appreciated that the proposal hinged on the argument of giving the Europeans the balance of power, he felt that such a point 'could hardly be used publicly'[40] to defend the European share.

The distribution of seats under the Communal Award (published on 16 August) followed neither Samuel Hoare's nor the Governor's line of suggestions. Not only did the Viceroy reject the scheme for the distribution of seats between the two communities as proposed by the Secretary of State and the Governor; he declined also to accept the proposed share of the European seats.

What came to be regarded as the Communal Award, in terms of the distribution of the seats, is shown in Table 2.3.

The distribution in Table 2.3 shows that though the Muslims were the majority community, they were given only 47.6 per cent of the seats. The Hindus, with 43.3 per cent of the population, had only 32 per cent. This figure, showing Hindu share, is misleading because in it was included, after the Poona Pact, the share of the depressed classes (thirty seats). Thus in actual terms, the caste Hindus obtained only 20 per cent of the seats. The Europeans lost their strength in the legislature considerably: while they claimed 13.3 per cent, they were granted only 4.4 per cent of the seats.

The Award was unsatisfactory to the Hindus, the Muslims and the Europeans. Benthall, representative of the Europeans in Bengal, while writing about it in his diary, expressed utter dissatisfaction because the Award, once implemented, would reduce the Europeans 'to a non-entity in the Bengal Legislature'.[41]

Table 2.3 The Communal Award: distribution of seats

Groups	Number of seats
General*	80 (including 2 women)
Muslims	119 (including 2 women)
Anglo-Indians and Christians	4 + 2 (including 1 woman)
Europeans	11
Commerce, industry, mining and plantation	19
Labour	8
Others (including landholders and university)	7
Total	250

Source: IOR, L/PO/48(ii), Communal Decision, 16/8/1932.

Note
*Includes Hindus, plus social categories defined as 'untouchables'.

Muslims and the Communal Award

Though the Muslims were politically better placed under the Award, the number of seats allotted to them was not in proportion to their demographic strength in Bengal. Commenting on the *Indian Franchise Committee Report*, A. K. Ghuznavi, member of the Bengal Government, insisted on 'a statutory majority of 51%' for the Muslims, though on a population basis they were entitled to 'a majority of 54.85%'.[42] Ghuznavi apprehended trouble if the suggested number of seats (128) was not given to the Muslims. 'What the Moslem community wish to stress', he argued, 'is the fact that they are not likely to agree to being consigned to remain in a perpetual minority by artificial means where actually they are in a majority'.[43]

Even after the Award was announced, the Bengali Muslim leaders, Fazlul Haq and A. H. Ghuznavi, met John Anderson to try to convince him of the need for a statutory majority for the Muslims in Bengal.[44] Haq did, however, regard the Award as a 'distinct advance' and therefore was pleased with it.[45] He did not like the pattern of seat distribution because 'the result has been that the Muslims cannot run the administration of the province in which they are in an unquestioned majority without entering into coalition with or depending on the support of other parties'.[46]

The scheme was generally welcomed by Muslims all over India.[47] In Punjab, as the Chief Secretary C. C. Garbett reported, the Muslims were determined to adhere to the Award and to resist any negotiations which might 'diminish the solid advantages which they consider the Award gives them'.[48] In Bengal the response was favourable, though initially R. Ahmad, President of the Bengal Presidency Muslim League, was unwilling to accept reservation of seats for the majority community on the ground that 'dependence on an artificial prop, as the scheme is, will stand in the way of their being self-reliant and self-dependent and will thus retard the growth of manhood in them'.[49] At the twenty-third session of the All India Muslim League, Fazlul Haq moved a resolution confirming his support for the Communal Award.[50] The Muslim leaders of Bengal were more categorical at the all India Communal Award Conference, held on 24 March 1937. The Nawab of Dhaka, as its President, attributed the Award not to the 'evil design of the Machiavellian foreign government, but to the communalism of a section which had engendered deep distrust and acute apprehensions' among the Muslims.[51] Both A. H. Ghuznavi and Fazlul Haq approved the speech and had an active role in the formulation of the main resolution, which justified 'separate electorate for the Muslims in Bengal and Punjab in view of the fact that there is no better agreed scheme before the country'.[52]

Hindus and the Communal Award

While discussing the *Indian Franchise Committee Report*, P. C. Mitter, member of the Bengal Government, argued that 'education, wealth, contribution to the government exchequer, political and economic importance entitle the Hindus considerably in excess of their population.[53] Of the three principal sources to the government exchequer (stamp duty, land revenue and excise duty), Hindus, he noted contributed '60% to the total'. Furthermore, he argued: (1) since the Muslims by religion were precluded from 'excisable articles, a very large percentage of the excise revenue' came from the Hindus; (2) the majority of the landlords were Hindus and their contribution to the exchequer in land revenue was more than that of their Muslim counterparts; and (3) Hindus, as landlords and moneylenders, were found to have paid '91% of the total court fees.'[54]

Mitter's criticism of the Franchise Committee Report was the theme of a protest meeting after the announcement of the Award. At a meeting in the Town Hall on 4 September 1932, presided over by Devaprasad Sarvadhikari, Vice Chancellor of Calcutta University, resolutions condemning the Award as a means to 'deepen the foundations of communalism and to extend the principle in new directions contrary to all enlightened and democratic ideas of the age'[55] were adopted. In these meetings, as R. N. Gilchrist, Reform Officer of the Government of Bengal reported, it was emphasised that 'Hindus' superior wealth and education have been given no recognition and their political record has been discounted'. The Hindus believed, the report continued, that 'the decision is in effect a punishment inflicted on the Hindus of Bengal because of their past political record'. Instead of ensuring 'separate electorate' for the numerically preponderant community in Bengal, Hindus could only be safeguarded by reversing the decision.[56]

The Bengali Hindus preferred open agitation against the Award, but the all India pro-Hindu Congressmen, including Malaviya, Moonjee and Aney, sought a dialogue with the Muslim leaders to bring about an agreement in order to substitute the Award. The Muslim League responded. Accordingly, a Unity Conference was convened at Allahabad between 3 and 17 November, 1932. Ramananda Chatterjee, editor of the *Modern Review*, represented the Bengali Hindus, but no Muslim leaders from Bengal attended. The Conference agreed that in Bengal '51% of the seats will be reserved for the Muslims and 44.7% for the general electorate'. It was also decided as well that 'all reservations of seats and all special constituencies were to cease after 10 years'.[57] Neither the Hindus nor the Muslims of Bengal were prepared to accept the above: Ramananda Chatterjee, though reluctantly conceding the Muslim majority in Bengal, was insistent on the 'introduction of joint electorate'.[58] The Muslims did not want to surrender the privileges they had under the Award. To them, giving away the separate electorate even after 10 years would not guarantee a legitimate Muslim share in the ruling of the country, and 'hence can never be surrendered'.[59]

All India Congress and the Award

The polarisation between the two communities was complete. The Congress was in a dilemma: rejection of the Award meant a breach in the united front which was essential for successfully fighting the White Paper; acceptance would not only drive away the pro-Hindu congressmen but also dub the Congress as championing separatism. In an effort to solve this, the Working Committee at its Bombay sitting on 18 June 1934 defined the Congress attitude to the Award: 'The Congress claims to represent equally all the communities composing the Indian nation and therefore in view of the division of opinion can *neither accept nor reject the Award*'.[60] Gandhi defended the Working Committee resolution as 'faultless' and explained that 'non-committal is the only position the Congress can take-up ... because the more we tease [the communal boil], the worse it becomes'.[61] The Congress position was more clearly stated in the Congress Parliamentary Board Election Manifesto: '[T]he Congress cannot refuse to take into account the attitude of the Mussalmans in general who seem to want the Award, nor can the Congress accept it as Hindus and Sikhs reject it. No other policy than [being non-committal] is consistent with the aim and history of the Congress.'[62] The immediate consequence of this decision was that both Malaviya and Aney, members of the Congress Parliamentary Board, quit the Congress and formed the Congress Nationalist Party to redress the suggested wrongs to the Hindus of Bengal and Punjab.

Their first endeavour in that direction was the organisation of an Anti

Communal Award Conference towards the end of October 1934. The Hindus of Bengal were represented by B. C. Mahatab, Maharaja of Burdwan, and B. C. Chatterjee, R. K. Mukherjee and Ramananda Chatterjee, professionally successful Calcutta bhadraloks. The Conference condemned the communal decision as an attempt to 'ensure the indefinite continuance of foreign domination' by dividing 'the body-politic into separate and conflicting groups'. The Congress attitude towards the Award was nothing but 'virtual acquiescence in that decision'.[63] In order to campaign against the Award, the Conference formed an 'All India Communal Decision League'.[64]

The Conference and the formation of a platform for agitation seem to have augmented the anti-Award tempo. Once the Congress 'non-committal attitude' was announced, the majority of the Bengal DCCs, irrespective of factional differences, castigated the AICC decision.[65] With the formation of the Nationalist Party, the dissident Congressmen decided, as Satish Chandra Mishra of the Sylhet DCC reported to the Working Committee, 'to support the Nationalist Party in case of contest'.[66] Those less vocal were, as another letter from Dinajpur DCC shows, determined not to take part in the election until the Bombay decision (26–28 October 1934) of the AICC was revised.[67] Having foreseen the impact of anti Award sentiment on the local organisations, B. C. Roy, the leader of the BPCC, made a futile attempt to persuade Gandhi to allow the Bengal Congress to organise anti-Award agitation.[68]

The Hindu position in Bengal was precarious in another respect. With the conclusion of the Poona Pact in which Gandhi had a direct role, the legislative seats of the Hindus were further reduced. Zetland, the Viceroy, thus argued that 'the caste Hindus must find themselves in a serious permanent minority in a Presidency in which they play an outstanding part in the intellectual and political life of the people'. Although he apprehended that this concessional design 'will strengthen terrorism [because] Hindus of Bengal may run into despair', he found the arrangement 'politically expedient' to deal with the Hindus, 'who are now more divided than before'.[69] As early as January 1933, the Hindu bhadralok, in a memorandum to the Viceroy, 'expressed [themselves] very strongly against the terms of the Poona Pact as far as Bengal was concerned', and requested reconsideration of the decision on the ground that no representative from Bengal was present when the agreement was reached.[70] In another manifesto, issued from Calcutta, the Pact was condemned not because it reduced the Hindu share but for its discrimination against the real backward classes. In concrete terms, the manifesto argued, the arrangement would benefit '19.7% Rajbansis and 17% Namasudras who were not only well organized and in no sense backward but also succeeded in holding their own against the caste Hindus. Those who deserved real care (Muchis, Haris, for instance) would go unrepresented even after this electoral arrangement.'[71] The cumulative effect of the above was the failure of all seven Congress candidates in the Bengal Legislative election of October 1934. All seats were won by the Nationalist Party.[72]

Even after this defeat in Bengal, the Congress High Command not only reiterated its support of the non-committal position but also defended it by referring to the fact that the Congress victory in all general seats in Madras, Orissa, UP and CP 'conclusively proved that the Congress had the support of the vast majority of the Hindu electorate.'[73]

The All India Congress leadership accepted the idea of seat distribution on a population basis but was keen at the same time to find a substitute. The attitude of the AICC leadership was different to that of the League. Jinnah, who was critical of the constitutional scheme, expressed his unequivocal support for the anti-White Paper campaign. However, he felt that opposition could only be effective provided there was unity between the Hindus and Muslims,[74] Prasad, the Congress President, seized the chance and wrote to Jinnah on 23 January that the only way to break the stalemate was 'to jointly formulate some proposals which you and I could put before our respective organizations as jointly emanating from us'. He emphasised that if separate electorates which deprived the Hindus of Bengal and Punjab of their legitimate share on a population basis were retained, no progress was possible. Therefore, he put forward a formula following the Congress resolution adopted in Bombay 1931, which included joint electorates reservation of seats on a population basis with freedom for minorities to contest more seats, the franchise being so arranged as to reflect the proportion of various communities in the electorate.[75] The two leaders met in long sessions on 28 and 31 January 1935. The discussion though abortive, was revealing, because it showed that Jinnah, in conceding that a Hindu–Muslim joint effort was the only way to get rid of the scheme, had in mind the desire to ensure a Congress guarantee for a statutory Muslim majority in Bengal.

> Three points emerged from the discussion: first, Jinnah accepted the idea of a separate electorate in principle. Without separate representation, he felt, 'involvement of the minority in the government of the province could not be created'. He argued that through their representations in the 'institutions of power, they could exercise their responsibility'; hence the idea of weightage was logically apt. Second, with regard to Hindu representation, he admitted that the outcome of the scheme, especially after the Poona Pact, 'was unfair to the Bengali Hindus'. However, he was unwilling to concede when asked by Prasad to grant the share of the depressed classes out of 119 Muslim seats. Having accepted Prasad's claim as 'legitimate', he refused on the ground that 'if Mussalmans had a margin out of which weightage could be given

to satisfy the minority communities, including the Hindus', he would not hesitate to give it. Third, he suggested that joint efforts should be made to secure seats for both the Europeans and the depressed classes in order to ensure a Muslim majority for the Muslims and an increased Hindu share.[76] As to the distribution of seats obtained from the share of the depressed classes, Prasad pointed out that it would be unfair to the Hindus because 'the share of the depressed classes was included in the 32% which Hindus had against the [Hindu-inclusive of Harijans] population of 44% and if seats were available from the general electorate, it should be given to the Hindus, otherwise Hindu share would be reduced further.'[77] It was certain that Jinnah's proposal for substituting the Award would not receive support from the Nationalist Party. Malaviya, as its leader, insisted that 'till the Hindus of Bengal get their share in proportion to their population, they are not going to endorse the outcome of the talks'.[78] The Congress High Command accepted the demand in principle, and suggested that 'the Hindus and Mussalmans should jointly press for reduction of European seats. Any seats so obtained should be distributed between them'.[79] In line with the above, Prasad again sat with Jinnah on 13 February 1935, with a view to arriving at an agreed formula. It was a successful effort in the sense that though Prasad conceded Jinnah's demands in relation to Bengal and Punjab, he at the same time obtained Jinnah's approval for a joint electorate in all the provinces as well as in the centre.[80]

Both the Bengal Congress and the Nationalist Party were upset. In a telegram to Prasad, Indra Narayan Sen, the Secretary of the Nationalist Party, described the formula 'as nothing but selling Bengal to the Muslims'.[81] Even among Congressmen, the idea of a pact was unwelcome. C. R. Reddy of the Andhra PCC, for instance, argued that the very idea of communal settlement through a pact 'can never have permanence. They [Muslims] will soon be agitating for a revision of the terms with changes in population'.[82]

The entire exercise was abortive. Though the Congress High Command was in favour of a settlement even at the cost of the Hindus in Bengal and Punjab, the Muslim leadership never agreed to abandon separate electorates. Jinnah failed to persuade his colleagues to give up on a separate electorate. As he explained to Prasad, the Congress President, the Congress should reckon that 'what may have been possible some years ago was not possible today and those who made such suggestions ignored the basic fact of the Award being in favour of Mussalmans'.[83]

There was no sign of either the Hindus or the Muslims becoming less intransigent. The Hindu Mahasabha organised an all-India Anti-Communal

Award Conference in Delhi on 23 February 1935 to demonstrate that the Hindus were not ready to support any scheme as long as the Award prevailed.[84] The Conference resolved further (1) to appoint a committee 'to organize all India agitation against this';[85] and (2) to send 'a deputation to London headed by Pandit Malaviya to agitate against the Award'.[86] The Muslims organized a counter conference to defend the Award. In their all India Communal Award Conference, held on 24 March 1935, it was resolved that although the Award fell 'short of legitimate demands of Indian Muslims', it should be accepted because 'no better scheme was available before the country.'[87] In view of this clear polarisation between Hindus and Muslims, the talks between Jinnah and Prasad seem to have achieved nothing. On I March, in a joint statement, Prasad and Jinnah regretted that 'in spite of our best efforts, we have not been able to find such a formula [to bring about] communal harmony and concord'.[88]

The Communal Award was the price the British had to pay for making the maintenance of the Empire an easier task. It was, at the same time, a victory for them because by inserting the principle of a 'separate electorate' in the 1935 constitutional scheme, the Macdonald Plan seems to have brought the infighting within the Congress on the Award to a conclusion which was definitely conducive to continued imperial control. The non-committal position was the only stand the Congress as an organisation representing all-India interests could take, because even Lothian, Chairman of the Franchise Committee, understood 'if it sets out to upset the Communal Award, it will, in fact, be starting a civil war with the Moslems and other minorities'.[89] The Award not only created and sustained communal dissension; it also brought about a split within the Congress organisation by separating a group of Hindu leaders who, as shown earlier, having declined to conform to the non-committal attitude of the Congress, formed a party (the Congress Nationalist Party) of their own. The Congress leaders who had active roles in formulating the AICC decision saw in the Award a device to divide the communities. Nehru, for instance, believed that by balancing and neutralising one community against the other, the Award would perpetuate British control in India.[90] Even Gandhi who was instrumental in having the 'non-committal resolution' adopted at the 1934 Bombay session of the AICC, when writing in 1940 with hindsight condemned the decision 'as it has benefited no single party in India, but the British. If the Muslims flatter themselves', he continued, 'with the belief they have profited by it they will soon find that they were mistaken. If I could alter the decision and make it what it should be, I should do so this moment'.[91] The condemnation of the Award by the leaders in their individual capacities did not however, change the Congress' stand.

Bengal Congress and the Communal Award

The publication of the Award brought, different factions within the Bengal Congress together. *Liberty*, the organ of the Subhas group, condemned the Award as it would make the Hindus 'politically impotent'.[92] *Advance*, speaking for the Sengupta group, agreed that: 'the award has sacrificed the province to the Moslem and European communities and has left no real autonomy to the children of the soil'.[93] *Amrita Bazar Patrika*, not committed to any faction, but anti-Subhas, saw the Award as 'the most preposterous arrangement for representation that could ever be conceived'.[94] Notwithstanding this common view, the Bengal Congress, as will be shown below, had eventually to accept the scheme under the Award. The outcome was more or less pre-determined, because it was unlikely that a provincial wing would succeed when the High Command decided otherwise. In any case, weakened by reasons entirely internal to the Bengal Congress, it failed to push its demand as strongly as it strove for.

First, neither Subhas, who was convalescing in Austria, nor Sengupta, who died in 1932, was there to lead the Bengal Congress. As a result, the leadership was vested in Sarat Bose, B. C. Roy and K. S. Roy. At least the anti-Award sentiment brought the leaders together, however transitory the unity was. Soon, B. C. Roy, who was the only person from Bengal consulted by the High Command on the Award, realised that the price for fighting the centre openly was too high. His opposition to the Congress decision was confined to requests to the AICC for reconsideration of the decision. K. S. Roy more explicitly showed that he was not ready to support the Bose-led Bengal Congress which, he realised, was too fragile to rely on. He castigated Sarat Bose (who refused to a accept the non-committal stand) as an enemy of the official Congress policy,[95] presumably with a view to proving his credibility to the high Command. This division among the leaders definitely weakened the Bengal Congress, and Sarat, the only leader left with the responsibility of carrying on the campaign, was not as gifted a leader as his brother Subhas. In fact, he himself admitted that his decision and strategy in regard to the anti Communal Award agitation flowed from his brother.[96] Subhas, though far away from Bengal, detested the decision and wanted Sarat to 'unsettle the settled fact'.[97]

Second, the Bengal Congress was weakened as a result of the split that took place after the formation of the Congress Nationalist Party in 1934. Important Bengal congressmen – Dinesh Chakravarti, Indra Narayan Sen, Chapala Bhatacharyya, and Birendra Majumdar – joined the new party. The party was welcomed by the Hindu Mahasabha, whose Vice President, Narendra Nath Das, wrote of it as strengthening the movement for the repeal of the 'anti national and undemocratic Award'.[98]

Third, the Congress Nationalist Party's campaign had at least moved the Bengali Hindu notables. Rabindranath Tagore, for instance, approved of the agitation, and was pained at the failure of the Congress High Command to organise an all-India agitation against the Award.[99] In trying to revoke the decision, the Hindu nobles, including Tagore, Sarat Chatterjee (the writer), P. C. Roy (the chemist), Nil Ratan Sarkar (the eminent physician), S. P. Mookherjee (Vice Chancellor of Calcutta University), and B. P. Singh Roy (Former Land Revenue Minister), sent a memorial to the Secretary of State, Lord Zetland, which illustrated the extent to which they were frightened of being dominated by the Muslims. The memorial, representing a remarkable unity among the Bengali Hindu nobles, defended the opposition to the Award on the ground of the 'enormously predominant role that [Hindus] have played under British rule in the intellectual, cultural, political, professional, and the commercial life of the province'.[100] In concrete terms, the memorial went on, 'Hindus of Bengal though numerically a minority, are overwhelmingly superior culturally, consisting as much as 64% of total literate population and more than 80% of school going population. Their economic preponderance is equally manifest in the spheres of the independent professions and commercial careers making up nearly 87% of the Legal, 80% of the Medical and 83% of the Banking, Insurance and Exchange business'.[101]

The memorialists therefore protested 'strongly against the unfair and unprecedented provision to protect a majority community by conferring upon it a position of permanent and statutory predominance in the legislature and making that position unalterable by any appeal to the electorate'.[102]

In their effort to raise a protest throughout the province, R. K. Mookherjee and T. C. Goswami, signatories to the memorial, issued a circular to the districts 'to hold public meetings of the Hindus ... in order to pass a suitable resolution in support of the Memorial and the demands made therein'.[103] However only four districts – Burdwan, Hooghly, Mymensingh and Dhaka – cared to responded.[104] The favourable response from Burdwan and Hooghly can be attributed to the individual efforts of B. C. Mahatab of Burdwan and T. C. Goswami of Hooghly. In Dhaka and Mymensingh, the recent defeat of the Hindu candidates in 1928 District Board Elections explains largely the Hindu consolidation in favour of the memorial.

The poor response (four out of thirty-two districts) to the Hindu noble-sponsored anti-Award campaign was probably due to the fact that the grounds on which the Hindu share was defended were too technical to draw the sympathy of the newly enfranchised individuals at the localities. As a result, the campaign was from the outset insulated from the vast majority and thus remained a 'bhadralok affair'. Not only was the response poor; the Hindu bhadraloks themselves were also divided, a fact well exemplified in their opposition to the memorial. In a letter addressed to R.K. Mookherjee, the memorial was characterised as 'a futile and ill-timed one'.[105] By any stretch of imagination the letter went, the Hindu demands that 'representation may be proportional to taxation as far as possible in the case of each community' could not be justified 'in any democratic lower chamber'. This would serve no purpose now because 'the unity now displayed in signing a memorial ... was never in evidence when effective steps might have been taken in England or in India. Nor has there been any genuine attempt at arriving at an understanding with the Moslems'. What the memorial would do, the letter concluded, was 'to aggravate the enmity between the two communities'.[106] Satis Dasgupta of Bankura defended the AICC non-committal stand on the same ground.[107] It is true that the memorialists denounced the Award because it eclipsed the Hindu preponderance in the Bengal legislature. Inevitably, this step appeared to the Muslims as one derived from the parochial desire to deprive a majority community of their due. Referring to this, *Azad*, a daily publication from Dhaka, stated: 'as the Mussalmans were given their legitimate share under the Award, the Hindus irrespective of their principles, were united to reverse the decision. This suggest [ed] that the Hindus [would] never allow the Mussalmans to get what [was] due to them'.[108]

Nonetheless, the Muslim leadership in Bengal found in the memorialists potential allies among the Bengali Hindus for a post-election arrangement which seemed highly improbable in view of the failure of the talks between Jinnah and Prasad. The initiative came from A. H. Ghuznavi, who, in a letter to B. C. Mahatab, expressed himself willing to open a dialogue with the Hindu leaders for the 'communal settlement', particularly on the question of the 'communal Award'.[109] The all-India Muslim leadership had backed this attempt. The Aga Khan in particular directed, as the above letter shows, the Bengali leaders to go ahead with talks for a settlement at the provincial level.[110]

The Ghuznavi proposal was a modified version of the abortive Ghuznavi–Chatterjee Pact of 1933 (see above) in the sense that the new draft emphasised that the seat distribution under the Award could cease even earlier than ten years provided there was a mutual agreement between the communities to that effect.[111] B. C. Mahatab, President of the Anti Communal Award Committee, not only responded favourably but got the Ghuznavi proposal approved by the entire Committee at an emergency meeting on the day he received the letter.[112] In order to make it a success, Mahatab tried to persuade B. C. Roy to have the proposal accepted by the Bengal Congress.[113] However, this was futile because the latter declined on the ground that the Congress Nationalist Party, to which Mahatab himself belonged, was instrumental in defeating the Congress candidates in the 1934 Assembly elections and therefore no agreement was possible with an anti-Congress organisation.[114]

Like the earlier Pact, this attempt failed. What brought the Hindu and

Muslim leadership together, as the evidence shows, was not a sincere effort to solve the communal problem, but the selfish desire to protect their futures. For the Hindus, this was the last means of ensuring their position in the new constitutional set-up because their earlier attempt to have the Award rescinded by sending a memorial to the Secretary of State had been abortive.[115] The Muslim leadership, Ghuznavi in particular, consented primarily because of the Hindu sponsored anti-Award agitation which might, they apprehended, upset the Award. In his letter to Mahatab, Ghuznavi mentioned that the talk was possible only with the cession of anti-Award agitation by the Hindus.[116] The proposed agreement had another purpose. As the Bengal Governor anticipated, the discussion was likely to be centred on 'the question of equal shares in the ministry and in government services'.[117] Thus the talk aimed primarily at 'post-electoral' arrangements. Ghuznavi's initiative was, as explained by the Governor, opportunistic, because the decision to come to an agreement with the Hindus on the eve of the 1937 election was determined largely by Ghuznavi's desire to counter 'the present generation of Dacca family [and] the leaders of the United Muslim Party' from which he extricated himself at an early stage.[118]

Despite these and other divisions within the Muslim League leadership, there was nonetheless a fundamental agreement that the Award should be kept. Thus it was perfectly possible for Ghuznavi to attend the 1933 Howrah session of the All India Muslim League, which was attended not only by Fazlul Haq (who was always critical of Ghuznavi for his association 'with the Calcutta based Marwari business community')[119] but also by the leaders of the United Muslim party.[120] Furthermore during the All India Communal Award Conference of 1935, the fact that the Nawab of Dhaka presided deterred neither Fazlul Haq nor Ghuznavi from active participation.

Compared with this, the Bengal Congress suffered a great deal – first by the Award itself, and second by the dissension among its members as a result of the Congress High Command's non-committal stand. As shown above, the Award overrode the factional differences among the Bengal Congressmen. Even J. C. Gupta, the leader of the Sengupta group, 'transferred his allegiance', as Anderson reported, 'to Sarat Bose'[121] in order to strengthen the campaign, but what was gained thus could not compensate the loss of B. C. Roy and K. S. Roy, whose drift towards the High Command was quite apparent after the Bengal Congress' decision not to comply with the AICC. Not only was the Bengal Congress weakened as a result of the formation of a solid pro-AICC faction; it was also handicapped because it lacked able leadership. Subhas Bose, the *de facto* leader of the provincial Congress, was away; though he was in constant touch with the BPCC and appreciated the steps it took to revoke the Award, nothing happened.

Bose totally rejected Award. To him, it was not an award but 'a lesser evil than the partition of Bengal'.[122] 'Instead of transferring power to the Indians, this imperial device', Bose argued, strengthened the authorities 'by dividing India still further, so that the effect of the meager constitutional reforms may be sufficiently neutralized'.[123] By creating an artificial division, he continued, the British government aimed at splitting the Indian opposition in the Legislature. He believed that in devising such a scheme, the authority attempted 'to placate those elements – Moslem, for instance, who according to the official estimate, are likely to be more pro-British than others'.[124] Thus it is clear that, for Bose, the Communal Award was the result of *divide et impera*.

In Bose's view, the High Command's refusal to sanction agitation against the Award was 'dictated by the desire to placate Dr. Ansari and the nationalist Muslims'. Since the nationalist Muslims consistently condemned the communal electorate, 'how could' they, he asked, 'give up the opposition on the occasion of the Award?'.[125] However, Subhas' idea was not appreciated by the nationalist Muslims, who favoured rather than opposed the system of electorate as given under the Communal Award. Dr Ansari, for instance, explained that 'the Congress knows that while a large number of Hindus and Sikhs have taken strong exception to the Communal Award, a considerable section of Mussalmans, Harijans and Christians have accepted it for so long as an agreed substitute is found. The Congress will always strive to help to find a national solution of the question, but in my opinion such a solution of the question cannot be found except by a Constituent Assembly convened to frame a national constitution. Until then, the question of acceptance or rejection of the mode or proportion of representation as aimed in the Award does not arise'.[126]

Dr Syed Mahmud, Secretary to the AICC, was keener to reap the benefit of the Award for his community. In a statement of 10 October 1937, he assured the Muslims that 'the Congress may not have accepted the Award in principle but has practically accepted all in its real effects and thus the Muslims need not be scared'.[127] Caught in contradictory pressures, it seems fairly clear why the non-committal stand appeared to the High Command to be the only feasible solution. Subhas, having ignored the infighting within the Congress on the Award both at the national and provincial levels, insisted that 'at the time when the Congress was committing a grave folly, it is the duty of all right-thinking men to come forward and agitate against the Communal Award'.[128] His objection to the Award was not to its basis but to its effect. He would have approved the seat distribution under the Award had it recognised Hindu representation according to the population in Bengal and Punjab, he claimed, as was done regarding Muslim minorities in all provinces.[129]

With the approach of the 1937 election and the Congress decision to contest it, the question of the Communal Award became more important, especially in Bengal, where the Sarat Bose-led provincial Congress resolved not to comply with the non-committal stand. The All India Congress leadership was still in a dilemma. In its 1936 Lucknow session, Congress reiterated its rejection of the new constitution in its entirety. The Nationalist Party suggested an amendment to add 'including the Communal Award'[130] but was opposed by the Working Committee and was defeated. Although in their public statements the Congress leaders conformed to the 1934 Bombay decision, in the Election manifesto issued by the Congress Parliamentary Committee, it was hinted otherwise:

> [T]he rejection in its entirety of the New Act by the Congress inevitably involves the rejection of the Communal Award ... the communal decision is wholly unacceptable as being inconsistent with independence and principles of democracy; ... the attitude of the Congress is, therefore, not one of indifference or neutrality. It disapproves strongly of the communal decision and would like to end it'.[131]

Although Congress wanted to fight the basis of the Award, paradoxically in the same manifesto a ban was placed on '*agitation against the communal decision by the Congress organisation*'.[132] Accordingly, B. C. Roy, President of the Manifesto Committee, Bengal, issued the Bengal Congress Manifesto, emphasising that 'the [BPCC] Executive has resolved that congressmen in the province, both Hindus and Mussalmans, shall take such steps to end the Decision in order that this may be supplanted by an agreed formula based on joint electorate and adult franchise'.[133] This position of the BPCC as explained by Roy underwent a complete change when it was placed before the Executive Council on 2 September 1936. In the resolutions, it was emphasised that though the BPCC appreciated the AICC stand that 'rejection of the New Act involved rejection of Communal Decision', it condemned simultaneously 'the ban on agitation against the Award by Congress organisations'. The Council thus insisted that 'it is the duty of the provincial Congress organisation... to carry on agitation both in and outside the legislature for the rejection of the Communal Decision'.[134]

The Congress President, Nehru, though admitting 'how hard Bengal [had] been hit by the communal decision',[135] never approved of agitation against the Award.[136] Later, in a letter to Jagat Narayan Lal of the Nationalist Party, he explained the Congress decision banning agitation in the following terms (emphasis added):

> Firstly, the primary consideration for us should always be the issue of independence. Everything should be judged from that

point of view ... The Congress wishes to avoid any activity which diverts attention from the main to the other matters. Such other matters which fit in with the larger issue, then it should be pressed with all vigor. When owing to various factors, it does not fit in, a special agitation based on it will injure the larger cause by making it appear that we are really thinking in terms of changes within the framework of the New Act, that is British imperialism. *Secondly*, the agitation would depend on internal situation. It may be that an agitation, say carried in the main by the Hindus, leads to a rival agitation in favour of the 'Award' carried in the main by the Muslims. This results in creating a situation in favour of the retention of the 'Award', for such a conflict is inevitably exploited by the British Government against us. *Therefore the idea of one-sided agitation is not favoured by the Congress.*[137]

Having disregarded the AICC direction, Sarat Bose asserted that the Provincial Parliamentary Committee 'will run the candidates on the basis of the Executive Council resolution of 2 September', which, he thought, was 'in no way inconsistent with the Manifesto of the AICC'.[138]

The Congress High Command was stubborn too. Patel, president of the AICC Parliamentary Committee, in his zeal to assert AICC authority threatened to refuse Congress nomination to the candidates in Bengal until the BPCC rescinded the above Executive resolution.[139] The BPPC retaliated equally strongly. At its Parliamentary Committee meeting on 8 November, the BPCC adopted a resolution depriving the Working Committee of its power of nominating candidates.[140] Besides this open challenge to the AICC, Sarat Bose also decided to offer nomination to the Nationalist Party members because 'the Party in Bengal consists of congressmen only'.[141] Nehru wanted Sarat to revoke the decision because 'this Party is a part of the larger Nationalist Party which does not consist of Congressmen only and which is carrying on in some places a violent campaign against the Congress'.[142] The plea was ignored by Sarat Bose. The Nationalist Party members, Dinesh Chakravarti, Indra Narayan Sen, Chapala Bhattacharyya and Birendra Majumdar, were still in the BPCC and had, as K. S. Roy reported to Nehru, a major role in the formulation of the above controversial resolution.[143] Especially after the adoption of the above resolution, the Congress High Command, and Nehru in particular, seemed to have believed the Nationalist Party swallowed the Congress: '[Bengal Congressmen] were gradually converting themselves into a Nationalist Party'.[144] Nehru's apprehension was unfounded. As a Nationalist Party circular shows, it was decided by the Nationalist Party at its executive meeting of 22 November that since the objectives of both the BPCC and the Nationalists were identical and half of the nominated members to the AICC from Bengal belonged to the Nationalist Party, merger with the

Bengal Congress was highly appropriate.[145] This decision was perhaps due to the formal approval of Nehru who, at a general meeting of the BPCC on 8 November, supported a resolution 'sanctioning organizational agitation against the award as a part of the new constitution'. It was further decided that this resolution 'would be included in the Election Manifesto as the supplementary Manifesto for the province'.[146] In view of the secession of some prominent congressmen from the BPCC, it was probably a strategic gesture on the part of the High Command to prevent further split. Nehru's approbation of an agitation led to strong criticism in the Congress press. *The Kaiser-I-Hind*, a Bombay daily, for instance, characterised the AICC decision as an unconditional surrender to 'an arch rebel who not only defied the Congress resolution on Communal Award but also set up a strong agitation in Bengal ... allying himself with the most reactionary communal groups in that province'. This was, it continued, 'nothing but stabbing Gandhi in the dark'.[147]

1937 election

The election results were, given the 'separate electorate', predetermined. What is interesting is the apparent division in the Muslim camp. It was apparent because though the United Muslim Party (which represented the Muslim League in Bengal) and the KPP contested separately, they did not fight each other in the constituencies allotted to the Muslims, with two exceptions.[148]

Compared to its competitors, the Bengal Congress was better equipped. Since factional differences were patched up for the time being, the Congress was, as the Governor thought, 'the only organized and well established political party in Bengal'.[149] Among the Congress 'right wingers, Nalini Ranjan Sarkar of the Bengal Chamber of Commerce could be effective in gathering support' provided, the Governor argued, he succeeded 'in winning both the Roys (i.e. B. C. Roy and K. S. Roy)'.[150] Apart from these two groups, there were non-Congress caste Hindus and Scheduled Castes. Among the former, B. P. Singh Roy, a Mymensingh landlord, and M. N. Chowdhury, Maharaja of Santosh, were individuals of some influence. The Governor anticipated that they would form a coalition with the British India Association.[151] As regards the latter, the Governor, while writing to the Viceroy, mentioned that since the Scheduled Castes had no recognised leader, the majority of them would ally themselves with the 'Muslims whose interests like theirs are predominantly rural; the rest would be divided between the Congress and independents'.[152]

The election results reflected the diversity of the political groupings in terms of their respective shares in the newly constituted Bengal Legislative Assembly (see Table 2.4).

Table 2.4 Election results, 1937

Parties and groupings	Number of seats
1 Congress (including one independent Hindu):	43
Scheduled Castes:	7
Labour	4
2 Hindu Nationalists: (caste Hindus)	3
3 Hindu Sabha: (Scheduled Castes)	2
4 Independent Hindus	
Caste Hindus:	14
Scheduled Castes:	23
5 Muslim League:	39
6 Proja Party:	40
7 Independent Muslims:	42
8 European:	25
9 Anglo-Indians:	4
10 Indian Christians:	2
Total	248*

Source: IOR, R/3/2/2, Anderson to Linlithgow, 8/2/1937.

Note
*Two by-elections were pending.

Out of the newly franchised 6 695 483 voters,[153] 41 per cent[154] exercised their suffrage. Of the total Hindu votes, only 61.4 per cent were cast their votes; the percentage of the total possible Muslim votes cast was remarkably high at 85 per cent. The Muslims responded zealously; in terms of putting up candidates they were far ahead. In the case of the Muslims, the proportion of candidates to seats was almost 3:1 (342 candidates for 117 seats), while in regard to the Hindus it was just above 2:1 (193 candidates for 80 seats).

Concluding observations

The Communal Award of 1932 was the culmination of a debate that began with the Morley–Minto Reform of 1909 over the question of 'separate' versus 'joint' electorates for the principal communities, Hindus and Muslims. The reason why Muslims insisted on a 'separate' electorate can be located in the Congress' failure to absorb the Muslims into the nationalist movement. The Muslim demand for a separate electorate was born out of suspicion and distrust of the Congress as the sole representative political organisation of India. In Bengal, the electoral controversy was compounded by peculiar socio-economic conditions: the majority of the landlords were Hindus, the majority of peasants Muslims. Once the Muslims were drawn to this peculiar feature of rural Bengal, the division assumed a political significance to which none of the Congress leaders paid attention. The Congress was never able to devise a strategy to counter Muslim apprehension. In part, at least, this was true because the Bengal Congress had long been dominated by rentier Hindus. When these nationalists were forced to choose between their opposition to foreign rule and the loss of their long-standing social and economic class interests, most of them opted for protection of these class interests. Presumably this would have held true had the tenants and raiyats been fellow Hindus. The fact that most of them were Muslims made it easier for the Government to use the 'divide and rule' strategy.

Though the idea of separatism, which was stated clearly by the Muslim League in its Lahore resolution of 1940 demanding a separate Muslim homeland, was given a concrete shape in the Communal Award, it was not a new idea. The spirit of 'separatism' could be traced back to the 1916 Lucknow Pact. C. R. Das's Bengal Pact consolidated it by guaranteeing concessions to the Muslims for their uplift. The leadership did not perceive the fragility of agreements at the elite level, given the deep-rooted differences between the two principal communities in rural Bengal. Thus what prepared the ground for a separate Muslim state was not the failure of both the Hindu and Muslim leaderships to adopt an appropriate programme neutralising 'separatist' ideas but the socio-economic reality, which not only gave meaning to the divisive tendencies but also consolidated them.

Notes

1 Gallagher 1973: 615.
2 Seal 1973: 343.
3 West Bengal State Archives (WBSA), Home-Poll 689 (1–3)/1933, note on the report of the Commissioners' Conference, 1933, by the Commissioner, Chittagong, no date.
4 National Archives of India (NAI), Home-Poll 41/1/1932, note to the Commissioners and Collectors by the Government of India, no date.
5 IOR, L/PO/46 (ii). The Prime Minister, Ramsay Macdonald was quoted in the memorandum submitted by the Secretary of State to the Cabinet Policy Committee, 11/3/1932.
6 IOR, L/PO/78 (i) PM's statement for release in the afternoon of Tuesday, 16 August 1932 in time for preparation for publication in morning newspapers of Wednesday 17 August 1932.
7 Ibid.
8 IOR, L/PO/49 (ii), Lothian to the Viceroy, 8 August 1932.
9 IOR, CMD 2360, Vol. XVI, memorandum by A. K. Ghuznavi, p. 188.
10 IOR, L/PO/48 (ii) Muslim demands, including fourteen points of Jinnah, were placed at the open meeting of the All India Muslim League at Delhi in March 1929.

11 A memorandum to Samuel Hoare, Secretary of State, by the Aga Khan, enclosed with the letter of 2 March 1932.
12 Nehru Memorial Museum and Library, New Delhi (NMML), AICC, 2/1928, Subhas Chandra Bose to Motilal Nehru, 12 July 1928.
13 Ibid.
14 Haque 1931.
15 Haque 1931: 10–15.
16 The entire discussion is based on Haque 1931: 6–11.
17 All Parties Conference 1928, p. 11.
18 Haque 1931: 11.
19 *The Star of India*, 19 December 1933.
20 NMML, Hindu Mahasabha Papers (HMP), Madan Mohan Malaviya to Amar Nath Majumdar, 18 February 1934.
21 Bose 1964: 290–1.
22 IOR, L/PO/78 (i), Tgm. From the Secretary of State to the Viceroy, 8 September 1932. It is believed that the secret letter of B. R. Ambedkar to the Aga Khan of 17 April 1932 influenced the PM's decision to a large extent. Ambedkar wrote, 'the depressed classes have in your Highness their best friend and staunchest support of their claims and I have no doubt that your Highness will exercise all [his] influence with Sir Samuel Hoare and the Prime Minister in favour of a decision which will do justice to them. See IOR, L/PO/48 (i) Ambedkar to Aga Khan, 17 April 1932.
23 Ibid, Gandhi to Macdonald, 8 September 1932.
24 Ibid, Prime Minister to Gandhi, 18 September 1932.
25 IOR, L/PO/78 (ii) Poona Pact, 1932.
26 IOR, L/PO/48, secret Cabinet Minutes, C. I. 32 (2), 11 March 1932.
27 IOR, L/PO/49 (iii), Bengal Governor to Viceroy, 5 May 1932.
28 IOR, L/PO/49 (ii), Tgm., Bengal Governor to the Secretary of State, Samuel Hoare, 7 June 1932.
29 Page 1982: 256.
30 IOR, L/PO/49 (ii), Tgm., Viceroy (Willingdon) to Samuel Hoare, 14 June 1932.
31 IOR, Templewood Collection, Eur 240/5, Willingdon to Hoare, 10 July 1932.
32 IOR, L/PO/49 (i), Tgm., Bengal Governor to Viceroy, 20 July 1932.
33 Ibid.
34 IOR, L/PO/49 (i), Tgm., Bengal Governor to Viceroy, 29 July 1932.
35 Ibid.
36 IOR, L/PO/49 (ii) Prime Minister to Secretary of State, 21 July 1932.
37 CSASC, Benthall Papers, suggested solution to the communal question in Bengal by Benthall, 21 January 1931.
38 Ibid.
39 IOR, L/PO/48 (i), memorandum presented by Samuel Hoare to the Cabinet Committee, India Round Table Conference (printed), 9 November 1931.
40 IOR, L/PO/49 (i), Tgm., Bengal Governor to the Viceroy, 26 July 1932.
41 Benthall Papers, Benthall's diary notes, 28 August 1932.
42 IOR, L/PO/49 (iii), a brief analysis of the Indian Franchise Committee Report with a few criticism by the Hon'ble Alhedy Sir Abdul Karim Ghuznavi, member, Bengal Government.
43 Ibid.
44 NAI, Home-Poll 41/4/1932, Tgm., Bengal Governor to Viceroy, 25 August 1932.
45 Ibid.

46 A. K. Fazlul Haq's speech on the special session of the All India Muslim League, Calcutta, 1938 (Pirzada 1970: 286).
47 Ahmad 1970: 83.
48 NAI, Home-Poll 41/4/1932, C. C. Garbett to Viceroy, 24 September 1932.
49 IOR, L/PJ/7/305, R. Ahmad to Secretary of State, 9 April 1932.
50 Pirzada 1970: 203.
51 Indian Annual Register (IAR), Vol. 1, 1935, presidential address, p. 326.
52 Ibid. resolution no. 1.
53 IOR, L/PO/49 (ii), a further note by P. C. Mitter on the Indian Franchise Committee Report, 8 June 1932.
54 Ibid.
55 NAI, Home-Poll 41/4/1932, resolutions of the meeting at Town Hall, 4 September 1932.
56 Ibid, Gilchrist to Viceroy, 16 June 1932.
57 NMML, M. S. Aney Papers, draft report of the Committee of Unity Conference, Allahabad, 3–17 November 1932.
58 Ibid, a note by Madan Mohan Malaviya, 4 November 1932.
59 *Azad*, Editorial, 19 November 1932.
60 Cited in A. D. Chakarvarti and C. Bhattacharya, *Congress Policy on Communal Award*, The Congress Nationalist Party, Bengal, August 1939, p. 125 (emphasis added).
61 NMML, Aney Papers, Gandhi to Aney, 12 July 1932.
62 See Appendix A in D. Chakravarti and C. Bhattacharya, *Congress Policy on Communal Award*, The Congress Nationalists Party, Bengal, August 1939, p. 127.
63 NMML, AICC, G24/1934–36, resolutions adopted in the anti-Communal Award Conference, Bombay, 25 October 1934.
64 Ibid.
65 NMML, AICC, G24/1934–36, Tgms., from Barisal, Chittagong, 7 September 1934, Mymensingh, Birbhum, Hili and Khulna, 8 September 1934. See also G23-24/1934–36, Tgms., from Noakhali, Dacca, 24 August 1934 and Pabna, 27 August 1934.
66 NMML, AICC, g24/1934–36, Satish Mishra to the Congress Working Committee, 26 August 1934.
67 Ibid., Nitish Nath Kundu, Vice President, Dinajpur DCC to Vallabhai Patel, 4 September 1934.
68 NMML, B. C. Roy Papers, B. C. Roy to Gandhi, 22 August 1934 and Gandhi's reply, 30 August 1934.
69 National Archives of India, new Delhi (NAI), M. R. Jayakar Papers, File No. 142, Zetland's letter to M. R. Jayakar, 30 May 1933.
70 IOR, L/PO/78 (ii), an extract from a private letter from Willingdon to Samuel Hoare, 15 January 1933.
71 IAR, Vol. 1, 1934, The Manifesto, issued by the representative Hindus of Bengal, Calcutta, 7 January 1934.
72 NMML, B. C. Roy Papers, B. C. Roy to Vallabhbhai Patel, 7 September 1934.
73 NAI, RPP, 1/35, AICC report, Allahabad, 28 February 1935, *The Congress and the Communal Award*.
74 IAR, Vol. II, 1934, p. 319.
75 NMML, AICC, G65/37, Rajendra Prasad's Diary Notes, 28 February 1935.
76 Ibid., notes of conversation held between M. A. Jinnah and Rajendra Prasad on 28 January 1935 at Ashoka Road, New Delhi between 2.30 and 3.30 pm.
77 Ibid., notes of conversation on 31 January 1935.

78 Ibid.
79 Ibid., notes of conversation between Madan Mohan Malaviya on the one side and Patel, Bhulabhai Desai and Prasad on the other, 31 January 1935.
80 Ibid., notes of conversation between Jinnah and Prasad, 13 and 14 February 1935.
81 NAI, RPP, III/35, Tgm., Indra Narayan Sen to Prasad, 15 February 1935.
82 Ibid., Reddy to Prasad, 17 February 1935.
83 Ibid., Vol. IV, 1935, Prasad's daily notes, 17 February 1935.
84 *IAR*, Vol. I, 1935, p. 314 (a)
85 Ibid., p. 325.
86 IAR, Vol. I, 1935, p. 328.
87 Ibid.
88 NAI, RPP, IV/35, Joint Statement of Prasad and Jinnah, 1 March 1935.
89 IOR, L/PO/49 (ii), The Communal Settlement Report by John Lothian, 18 July 1932.
90 Nehru 1941: 576.
91 Gandhi was quoted in *The Modern Review*, Vol. LXVII, No. 3, March 1940, p. 362.
92 *Liberty*, 18 August 1932.
93 *Advance*, 18 February 1932.
94 *Amrita Bazar Patrika (ABP)*, 23 September 1933.
95 NAI, RPP IV/36, K. S. Roy to Jawaharlal Nehru, 6 August 1936.
96 NMML, S. M. Ghosh (Oral Transcript), p. 305.
97 Subhas Chandra Bose to the Secretary, BPCC, 29 July, 1935 – cited in D. Chakravarti and C. Bhattacharya, *The Congress Policy on the Communal Award*, p. 26.
98 NMML, HMP, C/8, N. N. Das to Indra Narayan Sen, General Secretary, Congress Nationalist Party, Bengal, 24 August 1935.
99 ABP, 16 November 1936.
100 NMML, HMP, C/8, a copy of the memorial signed by 126 individuals including retired District Magistrate, editors of the newspapers, representative Hindu leaders, Chairmen of the municipalities and members of the Bengal Legislative Council.
101 Ibid.
102 Ibid.
103 Ibid., a circular to the districts, signed by R. K. Mukherjee and T. C. Goswami, 5 June 1936.
104 Ibid., replies from the districts, 11 June, 13 June and 14 June 1935.
105 Ibid., an anonymous letter to R. K. Mukherjee, 14 June 1936.
106 Ibid.
107 NMML, AICC G24/1934–36, Satis Dasgupta to Jawaharlal Nehru, 7 June 1936.
108 *Azad,* 18 June 1936.
109 IOR, L/PO/40, A. K. Ghuznavi to B. C. Mahatab, 17 December 1936.
110 Ibid.
111 Ibid.
112 IOR, L/PO/40, Mahatab to Ghuznavi, 18 December 1936.
113 NMML, B. C. Roy Papers, Mahatab to Roy, 18 December 1936.
114 Ibid. Roy to Mahatab, 22 December 1936.
115 IOR, L/PO/40, Zetland to Mahatab, 22 June 1936.
116 Ibid. Ghuznavi to Mahatab, 17 December 1936.
117 IOR, R/3/3/2, Bengal Governor to Linlithgow, 17 December 1936.

118 Ibid.
119 Ibid.
120 Pirzada (no date), *Foundations of Pakistan*, Vol. II, p. 194.
121 IOR, R/3/3/2, Bengal Governor to Viceroy, 31 December 1936.
122 Subhas Chandra Bose was reluctant to call it an Award. To him, it was 'a lesser evil than the partition of Bengal'. See Sharma 1938: 25.
123 Bose 1964: 288.
124 Bose 1964: 289.
125 RPP, IV/36, Bose to the Secretary, BPCC, 29 July 1935.
126 *IAR*, Vol. I, 1935, Ansari's press statement, 21 May 1934, p. 296.
127 D. Chakravarti and C. Bhattacharya, *The Congress Policy on the Communal Award*, p. 38.
128 RPP, IV/1936, Bose to the Secretary, BPCC, 29 July 1935.
129 Subhas Chandra Bose, *IS*, p. 288.
130 D. Chakravarti and C. Bhattacharya, *The Congress Policy on the Communal Award*, p. 29.
131 NMML, AICC, 24/1936, The Congress Election Manifesto, 1937.
132 Ibid. (emphasis added).
133 Ibid. B. C. Roy issued the Bengal Congress Manifesto, 1 October 1936.
134 Ibid. a copy of the resolution, adopted on 2 September 1936.
135 NMML, AICC P6/Part 1/1936, Jawaharlal Nehru to the BPCC Secretary, Suresh Chandra Majumdar, 6 August 1936.
136 NMML, AICC, 24/1936, Jawaharlal Nehru to Sarat Bose, 26 September 1936.
137 Ibid., Jawaharlal Nehru to Jagat Narayan Lal, 30 September 1936.
138 Ibid., Sarat Bose to Jawaharlal Nehru, 19 September 1936.
139 NMML, AICC G24/1936, Vallabhbhai Patel to B. C. Roy, 9 October 1936. The content of this letter was quoted in D. Chakravarti and C. Bhattacharya, *The Congress Policy on the Communal Award*, p. 15.
140 NMML, B. C. Roy Papers, the resolution of the Parliamentary Committee, 8 November 1936.
141 NMML, AICC, P6/Part II/1936, Sarat Bose to Jawaharlal Nehru, 7 August 1936.
142 Ibid., Jawaharlal Nehru to Sarat Bose, 14 August 1936.
143 Ibid., K. S. Roy to Jawaharlal Nehru, 6 August 1936.
144 NMML, AICC, 24/1936, Jawaharlal Nehru to Sarat Bose, 4 October 1936.
145 NMML, B. C. Roy Papers, File No. 39, the Nationalist Party Circular *Nationalist Party's Attitude, BPCC and the Award: The Basis for Collaboration*, 22 November 1936.
146 D. Chakravarti and C. Bhattacharya, *The Congress Policy on the Communal Award*, p. 15.
147 NMML, AICC, E7/1/Part I/1937, excerpts from *The Kaiser-I-Hind*, Bombay, 6 June 1937.
148 IOR, R/3/2/2, Bengal Governor to Linlithgow, 6 March 1937.
149 Ibid., R/3/2/2, Bengal Governor to Linlithgow, 3 December 1937.
150 Ibid.
151 Ibid.
152 Ibid.
153 NAI, F120/33, Qualification of Electorates: (a) payment of not less than 6 *annas chaukidari* tax or 8 *annas* municipal tax of fee, (b) having passed the matriculation or the school leaving certificate or an examination accepted by the local government as equivalent, (c) being a wife of a person but will be on

the roll during the widowhood or until remarriage when she will cease to be qualified in respect of her late husband, (d) assessment of income tax and (e) being a retired, pensioned or discharged officer, non-commissioned officer or soldier of His Majesty's regular forces.

154 IOR, CMD 5589, Vol. XXI, 1937, Election Results, p. 12.

3
POLITICS OF ACCOMMODATION AND CONFRONTATION
The second partition of Bengal

Even after more than half a century, the 1947 second partition of Bengal continues to baffle the historians. There are multiple reasons. One of them is certainly the complexity of the processes that finally led to the emergence of a new nation following the Radcliffe Award. Apart from the British, who indulged in *divide-et-impera* for obvious reasons,[1] the Hindus and Muslims had also played significant roles in formally articulating the schism between them. Thus the story that gradually unfolded is multidimensional. The other factor defying a more or less agreed explanation is the radical transformation of the socio-economic milieu of Bengal that underwent a dramatic metamorphosis in the context of British rule. The environment in which the Hindu–Muslim chasm was articulated is also crucial. It is therefore historically inaccurate to suggest that the Bengal partition was simply the outcome of the movement launched by the Shyama Prasad Mookherjee-led Hindu Mahasabha in December 1946, when the Bengal Partition League was formed. It may be argued that the movement gained momentum probably because of a conducive environment in which the so-called communal slogans had an easy acceptance among those who fought Lord Curzon when he sought to divide Bengal in 1905. The reasons for the success of the movement for the second partition in 1947 thus lie in the changing socio-economic and cultural circumstances sustaining and strengthening the segregated Hindu and Muslim identities. The most significant development that decisively shaped Bengal politics in the decades before the second partition was undoubtedly the emergence of Muslims as a distinct socio-cultural group, and their importance in the political arena with the introduction of the 1932 Communal Award.

What is also striking is the changing perception of Hindus, who no longer remained as significant in the provincial politics as before. Although the role of the Muslim League was peripheral in popularising the demand for Pakistan, the Congress had, at least by the late 1930s, nonetheless become a party supporting the Hindu landlord as opposed to the Muslim peasants. In the absence of a class-based ideology, Islam appeared to have provided the Muslim peasants with a unifying principle against the landlords, who were mostly Hindus. Religion continued to remain significant in Bengal. In the movement against the first partition, its role was tempered by underlining the Bengali identity that nearly evaporated in the context of the second partition. What replaced the Bengali identity was the communal identity of the Bengalis who now preferred to be identified as Hindus or Muslims. This is, however, not suprising when observing the historical processes of the period that finally culminated in the vivisection of Bengal.

There are two crucial questions that need to be addressed to grasp the second partition. First, how is it possible to account for the changing political stance of the Bengali leadership, who agreed to accept partition as the best possible solution under those circumstances? What is conspicuous is that the movement for partition gained remarkable momentum once the campaign for a united Bengal took off.[2] As this movement was jointly organised by the League and the leading Congressmen of Bengal, like Sarat Bose and K. S. Roy, it was potentially strong enough to launch an effective campaign. That the united Bengal movement was a ploy, as the evidence suggests, to create 'a greater Pakistan' may have significantly damaged its potential. This was a catalyst presumably because of the pro-Muslim policies, consistently followed by the Bengal ministry since 1937. Thus what accounts for 'the shift from nationalism to communalism' is not due to the preoccupation of the Bengali bhadrolok's with 'narrower and more parochial concerns',[3] but the apprehension of a hegemonic rule drawing exclusively upon Islam. The second equally significant issue – which is, in fact, a follow-up of the first – concerns the role of the national leadership, the Congress and the League High Command in the Bengal partition. The Bengal Congress was sharply divided into those supporting the united Bengal movement and those who opposed it. Once the partition plan was approved by a majority of the Congress MLAs, in the aftermath of the 3 June announcement, the only option for the Congress High Command was to negotiate with the British government for division of the province following its demographic composition.[4] As a result, the provincial wing of the Congress never became a crucial actor in the transfer of power. Similarly, the Bengal Provincial Muslim League continued to remain probably the most powerful factor in Jinnah's campaign for Pakistan, and yet it hardly had any significant role in his negotiation with the British. Always subservient, the Bengal counterpart of the League was conveniently utilised by Jinnah to attain his goal of a separate Muslim homeland. The irony of history is that the provincial wings of both the League and the Congress appeared to be peripheral in the final negotiations with the British for the transfer of power, when Bengal was sacrificed to fulfil an agenda to which they hardly contributed.[5]

Given the complexity of the processes that finally led to the fragmentation of Bengal in 1947, the second partition is probably the most important episode at a critical juncture of India's socio-political history. In dividing Bengal, apart from the role of the colonial power, the League was as much responsible as the Congress. Attributing partition largely to Hindu communalists is, therefore, historically inaccurate and factually wrong. The primary aim of this chapter is to unravel the processes that unfolded in the decades before partition in which Hindus and Muslims emerged as competing blocs for power and privileges. The chapter also argues that partition was probably unavoidable in view of the well-nurtured socio-economic processes that placed Hindus and Muslims in watertight compartments at the grassroots long before this was articulated at the institutional level of politics.

The first and second partitions contrasted

Historians seeking to explain the second partition of Bengal generally begin by contrasting it with the 1905 partition.[6] What was puzzling to Nirad Chaudhuri was that 'the same class of Hindus who opposed Lord Curzon's partition have now themselves brought about a second partition of their country' which he explained as an example of 'inconsistency of a politically incompetent and emotionally unstable class'.[7] Presumably to identify the startling contrast in the articulation of the movement against the division, historians tend to underplay the context of these movements. The Swadeshi movement was organised to annul the Bengal partition, which was allegedly a sinister imperial design to cripple the Bengal-led nationalist movement. As the evidence shows, though it was announced as an administrative device,[8] it drew upon the concern for containing the revolutionary terrorist movement seeking to undermine the Raj. None other than Minto, the successor of Curzon, expressed clearly the basic objective of the partition plan by saying that partition 'should and must be maintained since the diminution of the power of Bengali political agitation will assist to remove a serious cause of anxiety. ... It is the growing power of a population with great intellectual gifts and a talent for making itself heard [which] is not unlikely to influence public opinion at home most mischievously'.[9]

The comparison is valid so long as it is confined to the organisation of the movement. The Swadeshi Movement was an example where the schism between the principal communities did not figure prominently, presumably because Muslims did not emerge as an independent community to challenge the Hindus. As a result, the anti-partition campaign attained success and the partition was annulled. Although 'the Swadeshi movement ... produced an explicit rhetoric of Hindu–Muslim unity as part of its evocation of nationhood, ... the nationalist imagination that flourished ... actually naturalised a conception of nation ... that was quite distinctly Hindu'.[10] The second partition took place when the Muslims emerged as a competing community due to a specific unfolding of history also involving an alien power that manipulated the religious division to its advantage. Thus it would be inaccurate to understate the importance of those factors, which for obvious historical reasons were simply non-existent when the 1905 anti-partition movement was organised. It is important also to grasp the processes that led to the growth of Muslims as a distinct community, and the failure of the Hindu political leadership to anticipate the circumstances following the revocation of partition in 1908. Thus the roots of the 1947 vivisection of the province lay not merely in the movement demanding partition, as Joya Chatterji seems to suggest,[11] but also in the period that unfolded in a rather complex fashion during which the role of the British government was equally significant. The comparison is further flawed because the nature of communalism had also undergone changes. It is true that the campaign opposing the 1905 partition drew largely upon the Hindu-centred slogans and imageries.[12] All these gestures were, as Rafiuddin Ahmed has shown, 'repellent to the Muslims, now distinctly conscious of their Islamic identity'.[13] It would, however, be wrong to surmise that the Hindu-centric nation[14] that was sought to be constructed was anti-Muslim. Muslims were very much a part of the nation that was likely to be crippled if Curzon's design was not altogether shelved. The situation was not, however, the same as soon as the Muslims' demographic preponderance became a crucial factor in determining the distribution of governmental power following the acceptance of the 1932 Communal Award. Two processes were at work. On the one hand, the imperial legislative decision based on demography undoubtedly contributed to the growth of Muslims as a competing power in provincial institutional politics. Once in power, their representatives adopted several plans and programmes to ameliorate 'the conditions of the Muslims, exploited over generations by the Hindus'.[15] The legislative acts, as seen below, were probably aimed at the Hindu vested interests but, given the circumstances, they were articulated as 'deliberate attempts to ruin the Hindus as a race'. The interpretation gained ground in an environment where the Hindu communalists, active on the political scene in the 1930s and 1940s, were engaged in organising the Hindus essentially on sectarian issues. There seems to have been a polarisation of interests, and Hindus, just like the Muslims, appeared to have accepted the Hindu communalists as being capable of protecting the interests of 'a dying race'. As P. K. Dutta argues, the rise and strengthening of a Hindu bloc in the 1920s in Bengal drew largely upon what was defined as 'the communal common sense of dying Hindu'.[16] The Hindu demographic strength was certain to decline, as the argument goes, in view of the proliferation of Muslims due to reasons connected with their social system. The fear of being outnumbered by the Muslims appeared to be an effective instrument for those engaged in mobilisation for an exclusive Hindu constituency. Equally important was the process that led to the construction of a Muslim bloc and consequently the 'othering' of the Hindus. With their economic prosperity at the grass-roots through jute cultivation, Muslims gradually emerged as key players in 'high politics', and demands were placed for reservations for seats for the community in educational institutions and government employment. Since the progress of people is evidenced 'by the increase of wealth and knowledge',[17] several leading Muslim intellectuals of various districts constantly emphasised on the necessity of material improvement for their community.

The other process that was equally significant in the rise of Muslims as a separate community unfolded with the efforts to seriously cultivate their distinctiveness, drawing exclusively on their exclusive religious identity. For instance, the effort of the Bengali Muslim intellectuals to islamise Bengal, probably with a view to showing a cultural affinity with Muslims elsewhere, is striking. Thus religious identity was further consolidated by creating a language rooted in Islamic tradition. This had obvious political repercussions, and the Hindu communal forces lost no opportunity in utilising this campaign to gain further in rural Bengal. There is a third reason why the comparison was untenable. The 1905 division was, at least on the surface, an administrative device to partition the province of Bengal. Though divided, Bengal was as much a part of a country as was the proposed province of east Bengal. Drawing upon the cultural homogeneity, the anti-partition movement consolidated the nation that was constructed around the distinctive identity of Bengal. The second partition was undertaken in a completely different situation. It was a political decision, executed by those who presided over India's destiny at a very critical juncture of her history. It was not the division of a province but division of a country, and east Bengal became part of a new nation, Pakistan. The analogy with the first partition therefore appears to be overstretched, because the 1947 partition was the culmination of a process that derived its sustenance from Jinnah's two-nation theory. In other words, that Hindus and Muslims were diametrically opposing nations was formally articulated in 1947 by creating two sovereign nation-states primarily on the basis of religion. This was an event in which (apart from the British) both the Congress and the Muslim League had significant roles, despite the opposition of the former to Jinnah's conceptualisation of Muslims as a separate nation.

The Muslim hegemony in the institutional arena

Until the 1935 Government of India Act was promulgated, the Hindus were the dominant force in all the institutional bases of power in Bengal, and so Hindu hegemony developed throughout the province, thus alienating Muslims from them and aggravating communal animosities. The 1935

Act changed the situation radically by recognising the numerical majority as the likely source of political power at the provincial level. As a result, the Muslims in Bengal, by sheer demographic preponderance over the Hindus, captured the institutions of power, patronage and influence.

Having achieved this, the Muslim leadership (the KPP and the Muslim League) adopted policies and programmes to counteract Hindu preponderance in all walks of life. These policies aimed ostensibly to redress the grievances of the Muslim masses as well as educated Muslims. The legislative acts and their implementation during the period are illustrative of this. For instance, the adopted tenancy legislations were aimed at protecting the Muslim intermediary landed interests. Similarly, in urban areas the Muslim leadership sought to ensure jobs for the newly emerging educated middle-class Muslims.

In the aftermath of the 1937 elections, the failure of an agreement between the KPP and the Congress contributed to the formation of a coalition ministry led by the KPP and the Muslim League. Once in power the ministry took some legislative steps, ostensibly to ameliorate the conditions of the Muslims. In a situation where Muslims constituted a majority but lived under the socio-economic domination of the Hindu majority, any attempt to improve the conditions of the former was bound to provoke opposition from the Hindus. When the Bengal Tenancy (Amendment) Act (1938), for instance, abolished abwabs, the landlord's transfer fee, and their right of pre-emption, and the Bengal Agricultural Debtors Act (1939) established arbitration boards to enable the debtors to obtain moratoriums, Hindu politicians both within and outside the legislature characterised them as well-engineered devices to squash the Hindus.[18] Both these legislations aimed at improving the conditions of Muslim peasants, who suffered due to the illegal exaction of the zamindars, a majority of whom were Hindus. Given the communally charged atmosphere, the class division between the landlords and the cultivators acquired a communal colour. The reaction was similar when the Bengal Money-Lenders Act (1940) was promulgated. By fixing rates of interest, abolishing compound interest and providing for repayment of loans by instalments, the Act sought to protect the debtors against the creditors. The scope of the Act was, however, restricted by excluding the Wakf Boards, which were also involved in money lending in rural Bengal. On this issue, the Bengal Assembly was divided. Supporting the Bill, the Muslim members defended the exclusion of the Wakf Boards because they 'provide loan for religious purposes they should not be equated with the moneylenders, involved in money lending as a business to satisfy their greed at the cost of rural peasants'.[19] For the Hindu members it was a communal measure, since the Hindu *Debattor* Estates, engaged in similar activities, were not spared. Hence, 'through these excluding provisions, the jurisdiction of the Bill is being gradually narrowed and the very objective of the Bill might be, to a very serious extent, nullified'.[20] Apart from the blatant communal character, the Bill was also criticised for its failure to create sources of alternative and cheap credit in rural Bengal. Once the Bill was approved, the readily available sources of loans completely dried up as most of the Hindu talukdars and mahajans withdrew from money lending. Furthermore, 'by discriminatory measures in favour of the scheduled banks, the bill [also encouraged] the flight of capital from rural areas to Calcutta ... putting the masses of Bengali villages in a veritable financial deadlock'.[21]

Although a potentially positive step, the Act, as evident in the Assembly debates, placed the Hindus and Muslims in watertight compartments.[22] The campaign that was launched by the Hindu Mahasabha gained momentum, presumably because the Act was directed against only the Hindu mahajans and not other money-lending institutions. It was therefore a communal Act with a partisan aim of ruining the Hindus. Condemning the Act as a deliberate attempt to destroy the Hindus, the *Dainik Basumati* thus remarked:

> Banks, Insurance companies and societies for house-building purposes have been excluded. There is not reference even to Cooperative Credit Societies. New loans advanced by European firms are being put outside its scope. It must be noted that remainder of the creditors who come within the purview of the Bill are mostly Hindus.[23]

The other legislative bill that provoked Hindu–Muslim animosity further was the Bengal Secondary Education Bill, 1940. In a situation where there were consistent efforts to 'islamise' primary education by financially supporting maktabs (institutions imparting Islamic learning), the Bill acquired a communal character. That the Haq-led ministry was keen to strengthen the maktabs was made evident by a decree that not only recognised them but also allocated regular sums of money to them.[24] Criticising the government decision, the Congress legislator, Harendra Nath Chaudhuri argued that 'in this province, education is being tackled from a communal point of view, because the policy underlying the recent expansion of primary education has been a policy of *maktabising* the primary schools'.[25] This was the background when the Secondary Education Bill was tabled for debate and discussion. The House was clearly divided, and the arguments were made to advance the claims of the respective groups as forcefully as possible.

Since the primary objective of the Bill was to ensure a balance of Hindu and Muslim representation, it proposed to set up a board, consisting of the representatives elected on a communal basis. Of the fifty members, twenty-two were Hindus and twenty Muslims. With eight government nominated members, it was obvious that their support was crucial in the

Board's decision. As the League was a dominant partner in the government, the government nominees were likely to be those, sympathetic to the Muslim cause. Defending the application of the communal principle in the constitution of the Board, Fazlul Haq, the Bengal chief minister, thus stated: '[t]he Muslims are the majority community and they have vital interest in secondary education ... they can hardly be expected to tolerate a position in which their effective representation is not guaranteed as a right, but may be conceded by the goodwill of another community'.[26] The Muslim press openly supported the step as 'the one that was most desirable to change the bias ... in the secondary education ... so far controlled by the caste Hindus'.[27] Critical of the government, a majority of the non-League members of the house characterised the bill as 'another communal measure'. In his speech, Harendra Nath Chaudhuri therefore argued:

> communal composition of Board makes the Bill a communal measure *par excellence*. If better and more efficient secondary education is really desired then the Board should be composed of educationists and representatives of educational interests and the Board should be constituted on entirely academic and non-communal basis.[28]

Most of those who opposed the Bill drew upon the communal composition of the Board to defend their argument. Atul Chandra Sen, for instance, argued that 'we want peoples, Hindus and Mussalmans, in whatever proportion at any time, we do not mind if they be of the right sort, who have imbibed the spirit of the new culture and been elected on non-communal lines to guide the destiny of secondary education in the province'.[29] Although the Bill was approved *in toto*, it provided the Hindu Mahasabha with another powerful argument to blame the Haq-led government for its in-built communal bias. Not only was the Hindu press critical;[30] the Hindu Mahasabha leader, Shyama Prasad Mookherjee, in his speech in the Bengal Assembly, characterised the Bill as nothing but 'a part of the well-organised campaign of oppression of Hindus'. He further exhorted,

> [n]early 75 per cent of the children [studying] in Secondary Schools belong to the Hindu community and it will be our endeavour to see that the vast majority of these children should have nothing to do with any educational institution that will work under the domination of this Board. ... We Hindus should be given the liberty to develop our education in a matter we would consider best to [our] needs. ... [The] acceptance [of the Bill] specially means to us the end of education of the Hindus and a cry must go forth to every Hindu ... that if they are not to reduce themselves to a state of subservience in the field of culture as they

have been reduced in the economic and political spheres, they must be prepared to face this organised campaign of oppression at any cost whatsoever.[31]

The situation may not have been as severe as Mookherjee projected, but the speech is a clear indication of 'a mentality' that was nourished by the projected anti-Hindu bias of the League ministry – a bias that gained currency because of the categorical statements of the League leaders defending these steps as necessary to protect the hitherto peripheral majority community of Muslims.[32] Although it is difficult to ascertain the actual motive behind the framing of the Secondary Bill, Mookherjee's argument created and later consolidated a constituency for the Mahasabha in view of the various legislative acts to ameliorate the conditions of the majority who happened to be Muslims.

Of these legislative acts, the Calcutta Municipal (Amendment) Act (1939) was probably the most powerful intervention in undermining the Hindus in the Corporation. Seeking to ensure adequate Muslim representation, the Act proposed to introduce separate electorates following the arrangement that already existed in elections to the provincial assembly. The Calcutta press condemned the Bill as nothing but 'a well-designed device to weaken the Hindus in the Corporation'. As its aim was to curtail the share of Hindu seats, there was no doubt that, as Amrita Bazar Patrika exhorted, 'this Act clearly reflects the blatant communal bias of the Haq's pro-peasant [sic] ministry'.[33] R. N. Reid, the Bengal Governor, had therefore no doubt that 'the real question at issue [in the Calcutta Municipal Bill] under all the verbiage that has surrounded it, is how far Muslims will succeed in ousting Hindus from strongholds of political power, amongst which the Calcutta Corporation is one of the most important'.[34]

The main aim of the bill was to amend the original 1923 Municipal Act, which gave thirteen seats to Muslim, increasing to fifteen in 1927 and to nineteen in 1932. Election to these seats was based on the principle of a joint electorate[35] in order first to enhance the number of Muhammedan seats in the Corporation to thirty-two, and secondly to establish the principle of separate electorates in the election for these seats. The Bill created consternation in the Legislative Assembly. The debates during the passage of the Bill show the rival calculations of the Hindus and Muslims in relation to this important piece of legislation.

The Muslims defended the share of twenty-two seats as legitimate, 'because 22 out of 84 elective seats for the Muslims is in accordance with the proportion which the population of the community bears to the total population'.[36] Fazlul Haq, the premier, justified the Bill on communal grounds. He felt that 'a separate electorate is an absolute necessity in consequence of the fact that [Hindus and Muslims] are in watertight compartments. The watertight compartments are not the results of separate electorates but rather separate electorates are the results of watertight compartments that already exist'.[37]

Both the Congress and the Hindu Mahasabha opposed the Bill vehemently. Sarat Bose, the leader of the Congress party, characterised it as 'anti-national and anti-democratic', and argued that 'the Bill is opposed to all reason, common sense, to all ideas of justice and fair play and is calculated to prejudice the growth of civic freedom'.[38] The representative of the Mahasabha, S. P. Mookherjee, expressed his opposition to the Bill because he thought that 'the effect of the Bill will be to deprive the Hindus who form 70 percent of the total population of Calcutta and 76 percent of the total tax payers and 80 percent of total voters of the Corporation of the legitimate claims'.[39]

Among the Muslims, there were also dissenting voices. Nausher Ali, who was originally a member of the KPP but quit as a result of controversy over his appointment as a minister in the Haq cabinet, believed that the Bill 'will do nothing but increase the acrimoniousness between different sections of the citizens of Calcutta'.[40] Maulvi Haq Hussain Sarkar (himself a KPP member), while opposing the Bill, exposed the logical flaws of Haq's demand for a separate electorate as the only the means of securing the Muslim interests. He argued that 'Fazlul Haq himself was elected when the joint electorate system was introduced in the Calcutta Corporation on a Congress ticket. Is there anybody in the House who can say that the Honourable Mr. Haq did not represent the Muslim community in Bengal?'[41] Maulvi Hussain Sarkar was anxious as the Bill would secure

> the interests of the Urdu-speaking non-Bengalis, the Iranis, the Suhrawardy, the Siddiquis, the Adamjis and the Currimbhoys who are in a majority in Muslim Calcutta ... whose forefathers came to exploit Bengal alone, but seeing it now impossible, have joined the Campbells and the Morgans, the representatives of the European interests in Bengal.[42]

In spite of the opposition from the Hindus and group of Muslim leaders the Bill was passed, and the new statute, the Calcutta Municipal (Amendment) Act, provided forty-seven seats to non-Muslim voters (including four reserved for Scheduled Castes) in a House of ninety-three councillors. The principle of separate electorates was also introduced.[43]

The Corporation election under the new arrangement commanded public attention. Subhas Chandra Bose, who was trying to regain the strength he had lost as a result of his virtual removal from the Congress in 1939, came forward. Realising that in the changed circumstances an electoral alliance with the contending forces was the only way of maintaining his influence inside this civic body,[44] Bose forged an electoral alliance with the Hindu Mahasabha on the understanding that 'the election would be run in the name of the Joint Congress Corporation election Board, and that all those who would be elected would join the Congress Municipal Association.'[45]

The pact, though short lived, illustrates interesting trends in Bengal politics. First, on the part of the Mahasabha, conclusion of a pact with the Congress was sheer opportunism because the Mahasabha expressed disgust at the inclusion of the Congressmen (B. C. Roy and Sarat Bose) in a conference called by Fazlul Haq, the chief minister of Bengal, for the settlement of communal differences. The objection, as B. C. Chatterjee (a Hindu Mahasabha representative) explained, was based on the ground that 'the Congress does not represent any community and therefore it has no moral right to participate in talks dealing with the settlement of communal differences'.[46] This was opportunism in view of the fact that what drove the Mahasabha to agree to a pact with the Congress was not a principle but a consideration based on an assessment of how to secure Mahasabha's role within the Municipal administration.

Second, the agreement intensified communal feelings: Muslim opinion characterised this electoral deal 'as another instance of Congress and the Mahasabha being the same under different guises whenever a question affecting Muslim interests is at stake'.[47] Subhas Bose countered the allegation by saying that he effected the pact with a real Hindu Mahasabha (meaning non-political religious face of the organisation) and not with an organisation that sought to utilise Hindu orthodoxy for political mobilisation.[48] The pact collapsed nine days after it was signed, and the official Congress ridiculed it 'as a nine day wonder'.[49]

The above brief discussion of the legislations promulgated by the Bengal ministry reveals interesting trends in Bengal politics, which gradually became prominent. Once the principle of majority was recognised, the Muslim leadership lost no opportunity to utilise the government machinery to its advantage. Most of the legislative enactments aimed at the majority, who happened to be Muslims. Drawing attention to Hindu opposition to these endeavours as 'most natural' given their obvious communal bias, the League government easily mobilised support by underlining that:

> anything done for the improvement of the Muslims in Bengal had always been looked upon with suspicion by the entire Hindu Bengal; even the Hindus coming from the Muslim-majority areas always opposed economic measures designed for the improvement of the majority simply because bulk of the benefit will go the Muslims. The opposition to the amendment of the Tenancy Act of 1928 and 1939 and the Debt Settlement Board Act, the

Money-Lenders Act and the Rural Primary Education Act are illustrations. The Secondary Education Bill, meant for the improvement of the schools in the province (which by all opinion – Hindu and Muslim – need immediate improvement) [met] with combined opposition of the entire Hindu community on the sole ground that a very great portion of the benefit will be shared by the Muslims.[50]

What the League leadership at the institutional level undertook was further supported by the mullahs in rural areas. Not only were the Islamic festivals held regularly at their behest, they also distributed religious books and pamphlets to popularise the League ministry among the villagers in east Bengal. In their fatwas, the mullahs invariably linked the future of the Muslims with the continuity of the League ministry. The Muslims were therefore exhorted to strengthen the League as 'this is the command of the Quarn'. In another fatwa, widely circulated in Mymensingh, it was further insisted that the Muslims should strengthen the League because:

Islamic *Tamaddun* cannot exist without Islamic *Hukumat*. So this demand for Pakistan is based on the claim of justice. In the name of Independence the Muslims cannot tolerate slavery of the Hindu Congress. There are differences between the Hindus and Muslims in religion and *Tamaddun*. India should be partitioned into Pakistan and Hindustan for the development of these two nations.[51]

In compartmentalising the Hindus and the Muslims, the role of the Mahasabha was no less insignificant. The failure of the Bengal Congress to sustain its organisational hold in the districts for a variety of reasons, including internal squabbles,[52] was certainly an important factor in the growth of the Mahasabha that became a true representative of the 'declining' Hindus as the partition of Bengal drew close. Interestingly, unlike the League, the Mahasabha campaign was never structured around religious ethos or symbols; instead it drew upon the possible adverse consequences on the Bengali Hindus under the League ministry.[53] In other words, Hindus continued to suffer simply because of League's communal design. Thus what catapulted the Mahasabha on to the centre stage was a complex unfolding of events to which the League also contributed by pursuing policies striving seemingly to safeguard the interests of the Muslims as against Hindus.

The 1946 Calcutta and Noakhali riots[54]

Riots broke out in Bengal even before 1946.[55] What distinguishes these riots from the earlier ones is the scale of violence and the communal character so meticulously nurtured even during the height of mayhem.[56] Hindus and Muslims indiscriminately killed one another apparently to fulfil the grand design of the politicians, to which they hardly contributed. It is thus historically inaccurate to suggest that the decision to partition Bengal along religious–demographic lines actually involved the participation of the masses of people. The actual decision was made in the Bengal Legislative Assembly, which was constituted by a very restricted franchise, and was undoubtedly crucial in formally articulating partition of the province. What significantly influenced the course of events were, in fact, the communal killings in Calcutta in August 1946 and those in Noakhali just seven weeks later. These were probably the most powerful mass actions, planned by Hindu and Muslim communalists, contributing to the second partition. Those who were drawn to the riots appeared to have been swayed by what was projected as the goal of these unprecedented events. Some understood the 1946 communal violence as 'the cataclysmic sign of a general transition of power with its associated feelings of anxiety as well as of anticipation; [while] others took it to mean that Pakistan, whatever its precise legal or constitutional form, was inevitable'.[57]

How did the riot begin? In its Bombay meeting, held on 29 July 1946, the League adopted to observe 16 August as the Direct Action Day 'to get rid of the present slavery under the British and contemplated future caste-Hindu domination'.[58] According to Jinnah, 'Direct Action was a weapon of self defence'. The Bombay resolution was, as he further added, 'a reaction to the Congress direct action [that always aimed at] coercing and blackmailing the British to bypass the Muslim League and surrendering to the Congress'.[59]

August 16 was declared a public holiday. As a public holiday would enable 'the idle folk' successfully to enforce hartals in areas where the League leadership was uncertain, the Bengal Congress, in a debate in the Assembly, condemned the League ministry for having indulged in 'communal politics' for a narrow goal.[60] The League sought to organise a general hartal, while the Hindus tried to maintain a normal life.[61] The city was in the grip of tension, as everybody was apprehending trouble. In his diary, Major L. A. Livermore, an officer of the Eastern Command, thus wrote:

> there was a curiousness stillness in the air. The maidan was deserted and that artery of Calcutta, the famous Chowringhee, was as a street of the dead: not a vehicle or person in sight until about noon when a few people gathered in the vicinity of the

Ochterlony Memorial.... the silence was that of the air before the storm and that the crack of thunder would reverbate through the city at any moment.[62]

Minor confrontations were reported in the morning,[63] but disturbances started on a large scale in the afternoon in the aftermath of the meeting, organised by Suhrawardy, to observe the Direct Action Day.

Despite Jinnah's instruction to Muslims 'to conduct themselves peacefully and in a disciplined manner', the advertisement in the August 16 edition of *Dawn* was provocative enough to incite a confrontation.[64] Not only the wording but also the spirit the advertisement sought to convey were combative:

> Today is Direct Action Day
> Today Muslims of India dedicate anew their lives
> and all they possess to the cause of freedom
> Today let every Muslim swear in the name of Allah
> to resist aggression
> Direct Action is now their only cause
> because
> They offered peace but peace was spurned
> They honoured their word but betrayed
> They claim liberty but offered Thraldom
> Now, Might alone can secure their right.[65]

There was further provocation in the Muslim press in Calcutta. The Akram Khan-edited *The Morning News* began publishing editorials underlining the necessity for violence in case the Hindus conspired to defeat the campaign for Pakistan. Asserting that Muslims 'do not believe in the cant of non-violence', Akram Khan, in an editorial on 5 August, warned the Hindus of adverse consequences if the Pakistan proposal was not conceded.[66] Nazimuddin, another provincial League leader, also made statements threatening that 'there are a hundred and one ways in which we can create difficulties, specially when we are not restricted to non violence. The Muslims of Bengal know very well what Direct Action would mean so we need not bother to give them any lead'.[67] Apart from provocative statements clearly supporting violence, the League was also reported to have brought 'goondas from outside armed with sticks, spears and daggers [who] began to appear in the slums of Calcutta from the beginning of August'.[68] That the League was instigating the Muslims in Calcutta was clearly evident in a pamphlet written by the League Mayor of Calcutta, S. M. Usman, who exhorted:

> In the month of Ramzan, the first open war between Islam and Kafirs started and the Musslamans got the permission to wage jehad ... and Islam secured a splendid victory. ... According to wishes of God, the All India Muslim League has chosen this sacred month for launching this *jehad* for achieving Pakistan. We Muslims have had the crown and have ruled. Do not lose heart, be ready and take swords. Oh *Kafir*! Your doom is not far and the greater massacre will come.[69]

Attributing the participation of Muslims in the hartal to 'a holy duty' to Islam, a leaflet proclaimed:

> Awake, arise and unite under the banner of the Muslim League and make this hartal a success. ... Lead the procession [to Ochterlony Monument] with such strength and enthusiasm that even the blind, deaf, dumb can appreciate their strength and determination.[70]

The situation deteriorated in the afternoon of 16 August as the Chief Secretary requested the Bengal Governor to call the army immediately.[71] The Governor did not do so because he was not constitutionally authorised to do this without a formal request from the ministry.[72] The League ministry finally asked for its intervention on the second day. This force of about 8000 soldiers, if deployed in advance, could easily have stopped the carnage before it became unmanageable. The Government's unwillingness to call the army was characterised as 'intentional', especially when the situation deteriorated in the afternoon of 16 August. It is also possible that they asked for army help 'when they saw the game of killing was going against the Muslims'.[73]

The immediate provocation of a mass scale riot was certainly the afternoon League meeting at the Ochterlony Monument, which more than 100 000 Muslims were reported to have attended. As Major J. Sim of the Eastern Command wrote, 'there must have 100 000 of them ... with green uniform of the Muslim National Guard, with green hats and flags. Every man with a lathi – mostly so similar that they must have been bought especially for the occasion in bulk.'[74] Suhrawardy appeared to have incited the mob by making 'the most mischievous' statement and conveying that 'he had been able to restrain the military and police'. The Muslims interpreted this as 'an invitation to disorder'. That the Chief Minister's assurance provoked violence was confirmed by the incidents that began in the afternoon of 16 August. As the Governor also mentioned, 'the violence on a wider scale broke out as soon as the meeting was over', and most of those who indulged in attacking Hindus and looting Hindu shops were returning from the League meeting.[75]

The role of the Bengal Chief Minister was evident.[76] Not only did he ask the League supporters to be ready for the ultimate battle for Pakistan, he was also reported to have issued coupons 'bearing the chief minister's signature for the use of Muslim League lorries'. As minister in charge of the portfolio for law and order, he was believed to have arranged the transfer of Hindu police officers from all key posts. On the fateful day, twenty-two police stations out of twenty-four were in the charge of Muslim officials and the remaining two had Anglo-Indian officers.[77] The League made elaborate arrangements for first-aid stations and mobile units for the Direct Action Day. As Nirad Chaudhuri reminisces, '[i]n every Muslim quarter the Muslims were seen to sharpen their knives and spears and heard to utter threats. Well-disposed Muslims sent words to their Hindu friends to be careful and avoid trouble spots'.[78] Even the pro-League newspaper, *The Statesman*, was horrified by the sudden changes in the city when:

> [s]ome of those disrupting the city's peace were privileged. The bands of ruffians rushing about in lorries, stopping to assault and attack and generally spreading fear and confusion found the conveyances they wanted. On a day when no one else could get transport for their lawful occasions, these men had all they wanted; it is not a ridiculous assumption that they had been provided for in advance.[79]

The report of the Bengal Inspector General of Police, S. G. Taylor, is revealing. Struck by the attitude of Suhrawardy who was believed to have instigated the trouble, Taylor wrote (emphasis added):

> [t]he Chief Minister's own attitude during the rioting was reprehensible. During the height of the disturbances, he drove round Calcutta with the local army commander to assess the situation. As they drove, the Army Commander said, this is all extraordinary [since] in the Army Hindus and Mohammedans live and work very happily together. To this, the Chief Minister replied – *we shall put an end to all that*.[80]

On another occasion, the Calcutta Police commissioner lodged a complaint saying that 'the Chief Minister, with all kinds of hangers on (politicians of one community) had driven him and his staff nearly mad by sitting four hours at the Police H[ead] Q[uarters] interfering with every order and intercepting all information'.[81] Suhrawardy appeared to have restrained the police even during the height of the riot. As Tyson, the Secretary to the Bengal Governor reported, 'the police escort [of the Chief Minister] was amazingly lethargic about getting down from their vehicle and opening fire. The miscreants in each case were able to "complete the job" and slip away upside lanes before the His Excellency's convoy had covered fifty yards distance and drawn level with the place where these rioters and murderous mobs had been operating'.[82]

S. G. Taylor, the Inspector General of Police in Bengal, was equally disturbed when the Chief Minister ordered him to release those Muslims arrested in connection with rioting. As his order was 'illegal', Taylor refused to comply with it at the cost of making the Chief Minister angry, who now retorted that 'if he has occasion to arrest any Muhammedans in the future he will arrest at least as many Hindus!'.[83] 'It was extremely difficult for the police to deal with these dangerous situations', Taylor therefore concluded, 'with such irresponsible and unscrupulous persons in authority'.[84]

The 1946 riot[85] was distinctly different from its earlier manifestations in Bengal. It was more organised, directly connected with institutional politics, and hence, in the prevailing circumstances, 'more exclusively related to communal politics as well'.[86] As is evident, the League utilised the government machinery to mobilise the Muslims for the Direct Action Day.[87] While both the communities had, as an American intelligence report suggests, 'made preparations for self defence, it was Muslim provocation followed by instant Hindu retaliation' that caused the devastation.[88] The Muslims came off 'very much the worse through the Direct Action', as a contemporary report indicates, presumably because the population of the city was predominantly Hindu. Thus the Chief Minister made 'a tactical error in selecting Calcutta for his attack'. The scene now shifted to Noakhali in east Bengal, where 'the population was about 85 per cent Muhammadan'.[89]

Trouble began in Noakhali on 10 October 1946,[90] and spread to the villages of the Noakhali district,[91] Sandwip island and south-west Tippera district. The League ministry underplayed the nature of events almost for a week,[92] and the Bengal Governor was enjoying his holiday in Darjeeling.[93] Killings, conversions by force, abductions of women and looting were common. The pattern was uniform: at the head of the groups were ex-servicemen,[94] who organised the raids on the villages 'in quasi-military fashion'. The roving bands 'went about looting shops, burning houses, exhorting money and booty under threats, abducting women, forcibly converting Hindus and committing brutal murders wherever there was the slightest resistance'.[95] What affected the Hindu sensibilities most, both in Bengal and outside, was the mass forced conversion of Hindus in these areas. These conversions took place *en masse* and, as an official report elaborates:

> appear to have been carried out in several forms. In some cases, it appears to have been a fairly formal perfunctory affair involving merely the reading of *Kalma* and wearing a *lungi* instead of a *dhoti*. In other cases, initial conversion was steadily followed up

and converts were made to say their prayers regularly as Muslims and eat beef – anathema to Hindus. The women folk were generally herded into some central places like the village school and after the menfolk had signified their acceptance of Islam, the women were brought-out, their *tikka* mark on the forehead (the sign of a Hindu wife) rubbed out and their conchshell bangles broken. They were thus deprived of the outward symbols of their faith.[96]

It is difficult to ascertain the exact number of those who were forcibly converted during the riot because of the 'reluctance of the Hindus to admit that they have been converted'.[97] The horror of this in the eyes of orthodox Hindus must not be underrated. It seems clear, however, as the Bihar riot had shown, that events greatly exaggerated and subsequent excesses in other provinces were largely influenced by stories of Hindu women being abducted and bought and sold by Muslims.[98]

Hindus were invariably the targets of attack. After his tour of the district, the Bengal Governor confirmed that 'the Hindus were mostly affected and the Muslims were carefully left untouched'. While reporting on an incident in a village called Charhaim, the Governor had 'no doubt that the mobs ... did their work most thoroughly and systematically'. This village had, as he elaborated further, 'a prosperous bazar [sic] which was the economic centre of the neighbourhood. The bazar stood on Government land and the Government revenue office was untouched, as were a few Muslim-owned shops; but the rest was a desolate ruin of charred timber and twisted corrugated iron sheets'.[99]

The Muslim League may not have participated directly in the riot, but the main organiser of the mayhem happened to be Ghulam Sarwar, a former League member of the Bengal Legislature. Exhorting the Muslims to avenge the Calcutta massacre,[100] Sarwar urging the Muslims to join the National Guard and impose an economic boycott on Hindus. Muslims buying goods from Hindus were abused and beaten.[101] There were reports that Sarwar had conducted well-planned attacks on Hindu temples, desecrating idols and sacrificing cows on the lawn of these temples.[102] 'An uncrowned king' of the Muslims, he received support of the 'local school teachers, *Mullahs*, and the union presidents'. What Sarwar succeeded in doing was largely possible because of the involvement of the *Mullahs* who easily swayed the 'religious Muslim villagers' by their appeal, couched 'in Islamic terms'.[103]

Ghulam Sarwar's gang was estimated to be 1000-strong. A certain number of ex-army personnel were, a contemporary account underlines, 'reported to be adherents' who contributed by utilising their expertise in the use of 'sophisticated instruments for arson and blowing up roads and culverts'. The riot had also attracted a large number of local Muslim peasants from affected villages and contiguous areas.[104] The planning involved regular attacks on Hindu villages by Sarwar's striking gang.[105] The main gang, divided into smaller gangs of 150–200 members, followed a meticulously drawn plan, generally prepared by a group headed by Sarwar himself. The usual mode of action was to demand tribute from Hindus in various villages on pain of forcible conversion or death. Many paid, others were converted, most fled, and a large number who resisted were killed.[106] Hindus evacuated villages *en masse*, leaving their houses at the mercy of the gang, who looted and burned. As the police report shows, the areas in which the gang operated were 'Comilla, Fenny, Noakhali, Lakshimpur, Faridganj and Chandpur'.[107]

The complicity of the administration with the rioters was evident when steps were taken to track down Ghulam Sarwar and his major lieutenants. As Tuker, who was in charge of the operation, reported: 'there was no doubt in our mind that some subordinate officials were for communal reasons obstructing us in tracing and arresting Muslim evildoers'.[108] Sarwar remained at large for more than a fortnight after the outbreak[109] because the local police, presumably under instruction from the top, always helped him to disappear as soon as the army resorted to action.[110] On one occasion, when the army was, as report suggests, 'going to make a raid on a village to arrest [him] the police [were reported to have] given information of the intended move of the army and he had disappeared'.[111] What was even more discouraging was that, as Tuker reminisces, 'when we occasionally did catch red-hot goondas and send them to Chandpur for the case to be tried, nine out of ten of the local Sub-Divisional Officers would release them on bail'. Describing the procedure adopted by these officers to release those arrested as 'a travesty of justice', M. O. Carter, the Chittagong Divisional Commissioner, referred to a number of cases, commenting that: 'the indiscriminate and wholly improper release on bail of large number of Muslim suspects ... has had a most disheartening effect on the Hindus'.[112] What was most revealing was the involvement of the Chittagong District Magistrate, who happened to be a Muslim, in 'releasing an arrested absconder suspected of having committed murder in the Noakhali riot before the latter had even been produced in court'.[113] There was no doubt that 'the whole administration from top to bottom, was communally minded, supporting the Muslims to gain at any cost'.[114]

The involvement of the provincial League leadership in revamping the Muslim National Guard in Bengal raises question about its intentions. Suhrawardy, the Bengal Chief Minister, was reported to have attended meetings of the National Guard in Faridpur in July, where he urged the Muslim youth to strengthen the Guard in Bengal.[115] Whether the members of the Guard who were associated with Ghulam Sarwar acted in Noakhali on instructions from the provincial leaders is difficult to ascertain. What is clear, however, is that the carnage would not have assumed such devastating proportions without the participation of the Guard, which guided the Muslim hatred against Hindus in such a way as to cause 'a reign of terror for the Hindus'.[116] That a large number of ex-military Muslim personnel participated in the Noakhali outbreak is illustrative of its popularity among the discontented Servicemen in east Bengal. Attributing the carnage to 'superior brains', the Bengal Governor also underlined the role of the Guard in sustaining the riot beyond what was anticipated.[117] Therein lies the importance of organisation, which was partly automatic due to Muslim hatred against the Hindu businessmen who made a fortune by exploiting the Muslims during the 1943 famine[118] and partly due to considerable planning in linking the demand for Pakistan with the well-being of the Muslim masses.

The Noakhali–Tippera riot was neither sudden nor spontaneous, but had been deliberately planned with support and encouragement from the leaders of institutional politics. Thus *The Times* wrote:

> Noakhali was the outcome of enmity, aroused by the happenings in Calcutta. These feelings were played on by certain local Muslim leaders of doubtful reputation but with a large following whose motives were partly religious fanatacism and partly the desire to profit from the expulsion of Hindu elements. Disturbances took the form of seeking to establish a local Pakistan wholly Muslim in composition.[119]

Gandhi's presence in Noakhali for several months (6 November 1946–2 March 1947) temporarily quelled the situation, but did not radically alter the circumstances in which both the communities were placed. Sucheta Kripalani, who went to Noakhali and stayed there for seven months on Gandhi's request, felt that because '[t]he poison of ill-will and hatred, preached by the Muslim League leaders, the Mullas and Maulvis had gone so deep',[120] Gandhi's hope that people would 'cast off their fear and return to their homes was 'unrealistic'. It was unrealistic, she further added, because Gandhi 'did not realise that this was too much to expect from the Hindus who suffered so much and so grievously'.[121] By December the Mahatma had come to terms with reality because, as he himself admitted, 'distrust has gone too deep for exhortation'. Disheartened by his failure to bring back those who left, Gandhi articulated his emotions by saying that 'in spite of efforts exodus continues and very few persons have returned to their villages. They say [that] the guilty parties are still at large ... that sporadic cases of murder and arson still continue, that abducted women have not been returned, that burnt houses are not being re-built and generally the atmosphere of good will is lacking'.[122]

The Muslims did not like Gandhi's presence in Noakhali.[123] Attempts were made to prevent people from attending the regular prayer meetings by throwing night soil and glass on the path approaching where he lived.[124] Initially the local Muslims had shown enthusiasm for his prayer meetings, but later, especially from January onwards, the number suddenly dropped.[125] Suhrawardy and his League colleagues were critical of his decision to stay in Noakhali and charged him 'with the desire to make political capital out of an unfortunate happening'.[126] In his address to the students in Delhi, Suhrawardy accused Gandhi of being biased towards the Hindus, otherwise he would have gone to Bihar, which was tormented by communal riots following the Noakhali outbreak,[127] 'to see what his own nation had done to the members of the minority community' there.[128]

Unlike Nehru, who was very unhappy about the communal riots,[129] the League leadership did not condemn the events unequivocally.[130] Burrow's request to issue a statement met with a negative response. Insisting on a statement by the prominent League leaders, Liaquat Ali Khan escaped responsibility.[131] Apart from a news item in *The Morning News*, dissociating the League from Ghulam Sarwar (the principal leader of the Muslims in Noakhali),[132] neither was the riot condemned nor was an attempt to assuage the feelings of the Hindu victims. Instead, there was a constant endeavour to wish away the reports published in the Calcutta press. In the 19 October edition, *The Morning News* brought out, for instance, a report claiming that:

> public opinion in Noakhali is amazed and shocked at absurdly fantastic and inflammatory reports published in the Hindu Newspapers in Calcutta. They resent the highly exaggerated, coloured and false version of these reports which are meant to excite passions and set one community against another and are a concerted campaign to oust the Muslim League ministry by gangsterism.[133]

Seeking to fix the responsibility on the Hindus and Congress, Jinnah denied that the League had any role in the riots and suggested that they 'were organised by Congress leaders, not even excepting the most prominent'. Having seen the reports from his own sources, he was persuaded later, however, to accept that the 'communal riots in Calcutta were mainly started by Hindus, and *with the possible exception of Noakhali*, were of Hindu origin' (emphasis added).[134]

The carnage in Noakhali and Tippera (see Table 3.1) following the Calcutta massacre frightened the Hindus about their future in a Muslim-majority province. As Sitaramayya wrote in his history of the Congress, 'it was the variety and intensity of the crime in [Noakhali and Tippera] that attracted notice and roused *a sense of horror all round*, rather than the numbers of dead and wounded'.[135] The Hindus were favourably inclined to partition because 'only by partition can they escape the rule of ... "gangsterism", sponsored by the League'.[136] Apart from blatant communal

Table 3.1 Numbers of abducted women, dead and injured in the riots in Tippera and Noakhali

	Tippera	Noakhali
Abductions of women	6	2
Forced conversion	9895	3467
Women raped	11	7
Number of deaths	39 (Hindus), 26 (Muslims)	178 (Hindus), 42 (Muslims)
Number of injured persons	42 (Hindus), 16 (Muslims)	58 (Hindus), 26 (Muslims)

Sources: West Bengal State Archives, Calcutta, Home-Poll 49/47, E. H. LeBrocq, D. I. G. Police, Bakarganj to the Chief Secretary, Government of Bengal, 4 March 1947.

Note
These figures are definitely an understatement of what actually had happened because LeBrocq himself admitted that 'the correct figures can not be given at present since our force has not reached a large number of remote villages in both these districts'.

justifications, of which there were plenty, the division was defended by more sophisticated arguments underlining the probable strength of democratic-secular values in areas likely to constitute India.[137] In February 1947, the Hindu Mahasabha put forward the demand for dividing Bengal. The Congress High Command endorsed the idea as the best possible solution under the circumstances. Some of the Muslim League leaders and a handful of Bengali nationalists in the Congress fold continued their efforts to secure a united Bengal.[138] The proposal had few takers, and most seemed persuaded by Shyama Prasad Mookherjee's argument in favour of partition.[139]

By forming the Bengal Partition League in December, 1946, the Hindu Mahasabha began mobilising support for partition. The movement gathered momentum in the aftermath of the Tarakeswar Conference, held in April 1947; its significance lies in the fact that not only was it resolved to fight for partition; the meeting also 'authorised Mookherjee to constitute a council of action to establish a separate homeland for the Hindus of Bengal'.[140] While defending partition, N. C. Chatterjee, in his presidential address, declared:

> Traditionally and sentimentally the people of Bengal are against any move of dividing the province. But we shall be guilty of treason to the motherland if we merely quote old slogans without understanding their implications. The Anti-Partition movement in the Swadeshi days was a fight against imperialism which wanted to cripple the greatest nationalist force working for the Independence of the country by making the Bengal Hindus minorities in both the provinces. Our demand for partition today is prompted

by the same ideal and same purpose, namely, to prevent the disintegration of the nationalist element and to preserve Bengal's culture and to secure a Homeland for the Hindus of Bengal which will constitute a National State a part of India.[141]

The Bengal Congress did not lag behind. On the same day as the Tarkeswar Conference (4 April 1947), the Executive Committee of the Bengal Provincial Congress also urged the immediate setting up of two regional ministries and resolved that 'if the Government contemplated handing over power to the existing Government of Bengal, such portions of Bengal as wished to remain within the Union of India should be formed into a separate Province'.[142]

The campaign for partition immediately took off, though the League sought to scupper the movement from the outset. The Bengal Chief Secretary apprehended trouble, as 'a section of the Muslims at least are already busy collecting food and preparing plan for defence and offence, whichever is necessary, in the Muslim areas'.[143] Within a month of the Tarkeswar meet, the Mahasabha succeeded in mobilising a fairly wide support for its demand. As the fortnightly reports indicates,

> [i]n West Bengal, the movement for partition continues to gain momentum and all districts report growing confidence in favour of the scheme. In the Presidency division, meetings of Hindus in both urban and rural areas in support of the partition proposal continue to be held. In North Bengal, speculation generally favours partition. In Chittagong, there is interest in the idea and a general belief that the province will be partitioned.[144]

A careful study of the petitions for partition received by the AICC and the Mahasabha High Command reveals that Hindus were persuaded to support Mookherjee because of the blatant communal character of the League ministry. Their apprehension that the existence of the Hindus as a community 'will be in jeopardy in the Muslim-ruled state' gained credence probably in view of those policies with a clear communal tone and implications.

One of the issues that was constantly emphasised was the Noakhali riot, in which Hindus were butchered in a planned manner.[145] It was alleged that the calamity could have been stopped long before it was if the League government had called the military as soon as the trouble began. That the League ministry was 'communal' was evident when the local police helped Ghulam Sarwar, the main organiser of the riot, to escape arrest. Furthermore, the free availability of petrol and nitric acids during the Noakhali riot was not possible without the support of the local administration. 'How and from where do these goondas secure', the petitioners from Barisal asked, 'such a large quantity of petrol to burn houses and such a large quantity of nitric acid for throwing towards the pedestrians and passengers of trains, buses and other vehicles?'[146]

Another petition from Calcutta is more categorical in its characterisation of the League administration:

> Given the communal design of the League, Hindus are not safe any longer. The idea gained currency in view of the Calcutta and Noakhali massacre and ... unwillingness of the League officials to take strong action against the perpetrators of outrage, dilatory methods in rounding up the goonda element in Calcutta and Noakhali who rightly or wrongly feel that they have the support of Government at their back.

Furthermore, while the ministry did not pay attention to the rehabilitation of those Hindus who left Noakhali, they 'are sheltering thousands of Bihar Muslims in Western Bengal and feeding and clothing them with the ulterior object of showing an increase of Muslim population in Western Bengal in order to prejudicially affect the case of partition of Bengal'.[147]

The revamping of the Muslim National Guard compounded the Hindu fear of a communal backlash. Not only did Suhrawardy exercise his influence in releasing some of the members of the Guard when arrested in Noakhali; he was also instrumental in popularising the National Guard among the Muslim youth in rural Bengal.[148] Identifying the National Guard as 'a menace to the peace and tranquility of the province', a group of lawyers from Chittagong thus appealed to the Viceroy to force the League government 'to restrain before they strike again'. Equipped with firearms, they 'are terrorising the Hindus of Bengal', particularly in Muslim majority areas, by resorting to violence at the slightest pretext.[149] The British administration expressed resentment in view of the League's involvement in the activities of the Guard. What caused alarm to the Hindus was the government support to the League's proposal to recruit only Punjabi Muslims for the Calcutta Armed Police Force. Burrows defended his action by saying that 'since local Bengalis ... have never been much of a success in the Armed Branch ... our sources of recruitment of suitable material ... inside the province are limited'.[150] In communally charged circumstances, this action was likely to cause tension. Several meetings were organised in Calcutta and its suburbs highlighting the complicity of the Bengal Governor with the communal League ministry, more particularly its leader Suhrawardy.[151] What prompted Suhrawardy to recruit Punjabi Muslims was not difficult to determine. The Bengal Chief Minister was 'seeking to force the Hindus to withdraw the campaign for partition' by employing the Armed Guard 'to cause terror in the Hindu *mohallas*'.[152] They went around announcing that they 'were not ordinary "armed police", but men recruited by the Chief Minister, Suhrawardy for his own force and for a purpose that would be shortly disclosed'.[153] Not only did the ministry support Suhrawardy, 'their few rich merchant co-religionists also pampered 600 Punjabi Muslim Armed Guards by supplying good housing accommodation for their occupation when the Gurkhas [were] still inadequately housed in the barracks for years'.[154]

There are indications that the League felt threatened by the growing popularity of the movement for partition at the behest of the Mahasabha. To counter the campaign, the League was believed to have asked Suhrawardy to strengthen the Armed Police Force by immediately recruiting at least 30 000 Muslim ex-servicemen for Bengal. The Bengal Chief Minister was exhorted to meet, as an intercepted document shows, 'the hostile and rebellious [Hindu] force with superior force, superior strategy, superior generalship and superior morale'. The present Armed Police Force of the government of Bengal was inadequate simply because 'it was never raised or made for this job of checkmating civil war [sic]. We must therefore secure the services of war veterans, tough men, Muslim military officers – Brigadiers, Colonels, Majors, Captains, Lieutenants – and appoint them as D[eputy] C[ommissioner]s, A[ssistant] C[ommissioner]s and Commandants of Additional and Special Police forces'. Given the influence of the Gurkha League and the Congress among the Gurkha soldiers, they were 'a grave danger to the security of Bengal' and the Chief Minister was, therefore, asked not to recruit a single Gurkha for the Armed Police Force (see Table 3.2).[155]

The government report indicates that Hindus were also organised by the Mahasabha for a showdown in case of another communal riot. Preparations had been underway since the outbreak of the Calcutta riot. By March 1947, the Mahasabha had raised 'its own Home guards to protect the Hindus from the organised Moslem attack in near future'.[156] Moreover, 'in pursuance of their policy of watching over the interests of east Bengal Hindus, action has', as the Bengal Chief Secretary noted, 'already been initiated ... to organise minority committees in their area to protect the rights of Hindus'.[157] Such committees were instructed 'to send to the Mahasabha office detailed reports of Muslim atrocity'.[158]

As is evident, Hindus were in favour of partition to avoid Muslim rule. What strengthened the campaign was undoubtedly that 'the extreme communalism of the Muslim ministry over the last two years convinced the Bengali Hindus that they could not expect a square deal under a government which had a slight Muslim majority, and the partition of the Province has been accepted as the lesser of the two evils'.[159] The Congress had also received a large number of memoranda from Bengal preferring the division to Muslim rule. Apart from several organisations – like the Bangladeshiya Kayastha Sabha, the Assam Bengal (Indian) Tea Planters'

Table 3.2 Distribution of the 30 000 Armed Forces

Calcutta	
Additional Police Force	4000
Essential Services Protection Force	1000
Mills and Factories Protection Police	1000
Total	*6000*
Howrah	
Additional Police Force	2000
Essential Services Protection Police	500
Mills and Factories Protection Police	500
Total	*3000*
Hooghly	
Additional Police Force	1000
Essential Services Protection Police	200
Mills and Factories Protection Police	300
Total	*1500*
24 Parganas	
Additional Police Force	4000
Essential Services Protection Police	1000
Mills and Factories Protection Police	1000
Total	*6000*
Burdwan-Asansol	
Additional Police Force	3000
Mill protection Force	1000
Mines Protection Force	1000
Total	*5000*
Midnapore-Kharagpur	
Additional Police Force	2000
Border Police Force	1000
Railway Protection Police	500
Total	*3500*
Bengal Border Anti-smuggling Force	
Bengal-Bihar border districts	3000
For Railway Protection Force	
Midnapore, Burdwan and Calcutta areas	2000

Association, the Calcutta Motor Dealers' Association, the Bar Association of Barisal, Khulna and Khustia Municipal Commissioners' Association – the eminent Bengali intellectuals[161] participated in the campaign for partition.

Just like the Hindus, who zealously participated in the campaign for partition to avoid Muslim hegemony, Muslims also organised themselves to press for partition in those areas of east Bengal where Hindus constituted a sizeable section of the population. The League High Command received memoranda from Jessore, Khulna, Maldah, Rangpur and

Dinajpur, where Hindus were demographically preponderant in urban areas. The campaign in Jessore, Maldah, Rangpur and Dinjapur gradually fizzled out, presumably because of Suhrawardy's assurance of their inclusion in Pakistan due to a clear Muslim majority there.[161] As Khulna was declared 'a Muslim minority district', a massive campaign was organised to bring the district within Pakistan. On hearing that Khulna was likely to be part of Hindustan, 'the innocent peasant is bewildered saying, why is it so? I go to the fields, rivers, jungles, markets, courts and offices and find that most of the people who go there are Muslims'. In a petition to Quaid-i-Azam, it was therefore insisted that 'the sentiment of the common man, the tiller of the soil of Khulna, should be respected and considered ... before a final decision; otherwise, there will be disaster'.[162] Whether this campaign resulted in Khulna's inclusion in Pakistan is difficult to ascertain; since Muslims constituted a majority, the district was unlikely to have been included in India.

It is clear that the 1946 riots severely disrupted the communal chord[163] that appeared to have saved the first partition. Apart from the loss of lives, the Calcutta and Noakhali outbreaks created an environment of mutual suspicion and distrust that largely accounted for the panic among the Hindus in Muslim-majority areas and Muslims in Hindu-majority areas. Thus partition was due neither to the politicians' manipulation of events nor to communal chasm at the grassroots, but to a peculiar unfolding of socio-economic and political processes in which the division of the province emerged as the only alternative to avoid the further escalation of communal violence.

The 20 June meeting of the Bengal Legislative Assembly decided the fate of Bengal. The second partition of Bengal was formally articulated. The Muslims were 'enthusiastic that at last they have country which they can call their own'.[164] Those who had business in Calcutta felt that 'they are sacrificed by the League leadership to fulfil their narrow political ambition'. The Hindu reactions were 'guarded'. They were 'happy' because 'their campaign resulted in what they aspired for'.[165] With partition, the Hindus 'will now be able to maintain their own culture unhampered'. What caused discomfort among some of the leading members of the campaign was 'the realisation that in the council of Hindustan, they, the Hindus of a truncated Bengal will carry little weight'.[166]

Concluding observations

If it is contrasted with the 1905 partition, the second partition is a paradox of history. In 1905, the Hindus had opposed the division and the Muslims wanted it. In 1947, the Muslims were opposed to it while the Hindus were in favour. There was a complete reversal of the Bengali Hindu attitude. One of the immediate causes of this was certainly the communal rioting in Calcutta and Noakhali. After the killings in Calcutta, the idea of partition, as Nirad C. Chaudhuri reminisces, 'gained ground even among the Hindus ... and only in early 1947, East Bengal Hindus had become very zealous supporters of partition on account of the Hindu–Muslim feud from 1940'.[167] The Calcutta riot was the articulation of Hindu–Muslim animosity in its most virulent form. Describing 'the bestiality of the mob as simply incredible', an official report suggested, that '[b]oth sides seem to have set out to cause as many deaths as possible; they were not content with drawing blood or causing serious injury; they went on to crush and mutilate even a lifeless body'.[168] What had happened in Noakhali was worse, as Patel argued that 'the Calcutta incident pales into insignificance before Noakhali'.[169] These two riots in quick succession definitely contributed to the growing strength of the movement for partition as the only way to escape the Muslim atrocities. A contemporary memorandum to Jinnah clearly brings out the agony the Hindus in East Bengal by underlining that 'the Hindus of East Bengal ... have become nervous and panicky. They feel that their life, property, religion and honour will not be safe under the Muslim government. In fact, the Hindus seem to be completely paralysed. There is no denying that ... it is there, paralysing to no small extent the normal life of the Hindus in East Bengal'.[170]

Not only did the Hindus support the movement; the Scheduled Castes, the erstwhile ally of the League ministry, also came forward to bolster the campaign. The Great Calcutta Killing of August seems to have decisively shaped the Scheduled Caste opinion. The opposition of the Scheduled Caste members in the Bengal Assembly to the Congress-sponsored no confidence vote against the Bengal Chief Minister, Suhrawardy, outraged the opinion of the Bengal Scheduled Castes. Since J. N. Mandal was the only non-Muslim member in the Suhrawardy ministry, he was the principal target of attack. Asking him to resign, the following letter to the *Amrita Bazar Patrika* thus reveals,

> the fate of the Scheduled Castes of Bengal goes along with that of the Caste Hindus in a riot and they have suffered no less than the Caste Hindus. ... Hundreds of Scheduled Castes have been killed, hundreds wounded and hundreds of their houses and bustees have been looted and burnt. It is not the Muslim League ... but either the Hindu organisations or the Congress that have rescued [them] from the impending atrocities and hooliganism of the League. The riots of August 16 have compelled the Scheduled Castes of Bengal along with others to lose even the bit of faith they had in the League Ministry and its Government which are wholly responsible for the massacre of so many thousands of men, women and children.

[U]nder these circumstances we as your friends and followers hope that you would in no time cut off all connection with the League Ministry by tendering resignation ... and thus regain the sympathy and support of all'.[171]

What the experience of the 1946 riots had reinforced among the Scheduled Castes was 'a growing sense of Hindu identity which the communally charged general political atmosphere of the province during this time had definitely contributed to'.[172] This was evident in the debates in the Assembly when the partition proposal was placed for discussion. J. N. Mandal, who absolved the League of responsibility in the Noakhali riot,[173] argued against partition by saying:

If Bengal is partitioned, the scheduled castes will suffer most. The caste-Hindus of east Bengal are wealthy and many have salaried jobs. They will have little difficulty in moving from east to west Bengal. Poor scheduled caste peasants, fishermen and artisans will have to remain in east Bengal where the proportion of Hindus will decline and they will be at the mercy of the majority of Muslim community'.[174]

Mandal was in a minority, and his colleagues in the Assembly criticised him for extending undue favour to the League which was responsible for killing the Scheduled Castes in both Calcutta and Noakhali riots.[175] As Radha Nath Das argued in defence of the partition:

[t]oday if we say to our Namasudra brothers in Noakhali that they come to west Bengal where the government of the separate province of West and North Bengal will provide them with shelter and other economic necessities, then I am prepared to swear that Jogen Babu [J. N. Mandal] will not be able to keep a single one of his caste brothers in Noakhali. In other words, he will not be able to make them feel secure under Muslim League rule or Muslim League protection. I say the backward Hindus will be better able than others to leave east Bengal, since they have few possessions besides their tiny huts.[176]

During the voting, the Scheduled Castes were clearly polarised and a majority of twenty-five out of thirty of its MLAs voted for partition of the province. Clearly, when the time came for a strategic decision by 'a group organised as a minority within a minority, the hegemonic gesture of the Muslim League towards the scheduled castes proved inadequate'.[177]

Apart from the carnage in Calcutta and Noakhali, which undoubtedly influenced the Bengali Hindu opinion in partition's favour, what reinforced the Hindu fear was undoubtedly the legislative acts adopted by the Muslim ministry since 1937 to protect the interests of the majority community. As shown, since these acts had affected the Hindu adversely they were invariably identified as communal devices to uphold only the Muslim interests. In other words, in a communally charged political atmosphere the interpretation gained currency, especially in view of the in-built communal bias of most the legislations adopted by the Muslim ministry in Bengal. As a Congress legislator, Sasanka Sekhar Sanyal lamented:

> New sectional conflicts have been invented where there was none and old and decaying ones like the music before the mosque have been fanned into new dimensions and invidious sectional and communal discriminations seem to have been the key to the whole policy of the Government of Bengal ranging from the farthest village unions right up to the Dalhousie Square [the Bengal Government Head Quarters].
>
> An unprecedented toxin of communalism has put the entire province into a state of wild delirium and the passionate crusade of hatred against harmony has released disruptive forces which even the authors, however powerful they may be, cannot control.[178]

One area in which the Hindu representation was significantly slashed was the government services. Although the Bengal ministry, under Haq's tutelage, while recruiting for the government jobs always decried the reservation policy, Hindu candidates were generally bypassed to accommodate their Muslim counterparts. Two areas where most of the recruits were Muslims were education (particularly primary education) and in the revenue department. As minister in charge of the education department, the Chief Minister, Fazlul Haq, was always in favour of accommodating Muslims, since they 'were discriminated against for generations'. His government 'is morally committed to undo the wrongs of history by bringing the Muslims in line with the advanced Hindus'. Not only were the Muslims selected for scholarships to pursue education in schools, colleges and the university, they were also assured of jobs after completion of their studies.[179] As regards jobs in the government-aided primary schools in Bengal, Muslims obtained roughly 80 per cent of the jobs, as Haq's submission in the Assembly shows. Over a span of six years (1937–43), while Haq remained the Chief Minister of Bengal, out of 1137 primary school teachers there were 839 Muslims and the rest were divided between the Hindus and the Scheduled Castes.[180] Similarly, the revenue department had an overwhelmingly Muslim employees. The figures available for the period of 1937–43 also demonstrate the extent to which the recruitment policy was clearly tilted in favour of the Muslims. In response to a question, the minister in charge of the revenue department, B. P. Singh Roy, tabled the statistics of the new recruits. Within a span of seven years, out of 406 jobs the Muslims were offered 287, while the Hindus and the Scheduled Castes were offered just 85 and 21 respectively.[181] Describing this as part of the League's communal design, the Congress members expressed their resentment both within the Assembly and outside.[182] Hindu and Muslim members were clearly polarised, as the proceedings demonstrated. While defending the distribution as 'fair' and 'appropriate', Md Mozammal Haq of the Krishak Praja Party complemented the Bengal ministry for having undertaken correct steps to balance the Hindu and Muslim representation in the government jobs.[183]

What began under Haq's stewardship was further reinforced by his successors who led the Bengal government in the post-1943 period. Hindus were further eclipsed with the introduction of what was described as 'communalism in services'[184] as a report in the *Times* reveals:

> Muslims [have] reserved half the places in public services and more in the legislature. Consequently they control the public life of the province. The younger generation of Hindus instead of making government service or law its first choice for a career tends to feel frustrated by the Muslim predominance in public affairs. This may or may not be fair, but it means, in many cases, that merit is not the main criterion for appointment or promotion. Muslims must be appointed to the post of responsibility for which they are not always fitted.[185]

As is evident, what accounted for the growing popularity of the movement for partition in Bengal was certainly not soley Hindu communalism; the role of the Bengal ministry was also crucial in segregating the two principal communities into almost watertight compartments. S. N. Biswas, a Congress member of the Legislative Assembly, thus lamented: 'the system of separate electorate under the Communal Award has led our Muslim friends to gradually imbibe the spirit of absolute separatism everywhere it had a role to play'.[186] What is, however, significant is the contribution of the Mahasabha in mobilising the disgruntled Hindu opinion for a specific goal that was possible, presumably because there emerged an environment where the Hindu–Muslim schism was articulated only in communal terms. Already frustrated by those various schemes that the Bengal ministry adopted to safeguard the interests of the Muslims, the Hindus, regardless of their class position, were easily drawn to the campaign as probably the only option under the circumstances. The drive of the Muslim leadership to secure the privileges of the hitherto deprived socio-economic community (namely the Muslims) at the cost of the Hindus was what decisively shaped the articulation of the demand for partition.[187]

The publication of several blueprints for future Bengals is also striking. Earmarking primarily those areas where Hindus constituted a majority, *The Modern Review* produced, for instance, a detailed map of the proposed west Bengal separating largely the Muslim-majority areas of east Bengal.[188] Similarly, the pro-League *Star of India* and the *Morning News* published a detailed description of what constituted Pakistan, always including Calcutta[189] presumably because of its commercial importance long after it ceased to be India's capital. Despite the claims and counterclaims of the major political parties, what made the task of the Radcliffe Commission easier was the fact that Bengal was so populated that the province could easily be divided into two homogeneous units. Arguments were made to divide the province into two units, particularly as the two major communities were distributed in predominantly large numbers within the two different zones of the existing province. Ironically, those presiding over Bengal's destiny in 1947 now upheld the logic that appeared to have guided Curzon to demarcate the boundaries in 1905.[190]

Just like their urban counterparts, Hindus in rural Bengal were equally frightened by the riots of 1946. The League ministry may not have directly participated in the mayhem, although its role in shaping the events in a particular fashion cannot be glossed over. Both the Calcutta and the Noakhlai riots were communal, since Hindus were selectively butchered by the Muslims and vice versa. Not only were the British spared, the government offices were also hardly damaged. As an official report mentions, 'though Direct Action Day was intended as a gesture against the British, the riot took purely communal line and no attacks were made on European individuals or business premises'.[191] The same pattern was evident in Noakhali, as John Tyson, the Bengal Governor's Private Secretary, noted in his report that 'lately the preaching of hatred had been more communal than against the British'.[192] That the riot broke out on an auspicious day for the Hindus[193] is illustrative of the underlying communal tone of the Noakhali carnage. Muslims were mobilised against the Hindus 'by spreading grossly exaggerated stories of Hindu atrocities during the Calcutta riot'.[194] Both these riots are therefore an indication as well as confirmation of the rupture along communal lines that Bengal experienced during the penultimate year of her struggle against the British. The British divide and rule strategy had succeeded not only due to the peculiar structural characteristics of Bengal, but also to an equally peculiar unfolding of socio-economic processes in which those responsible for her political destiny had significant roles.[195]

Notes

1 Lord Dufferin's warning of 1887 that British attempts 'to divide and rule' would, as Anita Inder Singh wrote, 'recoil on them rang true in 1947. India paid [a heavy price] for the achievement of freedom, a consequence of the fact that communal forces were neither defeated nor unity totally achieved' (Singh 1987: 252). It is true that the British did not invent caste and religious community identities. What is true, however, is that the British policies of enumeration, as pursued through the census, had done much to harden these identities since the beginning of the census in 1872. As Cohn points out, 'what was entailed in the construction of the census operations was the creation of social categories by which India was ordered for administrative purposes'. Given the knowledge of the communities, enumerated in terms of both religious and caste identities, it was possible for the colonial power to fashion its strategy in such a way as to gain maximum out of these cleavages (see Cohn 1996: 8. Norbert Peabody, however, informs us that in the early nineteenth century castes were not at all classifying criteria in collecting data on human populations in India. Rather this style of classifying population 'appears to have crept into the colonial census in a somewhat backhanded manner owing to the reliance of British administrators on native informants and petty officials who were familiar with pre-colonial "household lists" that had long been caste-sensitive' (Peabody 2001: 841).
2 For details of the united Bengal Movement, see Chapter 4.
3 One of the powerful expositions of this argument is certainly Joya Chatterji's *Bengal Divided: Hindu Communalism and Partition, 1932–1947*. The central purpose of this study is, as she herself mentions, 'to understand how and why the bhadralok moved away from being the leaders of Indian nationalism and adopted instead a much narrower and less attractive (sic) communal stance' (Chatterji 1995: 17).
4 As early as 1945, Jawaharlal Nehru, in a speech at Lahore, had predicted that 'if Pakistan is given, then parts of Punjab and Bengal where the Hindu population is in a majority, will join Hindustan and both the Punjab and Bengal will have to be divided'. See *Jawaharlal Nehru Selected Works*, Vol. 14, Oxford University Press, Delhi, 1982, p. 165.
5 A commentator therefore wrote, 'though Haq in Bengal ... appeared to adhere nominally to the League in all India matters, Jinnah found [him] utterly intractable when it came to representing the League's policies at the provincial level'. Inder 1987: 237.
6 While dealing with the second partition of Bengal, Partha Chatterjee, for instance, begins by comparing with the 1905 or the first partition of Bengal (see Chatterjee 1997: 27–46.
7 Chaudhuri 1968: 218.
8 As Risley (who propounded the idea) argued, reorganisation was necessary to reduce 'the excessive burden' on the Bengal government and to enable at the same time an expansion of Assam which would 'give to its officers a wider and more interesting field of work [and] a maritime outlet in order to develop its industries in tea, oil and coal' (cited in Sarkar 1973: 12.
9 IOR, Minto Papers, M 1005, Minto to Morley, 5 February 1906, cited in Sarkar 1973: 20.
10 Chatterjee 1997: 29.
11 Chatterji 1995.
12 Many of the poems Rabindranath Tagore wrote around the time of the movement against the first partition made the country/nation vivid in the shape of

the Hindu goddesses, *Durga* and *Lakshmi*. Thus we get a description of Bengal as *Durga* in the following lines:

> The message of courage glows in your right hand
> Your left hand removes all fear
> While the eye in your forehead assumes the colour of fire
> O, Mother, I cannot take my eyes from you
> Your doors have opened on to a golden temple today.

Similarly, Bengal is moulded in the image of *Lakshmi*, the goddess of protection of domestic well being, in a 1898 poem of *Bangalakshmi* (Bengal, the *Lakshmi*),

> In your fields, by your rivers, in your thousand homes set deep in mangogroves
> In your pastures, whence the sound of milking rises, in the shadow of the banyan,
> in twelve temples besides the Ganges
> O, ever gracious *Lakshmi,* O, Bengal, my mother, you go about endless chores
> day and night with a smile on your face.

Chakrabarty 1999: 199–200.
13 Ahmed 1981: 181. Ahmed further argues, '[e]ven those who sympathised with the nationalist aspirations found the revivalist character of the anti-partition agitation too much to swallow. ... The Muslims and Hindus now belonged indubitably to two hostile camps. The Muslim educated class had achieved something out of this chaos; they had finally secured a real foothold in the politics of power in the new province with the prospect of better education, better employment, higher representation in the elected bodies, which they were eager to safeguard by all means. The foundation of the Moslem League in Dacca in 1906 at the initiative of the Dacca *Nawab* was partly a manifestation of this desire to protect what had been achieved and to pursue the gains further. With the gradual consolidation of their power base in the rural districts through the instrumentality of the *anjumans* and associations, Muslim politicians were now firmly in the saddle to direct a mass following as they wished. The Bengal Muslims were thus on their way towards close collaboration with Muslims in upper India as members of the same political community, in that they both were now confronting the Hindus for power and privileges.
14 The notion of 'Mother' was a cementing factor in the movement against the 1905 partition. Interestingly, the same analogy, which is absolutely anti-Islam, was drawn by a group of leading Muslim intellectuals who vehemently opposed the second partition. In its edition of 11 April 1947, the news magazine *Millat* accused the Congress and the Hindu Mahasabha of performing the role of Parashuram as they 'together raised a sharpened axe to slice the Mother into two'. For an elaboration of this argument, see Bose and Jalal 1997: 51–75.
15 Tamijuddin Khan, *Memoirs*, p. 18 (unpublished).
16 Dutta 1999: 22.
17 Dutta 1999: 71.
18 *Ananda Bazar Patrika*, 18 October 1946.
19 IOR, V/9/1318, Musharuff Hossain's speech in the Assembly duirng the passage of the Bill, 4 March 1940. Bengal Legislative Assembly Proceedings, Vol. LVI, No. 2, 1940.

20 IOR, V/9/1318, Nalinksha Sanyal's speech in the Assembly during the passage of the Bill, 4 March 1940, Bengal Legislative Assembly Proceedings, Vol. LVI, No. 2, 1940.
21 IOR, V/9/1318, Sasankha Sekhar Sanyal's speech in the Assembly during the passage of the Bill on 10 March 1940, Bengal Legislative Assembly Proceedings, Vol. LVI, No. 2, 1940.
22 The Commissioner, Dacca division, therefore mentioned that the act caused 'ill feeling between the Hindus and Muslims in most of the east Bengal districts'. WBSA, Home-Poll (Confidential), J1-3/41, the Commissioner to the Chief Secretary, Government of Bengal, 18 August 1941.
23 *Dainik Basumati*, 16 June, 1940, cited in Das 1991: 32.
24 In response to an enquiry, the Education Minister, Fazlul Haq (also the Chief Minister), reported that within a period of twenty years (1917–37) the number of Maktabs had risen from 6548 to 25739, an increase of 19191, while the corresponding increase in government primary schools was merely 360. Haq's reply to Harendra Nath Chaudhuri, 23 March 1941, Bengal Legislative Assembly Debates, Vol. 58, No. 3.
25 IOR, V/9/1318, Bengal Legislative Assembly Debates, Vol. 58, No. 3, Harendra Nath Chaudhuri's speech in the Assembly on 17 March 1941. According to the Eight-Quinquennial Review, 'Maktabs are general primary schools on Islamic basis intended for Moslem scholars. In addition to Quoran, Islamic rituals and Urdu are additional subjects, alternative to drill'.
26 IOR, V/9/ 1325, Bengali Legislative Assembly Proceedings, Vol. 57, No. 5, speech by Fazlul Haq, 3 September 1941, p. 45.
27 *The Star of India*, 18 June 1940. Akram Khan went a step further by suggesting a syllabus drawing upon 'the great Islamic tradition' of India. According to Khan, the Muslim representatives would render 'a great service to Islam', if the Board was 'forced' to accept the proposed syllabus (*The Mussalman*, 28 June 1940).
28 IOR, V/9/1325, A speech by Harendra Nath Chaudhuri in the Bengal Assembly, 2 September 1941, Bengal Legislative Assembly Proceedings, Vol. 58, No. 1.
29 V/9/1325, Atul Chandra Sen's speech in the Assembly on 3 September 1941, Bengal Legislative Assembly Proceedings, Vol. 58, No. 1.
30 Both *Ananda Bazar Patrika* and *Amrita Bazar Patrika* condemned the Bill as 'a clear design to cripple the Hindus of Bengal in education' (*Ananda Bazar Patrika*, 21 June 1940; *Amrita Bazar Patrika*, 20 June 1940). *The Statesman*, generally soft towards to the League ministry, was critical of the Bill, possibly because of its adverse impact on education if the syllabus was substantially altered on the basis of 'purely communal considerations' (*The Statesman*, 29 June 1940).
31 IOR, V/29/1310, the speech of Shyama Prasad Mookherjee, Bengali Legislative Assembly Proceedings, Vol. 57, No. 5.
32 Fazlul Haq, for instance, believed that 'the best solution of all the communal problems in the country ... lie in levelling up the Muslims, the Scheduled Castes and less advanced communities to the point which has been reached by the advanced communities'. See his statement in the Assembly on 15 December 1939, Bengal Legislative Assembly Proceedings, Vol. No. LV, No 3, 1939.
33 *Amrita Bazar Patrika*, 29 April 1939. *The Statesman* took a very ambiguous stand. Instead of expressing a judgment, it simply suggested that this particular act was likely 'to consolidate the communal elements within the ministry and League in a situation which was tense and volatile' (*The Statesman*, 28 April 1939).

34 IOR, L/PJ/5/144, R. N. Reid, the Bengal Governor to Linlithgow, 27 April 1939.
35 IOR, V/9/1289, Vol. LIV, No. 2, 1939, Bengal Legislative Assembly debate, speech by Shyama Prasad Mookherjee in the Legislative Assembly, 18 March 1939, p. 182.
36 IOR, V/9/1289, Vol. LIV, No 2, 1939, Nawab Khaja Habibullah Bahadur of Dacca, while introducing the Bill, justified the enactment, 6 March 1939, p. 19.
37 Ibid. speech by A. K. Fazlul Haq, 6 March 1939, p. 189.
38 Sarat Bose's speech in the Legislative Assembly (Bose 1979: 93).
39 IOR, V/9/1289, speech by Shyama Prasad Mookherjee, 18 March 1939, p. 35.
40 Ibid., speech by Nausher Ali, 27 February 1939, p. 35.
41 Ibid., speech by Maulvi Abu Hossain Sarkar, 27 February 1939, p. 30.
42 Ibid., speech by Maulvi Abu Hossain Sarkar, 27 February 1939, p. 31.
43 The Bengal Legislative Act, 1939.
44 IOR, R/3/1/13, J. A. Herbert, Bengal Governor, to Linlithgow, 7 March 1940.
45 Subhas Chandra Bose, editorial, 'Forward Bloc', in Bose 1983: 295.
46 IOR, R/3/2/13, Fortnightly Reports, first half of February 1940.
47 IOR, R/3/1/13, J. A. Herbert to Linlithgow, 7 March 1940.
48 Subhas Bose, editorial in *Forward Bloc*, in Sisir Kr. Bose (ed.), *Crossroads*, pp. 296–7.
49 IOR, R/3/1/13, J. A. Herbert to Linlithgow, 20 March 1940.
50 QAP, File No. 722/9-14, Notes on Eastern Pakistan by Hamidul Huq Chowdhury, 6 June 1947.
51 Md. E. H. Khan 1983, cited in Das 1991: 35.
52 For details of the processes that led to the decline of the Congress, see Chakrabarty 1990: 155–6. Jack Gallagher's explanation that the Congress declined due to factionalism does not appear to be tenable simply because the phenomenon, as shown in the above monograph, is too complex to be reduced to a single factor. Factionalism, based on vaguely defined but real ideological differences, partly accounts for the failure of the Congress, and this factor contributed to a process which began, in fact, at the beginning of the century with the Congress' lukewarm attitude towards the actors of the 'unorganised' world. The advantage was reaped by the KPP with its ostensibly pro-peasant stance. For details of Gallagher's argument, see Gallagher 1973.
53 In its twenty-first annual session in Calcutta, held on 30 December 1939, the Hindu Mahasabha therefore resolved to launch a campaign against 'the openly communal and reactionary policy of the present ministry in Bengal, as evinced by its various legislative enactments and administrative measures, calculated to curb the rights and liberties of the Hindus of Bengal and cripple their economic strength and cultural life' (see Tirmizi 1998: 967).
54 For a graphic account of these riots, see Tuker 1950: 152–60; Singh 1987: 188–202; Das 1991: 161–203; Mahajan 2000: 226–45.
55 For a detailed discussion of riots in Bengal since 1905, see Das 1991.
56 Hindu shops and houses were attacked simultaneously in different areas of Calcutta more or less in a similar fashion, while Muslim shops and house were marked 'to prevent from being looted by the Muslim crowd' (see Chaudhuri 1990: 25).
57 Chatterjee 1997: 38.
58 IOR, R/3/135, The Direct Action Resolution, adopted in Bombay on 29 July 1946. The resolution further mentions, 'the council directs the working [of the League] to prepare forthwith a programme of Direct Action to carry out the policy initiated above and to organise the Muslims for the coming struggle to

be launched as and when necessary'. Neither the Viceroy nor the Governors were very clear as to what the Direct Action Day would mean. In the Governor's Conference held on 8 August 1946, the Viceroy admitted that 'I have no idea what Direct Action is likely to mean'. See IOR, R/3/1/124, minutes of the Governor's conference of 8 August 1946. As late as 10 August, even Burrows, the Bengal Governor was 'in the dark as to the lines Direct Action is likely to take'. See IOR, R/3/1/124, Burrows to Wavell, 10 August 1946.

59 In an interview published in the *Dawn*, Jinnah further argued, 'The Congress has been and is organising itself to launch a struggle of mass civil disobedience. Preparations are and have been going on in full swing. The INA army men are requisitioned, enrolled, financed and sent all over the country.... We are, therefore, now forced for our self-defence and self-preservation to say good bye to constitutional methods and we have decided now as part and parcel of our policy and programme to prepare and resort to direct action as and when the time may come to launch' (see Jinnah's interview in the *Dawn*, 1 August 1946).

60 Even the Bengal government was not happy with the declaration of a holiday on the Direct Action Day because of the apprehension that 'the declaring of a holiday would encourage their men [the League supporters] to enforce a hartal on the Hindus who are likely to oppose'. See IOR, Tyson Papers, Eur E 341/41, Tyson's note on the Calcutta disturbances, 29 September 1946.

61 The government was criticised for declaring 16 August a holiday because 'by declaring a holiday, the Government was aligning itself with a political party and was creating a situation in which Hindu businesses were expected to close in order to observe a holiday, prescribed for political purposes by the Muslim League'. In support of this contention, it was argued that the disorders began when Muslims tried to force Hindu shopkeepers to shut their shops. The Bengal Governor, however, defended the decision of the ministry by saying that 'in his judgement, the disturbances would have been on an even greater scale had the Muslim League been forced to celebrate the Direct Action Day in defiance of the Government'. See IOR, L/PJ/8/576, Summary of events: the Calcutta Riot, 20 October 1946.

62 Personal reports on the killing on the Great Calcutta killing (extracts from the diary of Major L. A. Livermore), in Tuker 1950: 597.

63 An eye-witness account suggests that 'houses were burned in the north and east of Calcutta probably due to Muslim leaders compelling Hindu shopkeepers to close their shops and the rank and file pulling people off their bicycles and of the busses. The Hindus, on their side, were trying to prevent Muslim processions from marching through Hindu quarters of the city on their way to the meeting' (see Tuker 1950: 157). In his telegram to Pethick Lawrence, the Bengal Governor also confirmed that 'the communal trouble started as early as 7 am in Maniktola area'. See IOR, L/PJ/8/577, Telegram, Burrows to the Secretary of State, Pethick Lawrence, 16 August 1946.

64 Following the adoption of the Direct Action resolution on 29 July 1946, *The Dawn* regularly devoted a full page to justify the League demand for Pakistan and also warned the Muslims of the adverse consequences of opposing the Congress, which 'is bent upon setting up a caste-Hindu Raj in India with the connivance of the British. Hence, we [Muslims] shall fight for it, we shall die for it [and] take it we must or perish'. The L/PJ/8/655 series (of the India Office Records) contains these pages. For the quoted sentence, see *The Dawn*, 13 August 1946.

65 IOR, R/3/1/135, *The Dawn*, 16 August 1946.

66 *The Morning News*, 5 August 1946.
67 *The Morning News*, 11 August 1946.
68 Report of the Commissioner of Police on the disturbances of 16–20 August 1946, cited in Singh 1987: 182. Francis Tuker, in charge of the Eastern Command, which was called to help the police during the riot, also confirmed the influx of goondas from other parts of India (Tuker 1950: 1158).
69 IOR, L/I/1/882, proscribed pamphlets, the Muslim League pamphlet entitled, *Let Pakistan Speak for Herself*, the Muslim League, Calcutta, 1946. The pro-League *The Star of India* also drew upon the importance of the month of Ramazan while preparing the Muslims for the Direct Action Day. In its 13 August edition, *The Star of India* thus declared, 'Muslims must remember that it was in Ramazan that the Quoran was revealed. It was in Ramazan that the permission for *jehad* was granted by Allah. ... The Muslim League is fortunate that it is starting its action on this holy month' (see *The Star of India*, 13 August 1946).
70 Khosla 1989: 51–3. Large numbers of very provocative leaflets were in circulation. One of them, for instance, ran as follows: 'The Sword of Islam must be shining on the heaven and will subdue all evil designs. ... we, the Muslims, have had the crown and have ruled. Do not lose heart. Be ready and take your swords'. Asking the Kafirs 'to come to the arena with their swords', the other leaflet proclaims, 'we shall then see who will play with us for rivers of blood will flow. We shall have the swords in our hands and the noise of *takbir*, tomorrow will doom's day'. The Muslims should celebrate because, as another leaflet declares, 'God has granted to the Muslims in the month Ramzan what they have been clamouring for. The day for an open fight with the Kafir which is the greatest desire of the Muslim nation has arrived. ... The shining gates of heaven have been opened for [us]. Let us enter in thousands. Let us all cry out victory to Pakistan, victory to the Muslim nation, to the army which has declared a *jehad*'. G. D. Khosla's account drew upon the work of a Fact Finding Commission set up by the Government India to inquire into partition-related violence in Punjab. Regarded as too sensitive its report was never published, though Khosla had access to the records and the personnel by dint of his association with the Commission as a member.
71 Burrows to Wavell, 22 August 1946, Mansergh *et al.*, Vol VIII, 1979: 296.
72 The Bengal Governor was criticised for not having called the army immediately the trouble began. There was 'a loud and persistent demand for the recall of the Governor who, it was stated, had failed in his duty' (see Sitaramayya 1969: 805). On 25 October 1946, a protest meeting was, as an official report suggests, organised in London at St Martin's Art School in which a resolution was adopted demanding the removal of Sir F. Burros from the Governorship of Bengal and the removal of the Muslim League ministry in that province. See IOR, L/PJ/8/578, R. M. J. Harris (Private Secretary to the Secretary of State) to Penthick Lawrence, 26 October 1946.
73 Chaudhuri 1987: 810.
74 IOR, L/PJ/8/655, Major J. Sim to F. J. Errol, an MP of the Labour Party, 23 August 1946.
75 Burrows to Wavell, 22 August 1946, Mansergh *et al.*, Vol VIII, 1979: 297.
76 Tazeen Murshid absolves Suhrawardy of responsibility by glossing over his role in the riot. She attributed the massacre to the already prevalent animosity between the two communities, Stating that Suhrawardy did not organise the riot, and hence, 'his use of office vehicle to patrol the streets and offer protection to those [affected] was entirely misrepresented' (Murshid 1985: 214). As

shown above, the Chief Minister may not have been directly involved in the massacre that took the city by surprise; he did, however, undertake to shape the course of events in Calcuttta in a manner calculated to inspire awe in the minds of non-Muslims and to demonstrate to the world at large the strength and solidarity of the protagonists of Pakistan.

77 Khosla 1989: 49. As Percival Griffith of the Indian Police mentions, by 1946 80 per cent of the Police officers in Bengal were Muslims. Whereas in 1924 only three out of twelve officers were Muslims, there were thirty seven Muslim officers out of a total strength of forty eight in 1946. (Griffiths 1971: 427).
78 Chaudhuri 1987: 809.
79 *The Statesman*, 18 August 1946, cited in Singh 1987: 184.
80 Centre of South Asian Studies, Cambridge, Taylor Papers, S. G. Taylor's report on the 1946 Calcutta Riot (typescript), p. 9.
81 IOR, Tyson Papers, Eur. E 341/41, Tyson's note of 23 August 1946.
82 IOR, Tyson Papers, Eur. E 341/41, Tyson's note of 17 August 1946.
83 Centre of South Asian Studies, Cambridge, Taylor Papers, S. G. Taylor's report on the 1946 Calcutta Riot (typescript). p. 11.
84 Ibid.
85 According to a government estimate, 5000 died and 15000 were injured in the Calcutta massacre (see IOR, L/I/1/777, a report on the political situation in India, September 1946). Contradicting the official figures, the Congress estimate suggests that 'rough estimates of killed varied, ranging about 7000, besides many more thousand wounded'. (Sitamaramayya 1969: 805).
86 See Chaudhuri 1990: 25.
87 Muslims could not have 'secured even a partial hartal', wrote Tyson, 'had their leaders in Bengal not taken advantage of their position as Ministers to make improper use of the Negotiable Instruments Act'. See IOR, Tyson Papers, Eur, E 341/40, Tyson's note of 17 August 1946.
88 The American Consul General, Calcutta, to the Secretary of State, 31 August 1946, cited in Das 1991: 187. Wavell also corroborated this during his interview with Jawaharlal Nehru on 3 December 1946 (see IOR, R/3/1/128, Wavell's interview with Nehru, 3 December 1946).
89 Centre of South Asian Studies, Cambridge, Taylor Papers, S. G. Taylor's report on the 1946 Calcutta Riot (typescript), p. 14.
90 As early as 7 October 1946, apprehending serious communal strife in Noakhali, the Commissioner of the Chittagong division sought extra police 'to deal with the situation before it goes completely out of hand'. See IOR, Tyson Papers, Eur E 341/41, Chittagong Divisional Commissioner to Tyson, 7 October 1946.
91 As early as 1940, Benthall warned the government of Bengal of a possible communal outbreak in the district presumably due to the circumstances in which the Hindu minority was placed. As he categorically stated, '[i]n Noakhali where 80% of the population were Moslems, and are definitely making life intolerable for the Hindu majority, who, of course, are largely landlords'. CSASC, Benthall Papers, Box XIX, Benthall's diary notes of 20 February 1940.
92 Thus, Nirmal Kumar Bose reminisces, the outside world was kept completely in the dark about the event in Noakhali for over a week, for the government succeeded in imposing a strict censorship (Bose 1974: 33–4). Even the Home Ministry did not seem to pay much attention to the outbreak. The Special Branch of the Calcutta Police dismissed the magnitude of the events by characterising them as 'rumours'. In his 'Partition and Migration: perspectives on

1947', Basudev Chattapadhyay refers to this without identifying the source (see Chattapadhyay, 'Partition and Migration: perspectives on 1947', Occasional Paper 2, Peace Studies Group, Department of History, University of Calcutta, p. 12.

93 An irate Patel thus wrote to Stafford Cripps, 'would you believe that the Governor of Bengal has, all throughout these terrible happenings, been enjoying the bracing climate of ... Darjeeling?' See IOR, L/PJ/8/578, Patel to Cripps, 19 October 1946.

94 In his press statement, J. N. Mandal, the member-designate to the Interim Government, also underlined the participation of a substantial number of ex-servicemen 'who had prostrated their military training to base ends. About a dozen of those killed', as he mentioned, 'were in soldiers' uniform'. See IOR, L/PJ/8/578, J. N. Mandal's press statement, 25 October 1946.

95 Telegrams, Burrows to the Secretary of State, Penthick Lawrence, 16 October and 20 October 1946, Mansergh *et al.*, Vol. VIII, 1979: 743, 751. In its 18 October edition, the *Manchester Guardian* provides a graphic description of the riot: 'Eastern Bengal is aflame with the worst Hindu-Muslim riots India has ever known. The armed fanatical mobs of 20 000 strong', it further adds, are reported to be sweeping through an area of 250 square miles with fire and sword (*Manchester Guardian*, 18 October 1946).

96 IOR, L/PJ/8/578, a report prepared by A. Henderson, the Under Secretary, India Office, for presentation in Parliament on 3 November 1946.

97 IOR, L/PJ/8/578, Bengal Governor to Wavell, 3 November 1946.

98 *The Times*, London, 10 February 1947, thus argued that Noakhali triggered the communal outbreak in Bihar, where the stories of abduction and rape of Hindu women and the forced conversion were circulated to demonstrate the effect of Muslim rule in Bengal.

99 IOR, L/PJ/5/154, Bengal Governor to the Governor-General of India, 6 December 1946.

100 After his trip to the riot-ravaged Noakhali, J. B. Kripalani, the Congress President, confirmed that 'the Hindu population was told that the murder, loot and arson that went on was in revenge for Muslim lives in Calcutta rioting'. He further claimed that 'the attack on the Hindu population was previously arranged and prepared for. It was deliberate if not directly engineered by the Muslim League. Local evidence all went to prove that prominent League leaders in the village had a large hand in it. Organised bands, consisting of military men, under the leadership of an ex-MLA [Ghulam Sarwar] caused the disturbances'. See IOR, L/PJ/8/578, J. B. Kripalani's press statement, 26 October 1946.

101 IOR, L/PJ/8/578, Telegram, Burrows to Pethick Lawrence, 16 October, 1946

102 The tour diary of the District Magistrate, E. F. McInerney, published in *The Statesman*, is replete with examples of the activities of Ghulam Sarwar during and before the riot (*The Statesman*, 23 October, 1946).

103 Characterising the *Mollahs* as 'cog in the wheels of communalism', Tuker attributed the devastating nature of the Noakhali–Tippera riot to their involvement from the very outset (Tuker 1950: 614).

104 IOR, R/3/2/58, Burrows to the Viceroy, 8 November 1946.

105 Thus the Bengal Governor noted, 'the gangs appear to be organised. Roads have been cut in places and communication, difficult at any time of this period of the year, has become more difficult'. Telegram, Burrows to Pethick Lawrence, 16 October 1946, Mansergh *et al.*, Vol. VIII, 1979: 743.

106 This description draws upon Tuker 1950: 174–7. A large number of Hindus

were killed when the army moved in to track down 'the miscreants' involved in conversion. Rather than facing the consequences if caught by the army, they 'abolished the evidence by killing the converts'. Tuker's description of the operation of the gang in Noakhali corresponds with that of J. B. Kripalani, the Congress President, who undertook a trip to Noakhali within a fortnight of the outbreak. He reported that 'the modus operandi was for Muslims to collect in batches of hundreds and in some places thousands, and march to Hindu villages or Hindu houses with a mixed population. The crowds had their leaders and spokesmen. Those first demanded subscriptions for the Muslim League and sometime for the Muslim victims of the Calcutta riot. These enforced subscriptions were heavy, sometime amounting to Rs. 10 000 and more. Even after the subscriptions were realised, the Hindus were not safe. The same or successive crowd appeared on the scene later and looted Hindus houses. The looted houses in most cases were burnt. Those who resisted were killed. Sometimes, before the houses were looted, the inmates were asked to embrace Islam. The mollah or the priest of the local mosque always accompanied the crowd. However, the conversion did not give them impunity against loot and arson'. See IOR, L/PJ/8/578, J. B. Kripalani's press statement, 26 October 1946.

107 Bangladesh Secretariat Record Room, Dhaka, Home-Poll P10C–112/1946, Superintendent of Police to E. F. McInerney, the District Magistrate, Noakhali, 20 October 1946. Of these areas, Chandpur was devastated presumably because it was the only route for escape into West Bengal. A large number of Hindus were killed in Chandpur during their escape, since most of the roads and river exits were guarded by the armed Muslim National Guards (see *The Times*, London, 19 October 1946).

108 Thus the Noakhali District Magistrate, McInerney, mentioned, 'the police, especially the sub-inspectors and lower ranks seem to be openly taking sides in favour of their community and the people at large have little confidence in their impartiality and do not expect security from them'. See IOR, L/PJ/8/577, Wavell's interview with Divisional Commissioner, Chittagong (M. O. Carter) and District Magistrate, 2 November 1946.

109 That Ghulam Sarwar was arrested on 28 October 1946 was reported to the British Parliament on 29 October 1946. See IOR, L/PJ/8/578, report by A. Henderson, the Under Secretary, India Office, 29 October 1946.

110 Even the Viceroy was surprised at the inordinate delay in arresting Sarwar, which he attributed to 'the ineffective and demoralised lower rank police staff ... who were affected by communalism'. See IOR, L/PJ/8/577, Wavell's note on the interview he had with the Chittagong Divisional Commissioner and Noalhali District magistrate on 2 November 1946.

111 Tuker 1950: 178. Ineffectiveness of the police accounted largely for the devastation in Noakhali. The Viceroy himself admitted that the Sub-Inspectors and those below had openly collided with their community (J. M. G. Bell, 'Notes on recent experiences in Bengal',CSASC, Bell Papers, file No. 3 (4).

112 IOR, L/PJ/8/577, M. O. Carter to the Burrows, 7 November 1946.

113 While reporting on this, the Inspector General of Police, Bengal requested the Bengal Government to take adequate steps to avoid such incidents in future. IOR, L/PJ/8/577, the Inspector General of Police, Bengal, to the Additional Secretary (Home), Government of Bengal, 8 November 1946.

114 Tuker 1950: 609–10. There are instances where, as highlighted by M. O. Carter, the Additional Secretary (Home), the League ministry 'pressurised the police to withdraw the criminal cases, including murder, rioting and even

rape'. M. O. Carter, 'Trouble in 1946', see CSASC, M. O. Carter papers, pp. 10–11.
115 IOR, L/PJ/8/578, Burrows to the Secretary of State, 16 August 1946. Reporting on Suhrawardy's participation in a Faridpur meeting, Burrows also stated, 'mass meetings have been held in several districts in east Bengal urging Moslems to enrol in the National Guard. Some of the speeches were violent in character'.
116 Vallabhbhai Patel characterised the situation in Noakhali as 'a reign of terror' that seemed to have continued (Patel to Wavell, 25 October 1946, in Sardar Patel Correspondence, Vol. 3, p. 303). Seven months after the riot, the Chittagong Divisional Commissioner wrote, '[w]hat is happening is that a section of Muslims is taking advantage of the demoralised condition of the Hindus to insult, threaten and cow them down into a state of resigned submission, after which they fatten on their property and treat them as an inferior race. It is quite usual for the Hindus while moving about to be addressed as *malaun* or *kafir*. Sometime they are searched by parties of Muslims and deprived of anything the latter fancy. Cases have occurred of Hindus returning to their houses with their daily bazaar and having their purchases snatched away'. See WBSA, Home-Poll, 457/C. confidential report of the Commissioner, Chittagong Division, to P. D. Martyn, Additional Secretary (Home), Government of Bengal, 13 May 1947. In his memoirs, N. K. Bose also corroborated the 'helplessness' of those Hindus who survived the carnage by stating that 'under the surface, however, there is definitely tension and among Hindus a sense of insecurity. Hindus have not yet recovered their morale. They are apprehensive and suspicious'. See N. K. Bose 1974: 140, 152.
117 IOR, R/3/2/59A, Burrows to Mountbatten, 22 April 1947.
118 In his report, the Bengal Governor underlined this dimension while explaining the mass brutality against the Hindu businessmen. 'It is worth recording', he argued, 'that many of the shopkeepers had made fortunes in the 1943 famine, at the expense of the Muslim peasantry'. See IOR, L/PJ/5/164, Bengal Governor to the Governor-General, 6 December 1946.
119 IOR, L/PJ/8/573, *The Times*, London, 10 February 1947.
120 Kripalani 1978: 50.
121 Kripalani 1978: 81–2. She further adds, 'the social order having been destroyed, even the Muslims especially the poor had to suffer. All the markets, school, hospital, dispensaries had been destroyed. Bullocks had been killed and eaten-up and ploughs had been burnt. Even boats and fishing had been destroyed. Normal life was totally destroyed. Poor Muslim families were also starving. *Only the few at the top who had bloated with looted goods had gained by the riots*' (emphasis original; Kripalani 1978: 50).
122 Gandhi to Suhrawardy, 3 December 1946, CWMG, Vol. 86, p. 185.
123 The Bengal governor expressed anxiety for Gandhi's personal security. In his correspondence with the Viceroy, he thus wrote, 'I have redoubled the police precautions and since he pays no attention to my chief minister's repeated requests to quit Bengal I can only hope that he may tire of the ubiquitous constables and withdraw to a safer area'. See IOR, R/3/1/129, Governor to the Viceroy, 24 December 1946.
124 Kripalani 1978: 52.
125 Bose 1974: 132.
126 Mahajan 2000: 239.
127 As news of Noakhali spilled over into Bihar, a riot broke out in the province, which became violent, in the month of November 1946. Propaganda by the

THE SECOND PARTITION OF BENGAL

Hindu Mahasabha was believed to have added fuel to the desire for revenge. The most affected districts were Patna, Chapra, Mongher,, Bhagalpur and Gaya, killing more than 5000 people. Referring to the Bihar riot that began 'in revenge for Muslim atrocities in Bengal', a confidential report characterised the week-long disturbances as 'unprecedented [which] for ferocity, barbarity and size, seem to have surpassed all communal or political outbursts in recent Indian history'. See IOR, L/PS/12/1226, a confidential appreciation of the political situation in India, prepared under the authority of the Governor-General, 20 November 1946. Wavell, who undertook a trip to Bihar immediately after the riot, also confirms that what had happened in Bihar 'has been an outbreak of savagery and bestiality even worse than the Calcutta killings and more terrible than the Noakhali riots for which they were a revenge' (Moon 373). For details on the Bihar riot, see Damodaran 1995: 159–73; Mahajan 2000: 258–69.

128 *Jinnah Papers: Prelude to Pakistan*, 20 February–2 June 1947, First Series, Vol. 1 (part II), pp. 291–2. N. K. Bose, who stayed with Gandhi in Noakhali, also referred to this (Bose 1974: 130). Fazlul Haq indulged in personal vilification against Gandhi. In a public speech, he was reported to have compared Gandhi to gandhipoka, an insect known for emitting an odious smell, and urged the Noakhali Muslims to 'make it impossible for him to remain there' (cited in Das 1991: 202).

129 IOR, R/3/1/128, Wavell's note on his interview with Nehru on 3 December 1946.

130 Both the All India Muslim League and the Bengal Provincial Muslim League adopted resolutions condemning the acts of lawlessness, violence and murder in Noakhali for which the Congress and Hindu politicians were held responsible (see IOR, L/PJ/8/578). The tone in both the resolutions is uniform. The All India Muslim League adopted the resolution on 22 October 1946, and its provincial counterpart on 19 October 1946.

131 IOR, L/PJ/8/655, Burrows to Wavell 4 November 1946.

132 *The Morning News*, 26 September 1946.

133 *The Morning News*, 19 October 1946.

134 IOR, R/3/1/128, Wavell's interview with Jinnah and Liaquat Ali Khan, 3 December, 1946. Ayesha Jalal of course absolves Jinnah of all responsibility for the carnage in Bengal despite Jinnah's own recognition of the role of the Muslims in Noakhali riots. As 'a constitutional politician, a believer in rules enforced by rulers', Jinnah, as she argues, did not expect, and certainly did not want, anything like this to happen'. Ayesha Jalal, *The Sole Spokesman*, Cambridge University Press, Cambridge, p. 216.

135 Sitaramayya 1969: 806.

136 IOR, R/3/2/160, Burrows to the Viceroy, 19 June 1947.

137 The communists, for instance, supported the partition because 'in the given circumstances of 1946–7, the pressure to recognise the inevitability of a communal division was overwhelming' (Sengupta 1989, cited in Chatterjee 1977: 39).

138 See Chapter 4.

139 As late as January 1946, Shyama Prasad Mookherjee was, however, opposed to partition, before the communal violence of Calcutta and Noakhali. He was very unambiguous when he stated that 'we were not just willing to entertain any proposal to partition India. We objected [to the Viceroy's breakdown plan] because it meant the fragmentation of India. The Congress and the League only differed on the mode and extent of the country's truncation. ...

Only the Hindu Mahasabha had asserted that India should not be divided at any cost' (Mookherjee 1993: 105–7).
140 IOR, L/PJ/5/154, Burrows to Mountbatten, 11 April 1947.
141 NMML, Shyama Prasad Mookherjee Papers, Subject File no. 114/47.
142 IOR, L/PJ/5/154, Burrows to Mountbatten, 11 April 1947.
143 IOR, R/3/2/59A, The Chief Secretary's Report, second half of May 1947.
144 IOR, R/3/2/59A, The Chief Secretary's Report, first half of May 1947.
145 Apart from the newspaper reports, the stories of Muslim atrocities reached Calcutta as soon as refugees from the riot-affected areas began pouring into the city. According to an eye-witness account, 'hundreds of villages have been burnt, hundreds of people butchered or maimed, thousands made homeless and destitute and the two districts are now infernos of communal fury' (see IOR, L/PJ/8/578, *The Times*, London, 19 October 1946).
146 NMML, Shyama Prasad Mookherjee Papers, Subject File no. 114/147, petition from Barisal, 23 April 1947.
147 NMML, Shyama Prasad Mookherjee Papers, Subject File no. 114/147, petition from Calcutta, 7 May 1947. Even the Government of Bengal expressed alarm at the expenses incurred in providing shelter to the Muslim refugees from Bihar. The Bengal Chief Secretary, for instance, characterised this policy as 'illustrative of an intention to "Islamise" West Bengal, especially when the Government of Bihar was keen to take the Bihar refugees back' (see IOR, Mountbatten Papers, Mss.Eur F. 200/24, a note prepared by the Chief Secretary on the Future of Bengal).
148 As the government report suggests, the Chief Minister attended several meeting of the Guard just before the Noakhali outbreak. See BSRR, Dhaka, P10C-112/46, report on the communal disturbances in Noakhali and Tippera. S. G. Taylor, the Inspector General of Police, Bengal, remembered in his memoirs that Suhrawardy went out of the way to arrange the release of the Muslims arrested in connection with rioting. See CSASC, Taylor Papers, his report on the 1946 Calcutta riot. Confirming this, M. O. Carter, the Additional Secretary (Home), Government of Bengal, expressed disappointment when the Chief Minister took personal interest in releasing the 'miscreants'. See CSASC, Carter Papers, unpublished memoirs, pp. 10–11.
149 IOR, L/PJ/5/154, a petition from Chittagong to the Viceroy, 28 May 1947. Apart from the threat, the Guards organised processions shouting slogans in favour of Pakistan. Apart from Alla-ho-Akbar, the other two prominent slogans were '*larke lenge Pakistan*' and '*marke lenge Pakistan*'.
150 IOR, L/PJ/8/655, Burrows to Mountbatten, 11 April 1947.
151 Even the private secretary of the Bengal Governor, Tyson was critical of the Governor's permission to recruit Punjabi Muslims for the Calcutta Armed Police. According to him, 'it was a stupid thing to do politically if the Government wanted the trouble to die down and communal relations to improve'. See IOR, Tyson Papers, Eur 341/41, Tyson's note, 12 July 1947. Suhrawardy, however, defended the recruitment of 600 Punjabi Muslim Armed Guards 'to achieve equality in the balance of the city's police force' that was heavily tilted in favour of non-Muslims (presumably because out of a total of 1200 policemen there only 63 Muslims). See Suhrawardy 1987: 25.
152 NMML, Shyama Prasad Mookherjee Papers, Subject File no. 114/47, a petition from Calcutta, 28 May 1947.
153 *Amrita Bazar Patrika* of 9 June 1947 published several letters to the editor highlighting the activities of the Armed Guard in Calcutta and its vicinity. Tyson, the Secretary to the Governor of Bengal referred to their 'irresponsi-

ble' behaviour. See IOR, Tyson Papers, Eur E 341/41, Tyson, the Secretary to the Governor of Bengal, to the Viceroy, 12 June 1947.
154 IOR, Tyson Papers, Eur E 341/41, Tyson's note, 12 July 1947. The Bengal Governor, Fredrick Burrows, also noticed that the new recruits were provided with better accommodation than the Gurkhas owing 'to the accommodating spirit of a very rich Muslim'. See IOR, L/PJ/5/154-6, Burrows to Mountbatten, 11 April 1947.
155 IOR, L/PJ/8/655, This description draws upon the intercepted letter of Raghib Ahsan Huseyn, President of the Calcutta district Muslim League, to Suhrawardy, 13 April 1947.
156 NMML, Moonjee Papers, Subject file No. 74, B. S. Moonjee to Ashutosh Lahiri, 4 March 1947.
157 IOR, R/3/2/59A, the Chief Secretary's Fortnightly Report, second half of July 1947.
158 NMML, Moonjee Papers, Asutosh Lahiri to B. S. Moonjee, 3 July 1947.
159 CSASC, Bell Papers, file 3 (2).
160 Jadunath Sarkar, Meghnad Saha, Suniti Kumar Chatterjee, Kalidas Nag, R. C. Majumdar, among others. For details of the memoranda, see NAI, Rajendra Prasad Papers, 6-1/45-6-7, and also NMML, AICC, Bengal Partition Files, CL-8, CL-14C, CL-14D and CL-21. This reference is owed to Mahajan 2000: 271–2.
161 *The Star of India*, 22 June 1947.
162 IOR, QAP, F.9/2-21, S. M. A. Majeed, secretary, Khulna district Muslim League to Jinnah, 24 June 1947.
163 Even as late as September, the entire city was in the grip of panic for anticipated trouble. As an official report suggests, so panic-stricken were the Muslims that they 'were reluctant to board a bus, driven by a turban Sikh' since the Sikh community was 'involved in some of the ghastly killing of Muslims in the riot'. Furthermore, 'Muslim passengers were as unwilling to be dropped in Hindu areas as the bus drivers were to stop in Muslim areas'. See, IOR, Tyson Papers, Eur E 341/41, Tyson's note, 29 September 1946.
164 IOR, R/3/2/59A, Fortnightly Report, second half of June 1947.
165 The Hindus hailed the partition vote, John Tyson wrote, 'as a vote for freedom from Muslim dominance and as a vote of no confidence in the existing Muslim League ministry and in all past and possible future ministries in Bengal which had been or in the future would be Muslim-controlled'. See IOR, Tyson Papers, Eur E 341/41, Tyson's note of 5 July 1947.
166 IOR, R/3/2/59A, Fortnightly Report, second half of June 1947.
167 Chaudhuri 1987: 826.
168 IOR, Eur E 341/41, Tyson's note of 23 August 1946.
169 IOR, L/PJ/8/578, Patel to Stafford Cripps, 16 October 1946.
170 QAP, File No. 10/46-7, A. C. Dutta, member of the Bengal Legislative Assembly, to Jinnah, 17 July 1947.
171 *Amrita Bazar Patrika*, 4 September 1946.
172 Bandyopadhyay 1997: 205.
173 IOR, L/PJ/8/578, J. N. Mandal's press statement (on 25 October 1946) after his return from Noakhali. 'It is fantastic to impute political motives behind the recent outbreak and link political parties with disturbances. It was an uprising of violent elements pure and simple, and nothing but sheer lawlessness. No political parties are involved'.
174 J. N. Mandal's speech in the Assembly on 18 June 1947, Bengal Legislative Assembly Proceedings, Vol. 63, No. 3, 1947

175 Suhrawardy, for instance, admitted that 'there is no differentiation made where there is a communal struggle, as is evidenced by the fact that Muslims attacked the Scheduled Caste Hindus'. See IOR, QAP (microfilm), F 458/75–79, Suhrawardy to Liaquat Ali Khan, 21 May 1947.
176 Radha Nath Das's speech in the Assembly on 18 June 1947, Bengal Legislative Assembly Proceedings, Vol. 63, No. 3, 1947.
177 Chatterjee 1997: 40.
178 IOR, V/9/1318, Sasankha Sekhar Sanyal's speech in the Assembly on 10 March 1941, Bengal Legislative Assembly Proceedings, Vol. 59, No. 1, 1941.
179 Haq made this announcement in the 1939 Sirajganj conference. Reiterating his stance in his assembly speech, he thus retorted, 'I have devoted the best of my years of my life to advance Muslim education, not because I wish to treat Muslims as a favourite community, but I believe that the Muslims can come up to the standard to which we wish all other communities to come up if they get proper facilities'. Fazlul Haq's speech in the Assembly, 15 December 1939, IOR, V/9/1309, Bengal Legislative Assembly Proceedings, Vol. 55, No. 3, 1939.
180 *Amrita Bazar Patrika*, 11 July 1943.
181 IOR, V/9/1319, B. P. Singh Roy's speech in the Assembly on 11 July 1943, Bengal Legislative Assembly Debates, Vol. 59, No. 5.
182 B. C. Roy's speech in the Assembly, 15 July 1943. Interestingly, the Hindu Mahasabha found an ally in the Congress because the arguments, made earlier by N. C. Chatterjee of the Mahasabha, in the Assembly challenging the government recruitment policy were reiterated by Roy. N. C. Chatterjee's speech in the Assembly, 11 July 1946. Bengal Legislative Assembly Proceedings, Vol. 59, No. 3, 1943. Both the Congress and Hindu Mahasabha were severely critical of the Government. See *Ananda Bazar Patrika* (15 July 1943) and *Hindustan Standard* (16 July 1943).
183 According to Mazzamal Haq, the growing strength of Muslims in the government sector 'will naturally cause consternation to the Hindus who have so far been appropriating all benefits'. Muslims should get, as he demanded, jobs in proportion to their demographic strength in the province. He cited the case of Barisal, where Muslims though constituting 71 per cent of the district population had only 52 out 331 government jobs, while Hindus with only 21 per cent of the population grabbed the rest of the jobs. IOR, V/9/1319, Mozzamal Haq's speech in the Assembly, 18 July 1943, Bengal Legislative Assembly Debates, Vol. 59, No. 3.
184 Communalism in services was, as *Amrita Bazar Patrika* suggested, articulated in the Government policy of 'minimum qualification for the Muslims, fifty percent job reservation for them' and also 'importing Muslims from outside if Bengali Muslims were not available (*Amrita Bazar Patrika*, 17 and 21 October 1946). An otherwise pro-League daily, *The Statesman*, was also critical of the job reservation scheme that was clearly anti-Hindus and not at all proportional to their demographic strength in the province. Of the 50 per cent of jobs available, Scheduled Castes were allocated 15 per cent and the rest went to Caste Hindus and the remaining communities (*The Statesman*, 25 October 1946).
185 IOR, L/PJ/8/576, *The Times*, London, 19 October 1946.
186 IOR, V/9/1325, S. N. Biswas' speech in the Assembly, Bengal Legislative Assembly Proceedings, Vol. 59, No. 1, 1941.
187 In a memorandum to the Viceroy, signed by B. C. Roy, K. S. Roy (of the Congress) and Shyama Prasad Mookherjee (of the Hindu Mahasabha), it was thus

argued that 'ever since Pakisthan became the slogan of the Moslem League, communal feelings became further embittered. The entire official machinery has been sought to be utilised for strengthening the Moslem League in Bengal and for spreading militant ideas on Pakisthan'. See NMML, S. P. Mookherjee Papers, Subject File, 1946–47, Memorandum on Bengal by B. C. Roy, K. S. Roy and S. P. Mookherjee, 28 April 1947.

188 *The Modern Review*, February 1947.
189 *The Star of India*, 18 June 1947; *The Morning News*, 21 June 1947.
190 Thus, argues Sugata Bose, 'those who had blazed the trail of Indian nationalism a generation ago by doggedly opposing the partition of 1905 were now beset by Curzon's ghost' (Bose 1986: 229).
191 IOR, L/PJ/8/576, the summary of events: the Calcutta Riot, a report by R. J. Walker, Secretary to the Government of Bengal, 20 October 1946.
192 IOR, Tyson Paper, Eur E 341/41, Tyson's report, 8 September 1946.
194 One of the most popular religious festivals in rural Bengal was Laxmi Puja, which was observed in almost in every Hindu household. The Laxmi Puja for the year 1946 was held on 10 October when the famous meeting that reportedly triggered the riot was organised at the Sahapur English High School, Noakhali. About 15 000 Muslims attended the meeting. Addressing the meeting, Ghulam Sarwar, the main speaker 'exhorted the Muslims to attack the *kutchery bari* of Surendra Nath Bose, zamindar of Narayanpur and also the house of Rajendra Lal Chaudhuri, Karapra's zamindar' (see Khosla 1989: 71).
194 Khosla 1989: 67.
195 Warning his Assembly colleagues of the adverse consequences of disunity among the Hindus and Muslims, what M. Shamsuddin Ahmad of the Krishak Praja party said was most revealing. As he argued, 'our rulers are taking advantage of our communal frenzy by siding with the Hindus at one time and with the Muslims at another, thus perpetuating our bondage and slavery for all time to come'. IOR, V/9/1321, M. Shamsuddin Ahmad's speech in the Assembly, 9 April 1941, Bengal Legislative Assembly Debates, Vol. 58, No. 6, 1941.

4
AN ALTERNATIVE TO PARTITION
The united Bengal scheme

The 1947 British withdrawal from the Indian subcontinent led to the creation of two sovereign states: India and Pakistan. Drawing on the Hindu–Muslim chasm, the controversial 'two-nation theory' justified the great divide. Although Jinnah attained what he had long sought, the very basis of the partition was fragile, otherwise the erstwhile East Pakistan would not have seceded to form an independent state within less than three decades. Now, a number of studies have shown the extent to which religion was emphasised for political ends. Whatever the explanation, 1947 saw the vivisection of the subcontinent of India into two separate states. This chapter examines the short-lived proposal to create three and not two sovereign polities – India, Pakistan and United Bengal.

Between April and June 1947, top Bengali politicians such as Sarat Bose, K. S. Roy and H. S. Suhrawardy argued for a united Bengal comprising both east and west Bengal. Although they failed to generate adequate support in favour of the campaign, in their correspondence with the British authorities which has been published in *The Transfer of Power* volumes edited by Manseurgh and Moon, both the provincial Congress and Muslim League leaders made a strong case for an independent Bengal. Their efforts did not yield results, though the unity shown by them during the period was remarkable. Neither the British nor the Congress High Command thought the proposal viable in view of the deepening fissure between the Hindus and the Muslims at the grassroots level. What probably conditioned their decision was the experience of the devastating riots in and around Calcutta following the League's 'Direct Action' call on 16 August 1946.

The scheme for a third dominion

The idea of a united Bengal owed its origin to H. S. Suhrawardy, the then Premier of Bengal, who at a press conference in Delhi on 27 April 1947 argued strongly for 'an independent, undivided and sovereign Bengal in a divided India as a separate dominion'.[1] Although the Bengal Premier spelt out his views regarding an independent Bengal in the Delhi statement, he began floating the idea[2] with Attlee's historic announcement on 20 February 1947 that it was 'the definite intention' of the British to leave India by June 1948, even if that necessitated transferring power 'in some areas to existing Provincial Governments'.[3] Criticising the partition demand sponsored by the Hindu Mahasabha and the Congress as 'short-sighted' and a 'confession of defeatism',[4] Suhrawardy argued strongly for a united Bengal because Bengal was indivisible in view of its 'economic integrity, mutual reliance and the necessity of creating a strong workable state'.[5] In his view, Bengal continued to remain economically backward primarily because of the presence of a large group of non-Bengali businessmen who, in the name of earning their livelihood, exploited the people for their own benefit. Hence, he launched a campaign against them because he felt that 'if Bengal is to be great, it can only [be] so if it stands on its leg [sic] ... it must be a master of its own resources and riches and its own destiny. It must cease to be exploited by others'.[6] The Bengal Provincial Muslim League (BPML) corroborated Suhrawardy's argument, attributing Bengal's poverty to exploitation by the non-Bengali business interests. In a press statement Abul Hashim, the BPML Secretary, argued thus:

> Cent percent alien capital, both Indian and Anglo-American exploiting Bengal is invested in Bengal. The growing socialist tendencies amongst us have created fears of expropriating. ... They have the prudence to visualize difficulties in a free and united Bengal. It is in the interest of *the alien capital that Bengal should be divided*.[7]

Apart from the British-dominated Bengal Chamber of Commerce, there were three other organisations to protect indigenous commercial interests – namely, the Indian Chamber of Commerce, the Bengal National Chamber of Commerce, and the Muslim Chamber of Commerce. Of these, the Bengal National Chamber of Commerce, dominated by the Bengalis, had declined in importance by the first half of the twentieth century, probably because of the demise of its mentor C. R. Das and the consolidation of the Marwari business interests through the Indian Chamber of Commerce, which was in the forefront of the struggle against foreign capital. Although it 'had close contract with the Congress High Command and found in Gandhi the greatest guardian of an ordered society',[8] it was very hostile to the Bengal Congress for its radical tone and connections with revolutionary terrorism. G. D. Birla, the principal architect of the Indian Chamber of Commerce, on several occasions complained to Gandhi about the Bengal Congress.[9] In 1937 in particular, when the question of a coalition between the Krishak Praja party (KPP) and the Bengal Congress came up, it was Birla who persuaded Gandhi to withdraw his approval after having convincing him that the combination would have an adverse impact on the Marwari business community in Calcutta.[10] Similarly, the Muslim Chamber of Commerce, founded in 1932, was primarily an instrument for the protection of the non-Bengali (Muslim) commercial interests in Bengal. The Chamber, comprising Muslim merchants, manufacturers and bankers in Calcutta, including the Ispahani and Adamjee families, accounted for 890 members with a claimed capital of Rs 200 million.[11] It declared in 1934 – perhaps a wild claim – that apart form having a firm grip on the trade in salt, raw jute, rice and skins, its members controlled 75 per cent of Bengal's coastal trade;[12] although this claim seems somewhat exaggerated, the fact that it was a force to reckon with in so far as the coastal trade was concerned can be substantiated with reference to an application of the Chittagong unit of the Muslim Chamber of Conference for 'recognition from the Government of Bengal'.[13] The district administration was reluctant initially, because it was unclear whether the formation of a separate chamber of commerce was necessary since there were already commercial associations in existence of which Muhammedan merchants were members,[14] but it had to agree at the instance of the government of Bengal.[15]

In the context of divide and rule, the Bengal Chamber of Commerce, an association of European merchants and manufacturers in Calcutta, always supported the cause of the Muslims as against the Congress. In fact, with the publication of the 1932 White Paper, which recognised 'numerical strength' as the source of power, the European Association as the political wing of the Bengal Chamber of Commerce realised that the key to power was undoubtedly the solidarity of Muslims.[16] Accordingly, the Association decided financially to back *The Star of India*, the mouthpiece of the Muslims, with advertisements from European firms[17] so as to draw Muslim support against the nationalists.

The above summary shows the extent to which commercial interests appeared significant in Bengal's political arithmetic. By virtue of Birla's intimacy with Gandhi, the Indian Chamber of Commerce succeeded in most cases in pursuing its commercial goal despite the vehement opposition of the provincial Congress leadership. With the triumph of the anti-Subhas Bose faction in the Bengal Provincial Congress, it appeared to be plain sailing for Birla, primarily because the *ad hoc* committee which was installed in the wake of suspending the Sarat Bose-led Congress appreciated the role of the indigenous business houses in building the country's economic strength. Interestingly, the Indian Chamber of Commerce opposed the united Bengal movement from the beginning even though partition would destroy their commercial network in east Bengal. G. D. Birla, in his letter to the AICC,[18] insisted on partition because the Suhrawardy-sponsored united Bengal campaign was a ploy to create a greater Pakistan. The logic of the argument is easy to understand; what is puzzling, however, is Birla's unequivocal support for the division, which also meant a significant loss of market. Birla probably realised that his contact with the Congress High Command, drawing on national democratic ideology, would pay off with the departure of the British commercial houses. Also, his firm grip over Calcutta, the commercial capital of India, would enable him to explore both the national and international markets.[19] Partition would also rule out the possibility of the operation of other organised commercial interests, including the Muslim Chamber of Commerce – which, being well entrenched in east Bengal, was striving to extend into Calcutta and west Bengal. Thus the argument marshalled by the Muslim Chamber of Commerce in favour of the move appears to have stemmed from obvious commercial considerations. In fact, Jinnah's decision to support Suhrawardy was attributed to a large extent to M. A. H. Ispahani of the Muslim Chamber of Commerce, who was reported to have persuaded the Quaid-i-Azam to discuss the matter with the Viceroy.[20] It was certainly a master stroke, which transformed a regional political campaign into a national one by linking the national leadership with its regional counterpart. Jinnah perhaps saw in Suhrawardy's move the possibility of a greater Pakistan and was thus convinced, while Ispahani, a commercial magnate, decided to back the campaign financially, first with a view to neutralising the prevalent anti-non-Bengali feeling in Bengal, and second with the hope of becoming intimate with Jinnah – who, for obvious reasons, was to be crucial in Pakistan. Another consideration which probably prompted Ispahani to extend support to Suhrawardy was his long-cherished aim of controlling the jute industry in west Bengal,[21] then chiefly owned by British business houses and members of the Indian Chamber of Commerce.[22] Moreover, the decision that Calcutta was to be a part of India after the great divide caused alarm to Ispahani and his colleagues whose business careers had begun in Calcutta, which was likely to continue as an important business centre even after the transfer of power – hence the interest in keeping the city within Pakistan.[23]

Although Ispahani's indirect involvement in the campaign for a united Bengal strengthened Suhrawardy's argument to some extent, the very idea of separate dominion sparked off dissension within the BPML. Factional rivalry, which probably reached its zenith over the move for a united Bengal, was not new.[24] Suhrawardy's 27 April statement provoked the other faction in the BPML – (the Khawaja group, led by Khwaja Nazimuddin and Akram Khan) – to question the validity of such a move in the context of the 1940 Lahore resolution.[25] Abul Hashim, the spokesman of the Suhrawardy group, argued in a counter-statement strongly in favour of the campaign, which was justified in accordance with the Pakistan demand. Reiterating their faith in the Lahore resolution, he further elaborated that 'the resolution never contemplated the creation of any Akhand Muslim state', and on the contrary 'it stipulated that the areas in which the Muslims are numerically in a majority as in the North-Western and Eastern zones of India should be grouped to constitute "Independent States" in which the constituent unit shall be autonomous and sovereign'. Thus Hashim concluded that 'it gives Bengal ... complete sovereignty'.[26] Referring to the great tradition of Bengal as a distinct cultural identity and the richness of her language, the Hashim–Suhrawardy combination warned Bengali Muslims that 'in an Akhand Pakistan they would be under the domination of west Pakistanis and Urdu would be the state language. They could not expect a better position than becoming peons under the Urdu-speaking judges and magistrates'.[27] Interestingly, Akram Khan and his colleagues, who strongly deprecated the suggestion for a united Bengal movement at the outset, staged a *volte face* as soon as Jinnah accorded support to Suhrawardy's political campaign.[28] In order to save the situation, Akram, the spokesman of the anti-Suhrawardy Khwaja group, immediately announced that:

> as disciplined members of the All India Muslim League they opposed Suhrawardy vehemently because the United Bengal movement did not receive a favourable response from the High Command. Now, with Jinnah's opposition to the partition of Bengal, we will work hand in hand with Suhrawardy and his colleagues to accomplish the stipulated aim.[29]

The fight between the Khwaja group and the Hashim–Suhrawardy combination was merely a continuity of the rivalry between the newly emerged Muslim middle class led by Suhrawardy and the well-entrenched landed aristocracy under the leadership of Khwaja Nazimuddin, the Dhaka Nawab. Apart from the obvious social distance between the two groups, two events appear to have consolidated the differences in 1946. First, with the defeat of Nazimuddin as the parliamentary leader of the BPML, Suhrawardy formed a ministry in which the Khwaja group was not given adequate representation.[30] Instead of accommodating what he called 'the disgruntled and ambitious members of the Khwaja group', Suhrawardy lodged a complaint with Jinnah,[31] who apparently gave him a free hand in the formation of the ministry by referring to the practice of parliamentary democracy in which the leader chose his team-mates.[32] Jinnah's decision to back Suhrawardy against the Khwaja group was probably logical. As a tactful politician he could not afford to alienate the Bengal Premier, who, after Fazlul Haq, was the most popular leader, both in the BPML and outside, due to his image as the true representative of Bengali Muslims – an image that gained currency in view of the pronounced non-Bengali character of the Khwaja group in terms of language and other considerations.[33] Secondly, Suhrawardy strained his relations with the Khwaja group further by introducing the Bargadar Bill in the Assembly in April 1947, which, by stipulating to increase the share of the produce of the *bargadar* (sharecropper) from one-half to two-thirds, was a direct attack on the landed aristocracy in the context of absolute landlordism.[34] Although the Bill remained on paper,[35] its content caused alarm to the members of the Khwaja group who, in a memorandum submitted to Jinnah and Liaquat Ali Khan, the Chairman of the Central Parliamentary Board, insisted on the revocation of the bill.[36] For Suhrawardy it was a triumph because, apart from ensuring that the issues raised required serious thought, Jinnah did not either ask for the withdrawal of the bill or request the inclusion of the members of the Khwaja group in the ministry.[37]

Jinnah's role

As mentioned earlier, Suhrawardy gained remarkably owing to Jinnah's support for the united Bengal move. Although Mountbatten expressed uncertainty regarding Jinnah's role, Suhrawardy was confident that 'he could get Mr. Jinnah to agree that [Bengal] need not join Pakistan if it was prepared to remain united'.[38] While commenting on Suhrawardy's statement, Jinnah came out strongly in favour of keeping Bengal united: 'If Bengal remains united, ... I should be delighted. What is the use of Bengal without Calcutta[?]; they had much better to remain united and independent; I am sure that they would be on friendly terms with us'.[39] Jinnah was impressed by Suhrawardy's scheme, probably because it was a stepping stone towards attaining a greater Pakistan comprising provinces in which Muslims constituted a majority. In his view, 'the question of the division of India, as proposed by the Muslim League, is based on the fundamental fact that there are two nations – Hindus and Muslims – and the underlying principle is that we want a National Home and a National State in our homelands which are predominantly Muslim, and comprise the 6 units of Punjab NWFP [North Western Frontier Province], Sind, Baluchistan and Bengal'.[40] Opposing the government's move for the partition of Bengal and the Punjab, which meant 'a truncated or mutilated moth-eaten Pakistan', Jinnah argued that 'this clamour is not based on any sound principle except that the Hindu minorities in the Punjab and Bengal wish to cut up these provinces and cut up their own people into two in these provinces'.[41] Although he was aware that 'the caste Hindus and Sikhs don't want to be under a government in which the Muslims will be in a majority',[42] he nonetheless appealed to the Viceroy 'not to destroy the unity of Bengal and Punjab which had national characteristics in common, common ways of life; and *where the Hindus have stronger feelings as Bengalis or Punjabis than they have as members of the Congress*'[43] (emphasis added). Whatever the validity of Jinnah's contention, its logic appears unsatisfactory in the light of his insistence on the two-nation theory as the basis of the Great Divide. In fact, in response to the argument opposing partition, Mountbatten, by drawing Jinnah's attention to the implication of the two-nation theory, mentioned unequivocally that:

> by sheer logic if I accepted his [Jinnah's] argument in the case of India as a whole, I had also to apply them in the case of these two provinces [Bengal and Punjab] as well... and therefore I could not, of course, allow [his] theories to stop short at the provinces.[44]

Although Jinnah admitted[45] that what he was insisting on was not logical in the light of the two-nation theory, he strove to justify his demand by referring to what the plight of the Scheduled Castes in divided Bengal would be. He argued that the Scheduled Castes, constituting almost one-third of the total population, were opposed to the partition of Bengal because:

> they rightly say that they will be divided into two parts, one at the mercy of the caste Hindus in western and the other at the mercy of the Muslims in eastern Bengal. They dread the caste Hindus and it is well-known that they have suffered economical and social tyranny at the hands of the Hindus for which there is no parallel in the world.[46]

Having been drawn to the memorandum submitted by various Scheduled Caste groups in Bengal to the Viceroy in support of the partition, Jinnah seems to have been unnerved and probably realised that he was fighting for a lost cause.[47]

What probably lay at the root of Jinnah's concern was the fact that east Bengal as a separate state was not economically viable. He agreed with Suhrawardy that east Bengal 'although it has got a large enough population is so deficit in food grains that no amount of intensive cultivation will be able to produce a sufficiency'.[48] Not only would eastern Bengal suffer due to 'deficiency in food to the extent of 225 000 tons', its future as a viable economic unit was also at stake. As mentioned in the 1947 Governor's Conference: 'economically, [east Bengal] could not survive as all the coal mines, the minerals and the factories are in western Bengal, so are the jute processing mills with two exceptions'.[49] Jinnah's defence of the united Bengal proposal may have stemmed from the anticipation that it would secure Calcutta, the commercial capital of India, for the proposed dominion in which Muslims constituted a majority. Describing Calcutta 'as the heart of Bengal' around which 'the province has developed and grown', he insisted that 'Calcutta should not be torn away from Eastern Bengal'.[50] On another occasion, Jinnah mentioned that 'to divide the jute growing East Bengal districts from Calcutta will be tantamount to the destruction of

Calcutta within a few years'.[51] As is shown below, although Suhrawardy was confident, the united Bengal movement sparked off a counter-agitation which gradually became formidable both in terms of the grass-roots support and the strength of the arguments in favour of the partition. In view of this, Jinnah probably realised that the idea of a third dominion was futile and hence, he marshalled his arguments with a view to keeping Calcutta as part of east Bengal. He emphatically suggested that:

> if unfortunately, partition is decided upon and eastern Bengal is deprived of its only port of Calcutta which has developed its present position, in no case should it be allowed to go with the western Bengal, otherwise, it will follow as a corollary that western Bengal will go into Hindustan and His Majesty's Government will be making the present of one great port to Hindustan. In any event, if worst comes to worst, Calcutta should be made a free port.[52]

What prompted Jinnah was probably his desire to obtain the whole of Bengal for Pakistan. In fact, he was reported to have mentioned to the Viceroy that 'with its Muslim majority, an independent Bengal would be a sort of subsidiary Pakistan'.[53] Thus the idea that the 'cry for a sovereign and undivided Bengal' was nothing but a significant step towards creating a greater Pakistan is not without substance. Under the given circumstances, the call for a greater Pakistan was likely to be suicidal in view of the well-entrenched communal hatred following the Great Calcutta Killings of 1946,[54] hence the demand for a united Bengal comprising the economically advanced part of west Bengal including Calcutta, one of the most commercially important centres in India. He was optimistic that the move for a sovereign Bengal was likely to attain success in view of the 1905 precedent in which Bengalis, irrespective of religion, forced the British to revoke the partition. The unity between the Hindus and Muslims evident during the 1905 anti-partition campaign was attributed to the fact that despite differences in terms of religion, there lay a chord of unity between them because, as Jinnah himself mentioned, both the communities had stronger feelings as Bengalis.[55] Thus it was a grand strategy championing the cause of the Bengalis as such, which Jinnah devised to attract the Bengali Hindus as well. Convinced by Jinnah's argument in favour of a greater Pakistan, a person like Nazimuddin, who had opposed Suhrawardy from the outset, came out openly in favour of the united Bengal proposal, because 'an independent sovereign Bengal is in the best interests of its people, whether Muslims or non-Muslims ... and the partition of the province is fatal to the interests of Bengalis as such'.[56] So, Jinnah's support to the united Bengal movement was therefore part of a grand strategy of creating a bigger Pakistan comprising east and west

Bengal – which appeared attainable, since Bengal Congress stalwarts like Sarat Bose and K. S. Roy had decided to cooperate with the Suhrawardy–Hashim combination in this regard.

BPCC and united Bengal

The united Bengal issue caused a fissure within the BPCC. In consonance with the Congress High Command, a section led by Surendra Mohan Ghosh (the President) and Kalipada Mukherjee (the Secretary of the BPCC) opposed the united Bengal movement from the outset, as it was nothing but an act of 'provincialism'. Attributing the partition of Bengal to the two-nation theory, which sparked off communalism, they argued that 'an undivided Bengal in a divided India is an impossibility'.[57] The Indian Chamber of Commerce, representing the indigenous business interests, was opposed to the idea because 'the economic development to the province... [made] it imperative for Bengal to remain attached to an union'.[58] By insisting on the partition of Bengal a section of the Bengali intelligentsia, including Jadunath Sarkar, Rameshchandra Majumdar, Megnad Saha, Sisir Kumar Mitra and Suniti Kumar Chattopadhyay, accorded support to Surendra Mohan Ghosh, expressing 'no confidence in the Suhrawardy ministry which indulged in communal politics'.[59]

Despite opposition from within the BPCC, another section led by Sarat Bose and K. S. Roy agreed to support the demand for an independent Bengal, and accordingly started mobilising support in its favour. Perhaps emotionally carried away, both Bose and Roy saw in the idea the only possible way of protecting Bengali interests. Forgetting the adverse consequences of the Hindu–Muslim schism in rural Bengal, they were satisfied with a verbal assurance from the League with regard to an independent Bengal. Not only was Sarat Bose included favourably; Nehru too seemed willing to concede because 'he felt that a partition now would anyhow bring east Bengal into Hindustan in a few years'.[60] Bose's active involvement with the campaign for independent Bengal was probably the last effort of the BPCC to emerge as one of the significant political forces in Bengal. The situation seemed unfavourable: the 1935 Government of India Act guaranteed a separate electorate to the Muslims which, along with the Poona Pact concession to the backward communities, led to a total eclipse of Hindu strength in the legislature. The Bengal Congress was adversely affected in 1939–40, when its leader, Subhas Chandra Bose, was removed and the provincial Congress Committee was suspended. Between 1939 and 1945, apart from the War crisis, intra-party rivalry within the Congress plagued its activities. Only during the 1946 Calcutta riots did the party temporarily rise above the factional feud to combat the communal menace. Given the circumstances, the united Bengal formula appeared effective in mobilising support irrespective of religion. With

THE UNITED BENGAL SCHEME

Suhrawardy's favourable leaning towards a sovereign Bengal, the Sarat Bose–K. S. Roy combination seemed encouraging. Notwithstanding divisions within the BPCC, on 20 May 1947 a tentative agreement was reached between Sarat Bose and K. S. Roy on the one hand and Suhrawardy and a few other Muslim League members on the other. However, the absence of four members[61] of the six-member League sub-committee set up to negotiate the terms of an agreement with the Bengali Hindus is illustrative of the split within the BPMl. Thus, despite initial euphoria, the formula appeared to have added another dimension to the already well-entrenched internecine rivalry in both the BPCC and the BPML.

On 24 May, just ten days before the announcement of the partition plan, the agreement was released to the press.[62] The terms of the agreement[63] were as follows:

1. Bengal will be a Free State. The Free State of Bengal will decide its relations with the rest of India.
2. The constitution of the Free State of Bengal will provide for election to the Bengal legislature on the basis of a joint electorate and adult franchise, with reservation of seats proportionate to the population amongst the Hindus and Muslims. The seats as between the Hindus and the scheduled caste Hindus will be distributed amongst them in proportion to their respective population, or in such manner as may be agreed among them. The constituencies and the votes will be distributive and not cumulative. A candidate who gets the majority of the votes of his own constituency cast during the elections and 25 per cent of the votes of the other communities so cast will be declared elected. If no candidate satisfies these conditions, that candidate who gets the largest number of votes of his own community will be elected.
3. On the announcement by His Majesty's Government that the proposal of the Free State of Bengal has been accepted and that Bengal will not be partitioned, the present Bengal Ministry will be dissolved and a new Interim Ministry brought into being, consisting of an equal number of Muslims and Hindus (including Scheduled Caste Hindus) but excluding the Chief Minister. In his Ministry, the Chief Minister will be a Muslim and the Home Minister a Hindu.
4. Pending the final emergence of a Legislature and a Ministry under the new constitution, the Hindus (including the Scheduled Caste Hindus) and the Muslims will have an equal share in the services including military and police. The services will be manned by Bengalis.
5. There will be Constituent Assembly composed of thirty persons, fifteen Muslims and fifteen non-Muslim members of the Legislature respectively, excluding the Europeans.

THE UNITED BENGAL SCHEME

While explaining the terms of agreement, Sarat Bose mentioned that:

> the Free state of Bengal... will be republic and its nature and character will be socialist... by the 'free' [i.e. freedom] not only from political bondage but also freedom from social and economic servitude ... the basis for all legislation will be the economic, social and cultural interests of the people as a whole, and not the benefits of only a section.

He thus exhorted the Bengalis to 'seize the opportunity and combine to usher in a new era in the history of Bengal and eventually in the history of India itself'.[64]

Sarat Bose was also aware that without the backing of the Congress High Command, the movement was likely to be defeated. Bose's insisted that if the High Command accepted the plan, 'it would be easier to persuade the League High Command to agree to Suhrawardy's scheme of united Bengal which was virtually the same as his own plan'.[65] Despite his persuasive arguments, the Congress High Command never accepted the scheme because 'the independence of Bengal really means in present circumstances the dominance of Moslem League in Bengal. It means practically the whole of Bengal going into Pakistan area, although those who are interested may not say so'. Nehru, representing the High Command, further added that 'we can agree to Bengal remaining united only if it remains in the union'.[66] Expressing his disapproval of the scheme, Patel was unhappy with Sarat Bose and K. S. Roy, who had negotiated with Suhrawardy 'without the official authorization of the Bengal Congress'. He was disturbed when his attention was drawn to a number of pamphlets, alleged to have been circulated by the BPML, in which the united Bengal was identified as 'Azad Pakistan'.[67] Thus Patel urged Bose 'to take a united stand' with the Congress High Command on the issue of partition.[68] Instead of conforming to the High Command, Sarat Bose was equally emphatic in insisting on the united Bengal scheme because, according to him (emphasis added):

> It is not a fact that Bengali Hindus unanimously demand partition ... the demand for partition is more or less confined to the middle classes. When the full implications of partition are realized and when people here find that all they will get for western Bengal province will be roughly one-third of the area of Bengal and only about half of the total Hindu population in Bengal, the agitation for partition will surely lose support. I entirely agree with you that we should take a united stand; but I shall say at the same time that the united stand should be for a united Bengal. *Future generations will, I am afraid, condemn us for conceding divisions of India and partition of Bengal and the Punjab.*[69]

Reiterating that 'individual expression of men's views must fit into [the official Congress policy] and there should not be any discordant note',[70] Patel asked the Bengal Congressmen to withdraw from the campaign, because, according to him, 'the cry [of Suhrawardy] of a sovereign independent Bengal is a trap' to incorporate the Hindu-preponderant west Bengal into Pakistan. Hence he added, 'the only way to save the Hindus of Bengali is to insist on the partition of Bengal'.[71]

Notwithstanding the apparent unanimity over the terms of agreement at the outset,[72] dissension developed between Suhrawardy and Bose as the former publicly expressed the misgivings that the term 'socialist pattern of society' had aroused in him. 'This demand', he strongly argued, 'cannot be made if it is decided to keep Bengal as one and allow Bengal to frame its constitution'.[73] He was therefore unhappy with the revocation of separate electorates. The argument he put forward in public to support his contention was, however, strange. As a matter of principle, Suhrawardy was not willing to concede a joint electorate, which meant repudiation of Jinnah's two-nation theory.[74] The introduction of a joint electorate would, he was reported to have expressed, eclipse the Muslim preponderance in the legislature in the long run. Since the Muslims in general were not enthusiastic about participating in elections, Hindus, by their zeal to cast votes in favour of Hindu candidates, would gain remarkably by the joint electorate system, Suhrawardy apprehended.[75] His anxiety is probably not unfounded in view of the lack of interest among the Muslims in elections.

The division between Bose and Suhrawardy over fundamental principles led the former to dissociate completely from the united Bengal movement. With Bose's withdrawal, following Suhrawardy's reluctance to revoke separate electorates and adopt a socialist frame of government for Bengal, the movement received perhaps its most severe jolt, which weakened its claims considerably, because the other Congress leader K. S. Roy, as Suhrawardy himself admitted,[76] was too weak to counter the Hindu Mahasabha, which by then had captured the imagination of the Hindus on the issue of partition.[77] Although Suhrawardy had considerable support among his followers and he could bring his High Command to support his move for a united and independent Bengal, K. S. Roy had neither the capacity to persuade Nehru and Patel nor the political base to organise a campaign for the demand. In fact, this became evident when the Congress High Command ignored K. S. Roy's threat to resign if the demand was not conceded.

The Hindu Mahasabha and United Bengal

The success of the agitation for partition was attributed to a large extent to the preponderant Mahasabha and its leader S. P. Mookherjee, who spearheaded a fierce attack on the united Bengal scheme which was, he thought, a ploy to force the Hindus to live under Muslim domination. The situation seemed congenial because (1) the Congress High Command came to the aid of the Hindu Mahasabha, and (2) the disastrous consequences of the Direct Action Day (which had resulted in the 1946 Great Calcutta Killings) made the Hindus aware of a real threat under Muslim administration. Although the united Bengal movement gained ground following the agreement between Sarat Bose and Suhrawardy, it fizzled out gradually due to its internal weakness and Hindu mobilisation in favour of partition.

Arguing strongly against the united Bengal scheme, because 'Bengal Hindus have suffered terribly during the last ten years on account of communal misrule and maladministration', S. P. Mookherjee, the main Mahasabha supremo, argued that 'if ever an impartial survey is made of Bengal's administration during the last ten years, it will appear that Hindus have suffered not only on account of communal riots and disturbance, but in every sphere of national activities, educational, economic, political and even religious'.[78] Mookherjee also justified why the same Bengalis who had opposed the 1905 partition were insistent on it, because 'it is now realized that if communal-minded Moslem majority get the authority of perpetually ruling over the non-Moslem community, then their nationalism would be crushed.' He also added that 'the spirit underlying both the movements is the same namely, preservation of the national spirit, just as the Moslem League supported partition then and are opposing it now on the ground of strengthening their communal spirit'.[79]

Apart from highlighting the adverse consequences of a communally biased administration, S. P. Mookherjee in his letter to the Viceroy defended the partition of Bengal for several reasons. First, drawing on the 'two-nation theory', the partition of Bengal appeared most logical because, according to Jinnah, 'Hindus and Muslims are two separate nations and Muslims must have their homeland and their own state'. Therefore, Hindus in Bengal, who constituted almost half of Bengal's population, 'may well demand that they must not be compelled to live within the Muslim state'. Thus, Mookherjee concluded, 'the same logic and arguments applicable to Pakistan apply also to the partition of Bengal'.[80] Second, if Muslims, being 20 per cent of India's population, constituted themselves into such a formidable minority that their 'demand for a separate homeland and state' was irresistible, 'surely forty-five percent of Bengal's Hindu population', Mookherjee felt, 'is a sufficiently large minority which cannot be coerced into living within the [Pakistan] state against the will of the people'.[81] Finally, to the Mahasabha supremo, the idea of a sovereign undivided Bengal was not appealing because 'the sovereign undivided Bengal will be a virtual Pakistan'.[82] In an interview to the press, Mookherjee accused the Bengal Congress of hatching a conspiracy against Bengal because of 'Suhrawardy's undivided sovereign Bengal – a transparently political maneuvre designed to extend the frontiers of Pakistan'.[83] Referring to the past record of the Muslim League administration, Mookherjee was not willing to concede that Hindu interests would be better served in the proposed independent dominion. What had happened in the August killings (the 1946 Calcutta and Noakhali riots) was illustrative of the extent to which the Suhrawardy-led government encouraged organised violence, in Calcutta and elsewhere, against the minority community. In every major instance, the Hindu Mahasabha believed, 'the aggressive majority community feels that it is advancing its political aims by opposing the Hindus and depriving them of their due rights ... [and with] a government of their own in power which will not interfere with their acts of lawlessness and oppression,'[84] the task seemed easy. Thus, apprehending Muslim atrocities against the Hindus in various forms in united Bengal, in which the Muslims, (given their demographic strength), were likely to capture state power, the Hindu Mahasabha, by mobilising the Hindus at large, launched a fierce campaign for partition.

Whatever the authenticity of the facts and figures referred to by S. P. Mookherjee in his letter and memorandum, the Hindu Mahasabha opposition contributed significantly to the consolidation of pro-partition sentiments in the form of a campaign for partition. Drawing on the communal bias and the probable consequences of a perpetual Muslim League rule, those[85] supporting partition offered many arguments in justification of their claim.

First, the demand for partition was justified on the grounds of the evident communal bias of the League ministry. The Noakhali District Congress Committee, in a resolution urged the Congress leaders to insist upon a separate province for the Hindus in Bengal as the only alternative in the context of 'The Muslim League carrying out direct action and thereby strengthening the fight of Pakistan at the cost of the lives and properties of the minority community and the honour of the womenfolk'.[86] Secondly, the participation was justified in view of the deliberate attempt to champion the cause of the majority strength in the legislature. Hence 'all attempts by Hindus for punishment of riot makers, to bring peace by strict measures etc., are crushed by the League members by *brutal majority of votes*' (emphasis added). Therefore, in view of the general trend of the legislative and administrative policies of the government, 'there can be no doubt', as a resolution adopted in the North Calcutta DCC runs, 'that the Moslem Leaguers, by their anti-national and communal activities are determined to ruin the Hindu community socially, economically and culturally'.[87] Thirdly, referring to the 1946 Muslim League budget, which earmarked funds for the majority community, a memorandum signed by the students of Calcutta University highlighted several features justifying the contention that the Hindus had lost faith in the regime due to its discrimination against the minority community. The decision to sanction money for the Muslim refugees from Bihar, now settled in Calcutta and its vicinity, was identified as a deliberate policy to 'Islamise western Bengal'. The idea gained ground probably because of Suhrawardy's statement asking them to stay back despite 'Bihar government and Gandhi's repeated requests to the refugees to settle back in their villages'. Moreover, the government's decision to abandon the scheme for research facilities in the University College of Science, Calcutta University (for which originally Rs. 1 million had actually been sanctioned), in the context of the inauguration of the government-sponsored Muslim Educational Fund, gave credence to the charge of the League's communal bias. Thus, in the opinion of the signatories to the memorandum, 'the partition is the only answer to the oppression of the minority by the majority'.[88] Finally, condemning the move for an independent and sovereign Bengal as 'mischievous' because it 'is calculated to sabotage the movement of partition and which will lead to the establishment of Pakistan over the whole of Bengal',[89] a resolution adopted in a meeting in Jessore, an eastern Bengal district, exhorted the national and provincial Congress leadership to mobilise strength against 'the unholy alliance between Suhrawardy and Sarat Bose'.[90] To those supporting the resolution, 'no pact or alliance should be concluded with the League... so long as it will adhere to the policy of Pakistan and the two-nation theory and pursue the present anti-national and reactionary policies'.[91]

On the basis of an opinion poll conducted among literate Hindus and Muslims in Calcutta and other district towns by the Amrita Bazar Patrika, it is evident that despite Sarat Bose and Suhrawardy's sincerity regarding the goal of a united Bengal, the movement was an abortive one because more than 98 per cent favoured partition while a bare 0.6 per cent supported the scheme for an independent Bengal.[92] In the light of the mass agitation for partition and, later, Sarat Bose's withdrawal from the united Bengal campaign, the third-dominion movement which began in April 1947 soon lost its momentum. Suhrawardy too foresaw the collapse of the movement, and hence he was insistent merely on the inclusion of Calcutta in the Muslim zone.[93] Unlike Jinnah, who wanted to keep Calcutta in Pakistan owing to its economic importance, Suhrawardy defended his case by saying that 'Calcutta naturally belongs to the Muslim zone'. In his view, 'On the one side [Calcutta] touches the subdivision of Barasat where the Muslims are in a majority. There is no natural dividing line either other than the River Hooghly between the Hindu zone and the Muslim zone and this leaves Calcutta in the Muslim zone'. He further added, 'in Calcutta and the industrial areas, the Hindu majority is largely due to influx of foreign Hindu labour which it would not be fair to count'.[94] The Bengal Governor, Burrows, seemed willing to support Suhrawardy, because he felt that it would be unfair 'if all revenues went to one half of the province as the other half too had contributed to the prosperity of the city'.[95]

Nothing, however, changed the complexion of the transfer of power, because neither the Congress High Command nor the British government accepted the proposal.

Concluding observations

With the announcement of the partition plan on 3 June 1947, the saga of a united Bengal drew to a close. The statement provided the details relating to the partition of India as well as of the provinces of Bengal and the Punjab and the establishment of two dominions – India and Pakistan. The Bengal Legislative Assembly discussed the 3 June plan in its session on 20 June 1947. Members representing the Hindu majority districts (see Table 4.1) decided by 58 votes to 21 that Bengal should be partitioned, and the constitution of the state comprising these areas should be framed by the existing Constituent Assembly. In a separate meeting those from the Muslim majority districts (see Table 4.1) supported the sovereign Bengal proposal, by 106 votes to 34, that the districts in which the Muslims were demographically preponderant should join the proposed Pakistan Constituent Assembly.[96] Thus, eventually, a majority on both sides accepted the 1947 partition. Following the Congress acceptance of the 3 June declaration, prominent Muslim leaders of the Bengal Congress, including Ashrafuddin Ahmad Chowdhury, tendered their resignations from both the AICC and BPCC. Disillusioned by the Congress' decision to accept the Great Divide on a religious basis, they blamed the National Congress for having conceded Jinnah's two-nation theory, which considered the Muslims to be a separate nation. The Congress High Command, as Ashrafuddin Ahmad Chowdhury lamented:

> has thus cut at the very root of the national character of the Indian National Congress. Its leadership has shamelessly abandoned the long cherished ideal of the Congress and its tradition; ... they have badly let down their Muslim Congress comrades of long standing and stabbed them in the back unawares. Bengal and Punjab ... has [sic] been made a pawn in the power politics of these Congress leaders.[97]

Nonetheless, partition, though at 'a high cost',[98] was preferred by Congress leaders to a united Bengal which was simply 'a device of incorporating the Hindu majority west Bengal into Pakistan'.[99]

Notwithstanding the ultimate failure of the united Bengal movement, the three-month episode between April and June 1947 added an interesting chapter, relatively unknown, to Indian nationalism. Not only did it reveal a schism between the Congress leadership and an important section within the BPCC; it also illustrated the extent to which the imperial authority

Table 4.1 Percentage of Muslims and non-Muslims by district according to the Census of India 1941

Serial no.	District	Percentage of Muslims	Percentage of non-Muslims
1	Burdwan (1 890 732)	17.8	81.6
2	Birbhum (1 048 317)	27.4	72.8
3	Bankura (1 289 640)	2.3	95.5
4	Midnapur (3 190 647)	7.7	92.2
5	Hooghly (1 377 729)	15.1	84.9
6	Howrah (1 490 304)	19.9	79.9
7	24 Parganas (3 536 386)	32.4	66.4
8	Calcutta (2 108 891)	23.5	73.6
9	Khulna (1 943 218)	49.3	50.4
10	Jalpaiguri (1 089 513)	23.0	76.2
11	Darjeeling (376 369)	2.4	97.5
12	Rangpur (2 877 847)	71.4	28.5
13	Bogra (1 260 463)	83.9	16.0
14	Pabna (1 705 072)	77.1	22.9
15	Malda (1 232 618)	56.7	43.1
16	Dhaka (4 222 143)	63.3	32.4
17	Mymensingh (6 023 758)	77.4	22.5
18	Faridpur (2 888 803)	64.8	34.8
19	Bakargunj (3 549 010)	72.3	27.0
20	Tippera (3 860 139)	77.1	22.8
21	Noakhali (2 217 402)	81.4	18.6
22	Chittagong (2 153 299)	74.6	21.6
23	Chittagong Hill Tracts (247 053)	2.9	97.0
24	Nadia (1 759 846)	61.2	38.1
25	Murshidabad (1 640 530)	56.5	43.3
26	Jessore (1 828 216)	60.3	37.8
27	Rajshahi (1 571 750)	74.6	25.2
28	Dinajpur (1 926 833)	50.2	49.7
	Bengal (total) (60 306 525)	54.7	45.2

Source: Adapted from the figures given in the Constitutional proposals of the Sapru Committee, Bombay, 1945, p. 162A.

Note
Figures in parentheses show the total population in the district.

gradually became vulnerable in the face of the Congress High Command's defiance. Hence Mountbatten, who persuaded the India Office to make an exception for Bengal and allow it to become an independent dominion,[100] staged a *volte face* once Nehru had rejected the scheme altogether. Despite being instrumental in raising the call for a third separate state, the British administration's intervention appeared insignificant in this regard, as it was certain that 'Bengal will be sacrificed at the altar of Nehru's all-India outlook'.[101] The Congress High Command's resistance gained remarkably because of the Hindu Mahasabha's involvement in the movement opposing the Bose–Suhrawardy scheme. In fact, the pro-partition campaign, spearheaded by S. P. Mookherjee, swayed the Hindus elsewhere to the extent of expressing sympathy with the Mahasabha cause. In Maharashtra in particular, Savarkar launched a fierce campaign to support 'the demand for forming a Hindu majority province in Bengal' as the only means of 'checkmating any further treacherous attempt on the part of the Moslem majority'.[102]

Moreover, the united Bengal movement had an inherent weakness because it was confined exclusively to the organised world of politics. Suhrawardy's efforts to woo the BPCC reflected the age-old practice of sorting out issues at the elite level; in the context of mass politics the elite-level machinations appeared outdated, with dangerous consequences. By ignoring the unorganised world of politics in a changed scenario, the Bengali leadership, both in the BPML and BPCC, failed to rise above the limitations of bhadralok politics. Hence, despite its apparent viability, the idea of an independent sovereign Bengal had no mass appeal among either the Bengali Muslims or the Hindus. As a matter of fact, the Muslim League demand for the partition of India on the basis of Jinnah's two nation theory left little room for a non-communal independent Bengal. In other words, in the context of the two-nation theory, the basis for a greater Bengal appeared fragile. S. P. Mookherjee was thus perhaps right that there was no logic in the move for a united Bengal, especially when the two-nation theory was referred to constantly to justify the proposed Pakistan. Thus, despite the initial euphoria generated among the elites, the scheme had little to do with the aspirations of the Bengalis as such. In the organised world of politics, however, the BPML-sponsored scheme lost momentum considerably with Sarat Bose's withdrawal following Suhrawardy's refusal to adopt the socialist pattern of society and revoke separate electorates. Herein probably lies the justification of the contention that the united Bengal scheme was a well-calculated measure to carve out a greater Pakistan, incorporating economically advanced West Bengal.

Finally, the three-month campaign championing a united Bengal is significant because it reflected the in-built tension within the BPML between the Bengali and non-Bengali leadership. To be precise, the conflict between the so-called Khwaja group, led by Nazimuddin (the Dhaka Nawab), and the Suhrawady–Hashim combination surfaced over the campaign for a greater Bengal. Espousing the cause of the Urdu-speaking political and business interests, the Nazimuddin faction had always tried to curry favour with the Muslim League High Command, particularly Jinnah. The support the Khwaja group extended to the united Bengal movement was largely attributed to the possibility of a greater Pakistan, which was likely, given the demographic preponderance of the Muslims in Bengal. The roots of sub-nationalism can also be traced in this fight between the

Bengali and non-Bengali leadership in the BPML. The idea of an independent greater Bengal, floated by Suhrawardy, can be said to have projected the Bengali Muslims' desire to assert their regional identity, which manifested itself in the 1951 Language Movement in East Pakistan and finally in the creation of Bangladesh in 1971.[103]

Notes

1 *The Statesman*, Calcutta, 28 April 1947, p. 2; *The Star of India*, Calcutta, 28 April 1947, p. 2.
2 India Office Records, London (IOR hereafter), L/PJ/5/154, Fortnightly Reports (FR hereafter), first half of March 1947, Burrows to Wavel, 19 March 1947.
3 Mansergh *et al.*, Vol. IX, 1980: 774.
4 National Archives of Pakistan, Karachi (NAP hereafter), *Quad-i-Azam Papers*, (hereafter *QAP*), File No. 458, p. 65, which contains Suhrawardy's Delhi statement of 27 April.
5 Ibid., Suhrawardy to Liaquat Ali Khan, 8 May 1947.
6 Ibid., Suhrawardy's 27 April statement.
7 *The Star of India*, 30 April 1947; Hashim 1974: 139–43.
8 Saul 1966, quoted in Rajat K. Ray, 'Social Unrest and Political Conflict in Bengal', unpublished PhD dissertation, University of Cambridge, 1972, p. 11.
9 Birla 1964: 4.
10 Nehru Memorial Museum and Library (NMML), Padamkant Malaviya (Oral Transcript), p. 110.
11 West Bengal State Archives, Calcutta (WBSA hereafter), Government of Bengal Commerce Department Proceedings, B 155–61, File No. 3C2, February 1933.
12 Bangladesh Secretariat Record Room, Dhaka (BSRR hereafter), B Proceedings (Home) No. 67, Bundle No. 8 (1936, File No. 6C/11/36), letter from Secretary, Muslim Chamber of Commerce to the India Delimitation Committee, 5 August 1935.
13 BSSR, B Proceedings (Home), No. 72, Bundle No. 15, 1938, File No. 8A/13/37, letter from M. N. Islam, Secretary, Muslim Chamber of Commerce, Chittagong to the Secretary (Home), Government of Bengal, 10 June 1937.
14 Ibid., letter of J. D. V. Hodge, Commissioner, Chittagong Division to the Secretary (Home) Government of Bengal, 27 October 1937.
15 Ibid., a note by the Home-Poll department, Government of West Bengal (signature illegible), 19 February 1938.
16 Centre of South Asian Studies, Cambridge (CSASC), Benthall Papers, minutes of the meeting of European Association (Bengal Provincial Committee) between 20 July 1933 and 28 January 1935.
17 Ibid.
18 NMML, S. P. Mookherjee Papers, Subject File No. 139, a copy of the letter from G. D. Birla to Jawaharlal Nehru, 7 May 1947.
19 Given the Congress' explicit commitment to national democratic ideology, the national bourgeoisie had a free hand. For details, see Chakrabarty 1990: Ch. IV.
20 NAP, QAP, M. A. H. Ispahani to Jinnah, 17 April 1947. Jinnah, in his reply to Ispahani, appreciated the argument for a united Bengal. See Jinnah to Ispahani, 22 July 1947.

21 CSASC, Benthall Papers, minutes of the meeting of the European Association (Bengal Provincial Committee), 20 July 1933–28 January 1935.
22 Chakrabarty 1990: Ch. II.
23 The anxiety about losing Calcutta to India will be discussed later.
24 Harun-or-Rashid, 'The Bengal Provincial Muslim League, 1906–47', unpublished PhD dissertation, University of London, 1983, Chapters II and V.
25 *Millat*, 6 May 1947. For the 1940 Lahore resolution, see The Constitutional Proposals of the Sapru Committee, Bombay, 1945.
26 *The Star of India*, 7 May 1947.
27 *Millat*, 16 May 1947; *The Star of India*, 18 May 1947. In fact, the apprehension regarding the imposition of Urdu on the Bengalis was not unfounded because while presiding over the Urdu Conference, held at the behest of the Majlis Ittehadul Muslimeen at Hyderabad on 18 May 1947, Khaliquazzaman announced that Urdu would be the national language of Pakistan (*The Star of India*, 19 May 1947).
28 Mansergh *et al.*, Vol. X, 1981: 851, Jinnah's note containing his views on the draft announcement, 17 May 1947. His argument supporting the move will be discussed later.
29 *The Star of India*, 19 May 1947; *Amrita Bazar Patrika*, 19 May 1947; Hashim 1974: 143.
30 *Azad*, 3 April 1947; *Millat*, 11 April 1947.
31 NAP, QAP, File No. 458, Suhrawardy to Jinnah, 20 February 1947, pp. 54–6.
32 Ibid., Jinnah to Suhrawardy, 3 April 1947.
33 *Azad*, 3 April 1947; *Millat*, 11 April 1947. Editorials in these newspapers had, on several occasions, decried the statements issued by the Khwaja group championing Urdu and not the language of the majority (i.e. Bengali) as the probable national language in Pakistan.
34 IOR, L/PJ/5/154, Burrows to Mountbatten, 11 April 1947.
35 Ibid. The Bengal Governor, Burrows, expressed uncertainty regarding the implementation of such a Bill without reformulating any clear policy. The Bill, as Burrows concluded, was therefore merely an exercise on paper and not a serious design to improve the conditions of the sharecroppers.
36 IOR, QAP (microfilm, File No. 27–566) The memorandum of 11 April 1947, signed by six members of the BPML parliamentary party, was one of the many documents showing a clear polarisation between Hashim-Suhrawardy and Khwaja groups. In fact, the arguments, put forward by the signatories drew upon the age-old debate concerning the Bengali and non-Bengali schism, which had constantly been highlighted to undermine the indigenous leadership since the rise of Fazlul Haq in the mid-1930s.
37 Ibid., Jinnah to Habibullah Bahar, acting Secretary, BPML, 18 April 1947. Jinnah probably thought that it was not the right moment to encourage factional squabbles, and hence he urged them to 'remain united at this critical juncture of our history'.
38 Mansergh *et al.*, Vol. X, 1981: 448–9.
39 Mansergh *et al.*, Vol. X, 1981: 451–4. The interview between Jinnah and Mountbatten, 26 April 1947.
40 *Dawn*, 1 May 1947, reproduced in Mansergh *et al.*, Vol. X, 1981: 543.
41 Ibid.
42 Mansergh *et al.*, Vol. X, 1981: 852, Jinnah's views on the draft announcement, 17 May 1947.
43 Ibid, the interview between Jinnah and Mountbatten, 8 May 1947.
44 Ibid.

45 Ibid.
46 Ibid., Jinnah's views on the Draft Announcement, 17 May 1947.
47 IOR, L/PJ/10/79, Mountbatten to Burrows, 27 May 1947.
48 IOR, QAP (microfilm), File No. 27-566, Suhrawardy to Liaquat Ali Khan, 8 May 1947, quoted in Ikramullah 1991: 62. Jinnah was reported to have referred to this letter in his correspondence with Habibullah Bahar, the acting Secretary, BPML, 17 May 1947.
49 Mansergh *et al.*, Vol. X, 1981: 261–64, ninth miscellaneous meeting.
50 Jinnah's views on the Draft Announcement, 17 May 1947, Mansergh *et al.*, Vol. X, 1981: 852–3.
51 QAP, File No. 8/3-35, Jinnah to S. M. Usman of the Calcutta District Muslim League, 19 May 1947.
52 Mansergh *et al.*, Vol. X, 1981: 852–3.
53 Mansergh *et al.*, Vol. X, 1981: 896–901, minutes of India Meeting, 19 May 1947.
54 IOR, L/I/I/1777, a report on the 1946 killings: 5000 dead and 15 000 injured.
55 Mansergh *et al.*, Vol. X 1981: 159, the interview between Jinnah and Mountbatten, 8 April 1947.
56 *The Statesman*, Calcutta, 23 April 1947.
57 *The Statesman*, Calcutta, 2 May 1947.
58 *The Statesman*, Calcutta, 1 May 1947.
59 IOR, L/PJ/5/154. Tgm., signed by Sisir Kumar Mitra on behalf of others to the Secretary of State, London, 7 May 1947.
60 Mansergh *et al.*, Vol. X, 1981: 850, Mountbatten to Burrows, 16 May 1947.
61 Nurul Amin (Convenor), Habibullah Bahar, Hamidul Haq Chowdhury and Yusuf Ali Chowdhury were absent. Suhrawardy and Adul Hashim were present (Hashim 1974: 153–4).
62 *The Statesman*, Calcutta, 25 May 1947.
63 Bose 1970: 5–6.
64 Sarat Chandra Bose's press interview on 23 May 1947 (*The Statesman*, Calcutta, 24 May 1947).
65 *The Statesman*, Calcutta, 1 June 1947.
66 Mansergh *et al.*, Vol. X, 1981: 1040, Jawaharlal Nehru's interview on 28 May 1947.
67 NMML, AICC CL 14B/1946–47. On 13 May 1947, Ashrafuddin Ahmad Chowdhury, in his letter to J. B. Kripalani, referred to these pamphlets which were being circulated in east Bengal. While replying on 17 May 1947, Patel, mentioning the contents of the above letter, assured him of all help 'to deal with the situation effectively and benefittingly [sic]' (see Das 1972: 41).
68 Das 1972: 44, Patel to Sarat Chandra Bose, 22 May 1947.
69 Das 1972: 45–6, Sarat Chandra Bose to Vallabhbhai Patel, 27 May 1947.
70 Das 1972: 47, Patel to K. S. Roy, 21 May 1947.
71 Das 1972: 39–40, Patel to K. C. Neogi, 18 May 1947.
72 In fact, Sarat Chandra Bose, at a press conference on 23 May 1947, conveyed the impression that 'there is no difference as far as fundamentals are concerned between me and those with whom I had discussion on the subject' (*The Statesman*, Calcutta, 24 May 1947).
73 Mansergh *et al.*, Vol. X, 1981: 830, Suhrawardy to E. Mieville, Principal Secretary to the Viceroy, 15 May 1947.
74 IOR, QAP (microfilm) File No. 27–566, Suhrawardy to Liaquat Ali Khan, 21 May 1947.
75 Ibid., Habibullah Bahar to Jinnah, 27 May 1947.

THE UNITED BENGAL SCHEME

76 Mansergh *et al.*, Vol. X, 1981: 830, Suhrawardy to E. Mieville, Principal Secretary to the Viceroy, 15 May 1947.
77 The role of the Hindu Mahasabha will be discussed below.
78 NMML, S. P. Mookherjee Papers, Subject File No. 139, Mookherjee to Mountbatten, 2 May 1947.
79 Ibid., S. P. Mookherjee to Vallabhbhai Patel, 7 May 1947.
80 Ibid., S. P. Mookherjee to Mountbatten, 2 May 1947.
81 Ibid.
82 Ibid.
83 IOR, R/3/2/59A, Fortnightly Reports, first half of May, 1947.
84 Ibid., The Hindu Mahasabha memorandum to Mountbatten, 2 May 1947.
85 Both AICC and Hindu Mahasabha offices were inundated with memoranda urging the leaders to press for partition. See NMML, AICC CL8/1946 and CL/14B/1946–47, and also S. P. Mookherjee Papers, Subject File No. 141.
86 NMML, AICC CL/14B/1946–47, resolution of the Noakhali District Congress Committee, 19 April 1947.
87 NMML, AICC CL14B/1946–47, resolution of the North Calcutta District Congress Committee, 15 May 1947.
88 NMML, S. P. Mookherjee Papers, Subject File No. 141, Calcutta University Students' memorandum, submitted to J. B. Kripalani, President, Indian National Congress, 21 April 1947.
89 NMML, AICC CL 14B/1946–47, resolution of the Jessor District Congress Bengal Partition Conference, 18 May 1947.
90 Ibid.
91 Ibid.
92 *Amrita Bazar Patrika*, 23 April 1947.
93 NAP, QAP, Memoirs of H. S. Suhrawardy (unpublished), p. 22.
94 Ibid. Suhrawardy quotes his letter of 15 May 1947, addressed to E. Mieville. See Mansergh *et al.*, Vol. X, 1981: 831. Suhrawardy to E. Mieville, 15 May 1947.
95 IOR, L/PJ/5/154, Burrows to Viceroy, 18 April 1947; Begam Shaista Suhrawardy Ikramullah also referred to this letter in her biography of H. S. Suhrawardy Ikramullah 1991: 64.
96 *The Statesman*, Calcutta, 21 June 1947; *Amrita Bazar Patrika*, 21 and 22 June 1947.
97 NMML, AICC CL 21/1946, letter, written by Ashrafuddin Ahmad Chowdhury on behalf of the Muslim Congress leaders to J. B. Kripalani, the Congress President, 10 August 1947.
98 Jawaharlal Nehru, while reminiscing argued that 'we consented to [partition] because we thought thereby we are purchasing peace and goodwill though at a high price'. See his press statement of 18 July 1947, *The Statesman*, Calcutta, 19 July 1947.
99 NMML, Surendra Mohan Ghosh (Oral Transcript), p. 38.
100 IOR, Mss. Eur. E 341/46, Minutes of Viceroy's ninth miscellaneous meeting, 1 May 1947.
101 Mansergh and Moon 1981: 1025, Burrows to Viceroy, 28 May 1947.
102 NMML, S. P. Mookherjee Papers, Subject File No. 141, Tgm., from V. D. Savarkar to S. P. Mookherjee, no date.
103 Badruddin Omar has spelt out the argument in detail (Omar 1988: 60–4).

5

REDEFINING BORDERS

The Boundary Commission and the partition of Bengal

At the end of the Second World War (1939–45), the British politicians realised that the colonial rule in India could no longer be sustained. The Indian nationalists were dead against its continuation, and international opinion was also in favour of decolonisation. The perspective in which the Indian question had so far been articulated had thus radically changed. True to its pledge, the newly elected Labour Government also responded to the situation in a very different way. Illustrative of their commitment is the announcement on 20 February 1947, where Attlee, the British Premier, declared that 'His Majesty's Government wish to make it clear that it is their definite intention to take necessary steps to effect the transference of power to responsible Indian hands by a date not later than June, 1948'.[1] Accordingly, Mountabatten, the last Viceroy, was vested with all powers to devise an appropriate scheme to settle the Indian question. It was a difficult task. Nonetheless, the Viceroy convinced both the Muslim League and the Congress leadership to agree to the partition of Bengal and Punjab, and also assured completion of the process by August 1947 instead of June 1948, as decided earlier.[2] It was against this background that Mountbatten prepared a plan which 'was evolved at every stage by a process of open diplomacy with leaders'.[3] Harping on the commitment of the Attlee Government to withdraw from the subcontinent, the June plan, as it came to be known, elaborated the process as follows:

> [F]or the immediate purpose of deciding on the issue of Partition, the members of the Legislative Assemblies of Bengal and Punjab will sit in two parts according to Muslim majority districts and non-Muslim majority districts. This is the only preliminary step of a purely temporary nature as it is evident that for the purposes of or final partition of these provinces a detailed investigation of boundary questions will be needed; and as soon as a decision involving partition has been taken for either province, a boundary commission will be set up by the Governor-General. The members and terms of reference of which will be settled in consultation

with those concerned. It will be instructed to demarcate the boundaries of the two parts of the Punjab on the basis of ascertaining the contiguous majority areas of Muslims and non-Muslims. It will also be instructed to take into account other factors. Similar instructions will be given to the Bengal Boundary Commission. Until the report of the Boundary Commission has been put into effect, the provisional boundaries indicated in the Appendix will be used.[4]

Thus the plan made provision for the constitution of two Boundary Commissions – one for the Punjab and the other for Bengal and if necessary for Assam. In case of the award not being implemented before the transfer of power to the government of Pakistan in August 1947, the plan provided for 'the notional partition' of the provinces of Bengal and the Punjab purely on the basis of demographic composition of the provinces. It further stressed that the Commissions 'shall under no circumstances be conditioned by the provisional boundaries and instead look into the matter afresh'.[5]

The 3 June plan appeared to have guided the entire process of what finally culminated in the division of Bengal and Punjab. According to Mountbatten's statement, the provincial Legislative Assemblies of Bengal and Punjab would 'meet in two parts, one representing the Muslim-majority districts and the other the rest of the Province' to decide 'whether or not the Province should be partitioned'.[6] Unlike Punjab, where the Legislative Assembly met amidst demonstrations and communal disorders,[7] the voting in Bengal passed off in a comparatively peaceful atmosphere. First there was a joint meeting of the members from both the Muslim and Hindu majority districts, presided over by the Speaker of the House, Nurul Amin, in which a majority of 126 members endorsed the demand for a new and separate Pakistan constituent assembly while 90 members voted for participating in the existing constituent assembly that was elected in 1946. At the second stage, members representing Hindu and Muslim majority districts met separately. In a meeting chaired by the Maharaja of Burdwan, members from the Hindu-majority districts decided in favour of partition by 58 to 21 votes, while Members from the Muslim-majority districts, sitting separately, opposed partition by 106 to 35 votes.[8] However, when the results of the members from the Hindu-majority districts were made known to them, they decided by 107 to 34 votes that 'district with a clear Muslim-majority should join the proposed Pakistan constituent assembly'.[9]

The composition of the Boundary Commissions

The task before the Commissions was probably most arduous since both the Congress and the League demanded that the demarcation of boundaries should be performed following the well-defined formula. In order to make the Commissions truly representative of both the major players, the terms of reference clearly stated that 'each Boundary Commission shall consist of an equal number of representatives of the Congress and the Muslim League and one or more outsiders as impartial members'.[10] Given the obvious conflict between the claims of the League and the Congress, the role of the outside members was crucial. Under the changed circumstances, it was not possible for the Viceroy to impose a member of his choice unless he or she was acceptable to those involved in the process. Mountabatten therefore decided to consult both the Congress and the League to 'try to marry their ideas'.[11]

As regards the composition of the Commissions, M. A. Jinnah was consulted first and he was in favour of having three members of the Judicial Committee of the Privy Council to be appointed to each Commission as impartial members. He was, however, persuaded by the Viceroy to drop the idea, since such elderly persons would suffer miserably in the scorching Indian summer.[12] Later, the League insisted on having three non-Indian impartial members with experience of this work – perhaps from America, a France and a Britain to form each Commission at the behest of the United Nations – and also argued for the appointment of the assessors who would most effectively represent the case of the parties involved in this process.[13] While appreciating the suggestion as 'ideally the best', Mountbatten declined to accept as it was not feasible given the agreed date of the transfer of power, which was just 'a little more than two months' away. It was extremely important that the Commissions should submit their reports for implementation 'well before 15 August, 1947'.[14]

The formation of the Bengal Boundary Commission

In an official announcement on 30 June 1947 the Governor-General declared the composition of the two Boundary Commissions, one for Bengal and the other for the Punjab. The Bengal Boundary Commission was also entrusted with the task of drawing a boundary between east Bengal and Assam.[15] Cyril Radcliffe[16] was appointed Chairman of both the Boundary Commissions, to decide the frontiers in just seven weeks. Neither an officer of the Indian administration nor a person with prior experience in adjudicating disputes of this type, Radcliffe was an unknown entity, whose credentials as an eminent British jurist were 'invoked to compensate for his lack of knowledge and experience of the subcontinent'.[17] On his arrival in Delhi on 8 July 1947, he finalised the terms of reference for the task in consultation with Mountbatten and Claude Auchinleck (the Commander-in-Chief), the Congress and the Muslim League leaders. In a meeting held on 10 July, it was agreed that the final report was to be submitted at the latest by 15 August – less than a month after Radcliffe assumed responsibility. In response to a discussion concerning the importance of 'natural features' in the demarcation of boundaries, Radcliffe pointed out that it would be wrong to 'draw the boundaries on the basis of natural features [since] rivers which may appear to form suitable natural boundaries, frequently change their courses and so will not provide fixed boundaries'.[18] It was thus decided that no directive in addition to the terms of reference should be given to the Commission that would be supreme in interpreting the terms of reference.[19] Although the Commission had members to help the Chairman, it was virtually Radcliffe who dictated the terms of reference and decisions were taken accordingly. In fact Radcliffe, in his discussion with those involved in the Punjab Boundary Commission described 'the awards as the recommendations of the Chairman of the Commission, which would finally be sent to the Viceroy'.[20] This may have alienated Din Mohammad and M. Munir, members of the Commission who resigned because they felt 'humiliated' by being marginalised in the preparation of the final report that was to 'shape the future of two sovereign nations'.[21]

Proceedings of the Bengal Boundary Commission

The task before the Commission was 'to demarcate the boundaries of the two parts [of the province] on the basis of ascertaining contiguous majority areas of Muslims and non-Muslims' while taking into account 'other factors'.[22] As Table 5.1 shows, it was not difficult for the Commission to identify districts with a clear majority of either Hindus or Muslims.

In Bengal, as the 1941 census demonstrates, there were only two groups of districts which were not a cause of anxiety to the Commission. These were the indisputably non-Muslim-majority areas of Midnapur, Bankura, Hooghly, Howrah and Burdwan, and the Muslim-majority areas of Chittagong, Noakhali, Tippera, Dhaka, Mymensingh, Pabna and Bogra. Except for these, all the other areas, including Calcutta, were subject to contention and rival claims.[23]

Both the Hindu and Muslim representatives, while presenting their cases before the Commission, defended their claims for territories that could not be justified on the ground of 'contiguous majority areas' by reference to ambiguously worded 'other factors'.[24] Arguments were articulated in a highly legalistic and technical way, presumably because the counsels were all trained lawyers. Furthermore, the fact that all the commissioners were judges and the Chairman was a lawyer led to the widespread impression that the Award and the cases on which it was based were 'the product of legal expertise, resting on judicial (rather than political) rationality'.[25]

The Bengal Boundary Commission held its first meeting on 16 July 1947, at the Belvedere Palace, Calcutta. In order to complete the task within the stipulated dateline, the first step the Commission undertook

Table 5.1 Breakdown of population according to the Census of India, 1941

Division/district (total population)	Muslims (%)	Non-Muslims (%)
Burdwan division (10 287 369)	13.8	86.2
Burdwan (1 890 732)	18.4	81.6
Birbhum (1 048 317)	27.4	72.6
Bankura (1 289 640)	3.3	96.7
Midnapore (3 190 647)	7.8	92.2
Hooghly (1 377 729)	15.1	84.9
Howrah (1 490 304)	19.1	79.9
Presidency division (12 817 087)	44.5	55.5
24 Parganas (3 536 386)	32.4	67.6
Calcutta (2 108 891)	26.5	73.6
Nadia (1 759.846)	61.2	38.8
Murshidabad (1 640 530)	56.5	43.5
Jessore (1 828 216)	62.3	37.7
Khulna (1 943 218)	49.3	50.7
Rajshahi division (12 040 465)	62.5	37.5
Rajshahi (1 571 750)	74.6	25.4
Dinajpur (1 926 833)	50.2	49.8
Jalpaiguri (1 089 513)	23.8	76.2
Darjeeling (376 369)	2.5	97.5
Rangpur (2 877 847)	73.4	26.6
Bogra (1 260 563)	83.9	16.1
Pabna (1 705 072)	77.1	22.9
Malda (1 232 618)	56.7	43.3
Dacca division (16 683 714)	71.5	28.5
Dacca (4 222 143)	65.3	34.7
Mymensingh (6 023 758)	77.4	22.6
Faridpur (2 888 803)	64.8	35.2
Bakarganj (3 549 010)	72.3	27.0
Chittagong division (8 477 890)	75.3	24.7
Tippera (3 860 139)	77.1	22.9
Noakhali (2 217 402)	81.4	18.6
Chittagong (2 153 299)	76.6	23.4
Chittagong Hill Tracts (247 053)	2.9	97.1
Total: 60 306 525	54.7	45.3

Source: Census of India, Vol. IV, Bengal (Tables), pp. 2–3, 37–40.

Note
Figures in parenthesis show the total population in the division and the districts.

was to invite memorandum and representations from the leading parties stating their views on the demarcation of boundaries by 15 July. The Commission also held public sittings for a week between 16 and 24 July in which arguments were made to defend the claims of the key players, the Congress and the League. With regards to the district of Sylhet, where the referendum was scheduled to be held on 6–7 July 1947,[26] and adjoining districts in Assam, the Commission had open deliberations in Calcutta on 4–6 August in which the representatives of the major political parties defended the respective claims on Sylhet despite a clear verdict for joining east Bengal (see Table 5.2). Although the result of the referendum was unambiguous, the Commission was, at the outset, reluctant to recognise the outcome, presumably because of a large number of representations from various local Congress Committees alleging that 'the referendum was manipulated by the League activists'.[27]

Arguments of the Congress

As a constituent of the Coordination Committee that was formed to argue on behalf of the non-Muslims, the Congress played a crucial role. In addition to the Congress, the Hindu Mahasabha, the Indian Association and the New Bengal Association constituted the Coordination Committee. Initially an attempt was made to prepare a common memorandum for the Commission, which received a severe jolt because groups other than Congress insisted on demanding roughly 57 per cent of the total area of Bengal for only 46 per cent of the population.[28] Despite dissent, the Congress failed to change the formula since it was, with only two members, in a minority in the twelve-member Coordination Committee. Hence, the Congress decided to represent its viewpoints separately. Its representative, Atul Gupta, was convinced that to argue for the maximum area for less than half of Bengal's population would be suicidal since 'no one seriously thinks that it will be accepted by the Commission and it is, therefore, a bad legal strategy to argue a case that can so easily be shot down'.[29] Thus he was in favour of presenting 'a reasonable case' to gain as much as possible for west Bengal. None of the constituents agreed with Gupta's argument. As a compromise formula, Gupta put forward two different schemes. First,

Table 5.2 Voting pattern in referendum held on 6–7 July 1947

Name of subdivision	Total Muslim electorate	Total general electorate	Votes cast for east Bengal	Votes cast for Assam
Sadar	92268	48863	68381	38871
Karimganj	54022	46221	41262	40536
Habiganj	75274	60252	54543	36952
South Sylhet	38297	41427	31718	33471
Sunamganj	51846	39045	43715	34211
Total	311709	235808	239619	184041

Source: IOR, R/3/1/158, File No 1446/20/GG/143 – Referendum in Sylhet, Telegram from the Governor of Assam to the Viceroy, 12 July 1947.

the Congress Scheme – demanding a good number of Muslim-majority thanas on the basis of 'the other factors' – was not accepted as it fell considerably short of the claim already made. The other scheme, known as the Congress Plan, was drawn on the basis of 'contiguous majorities'. Neither of the schemes was satisfactory to the members who agreed to sever links with the Congress, which was not strong enough to press for maximum benefits due 'to internecine feud'.[30] Gupta also resigned from the Committee but agreed to act on behalf of only the Congress when requested by the J. B. Kripalani, the Congress President.[31] Thus the Commission finally received two memoranda – one from the Congress, which was prepared by Gupta, and another to which the Hindu Mahasabha, Indian Association and New Bengal Association had contributed.

Although the Bengal Congress was a divided house given the articulation of the united Bengal scheme, Atul Chandra Gupta sought to present the arguments on behalf of the Congress before the Commission as firmly as possible. Apart from the Burdwan division, the Congress insisted on including the whole of Presidency division (except small areas of Nadia, Jessore and Khulna districts), six districts[32] in the Rajshahi division and two districts (Mymensingh and Faridpur[33]) in the Dacca division. It also insisted on the inclusion of areas like Gournadi, Najipur, Sarupkati and Jhalakati – police stations in the district of Bakerganj – since they were contiguous to Hindu majority areas. Following the same logic, Gupta also put his claim for the subdivision of Gopalganj and the police station of Rajair (of the Madaripur subdivision). Since these areas were largely Hindu-dominated, the Congress defence appears to be consistent except in regard to Najipur, where the non-Muslims constituted a minority. What is striking, however, is that the Congress seems to have been swayed by the so-called 'natural factors' in excluding areas from west Bengal. For instance, Nadia lost five police stations of the Kusthia subdivision, presumably because the river Gorai set a natural boundary between east and west Bengal. Following the same criterion, the Congress agreed to part with four police stations of Jessore and Khulna.[34] As regards Jalpaiguri and Darjeeling, the Congress drew upon the demographic composition to defend their inclusion in West Bengal. The Congress also laid claim on two police stations of the Rangpur district, namely. Dimla and Hathibandha, because of their close proximity to Hindu-majority areas. In view of Muslim preponderance, eight police stations in the Malda and Dinajpur districts were identified as 'naturally belonging to east Bengal'.[35]

Justifying the inclusion of Calcutta in west Bengal in view of its Hindu majority, the Congress memorandum challenged the authenticity of the 1941 Census figures for Calcutta and its vicinity. Furthermore, a movement was organised at the behest of the New Bengal Association to demand that property consideration should also be taken into account while drawing the boundary. The movement never gained momentum in the province, presumably because the arguments endorsing the demand were vehemently opposed even by some of the Association members, who considered the entire exercise undertaken by the Boundary Commission to be 'a sinister design of destroying the Bengalees as a race'.[36] Since non-Muslims were preponderant in Howrah and 24 Parganas they should, argued Gupta, 'automatically come to West Bengal'.[37] though the Muslim leadership attributed this to 'the Congress design of control over heavy-waters, safety and security [and also to] ensure "a green belt" for the supply of food and other requirements of Calcutta'.[38] The Congress memorandum demanded for the inclusion in west Bengal of an area of 40 137 square miles with a total population of 28 032 000 – which constituted 45 per cent of the total population of Bengal in 1947.[39]

Arguments of the League

Unlike the Congress, which presented three separate memoranda to the Commission, the Muslim League, though divided between two factions led by Shaheed Suhrawardy and Khwaja Nazimuddin, presented only one memorandum since the former, because of his involvement in the United Bengal Movement, did not take interest in the activities of the Commission. Corroborating the difficulty, the League counsel, Hamidul Haq Chowdhury, thus recalls, 'I did not receive any assistance from Suhrawardy.... [A]s a result, during the Boundary Commission, I was left entirely to my own resource[s] without any assistance or help from the Suhrawardy group'.[40] Supporting the creation of a single Pakistan, Nazimuddin, at the outset, had also not shown any interest in the division of Bengal.[41] As soon as Nazimuddin realised that partition was inevitable he, as the leader of the faction with close ties with Jinnah and the All India Muslim League, organised several meetings in Calcutta in which the demand for the inclusion of Calcutta in the proposed Pakistan was strongly made.[42] However, the movement for 'keeping Calcutta in Pakistan' never gained momentum, probably because the League leadership was divided on this issue. One of the factors that weakened the campaign even before it took off was the declaration of Dhaka as the capital of east Pakistan on 10 June 1947 by the Bengal Premier, H. S. Suhrawardy. What probably decided the fate of Calcutta was the assurance of Rs. 330 million as compensation to east Pakistan if the League withdrew its claim over Calcutta.[43] The Nazimuddin-led Muslim League ministry that assumed power on 5 August 1947 expressed willingness to accept the amount to transform Dhaka into 'one of the best capitals in the world'. Thus the claim for Calcutta was immediately withdrawn by underlining that 'whatever is said, Calcutta is essentially a Hindu-majority area and Muslims are undoubtedly a minority. An area where Hindus constituted a majority cannot be forced to remain in a state where Muslims are demographically preponderant. This is against democracy'.[44] The assurance of Rs. 330 million turned out to be a hoax, argued Abul Mansur Ahmad, because in the final settlement recommended by the Partition Council – chaired by Mountbatten, where Vallavbhai Patel and H. M. Patel represented the Congress and Liaquat Ali Khan and Chaudhuri Mohmmad Ali represented the League – Calcutta was exchanged for Lahore and compensation was thus ruled out.[45]

Like the Congress, the Muslim League drew upon three criteria – contiguity of areas, demographic composition and unity of economic life – to make a case for a separate Muslim state. The proposed province was to include the whole of the Chittagong, Dhaka and Rajshahi divisions, and almost the entire Presidency division. The League counsel, Hamidul Haq Choudhury, did not stake a claim even for single police station in the Burdwan division, probably because of its demographic profile which, as is evident in Table 5.1, was heavily tilted in favour of the non-Muslims. Moreover, the task of the Commission was made easier by the presence of the River Hooghly (that later became the Bhagirathi and Brahmani) drawing a natural boundary between non-Muslim and Muslim majority areas. Choudhury also emphatically argued for the inclusion of Calcutta in east Bengal since it flourished as an economic centre largely due to jute, which was grown in east Bengal. Without jute, argued Choudhury, 'Calcutta will invariably decline in importance'.[46] Furthermore, he attributed the Hindu majority of the city to migrant labourers from the neighboring provinces, and it would therefore be wrong, Choudhury suggested, to characterise Calcutta on the basis of its existing population.[47] The League insisted that east Bengal must be given a share of provincial revenue proportionate to its share of Bengal's population, and this could only be achieved if Calcutta went to the east. While elaborating his argument, the League counsel thus underlined, '[t]he total revenue of Bengal is about forty crores [of rupees] of which thirteen crores are ... contributed by Calcutta alone. If Calcutta goes to West Bengal, the result will be that West Bengal with about one-third of the total population of the Province will appropriate 66.9% of the revenue, while East Bengal with two-thirds of the population will have at its disposal only 33% of the revenue'.[48] The claim for Calcutta was also justified by reference to the support of the Scheduled Caste population of the city. As Jogen Mondal, the Scheduled Caste leader, was the League's nominee to the Viceroy's Executive Council and was also a member of the League bloc in the Interim Cabinet, the League was certain to get Scheduled Caste support in defence of its demand.

The League also emphasised that the Jalpaiguri, Darjeeling and Chittagong Hill Tracts, identified as non-Muslim majority areas, were actually mere pockets in the Muslim contiguous majority areas 'having no contiguity to non-Muslim areas'.[49] Choudhury also put forward economic reasons for the inclusion of these three districts in Pakistan. For instance, as Teesta and Karnaphuli (two major rivers) were flowing through these districts, east Pakistan needed them to develop hydroelectricity for her industries; the hills of Jalpaiguri and Darjeeling were the only source of ballast supply for the maintenance of railroads in east Pakistan; and Jalpaiguri's forest was the only source of timber for this new state, which was likely to suffer if these districts were 'snatched away'.

The other powerful group was the Hindu Mahasabha, which also presented a memorandum to the Commission defending the inclusion of Calcutta in west Bengal. Their arguments were of two kinds: first, since Calcutta was 'a predominantly Hindu city',[50] the Mahasabha counsel argued, its inclusion in west Bengal was most logical; secondly, for the growth of the city, the role of the non-Muslims was formidable. For instance, while the Muslim share was merely 6.2 per cent non-Muslims contributed about 93.8 per cent of the total tax collected from the city. The majority of the industries in and around the city were also owned by the non-Muslim population. As regards the growth and development of Calcutta university, the contribution of the non-Muslim population was immense since almost 99 per cent of the endowments were made by them. The Mahasabha counsel also urged the Commission to take into account the property consideration, since the majority of property owners in Bengal were Hindus.[51]

The Radcliffe Award

Drawing a satisfactory boundary was simply impossible in view of the conflicting demands, well-defended by the representatives of the Muslims and Hindus. The task was further complicated since there was hardly a natural boundary between what later came to be known as east Pakistan and west Bengal. According to the terms of reference, the primary task before the Commission was the development of a balanced economic unit based on easy rail and road communications across the length and breadth of the new province. This, however, did not correspond with the demographic criterion, namely division of the province in terms of the demographic strength of Hindus and Muslims. In other words, areas in which Hindus were a majority naturally belonged to India, while Muslim-preponderant areas would automatically come to east Pakistan. The task before Cyril Radcliffe was not an easy one. Furthermore, he was never actually present when arguments were presented by the counsels, but made his recommendation on the basis of his 'careful study' of the memorandum and other relevant documents submitted to the Commission. After long discussions with the members of the Commission, who were also divided among themselves, Radcliffe was convinced that it would be difficult, if not impossible, to draw a satisfactory boundary between these two provinces. Hence, 'in the absence of reconciliation on all main questions affecting the drawing of the boundary itself', wrote the Chairman, he had no alternative but 'to proceed to give [his] own decision'[52] on the basis of what he deciphered from the claims and counterclaims of those who participated in the proceedings. Thus what came to be known as the Radcliffe Award was essentially the recommendation of the Chairman of the Boundary Commissions, Cyril Radcliffe, who drew up the boundary, single handed, against the background of claims and counterclaims.[53] In drawing the boundary, the primary consideration that ran through the exercise was 'to eliminate any avoidable cutting of railway communications and of river systems, which are of importance to the life of the province [though the Chairman was aware that] it is quite impossible to draw a boundary line under [the] terms of reference without causing some interruption of this sort'. Radcliffe, however, expressed hope that 'arrangement can be made and maintained between the two States that will minimize the consequences of this interruption as far as possible'.[54]

The Awards of the Commissions were due to be published well before 15 August so as to allow time for administrative and security arrangements to be made on both sides of the newly created provinces. The announcement was delayed because both Patel and Nehru expressed dissatisfaction over the inclusion of the Khulna and Chittagong Hill Tracts in east Pakistan, and also deplored the absence of any link between Darjeeling and the rest of west Bengal.[55] Neither Mountbatten nor the Chairman of the Commissions was in favour of reopening the issue, and the Award, which was ready by 13 August, was finally published on 17 August 1947. One of the reasons for the delay, as V. P. Menon (the constitutional advisor to the Governor General of India) suggested, was 'if the details of the Bengal Award were known to Nehru and Patel before 15 August, they might refuse to attend the meeting of the Constituent Assembly [which the Viceroy was to address on that day] or the state banquet and the evening party'. Mountbatten was reported to have instructed Menon to take all possible steps 'to deny access to the Radcliffe Report'.[56] Despite the great disadvantages of not knowing, at the creation of two sovereign states, what their precise areas would be, the publication of the Award was postponed 'to avoid turning a day of rejoicing over Indian and Pakistani freedom into one of mourning over disappointed territorial hopes'.[57]

As anticipated, the Radcliffe scheme satisfied neither the Hindus nor the Muslims. Characterising the Award as 'the latest blow' to the Muslims, Jinnah came out sharply by saying that:

> [n]o doubt we feel that the carving out of this great independent Muslim State has suffered injustice. We have been squeezed in as much as it was possible by the Radcliffe Award. It is an unjust, incomprehensible and even perverse award. It may be wrong, unjust and perverse; and it may not be a judicial but a political

award, but [since] we have agreed to abide by it [it is] binding on us. ... It may be our misfortune but we must bear up this one more blow with fortitude, courage and hope.[58]

Condemning the Award as 'self-contradictory, anomalous and arbitrary and as unjust to Hindus of Bengal and Punjab', the press in India was, however, hopeful that minor adjustments of boundaries would be possible by negotiation in the future.[59] Even a conservative newspaper like *The Statesman* expressed hope by stating that 'it is never too late for men of goodwill to take stock of realities ... by banishing all sense of fear and conflict [to] bring about for both countries enduring peace and progress'.[60] The Pakistani press was very critical and *The Dawn*, for instance, characterised the Award as 'a biased decision and an act of shameful partiality [through which] Pakistan was cheated'.[61] The wave of criticism and counter criticism was, however, short-lived, presumably because of the outbreak of riots and massacres in the wake of migrations – which were the outcome 'not of any particular frontier-drawing, but of partition itself and of the communal hate which had led to it'.[62]

Not only was the press critical of the Award; the Radcliffe arrangement also caused confusion and uncertainty since it was not well-publicised before it was implemented. As a result, neither the Hindus nor the Muslims had, at least at the outset, a clear idea about the newly-demarcated frontiers. They had little knowledge of how Mountbatten's Plan or the Radcliffe Award would change their destinies and tear them apart from their familiar social and cultural roots.[63] 'The English have flung away their *Raj* like a bundle of old straw', an angry peasant told the Punjab Governor, Malcolm Darling, 'and we have been chopped in pieces like butcher's meat'.[64] It was not therefore an exaggeration that the characters in Bhisham Sahni's story 'We have arrived in Amritsar'[65] did not know whether Lahore or Gurdaspur would be in India or Pakistan. The district of Malda probably presented an extreme case. For three days, between 12 and 15 August 1947, nobody knew for sure whether the district would finally be assigned to India or Pakistan. The Pakistani flag, as the district magistrate reminisced, 'fluttered over the collectorate until 14 August'. Three days later, the district, now reduced to ten pre-partition thanas, came to India.[66] Even after the formal declaration of independence in August 1947, the confusion and uncertainty regarding the boundaries continued to remain. For instance, there was a strong rumour in Nadia, even after the lapse of almost one year following the acceptance of the Award, that Nadia and Murshidabad would go to Pakistan in exchange for Khulna since non-Muslims constituted a demographic majority there.[67] There were innumerable instances where '[t]he pettiest incidents sparked-off brutal killings and the most unsubstantiated rumours cause people to flee their homes in their thousands'.[68] Realising that the Radcliffee boundary was vague in some areas, both

Nehru and Liaquat Ali Khan had signed an agreement to set up a tribunal, chaired by a Swedish judge, Algot Bagge, to resolve, once and for all, 'boundary disputes ... arising out of the interpretation of the Radcliffe Award'.[69] Despite the euphoria over its appointment,[70] the tribunal had a limited role to play because it was restricted to demarcating the boundary between Murshidabad and Rajshahi districts and to settling disputes about the course of the Mathabhanga river.[71]

Despite the vehement opposition of the League representative, Calcutta was given to west Bengal. Though Muslims were demographically preponderant in Murshidabad (see Table 5.3),[72] the district was placed under west Bengal following the logic of physical contiguity with the rest of the province. While including a part of Nadia (Table 5.4) and 24

Table 5.3 District of Murshidabad: proportions of Muslims and non-Muslims, 1941

Subdivision	Total population	Muslims (%)	Non-Muslims (%)
Sadar	499 749	60.0	40.0
Lalbagh	363 885	66.5	33.5
Jangipur	411 618	58.0	42.0
Khandi	365 278	40.5	59.5
Total	1 640 530	56.5	43.4

Source: Census of India, 1941.

Table 5.4 Demographic composition of each police station in the district of Nadia

Karimpur subdivision	Total population	Muslims (%)	Non-Muslims (%)
Karimpur	101 272	78.8	21.2
Gangani	72 405	82.2	17.8
Sadar subdivision			
Kaliganj	63 391	43.6	56.4
Nakasipara	66 827	52.1	47.9
Chapra	70 321	71.1	28.9
Nabadwip	54 208	22.3	77.7
Ranaghat subdivision			
Hansakhali	37 521	74.2	25.8
Haringhata	27 498	52.8	47.2
Ranaghat	82 073	41.9	58.1
Chakdah	63 862	40.3	59.7
Shantipur	55 036	31.7	68.3
Total	694 414	53.7	46.3

Source: Census of India, 1941.

Parganas (Table 5.5) in west Bengal where Muslims were in a majority, the Radcliffe Award sought to maintain a homogeneous land mass for the new province. Similarly, two police stations, namely, Bongaon and Gaighata of the district of Jessore (where Muslims constituted a majority), were placed within west Bengal. In north Bengal, the Malda and Dinajpur districts were almost evenly divided according to the demographic composition. While the task of dividing Dinajpur was relatively easier because of a clear-cut demographic configuration in each police station, the district of Malda posed a difficulty because only four police stations had a Muslim preponderance over non-Muslims (Table 5.6).

As the report shows, Radcliffe's primary consideration was not to

Table 5.5 Subdivisions of Barasat and Bashirhat: proportions of Muslims and non-Muslims, 1941

Barasat subdivision	Total population	Muslims (%)	Non-Muslims (%)
Habra	70718	58.5	41.5
Deganga	64700	69.8	30.2
Barasat	99064	59.9	40.1
Aamdanga	30196	57.2	42.8
Rajarhat	46583	34.8	65.2
Total	311261	57.6	42.4
Bashirhat subdivision			
Sarupnagar	57542	54.3	45.7
Baduria	83684	59.6	40.4
Bashirhat	125164	57.7	42.3
Haroa	90745	45.6	54.4
Total	357135	54.5	45.4

Source: Census of India, 1941.

Table 5.6 Demographic composition of police stations in Malda, 1941

Police station	Total population	Muslims (%)	Non-Muslims (%)
Kaliachak	194324	63.8*	36.2
English Bazar	83539	44.5	55.5
Malda	33978	34.5	65.5
Khorba	103062	59.4*	40.6
Harishchandrapur	99974	56.7*	43.3
Ratua	102985	56.8*	43.2
Bamangola	35973	42.4	57.6
Manikchak	64786	33.4	66.6
Gajole	73387	28.4	71.6
Habibpur	52307	13.2	86.6
Total	844315	49.1	50.9

disturb the communication channels, via road, railways and water, as far as practicable. This was why he recommended the transfer of almost 6000 square miles from east to west Bengal, and the districts of Murshidabad, Nadia, Jessore, Malda and Dinajpur were accordingly demarcated. The loss thus made was compensated for by assigning the sparsely populated district of Chittagong Hill Tracts, with a Buddhist majority, to east Pakistan. Similarly, to maintain the rail link in the north of the proposed province, Khulna, which had a substantial non-Muslim population, was assigned to east Pakistan.

Concluding observations

The Radcliffe Award largely conformed to the Congress scheme, as elaborated by Atul Chandra Gupta in his memorandum to the Boundary Commission, presented on behalf of the Congress.[73] Whether it was a coincidence or deliberate is difficult to ascertain, because the Chairman of the Commissions 'steadfastly refused to supplement or discuss his award' even after its publication.[74] It is also doubtful whether the Congress leadership exercised influence over the Chairman of the Commissions in view of his refusal even to discuss with Patel, who was a Partition Council member, why the publication of the Award was delayed.[75] As 'he was duty-bound to obey the specific terms of reference he had been given in demarcating the boundaries', Radcliffe felt it improper to share this information with Patel, who represented 'an interested party' in this exercise.[76] Though both the interested parties – the Congress and the Muslim League – were kept at bay, Mountbatten appeared to have asked Radcliffe to follow the terms of reference as far as 'practicable' and 'fairness of the eastern and western awards to the Muslims and non-Muslims respectively should be judged as a whole, so that disgruntlement in one area might be offset by satisfaction in another'.[77] This principle of 'balance' allowed the Chairman to redraw the boundary of the Punjab canal colonies in such a way as to sustain west Punjab, which would have lost its economic viability without those districts through which the irrigation canals passed.[78]

Amidst protests and demonstrations, the Award was made public on 17 August 1947. What led to the formation of the Boundary Commissions was the imperial initiative, articulated in the 3 June plan, that was ratified by the Legislative Assemblies of both Punjab and Bengal. For the British government, partition was probably the last resort in view of the failure of 'the major parties to cooperate in the working of the Cabinet Mission Plan of 16 May, 1946 and evolve for India a constitution acceptable to all concerned'.[79] Thus the appointment of Boundary Commissions was most logical under the circumstances. What is, however, striking is the haste with which the assigned task was completed. Arriving in India on 8 July, Cyril Radcliffe knew nothing about India other than the five perspiring weeks he spent there, trying with maps and pens to fulfil his impossible duty of devising a judicious cartography. The Commissions held their meetings over a period of eight days between 16 and 24 July without the Chairman. Though announced on 17 August 1947, the Award was ready by 13 August. Radcliffe did not visit the areas he was asked to demarcate, and nor did he undertake any effort to ascertain the viability of the proposed state of Pakistan as a socio-cultural and economic unit. The emergence of Bangladesh in 1971 confirms the apprehension that Pakistan, as it emerged in the aftermath of the partition, was not feasible. At another level, the line drawn by Radcliffe severely disrupted 'every aspect of existence for the rural community, criminalising the routine and customary transactions by which it survived'. It 'separated the peasant's homestead from the plot he had sharecropped in the last season and the peasant-proprietor from his holding'.[80] The local police stations in border districts in both east Pakistan and west Bengal were engaged, most of the time, in restraining those crossing borders illegally. There were innumerable instances of arrests and beatings by the police of *bhag-chasis* (sharecroppers) when they crossed the line to bring home their share of the crop. Thus, when a sharecropper of Kumarganj in west Dinajpur was returning from Phulbari with a maund of paddy that he earned, he was arrested by the east Pakistani militia.[81] Similarly, a Hindu zamindar of Kazipur in Nadia who, in January 1950, went to Damurhuda to realise rents from his tenants was arrested by the Pakistani border patrol and released with a warning never to return.[82]

The demarcation of a boundary is bound to be controversial, and more so because the task was undertaken by the Boundary Commissions when the schism between Hindus and Muslims was articulated not only in the public sphere but also in the social and cultural transactions in people's quotidian life that divided the Hindus and Muslims more effectively than resolutions of the League or speeches in the Congress sessions or political pacts. 'Socially', as Tamijuddin remarks, 'Muslims were in most respects untouchables to the Hindus ... and if therefore a Muslim somehow happened to enter the cook-shed of a Hindu, even if he did not touch food or utensils, all cooked food stored in the house along with the earthen pots were considered polluted and thrown away'.[83] In addition to this, the perception that because the landlords were Hindus they exploited the Muslim tenants[84] exacerbated the situation, given the composition of zamindars and cultivators in east Bengal. The socio-economic segregation of the two communities was so pronounced that they felt that they were 'two distinct communities in spite of fraternization in certain fields of activity'.[85] With the adoption of the 1932 Communal Award,[86] the Muslims realised, as Abul Mansur Ahmad, an erstwhile Congress member, noted, that 'where mere number counts, they must necessarily be a power'.[87] The Muslims began to 'feel that their language, culture and religion would be swamped,

[and] they also had the natural fears of a minority and kept demanding safeguards so as to preserve their own way of life and combat their impotence'.[88] Given the polarisation between the Hindus and Muslims at the grassroots, what the Radcliffe Award did was simply to formalise the chasm by drawing a line separating the communities as far as practicable. In a situation charged with communal tension the task of the Commissions was arduous; even more so because the time available to complete the demarcation was also limited. As shown above, Radcliffe was to submit the Award within less than a month after the first meeting on 16 July 1947. That the Award was ready on 13 August 1947[89] also underlines the haste in which the entire process was complete. No survey of the districts which were likely to be bifurcated was undertaken, and nor were those involved in the district administration consulted to ascertain the contiguity of the areas. Only the 1941 Census data[90] were taken seriously by the Commissions, to identify the essentially Hindu- and Muslim-majority districts. Bengal seems to have been divided on the basis of the claims and counter-claims of those operating within the public sphere. Drawing on probably the best available legal minds, the Award turned out to be an excellent technical document which, due to the utter negligence of the reality in Bengal, remained a bone of contention for both Bengals even in the aftermath of freedom. Radcliffe was perhaps aware of the fragile basis of the Award, saying while he was awaiting his flight for London: 'Nobody in India will love me for the Award about the Punjab and Bengal and there will be roughly 80 million people with a grievance who will begin looking for me. I do not want them to find me. I have worked and travelled and sweated – oh, I have sweated the whole time'.[91] Furthermore, although the Boundary Commissions undertook 'a surgical operation' (which Jinnah had insisted upon even before its appointment[92]) to create a separate Muslim homeland, its success was short-lived because within less than three decades Pakistan was dismembered following the emergence of Bangladesh in 1971.

Notes

1 IOR, R/3/1/157, Attlee's statement in the House of Commons, 20 February 1947. It was further underlined that 'His Majesty's Government are anxious to hand over their responsibilities to a Government which, resting on the sure foundation of the support of the people, is capable of maintaining peace and administering India with justice and efficiency. It is therefore essential that all parties should sink their differences in order that they may be ready to shoulder the great responsibilities which will be upon them next year [i.e., 1948]'.
2 In the new scheme of things, the transfer of power was to take place on 14/15 August 1947 instead of 30 June 1948. This was undoubtedly a momentous change, since it would ensure freedom for the subcontinent almost a year in advance, and the reasons are not difficult to locate in a radically different

milieu. Given the devastating impact of the 1946 Direct Action on interpersonal relationships, especially between Hindus and Muslims, the Congress leadership, particularly Patel and Nehru, came to terms with partition as the only solution. Mountbatten also had his role to play. Three important reasons appeared to have governed his insistence on an earlier date: (1) to take the credit for himself and thus expose the failure of the Cabinet Mission plan in understanding the reality in a proper perspective; (2) to earn the goodwill of the Congress leaders, particularly Nehru and Patel; and (3) because an early transfer of power would ensure India's participation in the Commonwealth, as the Congress had already committed. For details, see 1961; Campbell-Johnson 1951; Moseley 1961; Hodson 1988 (reprint of 1969 version).

3 Mountbatten made this remark in his press statement on 3 June 1947. Quoted in Hodson 1969: 204.
4 IOR, R/3/1/157, statement by His Majesty's Government, 3 June 1947, *Partition Proceedings I*, Government of India Press, New Delhi, 1949, p. 2 (reproduced in Menon 1993: 510–15).
5 *The Statesman*, Calcutta, 8 June 1947.
6 IOR, R/3/1/157, statement by His Majesty's Government, 3 June 1947.
7 The Punjab Legislative Assembly decided by 91 votes to 77 to join the new constituent assembly. The members from the Muslim-majority areas of west Punjab then decided, by 69 votes to 27, against the partition of the province; while the members from non-Muslim majority areas of east Punjab decided, by 50 to 22, that the province should be partitioned and that east Punjab should join the existing Indian constituent assembly (see Menon 1993: 388).
8 Those who voted for partition of Bengal comprised 48 Congress members, including thirteen Scheduled Caste members, four Anglo-Indians, two independents, 2 belonging to the communist party, one Indian Christian and one belonging to Hindu Mahasabha. All those who opposed were Muslim League members, including the Chief Minister, H. S. Suhrawardy. Of the 106 members who voted against partition, the Muslim League had 100 members, there were five Scheduled Caste members and one Indian Christian member. Those who defended partition included 34 Congress members and another belonging to the communist party (Burrows to Mountbatten, Telegram, 20 June 1947, in Mansergh *et al.*, Vol XI, 1980: 278).
9 *The Statesman*, 21 June 1947.
10 IOR, R/3/1/157, statement by His Majesty's Government, 3 June 1947.
11 IOR, R/3/1/157, Viceroy's personal report, 27 June 1947.
12 Ali 1967: 204.
13 IOR, R/3/1/157, Mountbatten to the Secretary of State, 9 June 1947.
14 Ibid.
15 IOR, R/3/1/257, Mountbatten's announcement of 30 June 1947, *The Statesman*, 1 July 1947.
16 Cyril Radcliffe accepted the Chairmanship of the Boundary Commissions on the following terms: (1) salary 5000 pounds sterling a year + tax-free allowances of 200 pounds sterling; (2) suitable accommodation without expenses; (3) free travel for Mrs Radcliffe; and (4) a competent personal assistant-cum-secretary. IOR, R/3/1/257, Secretary of State to the Viceroy, 2 July 1947.
17 Hasan 2000: 16.
18 *Partition Proceedings: Reports of the Members and Awards to the Chairman of the Boundary Commission*, Government of India Press, New Delhi, 1949, Vol. iv, p. 146.

19 IOR, L/PO/433, Viceroy's Fortnightly Report to the Secretary of State, 16 August 1947.
20 *The Statesman*, 23 and 24 July 1947.
21 Munir, 'Days to remember', *The Pakistan Times*, 22 June 1964; also Munir 1979: 12.
22 Statement by His Majesty's Government, 3 June 1947, in Mansergh *et al.*, Vol. I, 1970: 2.
23 The situation in Punjab was not different. As Menon reports, 'in the Punjab, there was much controversy and dispute over the three divisions of Lahore, Multan and Jullundur [Jalandhar], and also a portion of the Ambala Division' Menon 1993: 402.
24 The 'other factors' were not specified. Obviously they could include material considerations such as administrative viability, natural boundaries, communications or water and irrigation systems; but it was also open to the Commission to take into account less tangible influences. It was also decided that no direction beyond the terms of reference should be given to the Commission, which should interpret these at its own discretion. For details of what finally led to the formation of the Commissions, see Hodson 1988: 322–55.
25 Chowdhury 1989: 9.
26 The outcome of the referendum held on 6–7 July was in favour of joining east Bengal by a majority of 55 578 votes (239 619 votes were cast in favour of joining east Bengal while 184 041 voted for remaining in Assam).
27 NMML, AICC-I/CL-14(D)/1947–48, a memorandum signed by as many as twenty local congress members to the Congress President, J. B. Kripalani, 14 July 1947.
28 In addition to the ten Hindu-majority districts (Burdwan, Midnapur, Birbhum, Bankura, Howrah, Hooghly, 24 Parganas, Khulna, Darjeeling and Jalpaiguri), the Coordination Committee demanded that the two entire Muslim-majority districts (Malda and Murshidabad), large parts of Nadia, Fardipur and Dinajpur, and selected thanas in Rangpur and Rajshahi be annexed to west Bengal.
29 NMML, AICC-I/G-33/1947–48, Atul Gupta to J. B. Kripalani, 12 July 1947.
30 *The Statesman*, 14 July 1947. In a press statement on behalf of the members other than the Congress, S. P. Mookherjee attributed their decision to defend their scheme independently to 'the Congress's sinister design to weaken west Bengal ... by not pressing for those areas which naturally belong to [west Bengal]'.
31 NMML, AICC-I/G-33/1947–48, J. B. Kripalani to Atul Gupta, 16 July 1947.
32 NMML, AICC-I/CL-14 (D)/1947–48, The memorandum on the partition of Bengal was presented on behalf of the Indian National Congress before the Bengal Boundary Commission. Given their demographic composition and cultural characteristics, the following six districts, as Atul Chandra Gupta defended, should normally be included in West Bengal:- Rajshahi, Dinajpur, Jalpaiguri, Darjeeling, Rangpur and Malda.
33 Mymensingh and Faridpur should normally have come to west Bengal because they are contiguous Hindu majority areas though located in an area where Muslims are demographically preponderant.
34 Alfadanga and Muhammadpur Police Stations in the Jessore district, and the Police Stations of Morelganj and Sarankhola in the Khulna district.
35 NMML, AICC-I/CL-14 (D)/1947–48, *The Memorandum on the Partition of Bengal Presented on Behalf of the Indian National Congress before the Boundary Commission*.
36 *The Statesman*, 19 July 1947. It is, however, intriguing that the New Bengal

Association in its first memorandum of 1 July insisted on 'property consideration', though in another memorandum (*The Statesman*, 2 July 1947), signed by three out of seven members, it regretted having signed the original representation because the arguments made in favour of property consideration were either 'ignored or bypassed' while preparing the memorandum.

37 NMML, AICC-I/CL 14/(D)/1947–48, Atul Chandra Gupta to J. B. Kripalani, 12 July 1947. The arguments Gupta put forward before the Boundary Commission were elaborated in the *Memorandum on the Partition of Bengal presented on Behalf of the Indian National Congress*.
38 *The Statesman*, 17 July 1947.
39 As per the Congress demand, 32 per cent Muslims and 68 per cent non-Muslims (forming 45 per cent of the total demographic strength of Bengal) constituted the proposed province of West Bengal.
40 Chowdhury 1989: 118–19. For more details on the differences within the Muslim League on the partition issue, see Sen 1976: 203–45.
41 Hamidul Haq Chowdhury thus mentioned, 'Not for one single day, did any member of the party of the Ministry take any interest in the Boundary [Commission] proceedings in Sylhet or Bengal' (Chowdhury 1989: 119).
42 *The Statesman*, 10 August 1947: *Anandabazar Patrika*, 10 and 11 August 1947.
43 Ahmad 1988: 218.
44 *The Star of India*, 18 August 1947.
45 Ahmad 1998: 220–1.
46 Report of the Muslim members before the Boundary Commission, *Partition Proceedings* VI, Government of India Press, New Delhi, 1949, p. 78.
47 *The Statesman*, 18 July 1947.
48 *Partition Proceedings I*, Reports of the Members and Awards of the Chairman of the Boundary Commission, Government of India Press, New Delhi, 1949, p. 81.
49 Ibid. The argument does not, however, correspond with the reality, since both Jalpaiguri and Darjeeling were demographically Hindu-preponderant while Buddhists and several tribes with different religious beliefs constituted a majority in the Chittagong Hill Tracts.
50 Out of a total population of 2108891 in Calcutta, Muslims constituted only 23.5 per cent while the Hindu share was a staggering 76.4 per cent.
51 *The Statesman*, 2 July 1947. The argument drawing upon the property consideration was an afterthought, since it did not figure in the original memorandum. After having added this, the Mahasabha released a revised memorandum in the press which was published in almost all dailies on 2 July 1947.
52 IOR, L/PO/433, *The Bengal Boundary Commission Report*, Appendix II, p. 310. The pattern was the same in both the Boundary Commissions, since there was a complete lack of unanimity among the members regarding the demarcation of both Punjab and Bengal.
53 Under the Award, 36 per cent of the area and 35 per cent of the population were assigned to west Bengal while east Bengal got 64 per cent of the area and 65 per cent of the population. Of the total Muslim population of Bengal, only 16 per cent came under west Bengal, while as many as 42 per cent non-Muslims remained in east Bengal (Menon 1993: 402; *The Statesman*, 19 August 1947).
54 Report of the Chairman of the Bengal Boundary Commission in *Partition Proceedings I*, Government of India Press, New Delhi 1949, pp. 311–12.
55 Menon 1993: 402–3. Menon's argument was corroborated by Alan Campbell Johnson in his memoirs. According to Campbell Johnson, Menon had warned Mountbatten that the Award would surely annoy Patel and Nehru because

they were reported to have assured the delegates from Khulna and Chittagong Hill Tracts that 'there was no question of [these areas] being assigned to east Pakistan' (see Campbell-Johnson 1953: 152).
56 IOR, L/PO/433, V. P. Menon's daily report, 14 August 1947. Interestingly, Menon did not pursue this argument in his memoirs though he mentioned that the publication of the Award was delayed because Mountbatten so insisted (see Menon 1993: 402).
57 Hodson 1988: 351.
58 Jinnah 1963: 32–3.
59 The vernacular newspapers, like *Anandabazar Patrika* and *Jugantor*, brought out editorials in support of this argument, underlining that partition was possibly the best solution under the present circumstances of communal hatred and animosity (*Anandabazar Patrika*, 19 and 21 August 1947; *Jugantor*, 23 August 1947).
60 *The Statesman*, 19 August 1947.
61 *The Dawn*, 19 August 1947.
62 Hodson 1988: 355.
63 In his short story 'The champion of the people', the Bengali writer Satinath Bhaduri depicts vividly the confusion and uncertainty surrounding the precise terms of the Radcliffe Award. An English translation of this story is available Bhalla 1994.
64 Darling 1949: 307, quoted in Hasan 1995: 33.
65 In the words of Bhisham Sahni, 'The decision to create Pakistan had just been announced and people were making all kinds of surmises about the future. But no one's imagination went too far. The Sardarji sitting in front wondered whether after the creation of Pakistan Jinnah would continue to live in Bombay or settle in Pakistan. ... Similar guesses were being fielded about Lahore and Gurdaspur. Would they go to India or become part of Pakistan? No one knew which town to fall to the share of India and which to Pakistan's. People gossiped and laughed in much the same way as before. Some were abandoning their homes for ever, while others ridiculed them. Still others biding their time. They did what they thought right. They were not clear what the risks were. ... People believed that our troubles would cease automatically with the coming of independence ... [and] yet the darkness of uncertainty seemed to persist'. Sahni, 'We have arrived in Amritsar' (English translation), reproduced in Hasan 1995: 114.
66 Mitra 1991: 2.
67 West Bengal State Archives, Calcutta, GB/IB File No. 1238/1947–48, Superintendent of Police, Nadia to the Inspector General of Police, Government of West Bengal, 31 March 1948.
68 Chatterji 1999: 220.
69 West Bengal State Archives, Calcutta, Government of West Bengal, Home-Poll, 18 (KW)/1948, proceedings of the Inter-Dominion Conference held at Calcutta, 15–18 April 1948. The proceedings of the conference were also publicised in the press (see *The Statesman*, 19 April 1948; *Anandabazar Patrika*, 19 and 20 April 1948).
70 Not only did the local vernacular press, especially *Anandabazar Patrika*, welcome the setting-up of the tribunal; even the conservative newspapers, like *The Statesman*, defended the decision as probably the most appropriate to settle the boundary disputes amicably (*Anandabazar Patrika*, 19 April 1948; *The Statesman*, 19 April 1948).
71 Decisions given by the Indo-Pakistan Boundary disputes tribunal, 12 and 13

August 1948, *Partition Proceedings*, Vol. VI, p. 315, quoted in J. Chatterjee 1999: 220.
72 According to the 1941 Census, out of a total population of 1 640 530 in the district of Murshidabad, Muslims constituted 56.5 per cent and the non-Muslim share was 43.4 per cent.
73 Joya Chatterji has shown the similarities between the Radcliffe Award and the Congress Scheme in Chatterji 1999: 215–16.
74 Hodson 1969: 353.
75 NMML, AICC-I/G-33/1947–48, Patel to J. B. Kripalani, 13 August 1947.
76 Hodson 1969: 354–55.
77 Ibid., p. 354.
78 Ibid.
79 3 June plan, in Menon 1993: 510.
80 Chatterji 1999: 225.
81 Very common till almost the end of 1950, these incidents were frequently reported in the Fortnightly Reports on Border Incidents in West Bengal (see West Bengal State Archives, Calcutta, GB IB File No. 1238–A/47, Fortnightly Reports for second half of August 1950, cited in Chatterji 1999: 227).
82 West Bengal State Archives, Calcutta, GB IB File No. 1238–A/47, Fortnightly Reports for second half of January 1950.
83 Khan, *Memoirs* (unpublished): 35.
84 Ahmed 1970: 86.
85 Tamijuddin Khan, *Memoirs* (unpublished): 39.
86 For details, see Chapter 2.
87 Ahmad 1988: 61.
88 Nawaz, 'The heart divide', in Hasan 1995: 21.
89 Menon 1993: 402.
90 There were reports that the 1941 Census was doctored by the Muslim League ministry to inflate the Muslim demographic strength in Bengal (*Ananda Bazar Patrika*, 28 March 1942). S. P. Mookherjee pointed this out in almost all his press statements. *Amrita Bazar Patrika* was also apprehensive of the sinister design of the League ministry in manipulating the census figures (see *Amrita Bazar Patrika*, 4, 5 and 6 April 1942). Even the Muslim League was apprehensive of the census figures. For instance, in his letter to Jinnah, S. M. Majid, the secretary of the Khulna district Muslim League, mentioned that '[I]t was common knowledge that during the Census operation of 1941 a vigorous propaganda was started by the Hindu press inviting the attention of the Hindus to the importance of the census and they were indirectly asked to augment the figures. The result was that the Hindus who are the most politically conscious and educated people of the province left no stone unturned to show an inflated figure of population. Muslims, illiterate as they are in rural areas, were fully ignorant of the implications of the census and as such did not record their figures in many cases' (see IOR, *Quaid-i-Azam papers* (microfilm), 9/2-21, S. M. A. Majeed to Jinnah, 9 July 1947).
91 Khilnani 1997: 201.
92 In an interview with the Viceroy, Jinnah was reported to have said, 'you must carry out a surgical operation; cut India [into two halves] and give me the half that belongs to the Muslim League' (Mansergh *et al.*, Vol. IX, 1980. Jinnah's statement was quoted in the Viceroy's personal report No. 3, 17 April 1947, pp. 390–1.

6

CONSTRUCTION AND CONSOLIDATION OF IDENTITIES

The Sylhet referendum and partition

Louis Mountbatten's 3 June 1947 statement was a watershed in the history of India's emergence as a free nation, for at least three important reasons. First, the 3 June statement was a clear indication of the final British withdrawal from India. Not only was the date announced, the British government also put forward a scheme for the division of the subcontinent, according to what the newly appointed Viceroy thought was the best option available.[1] Secondly, as both the Congress and the Muslim League agreed upon partition, the statement provided for separation of Bengal and Punjab from India since Muslims constituted a majority in those provinces. Wavell, the predecessor of Mountbatten, had explored all the possibilities for maintaining an Indian Union, but to no avail.[2] The statement was therefore the culmination of a process that began with the adoption of the 1940 Lahore resolution defending a separate state for the Muslims.[3] Thirdly, apart from the partition of Bengal and Punjab, the 3 June statement also suggested a referendum in the North-West Frontier Province[4] and in Sylhet, a district in Assam. Sylhet was a difficult case because it was located in Assam, which was predominantly a non-Muslim province. Hence the Viceroy, in his 3 June statement, forcefully argued that:

> Though Assam is predominantly a non-Muslim province, the district of Sylhet which is contiguous to Bengal is predominantly Muslim. There has been a demand that in the event of the partition of Bengal, Sylhet should be amalgamated with the Muslim part of Bengal. Accordingly, if it is decided that Bengal should be partitioned, a referendum will be held in Sylhet under the aegis of the Governor-General and in consultation with the Assam provincial Government to decided whether the district of Sylhet should continue to form part of Assam province or should be amalgamated with the new province of East Bengal of that province agrees. If the referendum results in favour of amalgamation with East Bengal, a Boundary Commission with terms similar to those for the Punjab and Bengal will be set up to demarcate areas of Sylhet

THE SYLHET REFERENDUM AND PARTITION

district and contiguous Muslim majority areas of adjoining districts which will then be transferred to East Bengal. The rest of the Assam province will, in any case, continue to [remain] in India.[5]

As is evident, the decision to go for a referendum was conditioned largely by the peculiar location of Sylhet within British India. While defending a referendum for the district, the Viceroy was confident that this would enable the people to 'decide their fate themselves'.[6] Accordingly, appropriate steps were undertaken to complete the process before 15 August.

Given the complex unfolding of events immediately after the announcement, this chapter seeks to explore the processes that finally led to the transfer of the district of Sylhet. An attempt will also be made to grapple with what became prominent in the entire event. Notwithstanding the allegations and counter-allegations of both the Congress and the Muslim League, the British administration was not spared either. Not only was the administration held responsible for a low turn-out of voters in 'the interior', some of the Presiding and Polling officers were also blamed for being 'partisan' to the Muslims. Thus a thorough probing of the referendum will bring out the relatively unknown dimensions of India's freedom struggle that unfolded during the last phase of the transfer of power.

Sylhet: a profile

Located in Assam, a north-eastern province in India,[7] Sylhet (*Srihatta* in the vernacular) was 'a broad level valley bounded on either side by hills of considerable height. ... It is bounded on the north by Khasi and Jaintia Hills, on the east by Cachar, on the south by the state of Hill Tippera and on the west by the district of Tippera and Mymensingh'.[8] As shown in Table 6.1, the district was divided into five subdivisions and each subdivisions had several *thanas* within its administrative jurisdiction.

Table 6.1 Subdivisions of Sylhet

Subdivisions	Thanas
Sunamganj	Tahirpur, Sachna, Dharampasha, Dirai, Sunamganj, Jagannathpur, Chhatak, Sulle
Habiganj	Ajmiriganj, Nabiganj, Baniyachung, Lakhai, Madhavpur, Habiganj, Bahubal, Chunarighat
North Sylhet	Gosainghat, Jaintapur, Kanairghat, Sylhet, Biswanath, Balaganj, Golapganj, Fenchuganj
South Sylhet (Maulavi Bazar)	Maulavi Bazar, Srimangal, Kamalganj, Raj Nagar, Kulara
Karimganj	Karimganj, Beani Bazar, Barlekha, Pathar Kandi. Ratha Bari, Badarpur

Source: Census of India, Vol. IX, Assam, Government of India Press, 1943, pp. 2–3.

THE SYLHET REFERENDUM AND PARTITION

Demographic composition

Muslims constituted a majority in Sylhet. Apart from the Hindus, the district had a very small section of Christians (2418) and tribal population (69 907) (see Table 6.2).

Muslims constituted 60 per cent while Hindus were 38 per cent of the total population of the district. They constituted an overwhelming majority of 67 per cent in the north Sylhet subdivision, 'which was the first portion of the district to come to the [Muslim] possession'.[9] South Sylhet and Karimganj came less under the influence of the Muslim faith, and for many years 'were probably dominated by the Hindu kingdom of Tippera'.[10]

Although the district had registered an increase among the Muslims, their growth in North Sylhet was very dramatic, especially when the natural growth of the population 'was less than two per cent'[11] over a period of two decades. Furthermore, the sharp increase of Muslims was also remarkable because this was a subdivision 'in which the last census disclosed a serious decrease in the population'.[12] According to the Deputy Commissioner of Sylhet, 'conversion had little to do wth the growth of Muslims'. He further added, 'there is no organised propaganda of the faith and the few converts made are said to be Hindus of low castes who have been detected in intrigues with Muhammadans of the opposite sex'.[13] While explaining the higher rate of growth among the Muslims, the contemporary reports ascribes it to '(a) superior fecundity which is said to be due to greater physical vigour and a more nourishing dietary, (b) to the absence of restriction on widow remarriage, (c) to a less marked disparity between the ages of husband and wife and (d) to some extent, to the greater prevalence of polygamy'.[14]

Sylhet proper was not a homogeneous tract, but was scattered over the permanently settled area. There was a large number of estates which were occupied and settled at different dates, subsequent to the permanent settlement, while in the south of the district there were 'extensive tracts of jungle to [which] claims of a somewhat vague and dubious character were put forward by the neighbouring land-holders'.[15] The importance of Sylhet was largely due to the fact that it was one of the most important tea districts in Assam.[16] As tea was an important commercial crop, it had attracted a considerable number of Europeans. By the 1940s, the Europeans controlled almost 90 per cent of the tea gardens. While they were dominant in South Sylhet and Karimganj, there were also Indian planters in North Sylhet and Habiganj.[17]

Like any other tea-growing districts, Sylhet also attracted a large number of labourers from all over India. As the contemporary figures show, a majority of them came from the United Provinces. Since there was a constant flow of labourers from elsewhere, the production of tea was

Table 6.2 Demographic composition of Sylhet

Total population	Scheduled castes	General Hindus	Muslims
3 041 631	267 510	785 004	1 892 117
North Sylhet (67% Muslims)			
Goainghat	4678	5734	44 890
Jaintapur	1871	2734	12 642
Kanairghat	7500	2541	62 164
Sylhet	7929	39 690	133 588
Biswanath	4738	13 220	65 764
Balaganj	10 242	26 944	76 289
Golapganj	7081	15 167	74 740
Fenchuganj	2404	4393	20 019
Total	43 443	110 423	490 096
South Sylhet (39% Muslims)			
Maulvi Bazar	16 382	37 744	68 531
Srimangal	8183	47 274	22 000
Kamalganj	11 550	37 605	33 925
Raj nagar	9677	25 492	43 247
Kulaura	21 045	50 508	69 947
Total	66 837	198 623	237 650
Habiganj (53% Muslims)			
Ajmiriganj	10 522	12 646	23 129
Nabiganj	14 071	30 754	79 421
Bania Chung	19 348	28 578	74 765
Lakhai	10 839	11 824	38 523
Madhavpur	14 698	23 272	52 213
Habiganj	10 015	27 004	70 514
Bahubal	4223	16 594	44 638
Chunarighat	3695	21 788	51 156
Total	87 411	172 460	434 359
Sunamganj (55% Muslims)			
Dharmapasa	11 892	20 489	50 319
Tahirpur	4116	7428	21 753
Sachna	3302	7956	16 251
Dirai	11 980	24 264	45 282
Sunamganj	14 651	28 138	96 897
Chhatak	7854	21 165	115 131
Jagannathpur	8587	21 652	58 350
Sulla	10 962	13 554	13 421
Total	73 344	144 646	417 404
Karimganj (47% Muslims)			
Beani bazar	11 763	18 446	70 690
Barlekha	10 982	28 024	39 225
Pathar Kandi	5686	32 709	27 664
Ratha Bari	10 523	30 471	24 730
Karimganj	41 633	35 846	123 733
Badarpur	7402	9762	25 228
Total	87 969	155 258	311 270

Source: The Census of India, vol. IX, 1941, Assam, pp. 38–41.

never adversely affected despite the unhealthy environment in which they were forced to survive. One of the most important assets in the planter's favour in Sylhet, commented the B. C. Allen (who prepared the *District Gazetteer*), 'is the fact that he can obtain his labour at fairly moderate rates'.[18] As Table 6.3 shows, a majority of the plantation workers were from outside the province of Assam and Bengal. One of the factors accounting for the lower number of people from Sylhet and other adjoining districts of Bengal and Assam was probably the steady rise in the price of agricultural produce that 'has enabled the ordinary people ... to earn their living by agriculture'.[19]

Preparation for the Referendum

It was decided on 21 June to hold the referendum on 6 and 7 of July 1947. In a meeting of the District Officers, convened to decide dates, it was pointed out that the dates in the first fortnight of July were to be avoided because of the monsoon causing severe flooding almost every year in the district. As the district was likely to be flooded, it would be better to change the dates to the second half of July, otherwise people in the interior of the district 'are likely to be prevented from exercising their rights'.[20] Those who attended the meeting were convinced of the adverse consequences of flooding and were willing to consider alternative dates to enable most of the people in the district to defend their democratic rights. However, I. Stork, the Referendum Commissioner, argued that given the announcement of the date of final withdrawal, no negotiation of dates was possible. The Assam Governor, who realised the difficulty of mobility during the flood was 'helpless', as the Viceroy was committed to 'freedom' by 15 August. If the decision on Sylhet was delayed, it would undoubtedly 'upset the entire plan', and the British government was not willing to endorse this. It was unfortunate, as the Governor argued, 'that circumstances have compelled the holding of the referendum at a time when a

Table 6.3 Labourers from outside Sylhet

United Province	44 169 (28%)
Other parts of Bengal	22 067 (15%)
Chotanagpur	22 745 (16%)
Central provinces	12 681 (9%)
Madras	10 079 (7%)
Total	144 876

Source: IOR, R/3/1/158, K. N. V. Sundaram to G. E. B. Abell (the Private Secretary to the Viceroy) 18 June 1947.

Note
Figures in parentheses show the percentage in relation to the total labour force in the district.

large part of the district is flooded and a substantial percentage of polling stations will be in the flooded areas. Voters will have to find their way to them as best as they can'. The only help the government 'can give them is not to indent upon local transport' for its own requirement.[21]

The task was gigantic, and was expected to be over in less than three weeks. The entire administration was geared to prepare for the referendum. The difficulties the administration confronted were numerous. The actual business of preparing for the referendum was characterised as 'a headache' for the administration. One of the problems that bothered the Assam Governor most was to arrange for Presiding and Polling officer for the poll. While drawing the attention of the Viceroy to this, he emphasised that 'the whole province is being drawn ... to find 478 Presiding Officers and 1434 Polling Officers. This withdrawal of staff from their regular duties will mean that all work except essential services will be at a standstill in the province for about ten days'.[22]

There were other difficulties as well. The Muslim leadership felt that the Muslims would be under-represented in the referendum, since the voters list was prepared according to the number of electors who had participated in the last elections.[23] As Liaquat Ali Khan pointed out, 'the position is ... that while Muslims form 60.7 percent of the total population of Sylhet district, they form only 54.27 percent of the total electoral roll of the district'. On the assumption that the referendum 'will be confined to the electorates', he apprehends, 'it is clear that the Muslim votes will not reflect the true strength of Muslim opinion on the issue of referendum'. Liaquat therefore insisted that in order to secure this result, 'it will be necessary to multiply the number of Muslim votes by a factor which would equate the voting strength of the Muslims with their population strength'.[24] The request was turned down because the disparity 'which only of the order of 10 to 9 is in itself not so striking as to compel the adoption of some remedial measure'. Furthermore, to give the suggested weightage in this solitary case 'would be entirely against the general scheme of the statement of 3 June [that devised the principle of following] the composition of the Provincial Legislative Assemblies and the electoral *rolls as they stand at present* without importing any extraneous consideration whatever'[25] (emphasis original).

Similarly, there were disagreements among the leaders regarding the voting rights of the special constituencies like labour and tea planters. Endorsing the claim of the voters in the Labour and in the Commerce and Trade constituencies of the district, the Congress insisted on extending the right to vote to them.[26] The office of the Referendum Commissioner was inundated with complaints from several tea gardens. Of the labour constituencies, the Srimangal tea garden had probably the most organised union. In a representation to the Viceroy, the demand for voting rights was made on the ground that the labourers in this tea estate 'fulfilled the residential qualification' and hence they should be allowed to vote.[27] Not persuaded by this argument, the Referendum Commissioner defended his decision not to include them in the list by saying that the tea plantation labourers 'do not fulfil the requisite qualification ... of working as a permanent employee in one tea garden continuously for not less than 180 days. They thus represent a floating population with little or no stake in the district as such'. He, therefore concluded, 'there is no strong reason why the plantation labour should be given a special voice in the referendum which other labour, agricultural and industrial do not get'.[28]

Not only were the labourers denied the right to vote, the European planters were also excluded from the referendum on the principle that 'the special constituencies need not be permitted to participate in the referendum'. Objections were raised by drawing attention to the role of European planters in the overall development of the district. Memoranda were presented to the Assam Governor. The argument was not strong enough, as the Governor suggested 'to substantially alter the basic principle, announced by the Viceroy in his 3 June statement'. Accordingly, none of the European constituencies (for instance, the European Territorial Constituency, European Planting Constituency, and European Commerce and Industry Constituency) was allowed to take part in the voting.

The Assam Governor had received a large number of complaints touching on almost every aspect of the proposed referendum. Some of the serious complaints were as follows:

1   The appointment of H. C. Stock (the Secretary, Legislative Department, Government of Assam) as the Referendum Commissioner raised controversy because 'he was a prisoner in Turkey during the first world war and is notorious as being anti-Muslim'. As a result of his imprisonment, he 'is understood to have developed an aversion to the "Turkish cap" and whoever wears the headgear'.
2   One of the reasons for discontentment among the Muslim leadership was that the symbols for ballot boxes were decided without consulting them. Two symbols were selected: a *hut* for staying in Assam, and an *axe* for joining east Bengal. Critical of the symbol of an axe because, in local popular perception, it 'symbolises injury to oneself', the Muslims were also opposed to a hut as a symbol in view of its symbolical meaning of providing a shelter. The symbol became significant in the context of the referendum that was to be held to finally decide the fate of the Hindus and Muslims of Sylhet. In fact, the Congress was reported to have played 'on the popular superstition by telling the voters that if they want to live happily in their own huts or homes, they should put their votes in the boxes bearing the symbol, but if they want to put the axe to their limbs, i.e. commit an injury to themselves, they may throw their votes bearing the symbol of the axe'.[29]

3   There were complaints against the presence of military, mostly Gurkhas, in the district. Most of them came to contain the civil disobedience movement that was launched by the Muslims against the controversial 'Line system'. The military was alleged to be 'harassing the people without provocation'.
4   Criticism was also directed at the appointment of the Presiding Officers from among those serving the Assam government. It was therefore likely that these Presiding Officers were bound by those superior officers who were part of a government 'opposed to the rise of a Muslim nation state' in the aftermath of 15 August. A suggestion was therefore made to bring these Presiding Officers under 'the direct supervision of the Governor-General'.
5   Views were expressed against 'the date fixed for the referendum [which] is too early and the time given for voting too short'. Two arguments were used in support of this criticism: first, that the time span between the final announcement of the dates of referendum and the actual date of referendum was just two weeks, which that was too short to prepare the people for such a crucial decision; and second, time was too short for 'canvassing specially because of the floods now raging in large areas of the interior areas'.
6   The Muslim leaders also held the Assam government responsible for deliberately obstructing the League's campaign in most of the areas. They also charged the government with 'censoring the news as well as telegrams to outside League leaders and local leaders'. To demoralise those supporting the League's demand for a separate homeland for the Muslims, the government was reported to have 'arrested the best League workers ... under the Public Safety Act'. Apprehending that the aim of this Act was 'to stifle the Muslim League's campaign' by the Congress-led ministry, the Viceroy was urged to withdraw it[30]
7   A charge was levelled against the Viceroy for not having sent British military officers to supervise the referendum. It was alleged that since Baldev Singh, a member of the Governor's Council, was authorised to look after the security arrangements, he 'has sent a number of Sikh officers to actually collect information on the Muslim preparedness' under the pretext of ascertaining 'whether posting of more troops is needed for maintenance of peace before and after the referendum'. Under no circumstances were Sikh officers acceptable, and hence it was suggested in the complaint that 'a mixed troops – half Muslims and half Hindus – should be posted and the Gurkhas withdrawn'.[31]

Even before the Assam Governor addressed the issues raised in the complaints, the Viceroy made a special request to the Commander-in-Chief, Claude Auchinleck, to arrange for four British military officers of the Indian army of the rank of major or thereabouts to be associated with the

Referendum Commissioner. What led him to make this request was probably his apprehension that Muslims had reasons to be sceptical immediately before the transfer of power to two independent dominions. He was therefore 'forced to make this request as [he does not] wish to give the Muslim League any handle to allege that the referendum if it should go against them, has not been fairly run'.[32] The provision of troops for the referendum was immediately sanctioned as soon as the Viceroy had requested. Along with other officers from the British army, Lieutenant Colonel C. W. Pearson was given the command of Sylforce, a specially created force for the referendum. The purpose was to maintain law and order 'in a friendly manner, if possible during and after the Referendum, ... preventing intimidation of voters and to act as a mobile reserve to the police'.[33]

The sanctioned strength for the referendum was just one platoon, but that was not enough to patrol the district, especially in view of the 'peculiar topographical features of the district and vast expanses of water in nearly all the subdivisions'. In order to carry out his task properly, as Pearson explained, 'I decided that ... force under my command should be located at such places in the district that they could reach the place where trouble was expected in the shortest possible time, and that I should create *an illusion* of being here, there and everywhere' (emphasis added).[34]

Given the nature of the referendum in Sylhet, where both the communities expected to win, the Assam Governor apprehended communal disturbances. He therefore suggested making 'special arrangements for the use of army to preserve order and secure a fair vote'.[35] In his assessment, 'the First Battalion Assam Regiment would be a suitable instrument for this purpose'.[36] Interestingly, both the League and the Congress ministry welcomed the suggestion and agreed to co-operate with the army during the preparation for the referendum.[37] The Congress had reason to be happy because the army was called to control the League-sponsored civil disobedience movement in Assam against the Line system. Despite Jinnah's personal request for the army, the Assam Muslim League expressed resentment as the Assam Battalion was allegedly pro-Congress and pro-Hindus while discharging their duties during the civil disobedience movement.[38]

As soon as the dates were announced, both the major parties began campaigning for their respective goals. Unlike the Congress, the Muslim League was more organised and undertook the campaign in a planned manner. Even before the campaign for the referendum took off, the League had an organisation at its disposal, presumably because of its movement against 'the Line system'. Apprehending the adverse economic and demographic effects of unchecked immigration from East Bengal to Assam, the Congress ministry (headed by Gopinath Bardoloi) that came to power in February 1946 decided to evict 'the illegal immigrants' from

Assam following the Line system – introduced in 1920 – whereby all settlers beyond 1 April 1937 were to be evicted.[39] The Assamese Hindus welcomed the step, as 'the influx of Muslims from [east Bengal] was upsetting the population ratio and the Assamese wanted to retain a majority in the Brahmaputra valley'.[40] It was also suggested that the influx 'could be countered only by Bihar Hindus to settle down' in Assam.[41] The decision caused resentment among the Muslims, and a Committee of Action,[42] headed by Bhasani,[43] was immediately formed at the behest of the Assam Provincial Muslim League 'to oppose the eviction policy of the Congress Government all over the province'.[44] The movement did not gain momentum until 10 March 1947, when it was decided in a meeting, addressed by Liaquat ali Khan,[45] to start civil disobedience in all districts of Assam under the stewardship of the League.[46] A member of the working committee of the All India Muslim League, Chaudhury Khaliq-uz-Zaman, was deputed to strengthen the campaign while Habibullah Bahar of the Bengal Provincial Muslim League was invited to mobilise the Bengali Muslims who were the primary target of this system.[47] According to the Committee of Action, formed in the wake of the Congress-engineered eviction policy, it drew upon the fear that 'the immigration was aimed at increasing the Muslim population in order to turn the area into Pakistan'.[48] The Congress apprehension was absolutely unfounded, as the Committee of Action stated in categorical terms, since 'Assam is sure to be in Pakistan, so it is not true that the Muslim League is fighting to establish Pakistan in Assam'.[49]

For the Assam Premier, the Line system was probably the most appropriate system to halt Assam's decline as a socio-economic unit. In his letter to the Congress President, Rajendra Prasad, he elaborated further by underlining that 'the economic problem of the Province is bound up with this system. We cannot think that in the near future we shall have no spot of earth for our children and ultimately for ourselves and we shall be driven to the solution of acute difficulties which face some other provinces. The linguistic problem also increases the difficulties of an economic government, and what is worse, a source of constant friction resulting in violence, incendiarism and crimes of all kinds, naturally disturb the peace'.[50] What was most disheartening for the Premier was the League effort to design the movement in communal terms – which was 'natural in view of the League's declared objective of making Assam a part of Pakistan just like Bengal'.[51] The movement did not continue for long. It began on 10 March with the declaration of the Assam Day, when the League members courted arrest following the violation of the Section 144. Despite having successfully organised campaigns against the Congress ministry, the civil disobedience movement was immediately called off at Jinnah's behest following the announcement of the partition plan on 3 June 1947.

Preparation of the Muslim League

Once the dates of the referendum had been made public, Jinnah appointed a committee comprising M. A. Ispahani, Moazzamuddin Hussain and A. W. Baakza[52] 'to organise and help the Muslims of Sylhet in every way to face the forthcoming referendum'. He therefore requested all the leaders and workers of the Muslim League in Sylhet 'to get in close touch with the Committee and work in full co-operation and complete harmony as a united and disciplined people in a team'. As Muslims 'are in a powerful majority and if they vote solidly ... it will not only strengthen Eastern Pakistan [but it will also be] a boon to the Muslims of Sylhet'.[53] Apart from a personal appeal, Jinnah had also deputed Moazzamuddin Hussain, the Bengal minister, to act as a League observer. The decision to appoint an observer from outside was a response to a request of Moinul Haque Chaudhury, an MLA from Assam, who expressed a great difficulty in mobilising the Muslim MLAs for the referendum due to 'internecine feud among them'.[54] The selection of a Bengal minister for this role was probably strategically conditioned. The Muslim League was a ruling party in Bengal, and was capable of financially supporting the campaign for the referendum if required. Accordingly, he wrote to Suhrawardy, the Bengal Premier, to find out sources of funds 'that can be transferred to the Assam unit of the League without complications'.[55] As the League was not fully confident of the outcome of the referendum, a suggestion was made to him to sponsor the 'influx of Mussalmans from the neighbouring provinces or native States where the Mussalmans are in a hopeless minority and can never hope to lead a happy life'.[56]

The campaign was undertaken vigorously, and in every meeting an appeal was made to the Muslim voters 'to cast his or her votes in favour of the amalgamation of Sylhet with East Bengal – which will also carry with it the contiguous Muslim majority areas of adjoining districts which will then be transferred to Eastern Pakistan'.[57] To prove their identity as 'pacca Muslims', the Muslim voters were expected to vote in favour of joining east Pakistan.[58] If Sylhet was in favour of Pakistan, what would be her gain? Those addressed public meetings responded to this by saying that 'there would ... be a distinct gain to Sylhet if it joins East Bengal [because] Muslims of that area would become a part of the majority of East Bengal and cease to be a portion of the Muslim minority in Assam'.[59] Even if Sylhet decided against the amalgamation with East Bengal, Muslims 'need not be scared [because] Assam is certain to be part of Pakistan in near future given the rapidly growing demographic strength of Muslims here [owing] to both natural causes and migration from East Bengal'.[60] As the trends had shown, 'it is reasonable to expect that the in the course of next few years the number of Muslims in the Province shall be equal to the number of caste Hindus and that thereafter the Muslims will be the largest single community in the Province'. Even if Sylhet and its surrounding Muslim-majority areas decided to continue as parts of Assam, 'there is every prospect that with passing years Assam will grow closer to East Bengal and that at no distant date [she] will join East Pakistan'.[61]

The League left no stone unturned to organise an effective campaign in Sylhet just before the referendum. As a contemporary report mentions, '[t]he manner in which the Muslim League ... carried out their propaganda campaign was noticeable. Rowdy processions, shouting of slogans, drilling of young men were the order of the day'.[62] What was striking was the role of the Muslim National Guard, a para-military force,[63] during the campaign. So long as the local Muslim League leaders led the campaign, it was a low key affair. With their involvement, the League gained remarkably.[64] Jinnah was reported to have appreciated their contribution, and once this had been published in the leading dailies,[65] 'the Muslim National Guards flooded the district from outside'. Not only did they penetrate into the remotest villages they were also reported to have 'created panic in the minds of non-Muslim villages'.[66]

It is true that the presence of the Guards radically altered the nature of the campaign, and the local League leadership welcomed their entry. The difficulty arose as soon as the Guards declined to follow the instructions of the local Muslim League. As they were deputed by the central leadership of the League, they defended their independence *vis à vis* the Sylhet Muslim League. This led to a peculiar situation where the local unit of the League was completely oblivious of the activities of the Guards comprising members largely from United Provinces. There was hardly any communication, probably because of the language barrier between the Hindi/Urdu-speaking Guards and the local leadership, which was not conversant with either of these languages. As the campaign gained momentum, this resulted in a precarious situation when the local leaders appeared to have been disgusted with the Guards for having alienated even the Muslims by projecting them as 'the only saviour of Muslims'. Not only did this attitude hurt the feelings of the local Muslim leadership, it also provoked resentment and consternation among the local people, especially in the Muslim-majority Sylhet Sadar thana, for 'their arrogant behaviour and application of violence'[67] during the campaign.

The referendum was held on 6 and 7 July. The outcome was favourable to those demanding the amalgamation of Sylhet with East Bengal. As Table 6.4 shows, the overwhelming majority supported the League's claim.

Muslims constituted 60 per cent of Sylhet's population. As shown in Table 6.4, of the valid votes cast in the referendum, 239 619 (56.6 per cent) were in favour of Sylhet's amalgamation with Pakistan and only 184 041 (43.4 per cent) of an undivided Assam in India. The result was not unexpected, as it almost reflected the demographic composition of the district's population. As soon as the referendum was complete, complaints

Table 6.4 Results of the Sylhet Referendum, 6–7 July 1947

Name of the subdivision	Total Muslim electorate	Total general electorate	Votes for east Bengal	Votes for remaining in Assam
Sadar	92268	48863	68381	38871
Karimganj	54002	46221	41262	40536
Habiganj	75274	60252	54543	36952
South Sylhet	38397	41427	31718	33471
Sunamganj	51846	39045	43715	34211

Source: Mansergh et al., Vol. XI, 1982: 155, A. Hydari to Nehru, 14 July 1947.

regarding irregularities in its conduct began to pour into the offices of both the Assam Governor and the Viceroy. Jinnah made detailed complaints to the Viceroy about interference by the Assam ministry, and demanded an immediate enquiry.[68] However, he did not pursue the matter, presumably because he had indications that 'the referendum will go in favour of the League'.[69] The most serious allegation was made by Jawaharlal Nehru. According to him, '[r]eports submitted by many statements and other data indicate that in many interior areas state of lawlessness prevailed and thousands of Muslim National Guards from outside district prevented voters from voting. Large number of persons who had died in recent epidemics supposed to have voted. No sufficient protection given at most polling booths in the interior where intimidation rampant'.[70] Nehru's complaint was based on a large number of letters received by the All India Congress Committee. There were two types of complaints. The first was about the effort undertaken by the League to stop the genuine voters from voting by 'threats and violence'. It was also alleged that 'in almost all the centres, a large number of non-voters and unauthorised League members were allowed'.[71] The second type was more specific. For instance, a voter named Monorama Dasi, of Karimganj, sent a telegram to the AICC office stating that the European Presiding Officer in the Karimganj Town Female Centre 'snatched away the Ballot Papers from their hands and put them into the Ballot Box marked with Axe against their will'.[72]

As there were innumerable complaints, a suggestion was made to hold another referendum. In fact, Nehru in his letter also hinted at this possibility by saying that '[i]f any truth in these complaints, validity of referendum might be successfully challenged'.[73] On Nehru's request, the Sylhet District Congress Committee prepared a detailed report to defend the holding of a fresh referendum as it 'has been vitiated by Muslim League violence and grave irregularities which are too many to be catalogued here'. It was not a free and fair referendum, and 'the Hindus of Sylhet in all fairness cannot [therefore] be called to abide by the result of this spurious Referendum'. The demand was made to hold a fresh referendum 'which will be the concern of the people of Sylhet only and no one from outside should be allowed to complicate the issue'. The 'injustice' done to the citizens of Sylhet and specifically the Hindus 'ought to be set right by holding a fresh Referendum'.[74]

Interestingly, despite serious doubts expressed by both the Congress leadership and its counterpart in Sylhet, no attempt was made to organise a protest movement in the district, presumably because 'no one outside Sylhet is particularly anxious to retain the district in Assam'.[75] The opposition was confined to writing letters to the Viceroy or Assam Governor. Even Nehru, who was vocal immediately after the results were declared, accepted the verdict. To him, 'it seems clear both from the number of people who voted and the result of the voting that any irregularities that took place could not materially affect the result of the referendum'.[76] The outcome of the referendum, though unambiguous, did not ease the suffering of those suspected to have voted against Sylhet's amalgamation with East Bengal. Police reports indicate that 'the conditions in Sylhet are very insecure and general intimidation at the behest of the Muslim National Guard continues'.[77] In another report, a reference to the failure of the police is made by underlining 'that lawlessness in some interior areas ... may cause disaster if it is not immediately controlled. [It was alarming because] armed bands move about and threaten vengeance on those who might have voted against joining East Bengal. Most of these people who move about', the report highlights, 'are not residents of Sylhet district but have come from largely from the United Provinces'.[78] The situation did not appear to have changed radically even after the transfer of power. Several letters, written mostly by the Hindus not willing to move out of Sylhet, were addressed to Jawaharlal Nehru explaining the extent to which they were subject to intimidation and harassment by those who now felt that 'it is their Holy duty to evict the *Kafirs*[79] [i.e. Hindus] from Sylhet [which now was a part of East Pakistan] before it is too late'.[80]

The administrative preparedness

The report on the preparedness of the administration clearly suggests that the entire administration was geared to conduct the referendum as smoothly as possible. Given the involvement of the army, the role of the Congress-led Assam ministry was merely confined to supporting those especially deputed by the Viceroy to hold the referendum. It was not therefore surprising that the Home Minister, Basanta Kumar Das, characterised the referendum as 'a farce' and he had reason to be 'critical of those, associated with this'.[81] Not only did the Congress leadership act 'in a partisan way', the League members also 'fostered, and in some cases, started the alarmist rumours, [that] had caused severe disruption in the conduct of the Referendum'.[82] Although the relationship between various groups representing various shades of public opinion 'was far from satisfactory',[83] with the presence of the army to support the police, the situation never went beyond control, as the Superintendent of Police claimed.[84]

There were 239 voting booths and a minimum of three unarmed constables were deputed to each of these booths. Hence, a minimum of 717 constables were required, most of which came from the district with the remainder, brought in from outside. A number of polling booths needed more unarmed constables, since they were identified as 'dangerous spots', and here, addition to three unarmed constables, one officer and six armed constables were posted. Since the district force of armed constables was not adequate to meet the demand, the Assam Rifles and the Rail Force were also involved.[85] Armed police also patrolled in motor trucks on main roads and in boats in the interior.[86] These police patrols were in addition to patrols performed by the army, and the 'liaison between the military and police' was excellent.[87] Not only was the role of the army and police appreciated; the behaviour of the voters was 'admirable and restrained even under the constant bombardment of inflammatory and irresponsible statements made by their leaders'.[88]

Although the district police had a significant role, the presence of troops, as the Referendum Commissioner admitted, 'effectively prevented large scale intimidation and disorder and [their] energetic patrolling under considerable difficulties inspired confidence in the public'.[89] In response to an allegation that he brought a large contingent of army in connivance with the Assam ministry 'to terrorise those not supporting the amalgamation of Sylhet with East Bengal',[90] he argued that 'the number of troops actually available was small but this fact was less known to the people of the villages than the fact of their comparatively great mobility and their determination to strike when necessary'.[91] Given the distrust of the Muslims for the Assam ministry, the army was hailed because it was the Viceroy (and not the Assam government) that was responsible for its operation during the referendum.[92] Similarly, the Hindus also had reasons heartily to accept the army because of its capability of controlling the Muslim National Guard terrorising the Hindu voters, especially in the interior.[93] The presence of the troops almost everywhere in the district increased, as the Referendum Commissioner claimed, 'the confidence of the law abiding citizens who knew if there was any serious breach of law, army was instantly available. It was even rumoured', as he further elaborated, 'that army had at its command troop-carrying aeroplanes ready for aerial bombardment in case of emergency'.[94] Once the referendum was complete, the army was requested by both the Hindu and Muslim leaders 'to carry ballot boxes to the counting centres [probably because] mutual suspicion among local Hindus and Muslims had gone up to such a level that even police officers belonging to either community was not trusted by the people of other community'.⁹⁵ There were reports of intimidation of the minority by the majority community in some parts of South Sylhet and Karimganj, but the immediate arrival of the army in the affected areas helped control the situation.⁹⁶

As is evident from a contemporary report, 'there was no doubt that the Sylhet district was in the grip of the Referendum fever [and] the parties were carrying out the electioneering tactics'.⁹⁷ Charges and counter-charges were made by both the Congress and the Muslim League. It was clear even before the results were announced that 'the referendum will go', as the Assam Governor reported, 'in favour of the League'.⁹⁸ One of the reasons for League's success was certainly its involvement in the campaign from the day the plan for referendum was initiated. Not only was the local unit of the League actively participating in the campaign, the League High Command had also shown an equal interest in the referendum. It is true that the League had popularised its demand for Sylhet's inclusion in the proposed state of Pakistan, and at the outset the campaign was spearheaded by those who mattered in the League organisation. However, within a week of 20 June, when the dates for the referendum were announced, the campaign acquired a completely different character, especially in the villages, where Muslims irrespective of class 'participated in the processions [demanding] amalgamation of the district with East Bengal'.⁹⁹ Amazed by the presence of a large number of 'the half-fed and half-clothed villagers', the bhadralok press in Calcutta attributed this to the growing importance of Islam in mobilising the Muslims against the Hindus in Assam's remote villages.¹⁰⁰ Unlike Bengal, where the partition was forced upon the people once the members of the Bengal Legislative Assembly had decided by voting,¹⁰¹ Sylhet provided a completely different model where the decision was final only after it was endorsed by a majority of its population. No doubt there were instances of intimidation by the League supporters at the behest of the Muslim National Guard that radically changed the complexion of the campaign by clearly articulating the demand for Pakistan in essentially religious terms. This had an instant impact on the villagers who, by deciding to vote for the amalgamation, had actually supported 'a religious cause'.¹⁰² It is not therefore surprising that most of the slogans had a clearly religious overtone. Apart from the familiar slogan *Alla Ho Akbar*, the League organisers also picked up slogans highlighting the possible atrocities towards the Muslims if Sylhet was not made a part of East Pakistan. By casting votes in favour of 'a Muslim homeland', Muslims in Sylhet were actually contributing 'to strengthen the Islamic fraternity'. Thus the referendum was 'a golden opportunity' for them to prove their solidarity with 'fellow Muslims elsewhere'.¹⁰³

If some of these slogans were positive in their articulation, there were slogans highlighting the consequences of not supporting 'the Islamic cause'. The failure to support the amalgamation was sure to invite 'god's wrath' in one's life. Those defending the Hindu claim for keeping Sylhet in Assam were to be ostracised, as 'they had no reasons to be with their Muslim brothers'.[104] What was probably most effective was the slogan threatening 'social ostracism'. It was effective presumably because of the environment following the 3 June announcement when Pakistan became a real possibility. Just like their counterparts in Bengal, Muslims in Sylhet were emphasising a distinct communal identity linking them with Muslims elsewhere. Following the decision of partition of Bengal and Punjab, the notional state of Pakistan suddenly became a reality, providing a separate homeland for the Muslims.

In popularising the League demand, the role of the *Moulvis* was extremely significant. As in the case of Bengal, where Moulvis strengthened the League organisation in remote villages, Muolvis were very useful as soon as the campaign for the referendum began in Sylhet. Not as organised as their counterparts in Bengal, these individuals participated actively in mobilising support for the amalgamation. They usually operated at two levels. At a more organised level, their interaction with the local people was institutionalised within the well-defined structural limits of mosques. This had an advantage because, by being associated with the local mosques, these Moulvis had a stable group of followers who regularly attended Friday prayers. It was not therefore surprising that, during the campaign for referendum, the local mosques became the nerve centres of activity. Friday prayers were invariably extended because the Moulvi, apart from doing the routine job of interpreting *kalmas* from *Koran*, had also 'dwelled on the consequences of opposing the amalgamation of Sylhet with East Pakistan'.[105] The other level in which the Moulvis significantly contributed to the League campaign was not so formalised but was very effective in reaching out to those who remained peripheral to the entire campaign. These Moulvis regularly addressed the weekly local *hats* [markets], and in their speeches they always equated the vote in favour of Pakistan with 'a great service to Islam'.[106] On one occasion, as the Deputy Commisioner of Sylhet noted, 'the police was asked to disperse the people in a *hat* in Maulavi Bazar in the subdivision of South Sylhet since the meeting continued beyond the dusk'.[107] Moulvis were most effective in remote villages where the administration was either peripheral or absent, and the League had therefore succeeded in popularising its agenda without using its workers *per se*.

As is evident, the League had withdrawn the civil disobedience campaign as Jinnah requested it to do following the announcement of the 3 June plan. Probably because some of the League members felt 'betrayed' by this decision, there was clear dissension among its members. The Muslim League in Sylhet was therefore not as strong as expected before the campaign took off.[108] During the course of the campaign, however, not only had the League developed an organisation with tentacles even in the

THE SYLHET REFERENDUM AND PARTITION

interiors of the district, it had also succeeded in mobilising voters for Sylhet's union with East Pakistan. In some areas of North Sylhet, South Sylhet and Karimganj, the local units of the League undertook campaigns to popularise its demand, while in the distant villages what accounted for its growing strength was 'the Islamic bond' that appeared to have united the Muslims for a cause in opposition to the Hindus. The results were anticipated. Despite complaints by the Congress, the Referendum Commissioner never agreed to review the results, presumably because 'the demand was based on a partisan [assessment] of the situation'. He further added, '[i]n view of the fact that large percentage of voters and substantial majority are in favour of joining East Bengal, it appears clear that any irregularities and intimidation that may have taken place could not have affected the result of the referendum'.[109]

The reports on the polling reveal that, despite flooding, a large number of voters participated. Even on the first day, 6 July, a large crowd of voters and spectators 'assembled at the booths before the doors were opened'.[110] On account of inclement weather, as C. W. Pearson wrote, 'there was rush and stampede at the polling stations'. It appeared that the staff in the polling stations 'was not able to cope with voters at sufficient speed' and the police on duty 'failed to organise the entry of voters to the booth'.[111] There were reports of violence in South Sylhet and Karimganj. With the intervention of the army, the situation was quelled.[112] The polling was carried out 'more smoothly on the second day (7 July) largely because of the experience gained on the first day'.[113] It was noticeable that, as the Referendum Commissioner noted, 'a steady flow of voters was always passing in and out of the Polling compartments'.[114] Reports on violence came to the Sylhet Deputy Commissioner, but the timely intervention by police stopped 'the miscreants to disturb the polling'.[115] A serious incident was reported in Madhavpur in the Habiganj subdivision, where the Muslim National Guard 'obstructed the Hindu voters from entering the booths'. Even the military failed to restore order. The booths were shifted to a nearby school that made no difference and most of the Hindu voters stayed away presumably because 'of the panic created by the Muslim National Guard'.[116] The Hindu voters declined even when the army was willing to escort them to the booth, by saying that 'who will protect them when the army withdraws?'.[117] Similarly, the military escort for voters at Kurshi in the Habiganj subdivision was refused on the ground that 'nobody would protect them when the army went away'.[118] It is probable that in some areas there was either intimidation or fear of intimidation. What is striking, however, is the large percentage of Hindu voters in the referendum. As is evident, 78 per cent of the district's Hindus participated in the polling, and the scene was more or less uniform throughout Sylhet (see Table 6.5).

THE SYLHET REFERENDUM AND PARTITION

Table 6.5 Percentage of Hindus voting for remaining in Assam

Subdivision	Votes for remaining in Assam (%)
Sylhet Sadar	79.5
Karimganj	87.7
Habiganj	61.3
South Sylhet	80.7
Sunamganj	87.6

Source: IOR, R/3/1/158, The Report by Stock, the Referendum Commissioner, 26 July 1947.

Despite the alleged organised attempts to deter the Hindu voters from voting, the figures suggest that the effort was not as effective as was apprehended. Except in Habiganj, where Muslims constituted a majority, the proportion of Hindus who registered their votes was noticeable. The low percentage of Hindu turn-out in Habiganj is likely to be the result of stray incidents in which Hindus, as reported by the Superintendent of Police, 'were threatened by the Muslim National Guards of dire consequences' if their goal remained unattained.[119] The high percentage of Hindu votes is probably illustrative of 'one last attempt to support the claim for Sylhet's union with Assam'.[120] This is remarkable given the lack of interest of the Congress, presumably because Sylhet was to certain to go to East Pakistan given the Muslim demographic preponderance in the district. Nonetheless, the Hindus registered their opposition under adverse circumstances, especially when the League was present either in an organised way or through those sympathetic *Moulvis* who led the campaign in remote areas where the League was almost absent.

The referendum was conducted when both the League and Congress were busy in shaping the proposed independent dominions. The administration was careful not to be identified with either of the groups representing rival claims. This is evident in the detailed report of the Referendum Commissioner, who made an elaborate arrangement to avoid immediate sources of friction between the principal contenders. According to him, there were two contentious issues which he had sorted out even before the actual polling. The first issue concerned the appointment of the Presiding and Polling Officers. As each polling station needed two Presiding and at least five Polling Officers, the minimum requirement was 1673 officers to manage 239 polling booths. It was a serious problem when the number of officers in Sylhet was far below the requirement and hence, officers were brought from other districts as well as from the Assam Secretariat in Shillong. As far as possible, at least one Muslim officer (either as a Presiding or Polling officer) was allotted to each booth.

While commenting on the conduct of the administrative staff involved in polling, the Referendum Commissioner appeared happy with a qualifying note that 'most of the complaints against their conduct during the referendum ... arrived after the voting was over when it was manifestly impossible to make any kind of enquiry into them'. On one occasion, Stock visited a particular booth in Sylhet Sadar to find out the validity of a complaint against a Presiding Officer for compelling the voters to put their ballot papers in particular boxes. On enquiry, it was found out that the Officer in question 'was merely directing the voters to enter the booth alternatively in order to avoid congestion'.

The second issue that became decisive after the referendum was the security of the ballot boxes. The police were not trusted by the Muslims owing to their alleged complicity with the Congress–led Assam ministry. Therefore the army was employed to transfer the boxes to the Sylhet Sadar for counting. Every single box, with its seals, including those affixed by the parties, 'was subjected by representatives of the parties and a Gazetted Officer to minute scrutiny on arrival at the counting centre'.

As the result had to be kept secret till announced by the Viceroy, no representatives of the parties were allowed to witness the counting.[121] Two large rooms in the Deputy Commissioner's bungalow were specifically prepared for counting, the boxes marked with an Axe being counted in one room and those with a Hut in another. There was no access from one room to another. In each room, the counting agents, selected by the Referendum Commissioner himself from government offices in other districts, sat in pairs – a Hindu and a Muslim in each pair. Each pair was allotted the boxes of one station after another, and no fresh station was allotted till the one being disposed of was finished. All those involved in counting were under 'an oath' not to divulge 'anything they heard or came to know in the counting rooms'. To avoid controversy, neither 'tendered' nor 'challenged' votes were counted as valid votes. Once the counting was over, the results were prepared by the Referendum Commissioner himself.[122]

Assam divided

The results of the referendum were translated in favour of a division of Sylhet on the basis of its demographic composition. The Muslim-majority subdivisions were undoubtedly in favour of amalgamation with east Pakistan. Despite his misgivings about the outcome of the referendum due to the reported intimidation of the Muslim National Guard, Nehru accepted the verdict. As he himself explained, 'it seems clear both from the number of people who voted and the result of the voting that any irregularities took place could not materially affect the result of the referendum'.[123] His only concern was to get the report of the Boundary Commission before 15 August to ascertain that 'the process of transfer must be a single one after final determination of the area to be transferred'.[124] While demarcating the boundary, Radcliffe had however confronted a difficult situation. Inspired by the results of the referendum, the League presented a memorandum demanding the inclusion of Goalpara district into Pakistan since 'it is contiguous to the Muslim majority areas'.[125] There was another view, sponsored by the Hindu members of the Commission. According to them, the only districts of Assam that the Commission should consider 'are those that in fact adjoin Sylhet and that it is only the contiguous Muslim majority areas of those districts that should go with the Muslim areas of Sylhet to East Bengal'.[126] The choice was, however, very clear to the Chairman. He found it 'anomalous' to transfer those districts to East Bengal that had no role to play in the referendum and were not also 'neighbours geographically'.[127] Corroborating Radcliffe's interpretation of 'the terms of reference' for the setting the boundary, the Viceroy also held the view that 'only contiguous Muslim majority areas of districts adjoining Sylhet itself should be transferred to Eastern Bengal'.[128]

Keeping in mind the poll outcome, he recommended the transfer of the entire district of Sylhet to east Pakistan[129] with the exception of three thanas of Badarpur (47 square miles), Ratabari (240 square miles), Patharkandi (277 square miles) and a portion of Karimganj thana (145 square miles). Only these thanas with a total area of 709 square miles and a population of 23 million were retained in the district of Cachar in Assam. The Muslims seemed to have accepted the Award zealously, and with its announcement on 17 August the League organised Pakistan and a victory procession of 'at least 15000 people' that went off peacefully 'in a spirit of good will'.[130] As a result of the Radcliffe Award, Assam had undergone radical changes. On the one hand, though Assam's loss in area was negligible (only one-eighteenth of its existing area), it had lost nearly one-third of its population and along with it the vast paddy lands and the tea, lime and cement industries of Sylhet. On the other hand, Assam's topographical distinctiveness had been affected. With the amalgamation of Sylhet with Pakistan, the major portion of the Surma valley ceased to be part of Assam. Only a remnant of this old natural division, namely the Cacher district as now constituted (including the new truncated subdivision of Karimganj with thanas of Patharkandi, Ratabari and Badarpur and a portion of Karimganj thana), remains in the divided Assam.[131]

Concluding observations

That Assam was split following the 3 June statement is a relatively less known chapter of India's recent political history. Unlike Bengal and Punjab, where the Boundary Commission was primarily guided by the demographic complexion of the provinces, Sylhet provided an interesting case where the people themselves decided their fate by voting. Despite allegations and counter-allegations, the event itself is illustrative of the significant processes that are crucial in grasping the rise of both India and

Pakistan as independent nations. What is striking, as the above discussion shows, is the large-scale participation of both the Hindus and Muslims in the plebiscite, notwithstanding intimidation, violence or threats of violence. Even the flood that severely disrupted communications in most of the interior villages did not significantly affect the voter turn-out in the referendum. This indicates, *inter alia*, the extent to which people themselves were mobilised for their respective causes.

The Sylhet referendum was virtually a vote on the twin issues of the reorganisation of India on a communal basis and of Assam on a linguistic basis. As is shown, the Hindus, who had for decades agitated for amalgamation with Bengal, voted to remain in Assam, while the Muslims who had opposed the division of Assam till 1928, supported the partition. Apart from the religious schism, the ethnic division between the Bengalis and the Assamese significantly influenced the processes that led to the separation of Sylhet. Thus it was not surprising when Bardoloi, in his discussion with the Cabinet Mission, expressed his desire to 'hand over Sylhet to eastern Bengal'.[132] During the referendum, 'the Congress control was so correctly exercised that it hardly provided any advantage to the local Congress in its campaign to win the referendum'.[133] The Assamese had little stake in the future of Sylhet, which, as a Congress volunteer reminisced, 'they had for long been wishing out of the province'. The result of the referendum therefore provided the Assamese leadership with a grand opportunity to get rid of Sylhet and to carve out 'a linguistically more homogeneous province'.[134]

The Sylhet referendum also illustrates disjunction between the Congress local leadership and its national counterpart. The Congress appears to have confined its responsibility in dealing with the referendum in Sylhet largely to negotiating with the Viceroy and his associates at the highest level of administration. During the preparation of the referendum, none of the representatives of either the Congress High Command or the Assam Provincial Congress Committee visited the area. It is striking that not only did the League form a Committee of high profile members to guide the campaign; it also 'sanctioned adequate funds' at the behest of Jinnah to avoid difficulty. Although the Congress was organisationally strong in the Brahmaputra valley, it was confined to the subdivisionsal towns in the Surma Valley and the Hills. None of the prominent Congress leaders of Sylhet was there when the campaign took off. Both the provincial and national Congress leadership, a Congress volunteer reminisced, 'remained silent spectators, as if by design, and acquiesced the separation of Sylhet'.[135] Thus the pattern that emerged in Sylhet seems to have corresponded with what had happened in Bengal, where the Congress maintained a strategic silence when the Shyama Prasad Mookherjee-led Hindu Manasabha spearheaded a movement for partition.[136] Requests were made to the Congress High Command for money and organisational support, but to no avail. R. N. Chowdhury, of the district Congress Committee, thus lamented: 'Sylhet was sacrificed to fulfil the so-called national goal of the All India Congress under Jawaharlal Nehru and those of his colleagues who supported the British to divide India'.[137]

The Muslim League was also divided. Its campaign suffered initially due to a split between Bhasani and Saadullah. Despite his support for Pakistan, Saadullah was not as enthusiastic in the campaign as before, presumably because of the growing importance of Bhasani as an effective Muslim leader. Division in the Muslim camp also disturbed Jinnah, who instructed M. A. Ishapahani to persuade both these League leaders to work together for 'a broader goal of Pakistan'.[138] Given Bhasani's popularity among the Muslim masses, the indifferent Sadullah, who was basically an urban leader, hardly affected the League's performance in the campaign. Furthermore, the role of Mahmud Ali, a Sylhet-based Bengali,[139] was equally significant in projecting Bhasani as the leader in the campaign. It would not be wrong also to suggest that the Sylhet campaign was largely the brainchild of Bhasani, who, with Jinnah's support guided the campaign in accordance with his perception. Apart from the Muslim National Guards from the United Provinces, most of the League workers were from the eastern part of Bengal. Bhasani, it was alleged, therefore led 'a movement for a separate homeland for the Bengalis and not for Pakistan'.[140]

With a clear verdict in favour of amalgamation, the task of the Boundary Commission was relatively easier. It was not therefore difficult for Radcliffe to demarcate the boundaries of the Muslim majority areas of Sylhet. Neither the Muslim League nor the Congress succeeded in influencing the Radcliffe decision. Once its claim for the whole of Assam had been rejected by the Commission, the League submitted another memorandum demanding the district of Goalpara for Pakistan.[141] That was immediately shelved. Similarly, the Congress insistence on the inclusion of four thanas of Sylhet – Barlekha, Kulaura, Kamalganj and Srimangal – since they were Hindu majority areas also did not find favour with the Commission.[142] Even the suggestion of the Assam government regarding the demarcation of the the boundary following the river belt of Kusiara was dismissed as soon as it was made.[143] The Sylhet leaders were therefore discouraged when they tried to salvage two Hindu majority thanas of Ajmiriganj and Sulla 'through an effective representation to the Boundary Commission'.[144]

While demarcating a boundary for Sylhet, Radcliffe was guided solely by the outcome of the referendum and the terms of reference for the Boundary Commission. Thus not only did he reject the demand of major political parties, he also did not pay attention to the suggestion of even his Indian colleagues in the Commission. Both the Congress and League representatives in the Commission felt 'underutilised'.[145] Nothing seemed to have perturbed Radcliffe, who carried out his duty with the support of the

THE SYLHET REFERENDUM AND PARTITION

Viceroy.[146] At the end of the day, it was therefore neither the Congress nor the League but the colonial administration that remained supreme even as regards the delimitation of boundaries of the proposed independent states of India and Pakistan.

Notes

1 Mountbatten made it clear at the outset that he was prepared accept a division of the subcontinent if he could not get the two parties to agree on a political arrangement that would enable the British government to transfer power to a united India. See Minutes of the Viceroy's meeting with Indian leaders, 2 June 1947, in Mansergh et al., Vol. XI, 1982: 39.
2 In his discussion with Jawaharlal Nehru, Wavell expressed disappointment for his failure to maintain India's unity following the Cripps' model of federation. He mentioned that 'our attitude is not, as you seem to suspect, prompted by a desire to retain power for power's sake; but to give India the best possible chance of success as an independent India. We are giving you a chance of a united India, and I think, it may be the last chance and are prepared to give every possible help to obtain it'. See IOR, R/1/1/128, Wavell's personal note after his discussion with Nehru, 26 May 1946.
3 The resolution adopted at the annual session of the Muslim League at Lahore on 24 March 1940 was the first official pronouncement of the Pakistan or partition demand of the party. Though the term Pakistan is nowhere to be found in the resolution, it is nevertheless seen to have provided for the separation of Muslim majority areas in the north-western and eastern zones of India as 'sovereign' and 'independent states', and thereby formed the basis of the Pakistan demand (Roy 1990: 388). Even Nicholas Mansergh, while discussing the Lahore resolution, expressed surprise at the absence of the term 'Pakistan'. Despite this absence, what was significant was the reference to 'the Muslim homelands' and 'a Holy War' to defend them (see Mansergh 1999: 219).
4 The referendum in the North-West Frontier Province was held from 6 to 17 July. Of the total electorate of 572798, slightly over 50 per cent took part, 289244 voting for and 2874 voting against joining the new Constituent Assembly (see Menon (reprinted 1993) 1957: 389).
5 IOR, R/3/1/158, 3 June statement.
6 IOR, R/3/1/158, Mountbatten to A. K. Hydari, the Assam Governor, 18 June 1947.
7 For an elaborate discussion on the socio-economic profile of early colonial Assam, see Guha 1990.
8 Allen 1905: 1.
9 Allen 1905: 79.
10 Ibid.
11 The Census of India, Vol. IX, Assam, 1941, p. 8.
12 Ibid.
13 IOR, R/3/1/158, Report of the Deputy Commissioner, Sylhet, 6 May 1947.
14 Ibid. According to the Deputy Commissioner, Sylhet, 'the absence of restriction on widow remarriage is probably the most important factor in the dramatic rise of Muslims in North Sylhet'. He further explained, 'in 1931, there were only 31000 Muhammadan widows between [the ages of] 15 and 40, as compared with 60000 Hindu widows of this age, and Muslims had about 30000 more potential mothers, i.e, married women between [the ages of]

15 and 40 than the followers of the rival religion'. 'A difference such as this', he emphatically argued, 'is bound to produce a sensible effect on the growth of the population'.
15 IOR, R/3/1/158, Report of the Deputy Commissioner, Sylhet, 6 May 1947.
16 As reported in the *District Gazetteer*, wild tea was discovered in the Surma Valley in 1855 and the first tea garden was established in a place called Malnichara in Sylhet in 1857, (see Allen 1905: 135).
17 According to the Deputy Commissioner, in Sylhet, out of a total of 238 tea gardens in 1941, Europeans controlled 197 of them. In South Sylhet and Karimganj, Europeans had at their disposal 107 and 67 tea gardens respectively. See NAI, Home-Poll (Confidential), 18/11/41, Chief Secretary's Fortnightly Report, first half of March 1941.
18 Allen 1905: 137.
19 IOR, V/27/61/7, Assam District Gazetteer, supplement to Volume II, Sylhet, Assam Secretariat Press, Shillong, 1935, p. 3. As it was possible to survive on agricultural income, the difficulty of obtaining ordinary servants and ordinary labourers, as the *Gazetteer* reports, 'has increased greatly of late years'. Furthermore, '[many] people of this class from Karimganj, North Sylhet, and South Sylhet subdivisions have settled in Cachar where lands are more readily available and have taken to cultivation'.
20 NAI, Home-Poll (Confidential), C 69/47-II, report of the meeting, held on 19 June 1947, in which the Deputy Commissioner of Sylhet, the Superintendent of Police and officers in charge of the subdivisions participated.
21 IOR, R/3/1/158, A. Hydari, the Governor of Assam to the Viceroy, 23 June 1947.
22 IOR, R/3/1/158, the Governor of Assam to G. E. B. Abell, the private secretary to the Viceroy, 22 June 1947.
23 Both the Congress and the League leadership raised objections on this ground because the list of voters, unless updated, was unlikely to include the new voters and hence was not acceptable. V. P. Menon attributed the objection to the uncertainty of the both the Hindus and Muslims regarding the outcome of the proposed referendum (see Menon 1957 (reprinted 1993): 388).
24 IOR, R/3/1/158, Liaquat Ali Khan to Mountbatten, 11 June 1947.
25 IOR, R/3/1/158, N. Sundaram, officer-in-charge of the referendum to G. E. B. Abell, 13 June 1947.
26 Menon 1957 (reprinted 1993): 388.
27 IOR, R/3/1/158, Representation from the Srimangal Tea Estate to the Viceroy, 20 June 1947.
28 IOR, R/3/1/158, N. Sundaram to G. E. B. Abell, 18 June 1947.
29 *The Dawn*, 29 June 1947.
30 IOR, QAP (microfilm), File No 131/2–10, Jinnah to the Viceroy, 30 June 1947.
31 This section draws upon the complaints to the Viceroy. To his letter to the the Governor of Assam, A. Hydari, the Viceroy had attached more than one hundred complaints received by him, for the Governor to see. Interestingly, most of the charges were against the government for having failed to discharge its duties in a non-partisan way. The reference was probably to the Gopinath Bardoloi-led Congress ministry in Assam that never agreed to the idea of a referendum for Sylhet from the outset, since the district was an integral part of a province where Hindus were demographically preponderant (see IOR, R/3/1/158, Viceroy to the Governor, Assam, 28 June 1947).
32 IOR, R/3/1/158, Mountbatten to Claude Auchinleck, 2 July 1947.
33 IOR, R/3/1/158, a report by Lieutenant Colonel C. W. Pearson, 11 July 1947.

34 Ibid.
35 IOR, R/3/1/158, Telegram, Assam Governor to the Viceroy, 11 June 1947.
36 Ibid.
37 IOR, R/3/1/158, Jinnah to the Viceroy, 28 June 1947; Gopinath Bardoloi, the Assam Premier to the Viceroy, 29 June 1947.
38 IOR, QAP (microfilm), File No. 980/47, Abdul Hamid Khan (known as Maulana Bhasani), President of the Assam Provincial Muslim League, to Jinnah, 28 June 1947.
39 NAI, Home-Poll (Confidential), C213/39, *The Assam Gazettee Extraordinary*, No. 3, 4 November 1939, signed by S. P. Desai, Secretary, Government of India, Revenue Department, p. 3. A committee, presided over by F. W. Hockenhull of the European Party, was appointed in 1937 to review the Line system. Ratifying the 1920 Line system, the Hockenhull Committee, in its report submitted in February, 1938, stated, '[t]he restrictions constituting the so-called Line System which have been in existence in the province for over 10 years were primarily intended against the unending flow of Bengal immigrant cultivators and took the form of constituting certain areas in which settlement of land with such immigrants was prohibited. ... Within such prohibited areas so constituted immigrant cultivators shall not be allowed land either by settlement or by transfer of annual pattas, and any immigrant so taking up land or by squatting shall be evicted'.
40 Prasad 1957: 259–60. Corroborating the apprehension, the then Viceroy, Wavell, also realised that 'the chief political problem [in Assam] is the desire of the Muslim ministers to increase immigration into the uncultivated lands under the slogan of Grow More Food, ... but what they are really after is grow more Muslims. The native Assamese are ... likely to be ousted by more pushing but less attractive Bengali Moslems' (Moon 1973: 41).
41 Prasad 1957: 259–60. As a pioneer of this argument, Prasad also took steps. He, along with his brother and Anugraha Narain Sinha of the Assam Congress acquired 'a thousand acres of land and a tractor in a jungle-infested malarial tract' to encourage the Biharis to settle. The experience, however, failed (see Guha 1977: 259).
42 Members of the Committee of Action were 1) Maulana Bhasani, Chairman and Convenor, 2) Saadullah, 3) Abdul Kasem, 4) Md. Saleh, 5) Abdul Bari Choudhury, 6) Dewan Abdul Basit Choudhury, 7) Moinul Haque Choudhury, and 8) Badrul Hussain. See *The Star of India*, 21 February 1946; NAI, Home-Poll (Confidential), C 240/46, District Magistrate, Goalpara to the Secretary, Home Department, Government of Assam.
43 Maulana Bhasani, previously known as Abdul Hamid Khan, derived his name from *Bhasanir char*, an island in the *Brahmaputra*, where he settled along with his followers. He contested the 1937 elections and won with a massive majority (see Guha 1977: 215).
44 *The Star of India*, 21 February 1946.
45 Condemning the eviction policy of the Congress ministry, Liaquat Ali Khan thus sarcastically remarked: 'this way the Congress government in Assam serves the poor when they happen to be Muslims. Cruelty and inhumanity exceed all bounds in the Congress tyranny over the Muslim immigrants in Assam', See *The Star of India*, 11 March 1947; and also *The Assam Tribune*, 12 March 1947.
46 There were instances in which the Muslim Students' Federation were also involved in the agitation against the 'eviction policy'. After a meeting in Sylhet addressed by Maulana Bhasani, the members of the Federation were reported to have 'removed the Union Jack from the premises of the district

court and replaced it with the League flag' (see NAI, Home-Poll (Confidential), C69/47–II, Superintendent of Police, Sylhet to the District Magistrate, 18 April 1947). As the Superintendent of Police further reported, to disperse the League supporters disrupting the Railway in Sylhet, the army was reported to have fired – resulting in one death and several injured.

47 *The Pakistan Times*, 1 April 1947.
48 *The Pakistan Times*, 4 April 1947; Khaliq-uz-Zaman's report on the Assam League movement.
49 *The Pakistan Times*, 2 April 1947, a report of a meeting addressed by Khaliq-uz-zaman on 31 March 1947.
50 NAI, Rajendra Prasad Papers, File no 11/1946–47, Gopinath Bardoloi to Rajendra Prasad, 6 April 1947.
51 *The Pakistan Times*, 6 April 1947.
52 M. A. Ispahani was a businessman with a large stake in both Calcutta and Bombay. Moazzamuddin was a Minister for Revenue and Education, Bengal, and A. W. Baakza was an official of the Habib Bank, Calcutta.
53 *Jinnah Papers*, Vol. II, Jinnah's press statement, 26 June 1947.
54 *Jinnah Papers*, Vol. II, Moinul Haque Chaudhury to Jinnah, 25 June 1947.
55 IOR, Quaid-i-Azam Papers, File No. 496/ 6–7, (microfilm), Jinnah to Suhrawardy, 25 June 1947. Jinnah also made a written request to the Viceroy to sanction 'money from the Central Funds towards Referendum expenses' (see IOR, R/3/1/158, Jinnah to the Viceroy, 27 June 1947).
56 IOR, QAP (micrfilm), file 886/102–108, Moinul Haque Chowdhury to Jinnah, 28 June 1947. The plan to bring Muslims from provinces where they constituted a minority was probably part of a grand design devised by a Calcutta-based businessman, Zafarel Quarishi, who in his letter to Jinnah (on 13 March 1947) elaborated on the scheme further. He thus insisted: 'we should immediately start peopling these areas with Mussalmans as we have still 14 months to go before the final transfer of power takes place. *We have no time to lose* (emphasis original). We have to race against time. Wherever there may be a Muslim city or a big village in the district in dispute where enough space may be available, we should chalk out a plan for starting a factory there with its attendant scheme of housing the labour to be employed there. And only those Mussalmans who come from the minority provinces or states should be offered employment in those factories. Like the Jews of Palestine, we should concentrate on purely Muslim cities and places and thus swell our population ratio; and when the figures have reached the target, we should clamour for a plebiscite in case any party wishes to try conclusion [sic] for the partition of [Bengal and Punjab] on population basis'. See Zafarel Qureshi to Jinnah, 13 March 1947, Jinnah Papers, Vol. 1 (Part 1), p. 241. Part of this letter was published in *The Dawn*, 3 July 1947.
57 IOR, R/3/1/158; posters kept in this file clearly show the extent to which the campaign was organised in Sylhet on the eve of the referendum.
58 IOR, R/3/1/158, posters circulated in North Sylhet and Habiganj.
59 Jinnah Papers, Vol. II, President of the Habiganj District Muslim League to Jinnah, 4 July 1947.
60 Jinnah Papers, Vol. II. In his letter to Jinnah (Nawab of Bhupal had suggested this. Nawab of Bhupal to Jinnah, 8 June 1947).
61 Ibid.
62 IOR, R/3/1/158, Report by Colonel C. W. Pearson, 11 July 1947. Colonel Pearson was one of the four officers from the British Army who took charge of security during the referendum.

THE SYLHET REFERENDUM AND PARTITION

63 The Muslim National Guard, founded in United Province in 1931 as a counter-force to the Rashtriya Swyam Sevak Sangh, was rejuvenated at a meeting of the Committee of Action of the All India Muslim League held at Lahore in February 1944. Although the aim of the Guard was 'to organise Muslim youths with a view to infusing into them a spirit of tolerance, sacrifice and discipline', their role was not merely confined to this. They were reported to have instigated violence against the Hindus in the United Provinces and Bengal. While inaugurating a Training Centre in Faridpur, east Bengal, Suhrawardy (the Bengal Premier) announced that 'those who are being trained at this Centre will help Muslims in the event of enemy action as well as act as soldiers for the attainment of Pakistan'. In fact, during the Direct Action Day agitation, there were innumerable IB reports to show that the Guard had actively participated in the mayhem that ravaged Calcutta in August 1946. According to a Government report, the Guard were most active in almost all the British Indian provinces. Their presence was noticeable in Bengal (1132 members), Bihar (6979 members), Bombay (2710 members), the North West Frontier Province (5706 members) and the United Province (9,392 members). See NAI, File No. Home-Poll (I)–28/2/43 of 28 December 1944, Report on the activities of the Muslim League National Guard. This document is published in *Towards Freedom: Document on the Movement for Independence in India, 1943–44*, Part 3, edited by P. S. Gupta, ICHR and Oxford University Press, New Delhi, 1997, pp. 3284–8.

64 A contemporary police report reveals that the recruitment and training of the Muslim National Guard in Assam started in 1944. In a meeting of the Assam Provincial Muslim League, held at the League office at Sheikhghat, Sylhet on 1 October 1944, Arsad Ali was appointed as the commander-in-chief of the all Assam Muslim National Guard and he was vested with powers to recruit volunteers for this purpose throughout the province. In 1946 Badrul Hussain of Kulaura was made *salr-i-suba* [the provincial organiser] of the National Guard. He was reported to have recruited even ex-INA soldiers. Sylhet was the Headquarters of the Guards. See NAI, Home-Poll (confidential), File No. 119/46 (1) and also File No. 18/5/1946, Fortnightly Reports for the second half of May 1946; Home-Poll (confidential) File No. A.P.2/47/688, Superintendent of Police, Rangpur to the District Magistrate, Rangpur, 18 March 1947.

65 *The Dawn*, 25 June 1947. *The Statesman* of Calcutta did not bring out Jinnah's statement as a separate item, but had referred to it in a report on referendum (*The Statesman*, 29 June 1947).

66 IOR, R/3/1/158, Colonel Pearson's report, 11 July 1947.

67 This section draws upon reports submitted by A. Hydari, the Assam Governor, and Stork, the Referendum Commissioner to the Viceroy. See IOR, R/3/1/158, A. Hydari to the Viceroy, 14 July 1947; Stork to the Viceroy, 26 July 1947.

68 IOR, R/3/1/158, Mountbatten to Nehru, 13 July 1947.

69 A. Hydari to Mountbatten, 11 July 1947, Mansergh and Moon 1982: 104.

70 Jawaharlal Nehru's telegram to Akbar Hydari, 13 July 1947 (see Gopal 1985, Vol. III: 183).

71 NMML, AICC File No. 1/G 33/1947–48, R. N. Chowdhury, of the Sylhet District Congress Committee to Nehru, 17 July 1947.

72 NMML, AICC File No.1/G 33/1947–48, Telegram, Monorama Dasi to Nehru, 6 July 1947. The copy of this complaint was sent to the Governor, Assam. See IOR, R/3/1/158, A. Hydari's report on the referendum.

73 Nehru's telegram to Akbar Hydari, 13 July 1947 (see Gopal 1985, Vol. II: 183).
74 NMML, AICC Files No 1/G 33/1947–48, R. N. Chowdhury of the Sylhet District Congress Committee to Nehru, 17 July 1947.
75 IOR, R/3/1/158, The Assam Governor to the Viceroy, 1 July 1947. The Governor further wrote, 'all my ministers except from the Surma Valley ones are lukewarm and the Prime Minister has even been publicly criticised for his lack of enthusiasm in the matter of retaining Sylhet. The impression of a ministry strongly determined to keep it which is one of the objects of League propaganda to spread is [therefore] just not true'.
76 IOR, R/3/1/158, Nehru to Mountbatten, 15 July 1947.
77 IOR, R/3/1/158, a report by D. C. Dutt, the Deputy Superintendent of Police, Sylhet, 28 July 1947.
78 *Amrita Bazar Patrika*, 29 July 1947. Despite its pro-government stance, even *The Statesman* also referred to the several instances of atrocities, meted out to the innocent people in Sylhet by the Muslim National Guard (*The Statesman*, 29 and 30 July 1947).
79 Etymologically, *Kafer* refers to those with a different faith. In this context, it meant Hindus only.
80 NMML, AICC sub. Sylhet referendum 38/1947. The AICC had letters from the Sylhet district Congress Committee elaborating several instances of atrocities committed by the Muslim League-supported groups. The Sylhet subject file contains more than 100 letters from individuals not associated with the Congress at all. Some of them were teachers of primary schools, and shop-owners. The Hindu teachers were told to leave immediately, and those who declined were harassed and victimised; several shops owned by the Hindus were looted and gutted as well. The objective was 'crystal clear'. If the Hindus 'do not go away, they will be forced to leave Pakistan'. It is not possible to quote from all those letters. Here, those letters are quoted which are representative in character. For instance, in his letters of 18 July, 29 July and 21 August 1947, R. N. Chaudhury of the Sylhet district Congress Committee dwelled on the circumstances in the aftermath of the referendum in detail. What explains his consistent stance against the League was probably his hope that the Congress, especially Nehru, would finally insist on Sylhet's inclusion to India. The most illustrative of the situation in the villages are the letters writeen by N. Biswas, a primary school teacher, and Haran Dhar, a shop-owner. They were terrorised in Sylhet and sought Nehru's intervention to get jobs in India since they had decided to go there (see N. Biswas to Jawaharlal Nehru, 21 August 1947; Haran Dhar to Jawaharlal Nehru, 23 August 1947).
81 *Amrita Bazar Patrika*, 8 June 1947.
82 IOR, R/3/1/158, Pearson to Stock, the Referendum Commissioner, 11 July 1947.
83 IOR, R/3/1/158, C. W. Pearson's report, 11 July 1947.
84 See IOR, R/3/1/158, D. C. Dutt, the Superintendent of Police to Stock, the Referendum Commissioner, 19 July 1947.
85 Apart from the army, the district police force was strengthened by bringing police from outside the district. As the report of the Sylhet Superintendent of Police shows, Sylhet had 103 officers and 926 other ranks in the unarmed branch, and 6 officers and 330 other ranks in the armed branch. For the referendum, apart from 22 officers and 399 other ranks in the unarmed branch who came from outside the district, Assam Rifles provided 8 officers and 418 other ranks, and the Central Rail Force had 8 officers and 382 other ranks. See IOR,

R/3/1/158, D. C. Dutt, the Superintendent of Police to Stock, the Referendum Commissioner, 19 July 1947.
86 The government was reported to have seized boats, presumably to undertake effective patrolling in the interior. In his complaint to the Viceroy, Jogen Mandal, the member of the Governing Council, metioned that 'this act of the government at this time will surely create great resentment and dissatisfaction [because] seizure of boats will put the Scheduled Caste and Muslim voters who mostly belong rural areas to difficulty and also deprive them of exercising their franchise'. See IOR, R/3/1/158, Telegram, Jogen Mandal to the Viceroy, 4 July 1947.
87 IOR, R/3/1/158, D. C. Dutt, the Superintendent of Police to Stock, 19 July 1947.
88 Ibid.
89 IOR, R/3/1/158, Stock's observations on the Referendum, 21 July 1947.
90 IOR, R/3/1/158, Jogen Mandal to the Viceroy, 5 July 1947.
91 IOR, R/3/1/158, Stock's observations, 21 July 1947.
92 *The Dawn*, 29 June 1947.
93 NMML, AICC 1/G33/1947–48, R. N. Chowdhury of the Sylhet District Congress Committee to Jawaharlal Nehru, 28 June 1947.
94 IOR, R/3/158, Stock's observations, 21 July 1947.
95 IOR, R/3/1/158, Stock's observations, 21 July 1947.
96 IOR, R/3/1/158, D. C. Dutt's report, 19 July 1947. Despite being critical of the presence of the army in the referendum, nationalist dailies like the *Amrita Bazar Patrika* also hailed its role in restraining 'the Muslim League-sponsored hooligans' in Sylhet (*Amrita Bazar Patrika*, 21 July 1947).
97 IOR, R/3/1/158, C. W. Pearson's report, 11 July 1947.
98 Mansergh *et al.*, Vol. XII, 1982, A. Hydari to Mountbatten, 11 July 1947.
99 NAI, Rajendra Prasad Papers File No 11/1946–47, Basanta Kumar Das, the Assam Home Minister to Rajendra Prasad, 3 July 1947.
100 *Ananda Bazar Patrika*, 3 July 1947. It is significant that *Ananda Bazar Patrika* – which defended the partition of Bengal to avoid the Muslim domination – did not seem to be so zealous in Sylhet's union with Assam. One of the factors that appeared to have significantly influenced the Calcutta press was the demographic preponderance of the Muslims in Sylhet – a factor that invariably struck the balance in the Muslims' favour.
101 See Chapter 3.
102 NAI, Home-Poll (confidential), File No. C 133/1947, a report by the Superintendent of Police, Sylhet, 27 June 1947.
103 NAI, Home-Poll (Confidential), 6C/28/1947, a report of the Intelligence Branch, the Assam Police, 3 July 1947.
104 NAI, Home-Poll (Confidential), 6C/28/1947, a report of the Intelligence Branch, the Assam Police, 3 July 1947. *The Star of India* published several letters in its editions of 3 and 4 July noting that the best possible option for the Muslims of Sylhet was to be part of the future state of Pakistan as 'this will strengthen the Islamic fraternity'.
105 IOR, R/3/1/158, D. C. Dutt to Stock, the Referendum Commissioner, 28 June 1947.
106 IOR, R/3/1/158, Pearson to Stock, the Referendum Commissioner, 28 June 1947.
107 IOR, R/3/1/158, Deputy Commissioner, Sylhet to the Referendum Commissioner, 1 July 1947.
108 IOR, QAP (microfilm), File No. 886/102–108, Moinul Haque Chowdhury

of the Sylhet Muslim League to Jinnah, 9 June 1947. Chowdhury was disappointed when the majority of the executive members of the District Committee of the League in Sylhet were absent in a crucial meeting that was convened to prepare an agenda of action following the Viceroy's declaration.
109 IOR, R/3/1/158, Telegram, Stock to the Governor of Assam, 15 July 1947.
110 IOR, R/3/1/158, A report by Stock, the Referendum Commissioner, 26 July 1947.
111 IOR, R/3/1/158, C. W. Pearson's report of 11 July 1947.
112 Referring to the violence, *Amrita Bazar Patrika* reported that there had been a general breakdown of law and order and that the lawlessness had 'prevailed on a wide scale through out the district on the eve and during the referendum' (see *Amrita Bazar Patrika*, 9 and 10 July 1947).
113 IOR, R/3/1/158, C. W. Pearson's report of 11 July 1947.
114 IOR, R/3/1/158, A report by Stock, the Referendum Commissioner, 26 July 1947.
115 IOR, R/3/1/158, Deputy Commissioner to the Referendum Commissioner, 8 July 1947.
116 *Amrita Bazar Patrika*, 10 July, 1947. 'Hindu voters in Moslem majority areas', admitted the Referendum Commissioner, 'were afraid for safety of their houses and their women folk' and there were instances 'when the Hindus refused to go the polls even when promised escort by the military to the polls and back to their village'. See IOR, R/3/1/158, Stock, the Referendum Commissioner to the Secretary of State, London, 14 July 1947.
117 IOR, R/3/1/158, C. W. Pearson's report of 11 July 1947.
118 IOR, R/3/1/158, C. W. Pearson's report, 11 July 1947.
119 NAI, Home-Poll (Confidential), File No. C69/4711, Memo No. 502/47, Superintendent of Police, Sylhet, to the Deputy Commissioner of Police, Special Branch, Calcutta, 28 June 1947.
120 *The Assam Tribune*, 28 August 1947.
121 This caused consternation among the party representatives. To avoid untoward incidents, the military cordoned off the Deputy Commissioner's residence (which was selected for counting the ballots) even before the ballot boxes began arriving. IOR, R/3/1/158, D. C. Dutt's communication with the Referendum Commissioner, 9 July 1947.
122 The entire description of the arrangements made by the administration to conduct the referendum as smoothly as possible draws upon the extensive report prepared by Stock, the Referendum Commissioner. See IOR, R/3/1/158, A report by the Referendum Commissioner, 26 July 1947.
123 Mansergh *et al.*, Vol. XII, 1982: 167, Nehru to Mountbatten, 15 July 1947. An intelligence branch report also confirms Nehru's assessment by saying that 'in view of the fact that large percentage of voters and substantial majority in favour of joining East Bengal, it appears clear that any irregularities and intimidation that may have taken place could not have affected the result of referendum'. See IOR, R/3/1/158, Telegram, the Foreign Office to the Assam Governor, 15 July 1947.
124 Mansergh *et al.*, Vol. XII, 1982: 168, Nehru to the Viceroy, 15 July 1947. The confusion arose because the 3 June statement was not very clear on the fate of those areas likely to be separated if the Radcliffe Award was not published before the actual date of the transfer of power. Nehru therefore argued, 'from the June 3rd statement it appeared that such parts of Sylhet district as might be determined by the Boundary Commission would be transferred to East Bengal, this, of course, after the referendum had taken place and the major

issue decided. The Parliamentary Bill is not quite clear on this point and it might be said that in case the boundary has not been demarcated by the Commission by the 15th August, the whole district of Sylhet will be transferred. Subsequently, it might be necessary and indeed it is highly probable that certain parts of Sylhet district will go back to Assam after the report of the Boundary Commission. Obviously, *this transfer and retransfer will produce very great confusion and difficulty and will completely upset the life of the district and surrounding areas*' (emphasis added).

125 Assam Secretariat, Guwahati, Home-Poll (Confidential B) File No. C232/47, a report by the Superintendent of Police, Goalpara, to the District Magistrate, 2 August 1947. Endorsing this view, both the Muslim League members of the Boundary Commission insisted on including the district as, they argued, 'the adjoining districts should include all parts of Assam that join Bengal, even if they do not adjoin Sylhet and that the Commission is therefore intended to ascertain Contiguous Muslim areas of [Goalpara] and transfer to East Bengal'. See IOR, R/3/1/157, Radcliffe to the Viceroy, 2 August 1947.

126 IOR, R/3/1/157, Radcliffe to the Viceroy, 2 August 1947.

127 IOR, R/3/1/157, Radcliffe to the Viceroy, 2 August 1947. In his view, 'it would be, to some extent, anomalous that a referendum in Sylhet in favour of amalgamation with East Bengal should occasion the transfer to East Bengal of parts of other districts that have had no hand in the Sylhet decision and are not even its neighbours geographically'.

128 IOR, R/3/1/157, Telegram, the Viceroy to Radcliffe, 3 August 1947. The Bengal Governor supported Radcliffe's decision to demarcate those areas of Sylhet adjoining the district by underlining that 'the Boundary Commission must proceed on the basis that adjoining districts are adjoining districts of Assam that adjoin Sylhet and not any districts of Assam that adjoin Bengal'. See IOR, R/3/1/157, Telegram, the Bengal Governor to the Viceroy, 3 August 1947.

129 IOR, R/3/1/157, The Government Notification, 17 August 1947. This was the third time Sylhet was divided since 1874. The district was metaphorically described as 'the golden calf' sacrificed in 1874 'at the altar of the idol, called the province of Assam', in 1912 when the Bengal partition was revoked and finally in 1947 when the referendum was in its favour (see Kar 1997: 33). The expression 'golden calf' is, however, borrowed from the *Indian Statutory Commission Report*, Vol. XV, p. 321.

130 IOR, R/3/1/157, a report of the Superintendent of Police, Sylhet, 17 August 1947.

131 *The Census of India*, 1951, Vol. XII, Assam, Manipur and Tripura, Part 1 (Report).

132 Moon 1973: 234.

133 Guha 1977: 319.

134 Kar 1997: 49. Kar further writes that when the results of the referendum were declared, 'there was a feeling of relief in the Brahmaputra valley'. For an interesting historical account of the Bengalee-Assamese ethnic division, see Guha 1977: 256–63. Even Nehru was probably guided by 'the longstanding difference of opinion between the Bengalees and the Assamese' when he suggested a third Boundary Commission for Sylhet because he apprehended that the Congress representatives to the already prevalent Boundary Commission 'will naturally be inclined to view the question more from the point of view of Bengal than of Assam', presumably due to their ethnic roots (see Mansergh *et al.*, Vol. XII, 1982; Nehru to the Viceroy, 15 July 1947).

THE SYLHET REFERENDUM AND PARTITION

135 Kar, a young Congress volunteer who participated in the campaign against the partition of Assam (see Kar 1997: 48).
136 Although the Hindu Mahasabha was in favour of Bengal partition, in Sylhet its role was just the opposite. As a participant recollects, the Hindu Mahasabha volunteers who came just two days before the referendum supported the campaign for Sylhet's union with Assam (Kar 1997: 48). Despite its peripheral role in the referendum, the Assam question had always figured in the Hindu Mahasabha annual sessions. For instance, in its 1943 Bombay session a resolution was adopted stating: '[t]he Working Committee views with concern the influx into the province of Assam of Mahammedans from outside the province under the pretext of Grow More Food Campaign and requests the Government of Assam to help the Hindus from the districts of Sylhet and Cacher to settle in Assam valley and contribute to the food campaign and calls upon the Government to see that the Muslims who are rushing now, do not get any more facilities that Hindu cultivators and to extend full protection to the Hindu settlers'. See *Indian Annual Registrar*, Vol. 1, July–September 1943, p. 258.
137 *The Assam Tribune*, 29 August 1947.
138 IOR, QAP (microfilm), 886/102–108, Jinnah to Ispahani, 3 July 1947. M. A. Ishapahani was one of the three members appointed by Jinnah to organise the Muslims in Sylhet for the referendum.
139 Mahmud Ali of Sylhet joined the Assam Muslim League during its campaign against the eviction policy of the Congress in 1946. Opposed to Saadulla, he was one of the trusted lieutenants of Bhasani when the latter organised the League members to oust the former as the leader of the parliamentary wing of the party in 1946. A man of organisation, Ali rose to become the General Secretary of the provincial Muslim League. Along with Abdul Matin Chowdhury of Sylhet, he was most effective in mobilising Muslim support for Sylhet's amalgamation with East Bengal.
140 IOR, QAP (microfilm), 886/102–108, Ispahani to Jinnah, 2 July 1947.
141 Assam Secretariat, Guwahati, Home-Poll (confidential), C 232/47, The Memorandum of the Muslim League, 2 August 1947.
142 Bhuyan 1980: 291.
143 Aditya 1970: 31. Radcliffe ignored the suggestion because 'the rivers which might appear to form suitable natural boundaries in India frequently changed their courses and would not therefore provide a fixed boundary'. See IOR, R/3/1/158, Minutes of the meeting of the Partition Council held on 10 July 1947.
144 *The Assam Tribune*, 17 July and 23 July 1947. That the Assam Congress ministry never supported two of its militant leaders, Nilmono Phukan and Ambikagiri Chowdhury, when they decided to organise movements against the Radcliffe Award is indicative of the stance the party adopted just before formal partition. Despite his opposition to the referendum, which was in his view, a farce, and its outcome, the Home Minister, Basanta Kumar Das, was virtually hounded out of the cabinet when he was divested of his portfolio (*The Assam Tribune*, 28 July 1947).
145 IOR, R/3/1/157, Nehru to Mountbatten, 2 August 1947.
146 IOR, R/3/1/157, Telegram, Viceroy to Radcliffe, 3 August 1947. What the Viceroy confirmed was the reiteration of a decision taken in the Partition Council meeting held on 10 July 1947. It was agreed in that meeting that 'no directive in addition to the terms of reference should be given to the Boundary Commission; it should be left to their discretion to interpret their terms of reference'. See IOR, R/3/1/158, Minutes of the meeting of the Partition Council.

7
HISTORY OF PARTITION OR PARTITION OF HISTORY?

The fractured and wounded voice of the people

Partition is a story of re-negotiation or re-ordering. It is a resolution, at least politically, of 'a conundrum' involving Hindus and Muslims in the presence of 'a third party', namely the British. It is also an unfolding of historical processes into which people were drawn spontaneously or under compulsion and participated as significant actors in what was also 'a history of struggle' for survival in changed circumstances, following the construction of a new political identity as Indians or Pakistanis. Independence came in 1947, but with partition. The single most important event that interrogated the concept of 'nation' was the success of Jinnah in creating a sovereign Muslim homeland.[1] While the idea of an Indian or Pakistani nation was largely constructed or imagined, it had acquired distinctive characteristics in the struggle against imperialism. The imagined nation was influenced by history, memories of the past (both constructed and real) and the philosophical inclinations of India as a socio-cultural identity. This story can be told in two ways. The first is by focusing on institutional politics to map the unfolding of the events and processes that finally led to partition by linking the various levels of politics over a historical period. Undoubtedly significant, the importance of institutional politics, both in its 'high' and 'low' forms, may appear teleological unless linked with what had fashioned its articulation in a particular way. In other words, a critical engagement with the British political design to pursue the imperial goal is one of the ways of dealing with the outcome with reference to both its immediate and its ultimate background. The other interesting way is to capture the multiple 'voices' of those who were directly or peripherally affected following the sudden changes in the political map of India, some of them were passive but interested observers. Some represented the elite, but most were, argues Mushirul Hasan, 'ordinary folks whose fortunes and destinies were changed without taking into account their feelings and interests'. They spoke 'in different voices', expressed 'varying concern' and chose 'separate and distinct points of identification'.[2]

With the demarcation of boundaries, for those who had been uprooted the geographical space became a part of memory overnight. Partition was therefore a nodal point underlining a massive shift in conceptualising 'the self' and 'the collectivity' in relation to the politically demarcated boundaries. How is it possible to capture the 'shift', which was partly obvious given the changed complexion of the nation that had been transforming, ever since the articulation of Hindu–Muslim differences, to advance a political goal? Here, the creative writings of this phase are most crucial in capturing and meaningfully explaining the multifaceted voice of the people.

The immediate circumstances were a new social landscape in which communities were redefined in consonance with the political goals of the new states. Those who suffered in consequence were 'ordinary folks' who hardly had roles in the realm of 'high' politics. What figured prominently in the literary construction of the event was the break-up of an organic society and the resultant dislocation causing numerous cracks in both intra- and inter-communal relationships.[3] Critical in these narratives was not so much of the event of partition, but 'the impingement of its consequences on the consciousness of the individual – a defining moment that forces him/her to realize the pastness of the past and the presence of the here and now'.[4] The individual was torn between the lost past and an uncertain future, finding him- or herself rootless and homeless, a refugee 'who has to strive to relocate his/her identity in a radically different present, which, paradoxically enough, is shaped, influenced and conditioned by the very past which is irrecoverable'.[5]

There is no doubt that in articulating the history of partition, these voices are very important. Their recovery is not, however, unproblematic because (1) there are multiple voices, and (2) they are represented by the authors who interrogated partition from where they were located. In other words, the importance of the perspective is what invariably structured their sensibility and consequently the approach. What is critically imperative is to underline that the experiences of the creative authors are, after all, their representations, selectively highlighted by their concerns and priorities. The memory or the experience that inform them is a significant input while articulating the voice of the people that may not always correspond with the pattern elsewhere.[6]

This chapter selectively draws upon creative writings, primarily from Bengal, to map out the people's voice. There are two concern: first, since history written from archival sources is generally tilted in favour of the 'official' voice, the other side of the story, representing different political discourses where people figured prominently, remains peripheral, if not completely bypassed. Secondly, an attempt is made here not to place these voices against the 'conventional' and factual history of partition, but rather alongside existing history. In other words, the articulation of the people's voice is complementary to and not contradictory with what has been incorporated in the official records and documents.⁷ Underlying different voices lies a common note that informs nearly all the stories, novel and poems written about partition and its trauma. A note of utter bewilderment seems to be the basic theme that runs through these writings. Partition radically altered human life on both sides of the border, and 'the memories of their collective rites and traditions, stories and songs, names of birds and trees were permanently tinged with the acrid smell of ash, smoke and blood'.⁸

Hindu–Muslim quotidian life

The impact of partition was enormous in Bengal because not only was it politically divided; the province also witnessed a completely different kind of tension, nurtured and aggravated by communal differences. This is not to suggest that Hindu–Muslim chasm was articulated only during and after partition. In the quotidian life, as the contemporary literature illustrates, Hindu–Muslim separation was articulated simultaneously by highlighting the humanitarian dimensions that figured prominently in interactions involving the Hindus and Muslims. This may not be found in the characters Bankim Chandra Chatterjee created when constructing a Hindu nation in opposition to the Muslim rule. Since the 'old' Hindu had suffered from the absence of a combination of physical prowess and desire for self-rule, the 'new' Hindu, argues Tanika Sarkar, 'will only have arrived when he proves himself in a final battle that will overwhelmingly establish his superiority over the Muslims who had in the past always defeated the Hindus'.⁹ While Bankim had a goal for which a strong Hindu appeared to be the most important requirement, Rabindranath Tagore brought out the egalitarian principles of Islam in contrast with the constraint and injustices inherent in the caste system. In a short story, *The Tale of a Muslim Woman*,¹⁰ Tagore narrated the plight of Kamala, who had no alternative but to take shelter in a Muslim home when she was left behind by her husband and others during her journey to her in-laws house immediately after her wedding. Kamala here is a representative character articulating the agonies of those women who lost their parents and had to impose on relatives for survival. She had to agree to marry the son of a businessman who was 'a womanizer, involved in falcon-flying, gambling and bulbul fights'. On their way, 'the robber', Madhumuller, and his gang attacked the marriage party. Left by her new-found relatives, Kamala was rescued by Habir Khan, the local Muslim, who was widely respected. Khan brought her home. While describing Khan's house, Tagore brought out those features that are reflective of Hindu–Muslim composite culture, but had been forgotten due to the unfolding of peculiar circumstances nurtured and created by 'people' with narrow socio-political goals. That Kamala was surprised 'to find a Shiva temple equipped with all the paraphernalia for performing Hindu rituals' is not perplexing. Once Kamala expressed the desire to go back home, her decision was carried forward by Habir Khan with a cautionary note that she was 'not to be taken back home, and will be dumped on the road' simply because she had lived in a Muslim household. This came true and Kamala was hounded out of her old home, underlining that it was impossible for them to take her back because 'a fallen woman' who spent nights with Muslims had no place in 'a ritualistic pure caste society'. Kamala returned and arrangements were made for her to live like a Hindu along with Habir Khan's other children. Later in the story, Kamala converted to Islam to marry Habir Khan's younger son, whom she loved. She was now Meherjan, who became an integral part of Khan's household. Tagore concluded the story by re-enacting the incident in which a daughter of Kamala's uncle was involved. This time Meherjan rescued her cousin from the Madhumullar gang when the wedding party was attacked. 'Have no fear, sister', stated Meherjan. 'You'll be protected by one [Habir Khan] who does not make any distinction between religions'. She also made sure that nobody touched her cousin so as to avoid the plight she had suffered following her compulsion to live in Khan's family immediately after she was deserted by those who had accompanied her during the journey for her 'new home'.

As the story suggests, Tagore challenged the stereotypical image of Muslims. For him, Habir Khan is the epitome of a composite culture where boundaries between the communities were created and therefore unreal. The voice which the poet sought to create was neither Hindu nor Muslim but humane – a voice that was crippled by those swayed by narrow considerations of caste, clan or religion. That Kamala became Meherjan also indicates the difficulty of an inter-communal marriage without conversion. Overall, this 1941 story, informed by Tagore's own concern for Hindu–Muslim amity, is a significant comment on Bengal's socio-cultural profile at a time when narrow religious considerations were continuously highlighted to advance the interests of one community at the cost of others.

The other example drawn upon here to capture the neglected voice of history is *Mahesh*,[11] a short story written by Saratchandra Chattapadhyay, which depicts the extent of deprivation of the landless peasant in Bengal. Gafoor in *Mahesh* could have been a Hindu or a Muslim. For those who flourished by exploiting the landless peasant, whether the peasant was a Hindu or a Muslim hardly mattered. *Mahesh* is a comment on the inter-communal relations in Bengal, woven around the day-to-day life of Gafoor, a Muslim weaver who lost his livelihood as weaving was mechanised. He lived with his daughter, Amina, and *Mahesh*, a bull that grew up in the family despite severe poverty. Apart from the social distance between the Hindus and Muslims, reflected in the behaviour of the character, Tarkaratna, the village priest, the underlying theme of the story revolves around the author's indictment of the Hindu priest-zamindar combination in rural Bengal that thrived by exploiting the rural poor, irrespective of religion. Gafoor was constantly abused and taunted by Tarkaratna for having christened a bull *Mahesh*, another name of the Hindu pantheon god *Shiva*. Tarkaratna also found Gafoor at fault when he tied Mahesh to an old Acacia tree to prevent him from grazing in another's field. Just like the other family members, Mahesh was starving to death. One day he had 'broken loose from the tether and strayed into the zamindar's garden trampling the flowers. Then Mahesh had spoiled the rice left to dry in the sun and when tried to catch him he had pushed the landlord's youngest daughter and escaped'. Gafoor was called and badly humiliated by the zamindar. Gafoor went completely 'out of his mind and seizing the ploughshare that lay close by struck Mahesh violently on his bent head. . . . His whole body shook twice and then, stretching his hind legs as far as they went, Mahesh breathed his last'. The story comes to end with Gafoor leaving the village, along with Amina, in the darkness of the night to work in the jute factory in Fulbere, where he had declined to work because 'there was no religion, no honour and no privacy for women'. Although Gafoor had no complaints about his misery, he implored Allah to punish those 'who robbed Mahesh of the grass and the water that are your gifts to all creatures'.

Set in twentieth-century Bengal, these stories are clearly indicative of the milieu in which Hindu–Muslim relations were constructed. Underlying these stories lies a common theme that binds the exploiter and the exploited in a common frame, regardless of whether they are Hindus or Muslims. What is significant in these two stories is the fact that since Hindu and Muslims were differently placed in socio-cultural terms, it was easier for those with selfish motives to exploit the inter-communal differences to their benefit. Challenging the stereotypical description of Hindu–Muslim relations, *Mahesh* and *The Tale of a Muslim Woman* are illustrative of the multiple voices of people bound together by a reality where caste and religious prejudices determined inter-communal relations.

Woven around a four-poster bed, Narendra Nath Mitra's *Palanka* (The Four Poster)[12] is a powerful portrayal of Hindu–Muslim quotidian life in east Pakistan immediately after partition. What is emphasised here is the human bond that held the communities together even when most of the Hindus left for west Bengal. There was also a noticeable behavioural change among the Muslims, who realised how vulnerable the Hindus were in the changed circumstances. Once Rajmohan was heckled by the Muslims when he demanded that Makbul should return the bed since he had not paid enough, the local Hindus persuaded him not to pursue the matter because 'these Moslems are all one':

They have their secret support, or how could Makbul have the cheek to defy [Hindus]? You have to swallow it, there is no other way. The times are not good. You have lost a single bed. So many have given away their houses and lands practically for nothing. What does it matter really? ... You are not going to die for the loss of that bed.

Rajmohan seemed persuaded because 'it was now Pakistan and it would serve no purpose except to infuriate the big guns of the Moslem community'. Hindus had lost their pre-eminence and the fate of the poor Muslims did not change either. Hence Fatima, Makbul's wife, failed to understand why in 'Pakistan with a government of the Moslems', Muslims should starve. In response, Makbul articulates a powerful of history by saying that 'the poor like us have no Pakistan or Hindustan. The grave is the only place we have any right to claim'.

So far, the story has been woven around a familiar voice of the communities, which were socio-culturally demarcated. What finally triumphed was the human bond that matured and crystallised by being together even in circumstances when inter-communal relations were not at their best. When Makbul agreed to part with the bed for mere survival, he asked Rajmohan to take it back before it was resold. Rajmohan declined after having seen the children sleeping peacefully on the bed. For him, 'the bed was, [so far], just an empty pedestal. Today [he saw his] Radha and Govinda on it. My god has returned', he exclaimed. What is most revealing is the fact that despite fractured voices – perhaps a product of the prevalent socio-cultural differences, highlighted conveniently to further separate the communities – the human bond continued to tie the Hindus and Muslims together even when the political map of the subcontinent had changed.

The pangs of separation

The partition stories are more direct, depicting the agony and pain of those who underwent the trauma for no fault of their own. Based on their experiences of the trauma of the period, the creative writers have brought out the critical voice of the people who had to suffer simply because of the accident of birth by which they were identified as belonging to one particular religion. A new nation was born; antagonistic communities were constructed and justified by the exclusionist interpretation of Hinduism or Islam. The outcome was the suffering of human beings classified as Hindus and Muslims. Samaresh Basu's *Adab*[13] is a powerful portrayal of the agony that human beings undergo – whether Hindus or Muslims – when caught in a riot. In *Adab*, a Hindu weaver and a Muslim boatman meet not as deadly enemies, but as neighbours in suffering. The poor Muslim sees the poor Hindu as a friend, fleeing a common enemy – the riot. Set in the riot-torn Dakha, while escaping police firing, a Hindu worker takes shelter in a dustbin where a Muslim boatman is also hiding for safety. What comes through their conversation is a clear note of how 'the ordinary folks' endured the trauma as and when riots struck. 'I don't understand all this', remarks the boatman. He makes this point sharply when he further mentions:

> I am only asking as what will come about from so much killing. Some men from your side will die and some from mine. How will the country gain?. You might die or I, our wives and kids will have to beg.... Who think of us? Amidst all this rioting how will I earn who will give me food? Will I get my boat back? We are not human beings. We are like vicious dogs.

What is remarkable here is the articulation of a powerful human voice that surpassed the artificially created divisions along religion. Not only did the boatman and the weaver lose their sources of livelihood; they also became the victims of circumstances that never discriminated people according to their religion. In the story, the boatman, identified by the police as 'a dacoit' is shot dead because he runs away when asked to stop. Evoking the sufferings of the innocent, the story articulates a common theme underlying the experiences of people in similar circumstances where religion or community emblem hardly mattered.

Salil Choudhary's *The Dressing Table*[14] is a short story based on four letters written by Rahim to his wife, Amina of Howrah, when the former went to Khulna after partition in search of a job there. The letters were located in a dressing table by Nanda, for whom this was bought by her husband. Replete with references to Hindu–Muslim tensions in Khulana, Rahim was, however, confident that 'these days cannot last long. We must have faith in our hearts and continue to hope that one day humanity will win'.[15] He failed to understand when Amal, a college teacher in Khulna, decided to leave because Khulna belonged to Pakistan and it ceased to be his country. The incident that appeared to have led to Hindu–Muslim skirmishes involved primarily 'scheduled caste farmers and fisherman, united to fight the injustice and brutality of the Muslim zamindars'. The police came to arrest the 'leaders of the rebellious villagers – one of whom was a Hindu and the other Muslim'. With the villagers' refusal to handover the leaders, the police left but resorted to setting fire to several houses in the village. Taking advantage of the situation, a few goondas in the town looted and burnt the shops owned by the Hindus whilst shouting slogans like 'throw the Hindus out'. Not only was this incident presented in the local newspapers in a distorted form; it was also reported that 'not a single Muslim has been left alive in Calcutta'. More and more people, wrote

Rahim, 'are becoming suspicious of each other, losing faith in each other's integrity.... People seem to have lost even the last drop of humanity. Bestiality, in its most terrifying form, has been unleashed upon the town'.

In the first part of *The Dressing Table*, the author brings out the agony of those poor Hindus who had no option but to stay in what later became Pakistan. Once the story shifted to Ujanipura, Howrah, the scene was no different. Poor Muslims, including Rahim's family, were burnt to death in a brutal way. In the words of the author, 'one day, at midnight, the house was locked from outside and set on fire. There was a lot of firing, bullets were flying all around and it was impossible to step outside'. Amina, Rahim's wife, was presumed dead. This is one level of human agony, when those who failed to comprehend the sudden changes in their identity following partition experienced the highest form of brutality, including death. The other form was articulated by those who became *udvastu* [uprooted from home] or *sharanarthi* [shelter-seekers] as soon as the drive to identify the aliens began.[16] Muslims poured into Dhaka as they apprehended trouble in Calcutta, while Hindus came in groups to Calcutta, leaving their homes in east Bengal. In a dilapidated house, the author describes, 'there were at least twenty people inside. Some of them were sitting with their babies, and some lay on the floor. The conditions of the women seemed to be worse than that of the building. They were refugees from East Bengal'. Thus partition was a story of displacement of those people who neither articulated its form nor contributed to its devastating nature and yet became its innocent victims.

This theme is brought more sharply into focus by Homen Borgohain in his *In Search of Ismail Sheikh*.[17] The story, woven around the search of a character called Ismail, narrates the plight of the refugees who were evicted from east Bengal by force. The first part of the story is a graphic illustration of how a Brahmin father and his daughter lost everything, including their dignity, once they had arrived in Calcutta as refugees. The father became a destitute in Sealdah railway station, eating left-over food, while his daughter 'descended from the sacred height of a Brahmin's house to the depth of a prostitute's room'. Why did they leave east Bengal? 'It is because of the Muslim *goondas* who ruined our life. It is because of them that the daughter of a scholarly Brahmin is a prostitute'. So bitter was the woman that even a Muslim name rattled her as she herself was brutally tortured by the Muslim goondas. The second part of the story revolves around Ismail Sheikh, a Muslim immigrant who left east Bengal in search of a better opportunity in Assam. He came to Assam with the hope that he would own land as he heard of 'millions of acres of land lying fallow'. He was soon disillusioned and became virtually a slave of the landowners. Later, he 'set up settlements in the dense Assam forests where life was a constant struggle with nature'. In the course of time, Brahmaputra, the mighty Assam river, swallowed the settlement which

Ismail and his 'comrades' had built up by hard physical labour. They applied for land to the government but were refused, and hence they encroached upon the government land for sheer survival. In order to reclaim the land, the government ordered that the huts be pulled down by elephants. In the process Ismail lost two of his children, who could not move out of the hut as they were ill with smallpox.

The story has a very poignant end, with a message that illustrates a particular phase of history. The victims – whether of partition or poverty – have no nationalities. The tears shed out of pain and suffering have no religion. They are neither Hindu nor Muslim. Similarly, the colour of blood is red – whether the victim is a Hindu or a Muslim. Whether in Dhaka or in Delhi, the colour remains unchanged. What comes out of this story is a familiar theme of human suffering in a different location. How is it possible? 'It is a conspiracy of history', the author argues, 'in which a handful of landlords and capitalists play crucial roles in fomenting communal frenzy or dividing people in religious terms simply to sustain the rule of the few'. The Muslims in east Bengal, as the story concludes, 'stained their hands with Hindu blood in the name of religion. The fact is that the leaders had made them drunk on the wine of religion. If not dead-drunk, how could one rape a woman about to give birth to a baby'?

The silent majority continue to suffer. In a metaphorical way, Jayanta De, in *The Pendulum*,[18] links the pangs of partition with the agony of the people who had confronted the demolition of the Babri Masjid in 1992. In the name of respecting a faith, innocent people suffered in an event which they had neither desired, nor had they contributed to its articulation. In the form of a dialogue between a father and his son, the story brings out the pernicious impact of these political actions on those who simply become the victims of circumstances – whether of partition or the Babri Masjid demolition. During the 1946 partition riots, Calcutta saw the peak of communal frenzy and Hindus and Muslims were placed as adversaries. 'We also decided', as the story continues, that 'for every Hindu killed we shall kill ten Muslims'. What had provoked the Hindus was the desire to retaliate against the Muslim leadership for having created a situation in which Hindus and Muslims simply became enemies. This is also a story showing the emergence of the Hindus as a bloc despite obvious internal schisms. Under those circumstances, the Hindu voice was amazingly singular. What brought them together against the Muslims was the slogan *Bande Mataram*, apart from the 'vengeance for the killing of Hindus'. Decades have passed and *The Pendulum* continues to swing in the same way, probably to indicate that inter-communal communication has not improved to the extent expected. In 1946 it was partition and in 1992 it was the Babri Masjid demolition that substantiate the point beyond doubt that Hindus and Muslims continue to emerge as adversaries even after several years of experience of democratic values.

The White Horse[19] is an absorbing story of how a horse became a victim in the bloodbath of the 1946 Calcutta riots. This is not merely a story of an animal; through the symbolical representation of a horse, Ramesh Chandra Sen wove the feelings of those who simply became victims in an environment which was not their creation. Who suffered most? The innocent people – both Hindus and Muslims – bore the brunt of the political decisions, taken by the leaders without taking their views into account. The white horse is perhaps a symbol bringing together the people from both the communities. When alive, the white animal 'brings a fresh whiff of life into the riot torn locality. The boys are totally absorbed in the horse. The small ones are delighted at its sight. The bigger ones come close and caress its body'. When dead, Shorab, the horse, brought Hindus and Muslims together to ponder as to who caused his death. Was the soldier who fired responsible, or the crowd who provoked the army to resort to firing, or the coachman who allowed Shorab to move freely? The alternatives were many, but the answer remained unclear.

There are two clear voices in this story. The one that is quite familiar delves into the stereotypical description of Hindus and Muslims who were at loggerheads due to religious schism. Thus the riot was inevitable as the culmination of Hindu–Muslim animosity. This was evident when the crowd was insistent in killing the Muslim coachman, who came to a Hindu locality in search of Shorab, as vengeance for the brutal murder of Hindus in Metiabruz. Opposed to this was the other critical voice, which spoke in a language without rancour. When a number of people advanced from the crowd to kill the coachman, Jamuna, Nontey, Habul and other boys made cordon round the old man to resist the attackers though 'the old man does not seem to find reassurance in the hundreds of cruel eyes turned in his direction'. What made them protect the coachman was the concern for humanity, which became the first casualty in communal frenzy. Articulating both the mutually exclusive voices, *The White Horse* also reiterates the difficulty in conceptualising partition as the inevitable, and possibly the best, outcome of circumstances when Hindus and Muslims became permanent adversaries.

The boundary confusion

Two new nation states were born and the boundaries demarcated in just seven weeks. Those affected – Hindus, Muslims and Sikhs – had no idea of the national borders, yet they were the ones drawn into the new nation with completely different labels of identification. Some became Indians and some became Pakistanis – new labels of identity which they neither created nor easily accepted. There were uncertainties, and no one seemed to know the fate of the place in which they were located. As the novelist Bapsi Sidhwa graphically illustrates in *The Pakistani Bride*:

> Hysteria mounted when the fertile, hot lands of Punjab were suddenly ripped into two territories – Hindu and Muslim, India and Pakistan. Until the last moment on one was sure how the land would be divided. Lahore, which everyone expected to go to India because so many wealthy Hindus lived in it, went instead to Pakistan. Jullundur, a Sikh stronghold, was allocated to India.[20]

This is probably the most apt description of how the 'the shadow lines', to borrow the espression from the novelist, Amitav Ghosh, were contextualised in the contemporary articulation. People simply failed to comprehend the implications of the Radcliffe exercise for them. Totally unaware of the plan, they expressed shock and utter bewilderment at the way boundaries were drawn separating people on both sides who had a long history of cultural and social contact. This was most vividly expressed in Satinath Bhaduri's *The Champion of the People*.[21] Located in Aruakhoa, a small village situated between districts of Purnea and Dinajpur, the story clearly brings out the predicament of those who did not know whether this village belonged to Pakistan or India. The village had a mixed population of Hindus and Muslims and was affected by the 1946 Calcutta and Noakhali riots. Within a year, the scars had healed and 'the compulsion of habit and livelihood once again pulled their patchwork lives together'. This was the context when the Boundary Commission was involved in the demarcation of boundaries.

The story is told through a character called Munimji, the local agent of Johurlal Dokania, who owned the Sudhani depot. The story began with Munimji's disclosure that Dinajpur and Malda had already become part of Pakistan. The information spread like wildfire, and people gathered in the market to collect as much rice as possible to survive at this hour of crisis. In view of sudden demand, Saoji, the local trader, immediately raised the price to take advantage of the distress of the local people despite protests from Haji Sahib, who seemed to have lost the moral authority which he had held just a week previous to Munimj's revelation:

> The panic in the air could make even the strongest of minds unsure of himself. The narrow eyes of the Rajbanshis, the local dwellers, dilate with terror. Now, Arukhoa wears a changed look. It used to host a market only once a week; now there is miserable crowd of terrified men and women at all hours of the day and night. Cart after cart trundles across the bridge from the direction of Sripur, another village nearby. Droves of women, children, cattle and goats come on foot. Even a little boy carries a pile of pots and pans on his head. A man struck by *kala-zar* staggers along, gasping for air, a cat held in his scraggy arms. An asthmatic crone goes wheezing past, about to cough up her life, it seems, in

her desperation to escape Pakistan. All this time the world of these people was small. Today, however, some of them will move like hunted deer to an uncertain address, after a brief halt at the market place.[22]

Located in two independent nations, India and Pakistan, the people celebrated Independence Day on 15 August with great enthusiasm. The bridge separating Aruakhoa and Sripur had suddenly become 'unreal', apart from its importance in dividing two nations. This was a poignant moment for those who left Sripur to escape Pakistan. To Darpan Singh of Sripur, the bridge was not merely a physical link between India and Pakistan, it was also 'the only link between his soul and body'. 'It was because of the bridge that he could escape in time; he might go back to his own country, God willing. Or, is it the will of the [Radcliffe] Commission? Could the Commission be mightier than God', he exclaims.[23]

What radically altered the somber scene was Munimji's announcement that the Commission incorporated the district of Malda, including Sripur in Hindustan. It electrified the atmosphere. Darpan Singh, who left his estate in Sripur, 'flings his arms round the Munim'. His father 'bows low to God and the Commission', happy now because 'he will be cremated in the land of Hindus'. Pora Gossain, the religious man, had reasons to curse God since the Titlia thana of Jalpaiguri, where he lived, was included in Pakistan. 'Oh God, did you have to do this? Now I am going to be buried when I die. The Mussalmans won't even let me go to the temple'. Like the Hindus who were forced to leave home because they were reported to have been integrated into Pakistan, Muslims also were relieved when Haripur and Mirpur were included in Pakistan. The experience of those Muslims who stayed back in Mirpur is illustrative here. On hearing that Mirpur was in Pakistan, 'Achhimaddi starts to cry. We were running towards Haripur. Mirpur has been Hindustan for the last two days. The Hindus say [that] they will be forced to pray facing east, that they won't let us kill chicken. So, we cleared out everything behind'.

The voice that comes out is unambiguous. Hindus were scared because of the possible Muslim atrocities once the Muslim administration took over, while their Muslim counterparts also apprehended difficulty in areas brought under Hindustan. The contrasting examples also demonstrate the extent to which the stereotypical Hindu–Muslim perception governed the expression of those affected. What had upset the Hindus most was the possibility that they would be buried not cremated, while to the Muslims it was most un-Islamic if they were forced to pray facing east. The impact of the Commission verdict was therefore well anticipated. Here the boundary between the communities seemed to be clear and not fuzzy, as was the case elsewhere in Bengal, presumably due to the 1946 riot that affected the inter-communal socio-cultural contact adversely. Muslims were scared because the 1946 Bihar riots had shown the ugly face of Hindu communalism while the Hindus apprehended Muslim revenge once partition formally recognised a Muslim state.

People suffered, as the story clearly shows. Who had gained? The rural elite – whether Hindus or Muslims – took full advantage of the confusion created by Munim himself when he informed the villagers of the eventual contour of the area. Saoji raised the price of rice once villagers apprehended a crisis following the reported verdict of the Commission. Munimji, of the local elite, made money by re-selling national flags of India and Pakistan to both the Muslims and Hindus – that was made possible due to the uncertainty, in which he had a role, regarding the status of these villages. As Satinath Bhaduri eloquently puts it:

> The Pakistani flags he had sold are handed back to him. Tomorrow, these need to be taken to Titlia, Munimji tells himself. ... These flags will have to be sold there, and the Hindustani flags taken back. The same goods are to be sold twice. He tries to reckon what his profits will add up to. The Commission has given a lot to some people; from others, it has taken a great deal. But it has not failed him; he has extracted his fair share from its verdict. He got the Commission right; there was no mistake.[24]

While Satinath Bhaduri illustrated the complexity of life both the communities confronted due to uncertainty over the verdict of the Boundary Commission, Jibananda Das, in a 1948 novel *Jalpaihati*,[25] dwells on the Hindus' predicament since the fate of Jalpaihati was not decided yet.[26] The principal characters are Nishith, a professor of English in a local college, and his son Harit, who is inclined toward communism. Nishith came to Calcutta in search of a job in a college that was opened by Joynath, a rich man who made money by providing admission to the students from east Bengal who thronged the city apprehending massive Muslim retaliation after partition. Harit's purpose was different. 'Although nation is free, its true freedom requires a major revolution indeed', Harit felt. Both Nishith and Harit were disillusioned because neither was Nishith absorbed in the college, and nor did Harit meet anybody in Calcutta to appreciate his revolutionary zeal. They were in a limbo. 'They can't go back to Jalpaihati because as Hindus they would hardly be welcomed there'. Although they realised that Jalpaihati was a better alternative, the uncertainty that prevailed over the village pushed them to decide otherwise. Calcutta was equally distressing. 'There are no houses, no jobs or food in Calcutta. Death certainly lies waiting – yet like deformed children they came, only to fall flat on their faces in the alleys, corners and footpaths of this unwelcoming city'.

Once the story shifted back to Jalpaihati, the scene was familiar. Hindus were leaving the village despite the request of the Congress leader, Abani Khastagir, not to desert in panic. What disturbed the Hindu sensibilities most adversely was the free movement of the Muslims in Hindu households, asking for *bidis* and seeking matrimonial alliance with the Hindus. Hitherto unseen, this dimension of the emergence of Muslims as equals in social interactions was probably the most serious socio-cultural affront to the Hindus. It is this attack on the Hindus and the reversal of rituals of deference that 'becomes the moment of realization of the inevitability of migration for the bhadralok families'.[27]

Both *The Champion of the People* and *Jalpaihati* have one common voice, the voice of the deeply hurt Hindus. Apprehending that he was not be cremated on his death, Pora Gossain of Titlia was terribly upset once he was told that it was included in Pakistan. This was a serious affront to a Hindu, for whom 'cremation was the only way of relief from the mundane human existence'. Similarly, the free access of Muslims to a Hindu household and their expressed desire to marry Hindu girls in Jalpaihati were equally disturbing to the Hindus, who preferred migration to Calcutta to avoid their imminent cultural degradation. Despite hardships in a new city, which was not at all friendly, the option of going back to their home was never suggested even once by Nishith or Harit. They confronted the present as unavoidable for a new beginning in the near future.

As in the novels and short stories, the predicament of the refugees constitutes an important theme in contemporary Bengali plays.[28] Of these plays, Salil Sen's *Natun Ehudi* (The New Jews), published in 1950, is probably most subtle in elaborating the text of partition and the sub-text that followed in the aftermath of the division of Bengal. The play is about a refugee family who became the quintessential outsiders in Bengal, just like the Jews, in what traditionally belonged to them. This is also an extensive comment on the city of Calcutta, which continued to remain alien to this family from east Pakistan. Manmohan Bhattarchya, a Sanskrit teacher in a village school, lost his job once the Muslim-dominated School Committee declined to continue with certain practices that were evidently Hindu. Sanskrit was first target since it was 'a sacred language' of the Hindus. The playwright has brought out the historical context, because the Muslim ministry undertook specific steps to increase Muslim members in various school boards to purge schools of Hindu influences. In order to tune the school curriculum to Islamic teachings, the syllabi were radically altered as well.

Partition made the teacher's decision to migrate to Calcutta easier. Manmohan obtained some money by selling his house. Along with his wife and three children, He spent several days in Sealdah station. He was hopeful that the city, his new home, would provide an appropriate source of livelihood in no time. He was soon disillusioned. For sheer survival, Manmohan accepted the offer to serve as an assistant to the cook in marriage feasts. This was most degrading for a Hindu bhadralok, who also felt humiliated by the day-to-day insolent behaviour of the employer. Manmohan failed to thrive and soon died after a brief illness. Dukhia, his son, involved in petty criminal activities after Manmohan's demise, was killed in a road accident, and his daughter, Pari, was lured into prostitution. That was the end of the family that remained alien in the city due to unfolding of historical circumstances which they had neither created nor had any role in designing.

Concentrating on the agony of the refugees, metaphorically called *Nutun Ehudi*, the play captures one particular voice – the voice of the refugees. It is therefore a commentary on the sub-text of partition, dwelling on how refugees confronted their new status and at what cost. Interestingly, the basic theme – the plight of the refugees – that runs through the play is in clear correspondence with that of *In Search of Ismail Sheikh*, though this revolved around the Bengali immigrants in Assam. Sharing the same profession, teaching Sanskrit in village school, Anandacharan Mukhopadhyay in the latter and Manmohan Bhattacharya in the former had to accept jobs not befitting their caste and class status. Interestingly, their daughters suffered the same fate; both of them were forced into the flesh trade. The voice in both these creative works is subtle. In the story of Ismail Sheikh, the daughter of Anandamohan attributed her becoming a prostitute to the Muslims who forced her family out of their home during the partition riot, while Pari, Manmohan's daughter, had to accept prostitution as a profession just for sheer survival in Calcutta. Juxtaposed with the plight of Ismail Sheikh, Homen Borgohain, the author brought out most significant voice of history, namely, these families suffered and were wiped out not because of Partition but because of 'a conspiracy of history' that was articulated in different forms, and partition is one of them. Ismail Sheikh was unable to save his family, including his two severely ill children who were crushed to death when the government officer ordered an elephant to pull his thatched house down to remove encroachment onto government land. Partition was remotely linked with Ismail Sheikh, who came to Assam from east Bengal for survival, and yet he experienced the same fate as the partition victims. *Nutun Ehudi* is more explicit and spelt out what was described as 'the conspiracy of history' at the end of the play when Mohan, the only son of Manmohan who survived, exhorted,

> [b]ut the causes that led to the death of his father and brother still persist, and they have left us to demand an explanation. ... So be one with the oppressed and take a vow that you will punish the selfish and the greedy and those who are playing with the lives of all of you. Take a vow that you will end the exploitation of the cruel oppressors.[29]

The multifaceted or fabricated public face(s)?

Childishness[30] is a sarcastic commentary by Manik Bandyopadhyay regarding those adults who, by magnifying the Hindu–Muslim divide, articulated and defended partition. The story is told at two levels. At a rather mundane level, the author believes that the communal divide was temporary and it was therefore childish to attempt a serious discourse; at a more philosophical level, the author was persuaded to accept that the Hindu–Muslim schism was deep rooted with well-entrenched prejudices and distrust for each other. That Hindus killed Muslims and vice versa in riots clearly reveals that the inter-cultural penetration was largely superficial and not organic.

The story is woven around two families – one Hindu and the other Muslim – located in the by lanes of Calcutta. Although they lived in two separate areas of the same building, the wall dividing the area was too small actually to detach the families. Both the families had the same predicament and compulsions. Tarapada and Nasiruddin both went to work in the morning and came home exhausted at the day's end: 'The same blighted dreams and eager imaginings piled up day by day in both their hearts, the same anger against the same forces grew intenser every day'. The wives, Indira and Halima, were no different in lifestyles, as they were placed under identical socio-economic circumstances. Nonetheless, there was hardly communication between the families until children were born to them. Indira's daughter Gita and Halima's son Habib shattered the division 'with their denial of any unnatural man-made remoteness'. They drew the families closer.

Intimacy between the families developed. One day when Gita ate beef from Habib's plate, neither Tarapada nor his wife took notice since it was quite normal among the children. Indira, Tarapada's wife, justified it by saying, 'if beef doesn't harm Habib why should it harm my daughter? What does it matter if she's eaten some – a tiny girl like her'. It may not have affected their Hindu sensibility. They were, however, aware that their approbation might not go well in the locality, since beef-eating is a taboo for the Hindus. Hence, Indira warned Halima 'don't tell anyone sister'. The incident clearly shows the predicament of the familes which, despite being so intimate otherwise, are governed by deep-seated prejudices against each other. Not only did Indira take cognisance of the incident, Halima felt bad since Gita had eaten beef from Habib's plate. Similarly, the fact that Habib offered flowers and had prasad at Saraswati Puja did not make any difference to Tarapada and his wife, but it was made to happen when 'there is no one in the room'. Again, this demonstrates that in the private sphere this type of inter-communal exchange is perfectly tuned to Hindu sensibilities in a form not at all vitiated by the campaign in the public domain. It is, however, difficult, if not impossible, to argue that the nature of public and private interaction between the communities is uniform simply because the pattern radically varies from one location to another and from one phase of history to another. For Gita and Habib, it was simply beyond their comprehension as to 'why there should so much fighting and killing all around; why it [riot] should suddenly rear its head in such ugly shape? They were bewildered and terrified; their hearts quavered'.

Apprehending a riot, the locality instituted a Joint Peace Committee, not because of 'idealistic outpouring of Hindu–Muslim unity' but because of 'the simple material truth' that 'violence in this mixed area would be equally dangerous for all'. The idea of an impending riot became real in the public sphere. The families were drawn into this, but for the children, the riot provided a specific type of game in which they utilised knife and razor to give it a real look. In the process, one of them was slightly wounded. This led to a situation where 'the two obstinate, unruly children began stabbing and lunging at each other with a blunt knife and a blunt razor, crazed by pain, rage and resentment'. What appears to have given this story an extra dimension were the involvement and counter-accusations of the families holding one another responsible for the incident. One thing led to another. Indira and Halima rushed like 'madwoman; their heads knock together; they look at each other with savage eyes, like two tigresses about to attack'. Tarapada and Nashiruddin were not left out. Threatening each other with dire consequences, they appear to have been drawn to the public sphere, drawing sustenance from the unbridgeable communal distinction between Hindus and Muslims. The situation became worse in the evening, when neither Gita not Habib was found in the rooms where they slept. When the search did not yield results, both the families began accusing each other for having 'lured the children' away as a matter of vengeance. The message spread like wildfire. Drawing upon the mutual distrust between the communities, an atmosphere was created which gained credibility in view of the tension-prone environment of the city. As Bandyopadhyay describes:

> This time, there is no way to stem the tide: rumour and tension begin to spread like fire. All these days, for all their efforts, the provocations haven't been able to shown their fangs in the neighbourhood. They must have been waiting for just this chance, and now they spring. In trice, two bands of demented men gather in front of the two houses. This lot wants to attack that house, that lot this. But as there are two groups, neither can reach its target without first defeating the other in a street battle.[31]

The battle was about to begin when the children reappeared. They had climbed to the roof unobserved at some point of the day to play. This is the punch line of the story. Those who caused consternation among the families, so far living like a unit, were hardly affected by the growing separation between communities in the public domain. For many of those who 'had flocked there, out of their minds with homicidal rage, didn't even know [that] these two were the cause of the trouble'.

Appropriately titled *Childishness*, the story brings out multiple voices, articulated at different levels. For Gita and Habib, the riot was frightening, but amusing as well because it became a game different to these they were accustomed to. The families were split despite long social and cultural contact. What it shows is the role of the public sphere in clearly shaping a particular type of human response. The immediate environment had a role to play; what the story reiterates was the growing importance of a voice that loomed large under circumstances where narrow and parochial considerations were privileged to fulfil a specific socio-political goal. What is puzzling is why the individuals, not so much influenced by sectarian aims, merged their identities with those seeking to attain a goal in the name of a community. In *Childishness*, the inhabitants had lived side by side, mixed together, and the communal divide never became a factor in their day-to-day interaction. Perhaps, as the author laments, 'they had not, at all, mixed intimately'. The story reveals aspects of the Hindu–Muslim schism, and also the mutual distrust perpetuating the image and construction of the 'Other'. Living side by side does not necessarily mean living with each other. Is interaction on festivals, like *Saraswati Puja*, enough to hinder the exclusivist mindset built into the collective psyche of the people? The story has no conclusive answer, but simply underlines the structural ingredients of an environment in which the people's voice is fractured, foregrounding, on occasions, the human over parochial considerations.

The other side of partition

Violence seems to be one of the important dimensions of stories from the Punjab,[32] while in Bengali creative writings has generally been underplayed, presumably to highlight the mutually inclusive existence of Hindus and Muslims over generations. One Bengali writer who brought out this aspect of partition is Saradindu Bandyopadhyay. In his writings, partition violence constitutes an unavoidable aspect that suddenly became dominant in inter-communal interaction during those tumultuous days, particularly in Calcutta. There are five stories – two detective stories, *Adim Ripu* (Primeval Enemy), *Rakter Daag* (The Bloodstrain); a novel, *Rimjhim* (Pitter and Pitter); and two short stories, *Bisher Dhnoya* (The Poisonous Smoke) and *Dui Dik* (Both Sides)[33] – where the principal themes are violence and the resultant insecurity of the Bengali middle class. Of these, *Adim Ripu* is perhaps the most clearly documented narration of partition violence, where the underlying theme is the growing importance of the underworld in sustaining and fomenting communal violence in Calcutta. It is also where the author confronts the most chaotic part of history, which saw the growing distance between the two communities. How was this possible in view of the long-term social and cultural contact between Hindus and Muslims over generations? The author seems to have attributed the gory appearance of partition violence to the hegemonic role of the underworlds. His voice is from both the Hindus and Muslims, who unquestionably suffered equally with the march of events.

The underworld came alive under the cover of communal violence. To the fear of a knife held in the hands of the violent 'other' was added 'the fear of the goondas who extracted his own charge for the continued safety of the people in his locality'.[34] The author had to maintain a steady supply of cigarettes and tea to the goondas for the security of his family. There is no doubt that in the partition violence, it was the goondas who benefited most. Moreover, whether Hindus or Muslims, goondas were similar in their behaviour and activities. In *Adim Ripu* it was a Hindu, Bantul Sardar, who rose to prominence for having provided safety to the Hindus in Bowbazar area during the riot. No dissent to his order was acceptable. Even the Hindus who provided protection for the Muslims in the area were not spared. Bantul threatened Ajit, another character, who did not find any logic in killing Muslims because they were Muslims, with dire consequences if he continued to intervene in this struggle 'to finally settle the score with the Muslims'.

That goondas have no religion, no nationalities is further sharply restated in *Dui Dik*, where Noor Mian, a Muslim goonda, discharged similar kind of responsibilities vis à vis Muslims in areas between Mechobazar and Badurbagan. His story revolves around a Hindu doctor who had a dispensary in this area. Once there was a rumour that Hindus had killed Muslims in other areas of Calcutta, Noor Mian plunged into action by butchering Hindus indiscriminately. At the outset, the familiar pattern of his action was to knife the Hindus who unknowing passed through his area or came to visit the doctor for treatment. Informed by his cronies, he could easily identify the Hindus from the Muslims. Later on the Hindus, especially the Marwaris, came as 'hunter, armed to the teeth' and the situation became worse.

So far, the story is confined to familiar terrain: Noor Mian's involvement in the riot is articulated in the binary opposition between Hindus and Muslims. The voice is undiluted and the explanation is mono-causal. Caught in a dilemma, given his Hindu identity and his profession, the doctor is probably the most significant character articulating the multiple voices of those who suffered in the same manner whether they were Hindus or Muslims. As his dispensary was located in a Muslim majority area, he had to submerge his Hindu identity as far as possible. His identity as a doctor who treated the wounded – whether Hindus or Muslim – was what allowed him to escape Noor Mian's wrath. Under the circumstances, the doctor's dilemma was resolved by underplaying his Hindu identity – which filled his mind with resentment. In other words, the voice that took precedence here was the deeply felt fear that engulfed the doctor who fathomed the consequences of a riot but failed to comprehend how 'human beings' who grew up together in the same area became so brutal.

There was another interesting twist when Noor Mian, fatally wounded by 'a *chotodhari* Hindustani', was brought to the doctor for treatment. The doctor was in a dilemma. He appeared to be happy because a Hindu had finally succeeded in showing his strength vis à vis Noor Mian, the architect of goonda raj in the area. 'I felt like letting the wretch lie there and die – as you sow, so shall you reap. Let him atone for his sins with his face grounded in mud', felt the doctor. Apprehending that 'he will be poisoned by the Hindu doctors in Mitya College', Noor Mian urged the doctor to treat him in his dispensary. Torn between his hate for Noor Mian and his professional duty to save an injured Muslim, the doctor himself was amazed at the way his conscious mind was clearly divided: 'when he wanted to give Noor Mian poison, he gave him fruit juice, and when the delirious man yelled out, *maro Hindus, maro Hindu*, [kill Hindus] he pressed ice bags to his head'.[35] The doctor in him won, and the Hindu self was contained – or, humanity prevailed over other parochial considerations. This became evident when Noor Mian insisted on paying a hefty amount to the doctor for having saved his life. 'You can't repay me with money, but you can repay me with something far more difficult that that', doctor said. Noor Mian pledged to do everything except abdicating his religion. The doctor sought an assurance that he would abdicate his career as a goonda and also give up his habit of imbibing cocaine. Noor Mina was astounded, but after a while said, 'Malik, you have just robbed me of the only life I have ever known, but your demand, I will do my best to obey'.

The partition riots were an occasion, as Bandyopadhyay chronicles, when the appearance of goondas as saviours tended to consolidate the separate Hindu–Muslim identities as contrasting, if not antagonistic, blocs. Moreover, when it comes to cruelty, neither Hindus nor Muslims differed from each other. How do they gain legitimacy? Hinting at the charged atmosphere due to the brutal killing of Hindus by Muslims and vice versa, the author seeks a possible explanation. The city was not clearly bifurcated along religious divisions. Even the doctor who saw Hindus being butchered by Noor Mian and his cronies at the doorstep of his dispensary faced a serious dilemma, though the Hindu in him was brutally hurt and would probably welcome vengeance when Noor Mian was under his medication. In his reconstruction of the past the doctor clearly saw that it was not merely his professional ethics but also his faith in humanity that ultimately determined his behaviour when Noor Mian was under his care. This is also evident as the doctor was inclined to forget those traumatic days as mere ripples in human history by saying that 'I do not see the least necessity of describing the macabre sight in detail; you had all been in Calcutta in those days, you have all witnessed a little or much of that I have seen'. Forgetting the past in a creative way was probably the best way of remembering meaningfully bygone days.

As the stories have shown, the voice of the people is clearly fractured, though there is an underlying thread of unity based on the trauma of partition. In other words, although clearly fractured, these multiple voices are nonetheless well articulated, underlying the defining moment in South Asian history due to circumstances beyond their control. Munimji in *The Champion of the People* and Noor Mian in *Dui Dik* are, for instance, not peculiar to partition; they always thrive in a situation of terrible uncertainty and dislocation. That a Hindu doctor saved Noor Mian's life shows that, even at the height of communal distance, human identity, justified in terms of professional ethics, prevailed over other narrow and parochial considerations. This also comes out of the recorded views of a large number of Bengali Hindu women who became easy targets once partition occurred.[36] They were certainly traumatised, but never held the entire Muslim community responsible for this event, presumably because several Muslims, individually as well collectively, both protected them and provided an escape route when trouble brewed in the locality. While narrating her story, Pramila Das, who had to leave east Bengal in the wake of partition riots in 1946, simply refused to blame the Muslims in general for the bloodbath. Once 'Muslims marauders attacked our house and butchered every member of my family – male, female and child', she reminisced, 'I fled secretly through a backdoor, ran breathlessly and reached a neighbouring Muslim house. They were kind enough to hide and protect me as a family member. It was they who informed my husband who rescued and took me back to Shilong'.[37] Similarly, Anupama Deb also encountered a situation during the height of the riots when her husband's student saved the family by shifting them to his house and later 'escorted them to Khulna that was relatively free from communal skirmishes'.

How do the voices explain the volcanic eruption of violence in Bengal, where Hindus and Muslims had been connected symbiotically over generations? The answer varied, though in their elaboration of the circumstances two factors appear to have gained enormous significance. First, as the explanation is couched in socio-economic terms, the primacy is given to the precarious economic conditions of the Muslim peasants vis à vis the Hindus, who were relatively well-placed. This was compounded by the growing cultural differences that engendered a deep sense of alienation among the Muslims from their Hindu neighbours. The second factor was the success of the local mullahs in attributing the Hindu attitude to their abhorrence to Islam. Once Islam seeped in, several Muslim families who were otherwise not antagonistic to their Hindu neighbours became aloof.

It was 'this indifferent silent majority' that made a significant differences to those who took full advantage of 'the chaos and uncertainty'.

Among the women, the impact of partition varied depending on their socio-economic status. Those who belonged to the rich or landed class, the educated middle class or the professional class were undoubtedly the victims of circumstances, but survived once they migrated to Calcutta. They were, however, dragged far below what they had enjoyed earlier. The serious economic difficulty they encountered was attributed to the dislocation from their 'homes'. What had caused severe mental trauma was 'the sense of loss' after they were forcibly uprooted 'from their birthplace, their home and hearth'. It was aggravated further when as refugees they were often ridiculed, as Prabharani recollected with agony by 'their neighbours in Calcutta'. The standard charge was that 'the city has become filthy due to the flooding of the refugees [who] have distorted the city's image by their dialect, their dress and they way they live'. This is one part of the story. The other part dwelt on the experiences of the relatively poorer section of Hindus in east Bengal who migrated to Calcutta in the wake of communal attacks on the Hindus. They were small traders, artisans, masons, carpenters and fishermen. Illustrative of their life in the aftermath of migration to Calcutta are the stories of Kusum and Kamala. They had a comfortable life with income from their husbands. Once in Calcutta, they took shelter on the railway platforms and in transit refugee camps. For them, partition completely disrupted their life and reduced them to 'destitutes'. There were hardly jobs for their husbands to apply their skills. Thus Calcutta became '*narak* [hell] for us after a week of arrival in the city [which] offered neither shelter nor allowed us opportunities to live in a respectful manner'. As there was no alternative, Kamala and Kusum were forced to take the job of maidservants in different households. Partition was thus not merely an event of August 1947 that caused immense misery to the east Bengal Hindus; it was also a constant reminder to these families of the sudden loss of their dignity and social status, which they had to compromise for sheer survival.

Partition is also the story 'of displacement and dispossession, of large-scale and widespread violence, and of realignment of family, community and national identities'.[38] Juxtaposed with the creative writings, the oral testimony of these women reveals the human dimension of the 'event' that not only brought about radical cartographic changes in the subcontinent, but also transformed the mental map of those who overnight became 'alien citizens' due to circumstances beyond their control. Partition therefore lives, as one commentator argues, 'in family histories ... where tales of horror and brutality, the friendship and sharing, are told and retold between communities, families and individuals'.[39] Gendered oral narratives also underline that the brutal story cannot only be articulated in binary opposition between a vulnerable Hindu woman and the Muslim aggressor; instead, there are innumerable instances where the Muslims came forward to protect and rescue the Hindu families. Not only have these instances challenged the 'cultural incompatibility' between the two communities, embodied in Jinnah's two-nation theory; they have also brought human considerations to the forefront, over other narrow and parochial considerations.

In contrast with the Bengal experiences, what comes out of the oral testimony of Hindu and Sikh women in Punjab is a mixed bag. On the one hand, Hindus and Muslims lived together without large-scale friction for generations, though they were segregated culturally in watertight compartments. As Urvashi Butalia argues, what alienated the Muslims was the way they were 'ill-treated' by the Hindus in their day-to-day interactions. For instance, 'if a Muslim guest came to [a Hindu] house, he was asked to eat from the earmarked utensils and also wash them. While serving, *rotis* were thrown away from such a distance to avoid being polluted by an accidental touch with the utensils'.[40] This is one side of the story; the oral narratives of Subhasani, whose father was murdered by the Muslims bring out the other side. This event became a reference point for any discussion by her regarding partition. She was happy when 'the Hindu community, imbued with the spirit of sacrifice and revenge ... wanted to take revenge for what was being done to our brethren in Punjab [though she felt bad] by the treatment meted out to Mussalman women and children. It was not a very pleasant experience', she underlined, 'to see Mussalman women and children being brutally killed'.[41]

The un-fractured Bengali sensibilities: the other side of partition

Partition marks the breakdown of that community that had defined the individual and his or her identity. This is the common theme running through most of the east Pakistani creative writings seeking to articulate the voice of the people. There is, however, a significant difference: while in most of the stories in the context of partition riots in the Punjab, violence seems to be an important (if not overarching), dimension of the human experiences, Bengali stories are relatively free from violence in its most crude form. Since violence is peripheral to most of these Bengali stories, killings are usually shown as 'isolated' events with a distant backdrop of partition riots. Even the death toll in Bengal was smaller than in the western part of India, and there were no parallel massacres of people in the trains or in refugee camps. Stories are plenty, though the theme is more or less similar, as Niaz Zaman has shown in *A Divided Legacy*.[42]

What is prominent in most of the stories is the articulation of Bengali cultural sensibilities that appear to have surpassed other parochial considerations based on a narrow interpretation of religion. The Bengali identity appears to have surpassed, on occasion, the religious distinction of the communities: 'Here no one is a Hindu, no one is a Muslim. We are Bengalis. We are one', proclaimed Shanti Muzumdar, the principal character in *The Mother of Dhirendu Muzumdar*.[43] She also warned that 'if the head and the body were separated, then like rahu and ketu will play a very destructive game. Both the sun and the moon will come under total eclipse'. While this was clearly a voice of opposition, the sense of loss and agony seem to be prominent in most of the stories. Set in the height of communal animosity, Syed Waliullah's *The Story of the Tulsi Plant*,[44] for instance, captures the emotional predicament of a family of Muslim refugees when a Tulsi plant, a Hindu religious symbol, was discovered in the house they barged into for shelter. The inmates of the house, which was deserted, had no problem so long as its allegiance was not known. With the presence of a Tulsi plant it was different, because 'this half dead, dried, insignificant Tulsi plant, caught unaware, had revealed the secrets of the house', so 'it has to be torn out because no Hindu symbols can be tolerated', as some members of the family insisted. The others thought of the woman who nurtured the plant religiously as an integral part of the household:

> They were not entirely familiar with Hindu customs; but they had heard that in a Hindu home, the mistress of the house lighted a lamp under the plant at dusk, and with the end of her *sari* wrapped her neck, made a *pranam*, bowing to touch the earth with her head. Though it was overgrown with weeds now, someone had lighted a lamp every evening under this abandoned Tulsi plant too. When the evening star, solitary and bright, shone in the sky, a steady quiet flame had burned red, like the touch of crimson paint on the bowed forehead.

The plant survived, and even the staunch Hindu-baiter in the family, who had wanted to destroy the plant at the outset, began caring for it as days passed by. The human voice had prevailed. What is pertinent is the underlying theme, articulated in the pain and agony of the Hindu family that had vacated the house and those who occupied it. Their plight was the same. Both the families are victims of circumstances beyond their control, and became homeless refugees for an uncertain future in an unknown place. For the Hindu housewife, 'tending the plant might have been a religious duty', for the refugees, who took care of the plant despite initial reluctance, 'it was a reminder of their common humanity, of the need for roots, for the ordinary rhythms of life which the political events and upheavals [violently] disrupt'.[45] Once uprooted, the *udvastus* became vulnerable even when they were 'the government's people'. With the requisitioning of the house by the state, the inmates were asked to vacate within twenty four hours as 'they have illegally occupied the house'. A shadow of gloom descended upon the house. 'There was no end to anxious speculations. Where could they go, they wondered'. This is where Waliullah is at his best, in focusing on the trauma of human beings who became the first victims of partition. Just like the Tulsi plant, which had a fresh lease of life due to the support of those who had occupied the house despite initial reluctance, the refugees – whether in Pakistan or India – were equally helpless in the radically altered circumstances. They were as 'vulnerable' as the Tulsi plant '[since] the life and well-being of the tulsi plant could not be insured by its own powers of self-protection'.

Abu Rushd's *Nongor* is another fine representation of the contrasting voices of the Muslims who happened to be Bengalis as well. Two major themes recurred in the novel. The first is the enthusiasm with which Pakistan was conceptualised. Pakistan was 'necessary' for Kamal, the principal character in Nongor, 'to understand that the entire world is mine. In its paddy fields, I find my own fragrance. I revivify in the electric violence of storms. Its fruits and flowers sustain and refresh me. Its breezes will lull my child to sleep. There my being is different, secure and unique'.[46] Kamal was happy because Radcliffe 'has promised Nazimuddin that Calcutta, from Sealdah to Park Circus, where the wealthy Muslims live – would go to Pakistan'. The second equally important concern of Rushd centers around the fate of those Muslims left behind. At least seven crores of Muslims 'will benefit', Kamal confidently mentioned. What will happen to those stuck in India, Kamal had no clue. This was true of the Hindus who stayed back in Pakistan even after the *batwara* (division)! Thus, 'the problem has not been solved', concluded Kamal.

In *Nongor,* partition constitutes the background and there was hardly a detailed commentary on this. Kamal left Calcutta not because of communal strife but for a better life that was assured to him as it was 'a Muslim land'. There are, however, stray references to partition that 'aroused suspicion and raised walls between the communities which till then had co-existed peacefully, if not happily'. However, what stands out is the Bengali identity, nurtured and refined by both Hindu and Muslim cultural ethos over generations. Hence Kamal, who most happily accepted that Pakistan never did compromise his identity, rooted in 'composite Bengali culture' by saying that 'supporting Pakistan does not mean that I will cut myself off from my entire past. My unique identity is inseparably made up of my past, present and future. After I finish my life on earth perhaps I shall return as a lotus flower, or a cock to wake up people in the morning, or perhaps even a star to shine up above'.[47]

Concluding observations

Partition was a watershed in the construction of nations in the aftermath of British rule in India. Redefining Hindus, Muslims and Sikhs as Indians or Pakistanis, the 1947 division is a story of renegotiation and re-ordering of the identity of the individual or the community. It was not merely a history of violence, or victimhood or of madness; it was also 'a history of struggle of people fighting to cope, to survive and build anew'.[48] What appears to have emerged in the context of partition were two mutually contrasting tendencies: on the one hand the clamour for partition, supported by both the Congress and League High Command, clearly demarcated the Hindus and Muslims at every levels of their existence despite having lived side-by-side over generations; contrary to this, there is another layer of existential experience where Hindus and Muslims remained organically linked with one another as human beings despite the well-designed attempts to segregate the two.[49] As is shown, examples abound in the creative writings of the period from both sides of the border. By focusing on individuals and their agony, pain and sorrow in particular historical circumstances, these stories become representative of the time and its predicament; they thus provide 'a mental map' of partition. Because literature transcends time, these stories 'are relevant ... as they vividly portray the existential absurdity of the hatred [and also how they] negotiated the complexity and liminality of expression of people, caught in the competitive savagery of Partition'.[50]

The literature of partition affirms that 'the subject of Partition was first the human being – not the Hindu human being nor the Muslim, nor the Sikh – [and] the experiences of each community distinctly mirror one another, indeed reach out to and clutch at one another'.[51] Sadat Hasan Manto's Toba Tek Singh was at a complete loss once the country was divided and people were labelled as Hindustani and Pakistani: '[A]ll the inmates in the asylum found themselves in a quandary; they could not figure out whether they were in Pakistan or India, and if they were in Pakistan the how was it possible that only a short while ago they had been in India when they had moved from the asylum at all'.[52] Most of the characters are not reconciled to borders being drawn and people being uprooted from their familiar socio-cultural milieu. They remind us time and again, as Mushirul Hasan succinctly puts, that 'regardless of religious passions being heightened by the politics of hate and of the fragile nature of inter-community relations in the 1940s, most people had no clue whatsoever' of the nature of the forthcoming division.[53] Perhaps the most significant point is how the boundaries arbitrarily dissolved older identities as towns, cities and villagers were 'mercilessly scattered right or left as the juggernut of Partition etches its way across the face of the country'.[54] Nothing is more explicit than the growing unease of Toba Tek Singh regarding the 'whereabouts' of his village.

> He began asking people where Toba Tek Singh was, for that was his home town. But no one could answer that question for him. And if someone did make an attempt to figure out the present

status of Toba Tek Singh, more confusion would follow. It had been rumoured that Sialkot, which was once Hindustan was now in Paksitan; who say where Lahore, which was in Pakistan today, would be tomorrow, and was there anyone who could guarantee that both Pakistan and Hindustan would not disappear someday?[55]

It is evident that the high politics of partition constitute the background of the majority of the stories. People affected in a variety of ways stand out even in the context of severe uncertainty following the transfer of power. Dwelling on 'the affective experience of the events and their consequences for the ordinary people', these stories have not only brought out 'the ways the partition felt', but also articulate 'the historical memory' of a phase in which human beings suffered, both physically and emotionally, for reasons beyond their control.[56] It was not only that 'the country was split into two – bodies and minds were also divided'. Ismat Chughtai, the creative Urdu writer, further notes,

> Those whose bodies were whole had hearts that were splintered. Families were torn apart. One brother was allotted to Hindustan, the other to Pakistan; the mother was in Hindustan, her offspring were in Pakistan; the husband was in Hindustan, his wife in Pakistan. The bonds of relationship were in tatters, and in the end many souls remained behind in Hindustan while their bodies started off for Pakistan.[57]

There is a familiar theme in all the stories, whether they are from the east or west. People suffered due to circumstances of which they were the victims. Arbitrary boundaries were drawn and two nations became sovereign after a protracted struggle against colonialism. The colonial atmosphere created an imagined collectivity in response to a political campaign for separate nation-states. In other words, the collectivity that came into being was a political construct – products of human interaction and human imagination drawing upon particular historical circumstances. It would not be an exaggeration to argue therefore that movements both for and against partition had an adequate support base in certain quarters, including those who mattered at the level of high politics. As shown, both in Bengal and Assam partition emerged as the best possible solution to avoid an imminent bloodbath on a mass scale. This is an equally important part of the story of partition that simply cannot be wished away while grappling with the 'events' and the consequences thereafter. The creative writings, which are a powerful portrayal of a fragmented and a wounded society, act as complementary sources to piece together the relatively unknown dimension of those tumultuous days when the religious description of the community appeared to have been privileged. The aftermath of partition is what constituted the backdrop to most of the stories, underlining the impact of displacement, uprootedness and alienation of the inner self and the renegotiation of identity within a radically altered milieu. In this sense, they serve a useful historical purpose in grasping the processes manifested in the articulation of a new identity both for the nation and its citizens – where past, present and the future come together to mutually redefine themselves through equally intricate processes of contestation and adjustment.

Notes

1 There was a parallel attempt by the 'depressed classes' to construct an independent identity, Urvashi Butalia informs. According to her, 'a sense of separateness seemed to have become essential to establishing a sense of identity. Thus the fear of conversion at the hands of "others" – Muslims, Sikhs [and] Christians. Conversion was suspect because it was done, clearly with a view to increasing their number solely for political purpose. A demand for separate electorates, for proportional political representation, for a presence in the important decision making bodies, these were some of the broader realities that underlay the sense of difference [and] of separateness. ... And lest this seem like a chimera, they had provided a rationale, and invented a name for this imaginary homeland: Achhutistan, the land of the untouchables' (Butalia 1998: 238–9).
2 Hasan 1995: 26.
3 Mushirul Hasan thus argues, 'the intellectual resources made available to us by such creative writings ... provide a foundation for developing an alternative discourse to current expositions of a general theory on inter-community relations' (Hasan 2000: 39–40).
4 Prakash 2001: 75.
5 Prakash 2001: 76.
6 There is a great difficulty in articulating people's voice through these narratives. As Urvashi Butalia argues, there is invariable a gulf between how people define their identity, for instance, and how they are represented in accounts written by others. The representation of experiences of women, children and Scheduled Castes at partition are, after all, her construction, selectively illuminated by her concerns and priorities. 'To me', she argues further, 'these make for another voice: a voice that reads into, and interprets other voice' (Butalia 1998: 265).
7 This is more or less true. As is evident in the recent publication of short stories, novels, plays and poems, the creative writers interrogating partition were largely traumatised both by the suddenness of the event and by its pernicious impact on the inter-communal relationships involving the Hindus, Muslims and Sikhs – which was explicable but not acceptable given the historically tested organic unity among the communities under normal circumstances. The most important and exhaustive collections are include Cowasjee and Duggal 1987; Bhalla 1994; Hasan 1995; Memon 1998; Hasan and Asaduddin 2000.
8 Bhalla 1994: ix.
9 In Ludden 1996: 163.
10 Rabindranath Tagore, 'The tale of a Muslim woman', translated by M.

Asaduddin and reproduced in Hasan and Asaduddin 2000: 48–52. All the following quotations are from this volume.
11 Saratchandra Chattapadhyay, *Mahesh*, translated by M. Asaduddin and reproduced in Hasan and Asaduddin 2000: 17–27. All the following quotations are from this volume.
12 Narendra Nath Mitra, 'The Four Poster', in Cowasjee and Duggal 1987: 114–42. All the citations are from this volume unless otherwise stated.
13 Samaresh Basu, 'Adab', in Bhalla 1994: 21–8. All the citations are from this volume unless otherwise stated.
14 Salil Choudhary, 'The dressing table', in Bhalla 1994: 25–38.
15 Salil Choudhary, 'The dressing table' in Bhalla 1994: 33.
16 For a detailed and critical exposition of the refugee problem in West Bengal, see Samaddar 1999.
17 Home Borgohain, 'In Search of Ismail Sheikh', translated by M. Asaduddin and reproduced in Hasan and Asaduddin 2000: 226–37. All the following quotations are from this volume.
18 Jayanta De, 'The Pendulum', translated by Hiten Bhaya and reproduced in Hasan and Asaduddin 2000: 156–68. All the following quotations are from this volume.
19 Ramesh Chandra Sen, 'The White Horse', in Bhalla 1994: 126–33.
20 Bapsi Sidhwa, *The Pakistani Bride*, Penguin, New Delhi, 1983 quoted in Hasan 2000: 15.
21 Satinath Bhaduri, 'The Champion of the People', in Bhalla 1994: 209–28.
22 Satinath Bhaduri, 'The Champion of the People', in Bhalla 1994: 216.
23 Satinath Bhaduri, 'The Champion of the People', in Bhalla 1994: 225–6.
24 Satinath Bhaduri, 'The Champion of the People', in Bhalla 1994: 228.
25 *Jalpaihati*, taken from *Jibananda Samagra*, Mitra Prakashan, Calcutta, 1985. All the citations are from this volume unless otherwise stated.
26 Tapati Chakravarty made a very illuminative discussion of this novel along with *Swaralipi* (1952) by Sabitri Roy and Pratibha Basu's *Samudra Hriday* (1959) in her 'The paradox of fleeting presence: partition and Bengali literature', in Settar and Gupta 2002: 261–81.
27 Tapati Chakravarty, in Settar and Gupta 2002: 270.
28 Jayanti Chattapadhyay attempted a very useful content analysis of Salil Sen's *Nutun Ehudi* (The New Jews), 1950 and *Banglar Mati* (The Earth of Bengal), 1953 by Tulshidas Lahiri in her 'Representing the Holocaust: the Partition in two Bengali plays', in Settar and Gupta 2002: 301–12.
29 Salil Sen, Nutun Ehudi, Scene XVII – quoted from Jayanti Chattopadhyay, in Settar and Gupta 2002: 305.
30 Manik Bandyopadhyay, 'Childishness', in Bhalla 1994: 127–36.
31 Manik Bandyopadhyay, 'Childishness', in Bhalla 1994: 135.
32 Of all the writings, Sadat Hasan Manto's 'Siyah Hashye' [Black Margins] is perhaps the most revealing exposition of violence in the context of partition and its aftermath. For this, see Hasan 1995: 88–99.
33 *Saradindu Omnibus*, Vols. I–XII, Tuli Kalam, Calcutta, 1977. All the citations are taken from this collection, unless otherwise stated. *Adim Ripu* was published in 1955, *Rakter Daag*, *Rimjhim*, and *Bisher Dhnoya* in 1961, and *Dui Dik* in 1964.
34 Anindita Mukhopadhyay, in Settar and Gupta 2002: 212.
35 Anindita Mukhopadhyay, in Settar and Gupta 2002: 215.
36 Care must be taken with these oral testimonies, as Mushirul Hasan warns. Because they are conducted over space and time by writers who have an

agenda of their own, oral interviews cannot be a substitute for archival research. Hence gender narratives, personal and collective memories can at best enrich partition debates and not constitute an alternative discourse to the existing ones (Hasan 2002: xxxix).

37 The interview with Pramila Das has been reproduced from Monmayee Basu, 'Unknown victims of a major holocaust', in Settar and Gupta 2002: 153.
38 Menon and Bhasin 1998: 9.
39 Butalia 1998: 8.
40 Butalia, in Settar and Gupta 2002: 136.
41 Nonica Datta, in Hasan and Nakazato 2001: 43.
42 Zaman 2000. Perhaps the most exhaustive study of the Bengali novels, written by Bengali writers located in east Pakistan. All the citations will be from this volume unless otherwise stated.
43 Lalithambika Antharjanam, in Bhalla 1994: 203. All citations are from this volume unless otherwise stated.
44 Syed Waliullah, in Bhalla 1994: 191–8. All citations are from this volume unless otherwise stated.
45 Zaman 2000: 132–3.
46 Rushd 1967: 265.
47 Ibid.
48 Pandey 2001: 18.
49 It has now been well-established that there never has been, despite the rhetoric of theologians and publicists, 'a single, inalienable Muslim identity and that identities are inclusive and often rooted in local cultures, languages, oral traditions, influenced by complex historical processes (Hasan and Asaduddin 2000: 15).
50 Asaduddin, in Settar and Gupta 2002: 329.
51 Jason Francisco, in Hasan 2000: 392.
52 Sadat Hasan Manto 'Toba Tek Singh', in Bhalla 1994: 2. *Toba Tek Singh* is a story of the loss of identity against the backdrop of the communal massacre and transfer of population during partition. Viewing partition from the perspective of a lunatic, *Toba Tek Singh* is a powerful argument challenging the decision that finally led to separation.
53 Hasan 2000: 16.
54 Prakash, in Damodaran and Unnithan 2001: 77.
55 Sadat Hasan Manot 'Toba Tek Singh', in Bhalla 1994: 3–4.
56 Francisco, in Hasan 2000: 382.
57 Chughtai, quoted in Hasan 2002: xi.

CONCLUSION

The contradictory nature of the reality of 15 August 1947 continues to intrigue historians more than half a century after India was partitioned. Freedom was won, but was accompanied by the trauma of partition and the mayhem that followed immediately before the transfer of power was formally articulated. Thus India's independence represents a great paradox of history. The nationalist movement led to freedom, but failed to avoid partition. The success of the nationalist movement was therefore also its failure. Why did it happen? The answer lies in another paradox, namely the success–failure of the anti-imperialist movement, led by Gandhi and his Congress colleagues. In its struggle against the colonial power, the Congress had a two-fold task: moulding different classes, communities and groups into a nation, and winning freedom for this emerging nation. The Congress had succeeded in mobilising the nation against the British, which accounted for the final withdrawal of the British rule in India; it was, however, virtually unsuccessful 'in welding the diversity into a nation and particularly failed to integrate the Muslims into this nation'.[1] Underlying this conundrum – the success and failure of the nationalist movement – lies the roots of the paradox of independence that came along with the Great Divide of the subcontinent of India. Independence and partition were, as a commentator argues, 'but the reflection of the success and failure of the strategy of the [Congress-led] nationalist movement'.[2]

The study challenges the argument that the 1947 partition of Bengal was a consequence of Hindu communalism of the Bengali bhadralok.[3] It has been shown that the roots of the vivisection lay in a highly intricate unfolding of a process in which the British were as much responsible as the rising tide of Muslim communalism.[4] By institutionalising the separate facilities offered to the Muslims in the form of separate electorate, quota in government jobs and special education facilities, the colonial government initiated a policy of segregation from which it never retreated.[5] It has also been argued that the respective elites skilfully manipulated the doctrinal differences between the two principal communities to fulfil a political agenda.[6] With the assumption of power by the Muslim League in 1943, the effort was directed to organising Muslims at the grassroots along communal lines. Distributing posters showing that Hindus grabbed all resources in the campaign for the 1946 provincial election, the League also promised land and primary education to Muslims once Pakistan was created.[7]

Both Bengal and Assam were divided following the 3 June announcement of Louis Mountbatten, though the principles that determined the division were different. While Bengal was partitioned following largely the demographic composition of the areas – namely the Muslim-majority areas constituted the new province of Pakistan while the Hindu-majority districts formed west Bengal – Assam was separated as a result of a referendum in which Hindus and Muslims participated to create a new nation. The story of partition in Bengal and Assam clearly indicates the growing importance of religion at a critical juncture in India's political history. As the contemporary evidence shows, to the vast mass of small holding peasants living more or less under similar conditions, religion seemed to impart a sense of 'community'. By providing the basis for 'a national bond', religion became the rallying cry of a political organisation demanding the creation of a separate Muslim land. That the Muslim peasantry favourably responded to the appeals of Islam in both Bengal and Assam is illustrative, on the one hand, of the importance of religion in bringing them under the elite League leadership despite serious class differences. On the other, Islam also gave them a powerful ideological explanation of the exploitation by the Hindu landlords in exclusive religious terms, glossing over entirely the class dimension of the relationship between the landlords and peasantry. What it means is that the period had witnessed the convergence of (1) class and communal identities and (2) elite and popular communalism in the context of movements supporting partition. The outcome was the polarisation of Hindus and Muslims into two communal blocs, competing for their respective shares in the aftermath of the 1947 transfer of power. As the political mobilisation for a separate Muslim state gathered momentum in the late 1930s and 1940s, the larger Bengal cultural and linguistic identity increasingly became fractured along sectarian and religious lines.

Not only did the period between 1932 and 1947 witness a radical transformation in India's political landscape, it was also marked by significant changes in the prevailing ideological orientation of both the Hindu and Muslim political leadership. The 1935 Act definitely shifted the centre of political activity in Bengal to the east of the province – Not by virtue of any inherent superiority of the Muslims, but simply because, in a democratically elected legislature, as a contemporary report underlines, 'the weight of numbers tells and the teeming millions of East Bengal – sixty percent of their being Muslims outweighed in point of numbers the more educated

Hindus of the South, West and extreme north of the province'.[8] The migration of power to the countryside took place in the context of a major realignment in the social bases of political power. The deepening agrarian crisis, manifest in the collapse of jute and rice prices, polarised rural Bengal, and provoked conflicts between Hindu talukdars and mahajans and the overwhelmingly Muslim peasantry.[9] This explains why the economic issues figure prominently in the League campaign in Bengal in the 1946 provincial poll. Abul Hashim, the League Secretary, 'organised an extraordinary campaign amongst the poor peasants of Bengal on economic issues' where religious ideology seemed peripheral.[10] The massive and unprecedented landslide victory for the Muslim League was illustrative of how effective the campaign was. In a remarkable departure from the stereotypical League campaign, where the Islamic identity of the Bengali Muslims was crucial, Abul Hashim 'promised the peasants that the future of Pakistani government would be their government, a peasant raj ... [and] the Bengal peasant was led to believe that Pakistan was to be ruled by the peasants'.[11] The tragedy was that the peasant euphoria was, recounts Alavi, short-lived and 'the feudal forces in the League, namely the Dhaka Nawab group' captured state power in the aftermath of the election by sweeping the peasant issues under the carpet and pushing the architect of the League victory, Abul Hashim, into the periphery.

Once in power, the Muslim leadership utilised the state machinery to its advantage. The clearly devised and carefully drafted legislative acts and regulations during the period before partition soon attracted considerable support from the Muslim businessmen[12] and intellectuals.[13] With Fazlul Haq's decision to join the League in the aftermath of the 1946 Calcutta riot to safeguard the Muslim interests,[14] the party was 'greatly assisted in acquiring the agrarian base, it had lacked for so long'.[15] It has also been well established now that what accounted for the most virulent Hindu–Muslim riots in the 1940s was undoubtedly 'the imminent prospect of the withdrawal of British influence and the handing of power to Indians'.[16] What it reflected was the desire of both the League and Congress to grab as much as possible under those circumstances. It was 'as if a starving prisoner', as Wavell graphically described by drawing an analogy, 'was suddenly offered unlimited quantities of food by the gaoler; his instinct is to seize it all at once and to guard against its being taken away again [and] also to eat as much as quickly as possible, an action which is bound to have ill-effects on his health'.[17]

The height of communal animosity was witnessed in the Calcutta and later Noakhali riots. Hindus and Muslims were largely polarised into two opposite blocs. Although these riots were the culmination of a well thought out plan, its roots can be traced back in the failure of Jinnah's talk with the Congress leadership for a probable settlement of the constitutional question. In fact, as early as May 1946 Wavell, the Viceroy, apprehended 'trouble in the form of serious communal rioting owing to the Congress and Muslim League being unable to come to terms'.[18] With the outbreak of riots and the indiscriminate killing of Hindus and Muslim in Calcutta and Noakhali, a helpless Tyson, the Private Secretary to the Bengal Governor, thus lamented, '[i]t is a heavy price to pay for the failure of Jinnah and Congress leaders to come to terms'.[19]

That the administration failed to contain the devastation in the riot-affected areas of Bengal was symptomatic of its growing weakness in the closing years of colonialism. Riots therefore significantly undermined the British administration, although they were not directed against it. The bureaucracy did not appear to be as reliable as before. By late 1946, a majority of the officers at the top of Indian bureaucracy were Indians since 'there has been no British recruitment since the war began'. As the administration went 'down hill', Tuker reminisces, 'its prestige went with it, and the British could not have administered India much longer with such an unsuitable instrument through which to exercise their rule'.[20] The Indian members of the Services looked more cautious, presumably because of the announcement of the imminent British withdrawal: 'there is a general belief the power of the Secretary of State to protect his Services will rapidly weaken as it has already manifested in the Provinces after an interim government assumes office'.[21] While the officers in the top echelon were indifferent those at the bottom were evidently communal, as their role in the riots had clearly demonstrated. It was therefore difficult, if not impossible, to manage the affairs in India as efficiently as earlier simply because 'the administration has almost collapsed from which it is unlikely to recover' given the contemporary political environment.[22] The situation was already alarming, as the British Indian Army had also shown signs of cracks following the conclusion of the Second World War. The factors affecting reliability were 'mainly political and not military'. What affected the morale of the army, as Auchinleck wrote, was 'the Congress praise of men of the so-called Indian National Army as true patriots and [its] extravagant anti-Government abuse. If morale were to deteriorate gravely owing to continued propaganda', the Chief of Army Staff even apprehended a general mutiny in India.[23]

Why did the Congress accept partition despite its consistent challenge to its very foundation, the two-nation theory? With his first-hand experience of the dismantling of the Raj, Nicholas Mansergh explains this in terms of three reasons. First, the Congress always favoured a strong government, which was not possible so long as Muslims remained within a united India. Hence they 'sacrificed' the unity of India for 'a strong central government'. Secondly, the perception held both by Patel and Nehru that Pakistan 'would not endure long' may have influenced the Congress leaders to support India's bifurcation. Thirdly, the Congress leaders were

CONCLUSION

believed to be 'impatient'. As they were 'aging', they were not prepared 'to delay independence further'.[24]

The acceptance of partition by the Congress leadership is perhaps illustrative of a distinct change in its assessment of the Congress Party which failed to represent the Indian Muslims at large. The acceptance was also the final act of a process of step-by-step concession to the League's communally orchestrated demand for a sovereign Muslim state. Each concession by the Congress consolidated communalism further. On the one hand it had strengthened the claim of the Muslim League as the 'true' representative of Muslims; on the other, it had weakened its position vis à vis the secular Hindus by paving the ground for the Hindu communalists, particularly the Hindu Mahasabha, to thrive. One of the direct results of the communal tension, as an official report underlines, was 'the growth of communal organisations like the Rashtriya Swyam Sevak Sangh and the Muslim National Guards in most of the provinces'.[25]

By endorsing the 3 June plan, the Congress put their Muslim leadership in east Bengal in a most precarious situation. Hindus suspected them as Muslims; Muslims hated them more than they hated the Hindus for they regarded them as 'renegades'.[26] Dismayed by the Congress decision to accept the bifurcation, Ashrafuddin Ahmad Chowdhury, a member of the All India Congress Committee expressed his agony by saying that:

> the Congress leadership whether willingly or unwillingly, has agreed to the British declaration of the 3rd June, '47 with the terms contained therein, partitioning India on religious basis. They have for all practical purposes accepted the Muslim as separate nation thus conceding to two-nation theory of Mr. M. A. Jinnah. The High Command of the Congress has cut at the very root of the national character of the Indian National Congress. Its leadership has shamelessly abandoned the long cherished ideal of the Congress and its tradition by accepting the 3rd June declarations of the British Government. Besides, they have badly let down their Muslim Congress comrades of long standing and stabbed them in the back unawares. ... Bengal and Punjab have been made a pawn in the power politics of these Congress leaders.[27]

Unlike the earlier communal outbreaks, by the 1940s the riots in Bengal had assumed an overtly communal character.[28] The crowd – Hindus and Muslims – came to be primarily motivated by the sectarian goal – Pakistan for the Muslims and partition for the Hindus. It is therefore difficult to suggest that only Hindu communalism was responsible for the partition of Bengal. In fact, a thorough scan of Bengal's political history since the assumption of power by the KPP–League ministry in 1937 amply demonstrates the equally significant role of the provincial Muslim leadership in articulating governmental decisions in clearly communal terms.[29] It is now clear that communalism of whatever variety was responsible not only for the Calcutta riot and the persistent tension in many other towns in Bengal, but also 'for poisoning the life stream of the province ... just like "the purple devil" or water hyacinth, which grows rank and luxuriant in waterways and ponds throughout Bengal hindering irrigation and navigation'.[30]

Bengal: a distinct political entity

Bengal was characteristically different from the rest of India. The fact that it was more thoroughly 'colonised' than other parts of India marks it out from the rest. Thus it should be emphasised that Bengal's socio-economic development was influenced significantly by the conditions imposed under colonialism. The British system of land tenure, the lack of industrial development and the destruction of indigenous manufacturing contributed directly to the formation of a 'middle class' who became 'rent-receivers', virtually divorced from land except in some cases as suppliers of credit. With a gradual decrease in rental income this social category responded energetically to English education, which provided them with an alternative source to supplement or increase their earnings. The fact that this group, comprising principally Hindu upper castes, continued to depend English education not only maintained but also extended the distance of this group from the agricultural production process. The entire socioeconomic and cultural context thus created a new social category, identified neither with the class owning the means of production nor with those selling labour for survival.

Similarly, the heterogeneous demographic composition of Bengal and the disproportionate economic development of Hindus and Muslims created unique political tensions. The combination of religious appeals with the economic grievances of the Muslim peasant led to a situation in which conflicts, which were primarily agrarian in character, assumed communal dimensions. The problem was aggravated by the growing desire of the educated Muslims for a share in government jobs and learned professions hitherto monopolised by the upper-caste Hindus. As a result of a temporary accommodation of the newly emerged Muslim middle class by agreement at the elite level, C. R. Das built a united anti-British platform involving both Hindus and Muslims following on from the Non-Cooperation–Khilafat movement. The unity forged between the Hindus and Muslims in the context of the anti-British agitation was indicative of a new phase in provincial politics.[31]

The unity, however, appeared ephemeral, with the shifting of the centre from Calcutta to the villages and small towns with the introduction of the

1935 Government of India Act. The formation of the Praja Samiti, and later of the Krishak Praja Party (KPP) which had declared the objective of protecting one community against the other, drew a large number of Muslims from the Congress. By highlighting the uneven development of the two religious groups, the newly emerged Muslim leadership developed its support base quickly among the Muslims irrespective of socio-economic differences. The Congress' intimate ties with upper-caste intermediary landed interests and its explicit policy of protecting them through institutional means,[32] consolidated the division further. Constrained by its communal aims, the KPP was, however, unable to link the agrarian questions with the broader anti-imperialist struggle and thus was confined to east Bengal Muslims. Because the KPP leadership saw the explanation of Muslim backwardness in the disproportionate Hindu dominance in all spheres of life, it failed to perceive the nature of contradictions in a colonial society, and therefore the possibility of a movement involving the underprivileged, regardless of religion, was unrealised.

Furthermore, the inherent political differences between the KPP and the Bengal Provincial Congress provided the colonial state with an autonomous character. By enacting agrarian legislations, the state strove to demonstrate its willingness to ensure the economic interests of a relatively underprivileged section of the agricultural population. The Congress's opposition to the 1928 Bengal Tenancy (Amendment) Act and neutrality on the 1938 Amendment not only alienated the peasant masses from the Congress; it also projected the image of the state as an arbiter of justice in view of the ameliorating stance of the above legislations. The peasantry as a constituent was therefore almost ruled out because of the pronounced bias of the Bengal Congress toward intermediary landed interests – a bias utilised by Muslim political groups to consolidate the anti-Congress platform, especially in east Bengal, where a significant proportions of *mahajan* and *talukdar* were Hindu. What finally eclipsed Congress' power was the emergence and consolidation of Muslim political groups under the KPP–League alliance on the basis of communal sentiments. Not only were the urban Muslims organised, the vast majority of east Bengal Muslim peasants were also brought under its banner to end Hindu-dominated Congress hegemony in the province.

The changing profile of Assam

In contrast with Bengal, Assam provides an interesting chapter in India's freedom struggle during its final stage, for two important reasons. First, although the 3 June announcement suggested the division of Assam, particularly the district of Sylhet, the province was partitioned only after the referendum in which a majority of its population endorsed the separation. As the Muslims constituted an overwhelming majority in the district,

CONCLUSION

the outcome of the plebiscite was more or less anticipated. A unique experiment in the context of colonialism, the referendum brought out interesting dimensions of Hindu–Muslim communalism. Secondly, for the Muslims, the campaign during the referendum was a continuity of their movement opposing the Assam Government since it had decided stringently to follow the controversial Line system in 1946. As described earlier, the Line system was a device introduced by the government in the 1920s to halt the migration of Bengali Muslims into Assam. Muslim immigrants were instantly mobilised for the 1947 referendum, and the campaign gained momentum once a Bengali Muslim *Pir*, Maulana Bhasani, assumed the leadership.

In Sylhet, the League leadership demanded partition of Assam – unlike its counterpart in Bengal, which never endorsed the separation. With the announcement of the dates for referendum, the League High Command constituted a committee comprising the important leaders of Bengal and their representative, Khaliquazzaman, to mobilise Muslim support for Sylhet's amalgamation with Pakistan. Presumably because the League was uncertain about the outcome of the referendum, Jinnah, who broached the idea of the committee, preferred to organise the Muslims in the Surma Valley (of which Sylhet was a district) from the very outset. That he monitored the movement through his representatives also shows the uncertainty he felt about the outcome. The other significant feature of the Muslim mobilisation was the nature of the local leadership that spearheaded the campaign. Jinnah chose Maulana Bhasani who became famous after his successful movement in Bhasani's *chars* (alluvial land) instead of the established provincial League leaders. As a religious leader, Bhasani invested the misery of the Bengali Muslims with a communal connotation. By choosing mainly mosque compounds or those in the vicinity as the venues for his meetings, he undertook a campaign in which the religious sentiments of the Muslims were utilised to his advantage. That he couched the demand for amalgamation of Sylhet with Pakistan in clear religious terms also underlines the significance of his persona as a Pir. It is not therefore surprising that the Muslims in Sylhet always associated Bhasani with a godsend *Poigambor* (a saviour).

Not only did Bhasani appeal to the religious sentiments of the people; the entire campaign was also organised in such a way as to gain maximum impact by drawing upon Islam. *Mullahs* from Bengal were brought in to go to the remote areas of the district. Village *hats* were the places where these Mullahs addressed the villagers. In these informal yet important gatherings, the support to Sylhet's union with Pakistan was always presented as 'a service to Islam and Muslim fraternity' elsewhere. Those who opposed the League agenda were also threatened with dire consequences. Apart from the divine punishment, what was most effective in garnering support was 'social ostracism', which acted like magic in the Muslim villages where survival was almost impossible without effective co-operation among those living there.

Unlike Bengal, where the members of the Legislative Assembly, elected on a limited suffrage, forced partition upon the people following its endorsement, Sylhet provided a completely different story where the decision was made final only after it had been approved by a majority of its population. No doubt there were stray instances of intimidation by the League supporters at the behest of the Muslim National Guard. What explains the massive support of the Muslims for Sylhet's amalgamation was the consolidation of a distinct communal identity drawing upon religious sentiments. By skilfully playing on the Hindu–Muslim socio-economic differences at the grassroots, the League and its representatives succeeded in clearly segregating both these communities in the final phase of the freedom struggle. Hindus appear to have anticipated the outcome of the referendum, given their demographic strength in Sylhet. In spite of an impressive turn out of Hindu voters, the result of the referendum went in favour of the Muslims, as they constituted a majority.[33]

Apart from its distinctive historical character, the Sylhet referendum underlines a significant process of community formation. In contrast with Bengal, where linguistic homogeneity failed to cement the bond, language proved to be a strong binding element along with religion. This acted in both ways. For the Muslims in Sylhet, a vote for amalgamation was also an opportunity to integrate with east Bengal, where their linguistic identity would both be upheld and protected. For the Hindus of Assam, the separation of Sylhet was a boon in disguise since it would create a linguistically homogeneous province excluding the Bengal-speaking Sylhetis.[34] Thus it was not surprising when the Assamese Hindu leadership hailed 'the separation of Sylhet ... and [thus] the restrictions on land-hungry Muslim peasants immigration from Bengal into the Assamese homeland' presumably because it paved the ground for the rise and consolidation of Assam as an independent entity in free India.[35]

The complex nation

The story of partition in Bengal and Assam directs our attention to a process of nation formation, which was not derivative but contingent on the prevalent socio-economic milieu. In the context of the first partition of Bengal, Hindus and Muslims constituted a nation that was imagined into existence by taking into account the Hindu–Muslim composite culture. Glossing over communal differences, the Swadeshi Movement led to the rise of a nation drawing on an anti-imperial ideology. The nation that emerged had serious internal contradictions, presumably because Muslims were mobilised in a movement based primarily, if not exclusively, on the Hindu ethos. Despite its success in revoking the first partition, the

CONCLUSION

Swadeshi Movement laid the foundation of the Hindu–Muslim chasm that became unbridgeable as history unfolded.[36] In contrast with the first partition, two nations arose in the context of the second partition – one drawing upon the two-nation theory, while the other opposed it. Both in Assam and in Bengal the division of India was justified, even in popular parlance, in terms of the distinctive socio-cultural characteristics of both the communities. In the construction of the respective nations, religion appears to have united the disparate masses irrespective of socio-economic differences. The 1946 riots in Bengal confirmed the perception that the Hindus were not safe under Muslim rule, and hence it was probably easy for the Hindu Mahasabha successfully to organise the campaign for partition. What brought the Bengali Muslims in Assam to the polling booths during the plebiscite was probably the concern for maintaining their separate identity, which was at stake in the Bordoloi administration. In both the cases religion provided a sense of national bond, bypassing completely the obvious socio-economic differences among those who became the natural constituents of the nation-in-the-making. While the linguistic homogeneity strengthened the religious fraternity in Assam, it never became an important issue in Bengal – presumably because of the constant Muslim propaganda in favour of constructing a language drawing upon the Islamic tradition. As shown in Chapter 3, the growth of the Mussalmani Bangla and revamping of *Punthi* literature aimed at culturally segregating the Muslims from the Hindus. What is common among the Muslims in both Bengal and Assam is the importance of religion as a cultural-demographic element in the formation of a hegemonistic nationalist ideology. And religious identity continued to remain significant in the cultural construction of the national identity.

The partition riots created a panic among the Hindus in east Bengal. What is significant is that the sense of vulnerability cut across the internal division among the Hindus. They responded to the situation as a homogeneous community. Even the Namasudras, the erstwhile League allies, supported the campaign for partition because they became suspicious of the Muslims following the Noakhali riot.[37] A new concept of 'homeland' emerged in the lexicon. While the lower castes found it difficult to stay when their upper-caste patrons (*Kartas*) were leaving, the well-off and upper caste sections migrated because 'in west Bengal they would at least die in dignity'.[38] The 1947 partition was therefore not merely a physical division of the subcontinent; it also radically altered its complexion by seeking to define its members in conformity with the constructed political boundary in the aftermath of the transfer of power. For the Muslims, 1947 was not merely about partition, it was also about freedom from both the British and the Hindu ruling authorities. For the Hindu-Bengalis, it created a sense of home[39] – where they were safe and protected.[40]

CONCLUSION

Literature and partition

There is no doubt that the literary representation of the events in the wake of partition provides an alternative discourse supplementing the stories based on archival research. The history of partition is also the partition of history of communities. What apparently created a legitimate space for the two-nation theory were the 'cultural differences' between the communities which, though living side-by-side for generations, appear to have remained clearly separate from one another. This is, however, not to suggest that Hindu–Muslim separate identities owed only to existential cultural differences; instead, they were also rooted in colonialism and the economic changes of the decades preceding the transfer of power. What is emphasised is the fact that the 'distinct' Hindu–Muslim identities were not just products of 'divide and rule', but were created by communities themselves on the strength of inherited cultural resources and invented traditions. Thus the emergence of the Hindus and Muslims as distinct political communities was historically conditioned. What was seriously questioned in these creative writings was the displacement and dispossession of the innocent victims who failed to reconcile to the changed environment when separate homelands were created for separate communities which had so far co-existed. *Amma* (mother) in Ismat Chughtai's *Roots* was at a loss when she was told that where she had lived so far was not her country. She retorted, '[w]hat is this strange bird called, our country? Tell me, where is that country? This is the land where you were born, which gave birth to you; this is the earth on which you grew up; if this is not your country, how can some distant land where you merely go and settle for few days become your country?'[41]

Representative of the period, these stories are powerful devices to articulate the people's voice that so far has remained peripheral in recorded history. However, care must be taken because, though these texts articulating rupture and loss constitute important dimensions of historical memory, they were constructed within an individual perspective that might not have corresponded with what partition was all about. For the writer, 'the composite' Indian culture and history was violently broken by the 'madness' of partition. Seeking to recreate a shared past where Hindus and Muslims lived in harmony for centuries, these stories are representative of the age and well constructed with a specific agenda that was clearly peripheral, as the 'events' of partition clearly indicated. Bewildered as they were, these writers hardly offered explanations except by describing it as temporary madness, caused by unforeseen circumstances. The history of partition is also the history of deteriorating communal relations, and the propaganda and rumour that fuelled this. As Ishtiaq Hussain Quareshi while recounting his experiences of 1947 Partition riots in Delhi, mentions (emphasis added):

CONCLUSION

The fortified *mohalla* (as the quarters were called) developed into arsenals. One could see that an undeclared and unofficial civil war was in the offing. It became the practice to organize parties of able-bodied inhabitants into groups to man strategic places. At night the house tops began to bristle with armed men. This seems to have been a country-wide phenomenon and ultimately resulted in mass killings in many areas. ... *Under such circumstances, the meagre social relations which had survived among the members of the two communities came practically to an end.*[42]

Partition was also a merger of religious with national identity. In many parts of the new dominions of India and Pakistan, being a Hindu (on the one side) or a Muslim (on the other) 'had become virtually synonymous with being a refugee and a foreign national'.[43] One's religious label – be it Hindu or Sikh or Muslim – had suddenly become crucial in one's identity in the new nation states. What it means is perhaps the fragility of socio-cultural communication between the communities drawing upon the obvious points of similarities and differences. Partition was thus a moment of departure from what was described as 'an organic unity' between the Hindus and Muslims that appeared to have flourished due to living together side by side within a particular socio-cultural milieu. This was also a significant historical moment in which communities were constructed in a rather straightforward manner ignoring both their characteristic multiple shades and also the complex processes in their formation. Perhaps in a particular historical conjunction, the one-dimensional community was privileged to fulfil a political agenda that appeared to have translated the socio-political demands of one group of people against another. It was also possible that for the under-privileged Muslim community, particularly in east Bengal, religion acted as a cementing force in the movement for partition. In other words, aroused and inspired by the message of Pakistan, the Muslims, whether in Bengal or Assam, rallied behind the campaign for a separate Muslim homeland. This is, however, not to argue for a single, inalienable Muslim identity, for Islam in India, past and present, 'unfolds a bewildering diversity of Muslim communities'.[44] Instead, what is emphasised here is that the community – whether Hindus or Muslims – is malleable, fuzzy and contextual.[45] Conceptualising community as living and constantly changing experiences clearly suggests how partition influenced the process by foregrounding religious identity over others under specific circumstances. Thus partition was a significant input in the construction of India and Pakistan as nations and their constituents that had naturally undergone radical shifts in its aftermath.

GLOSSARY

Abhijata bhadralok	Aristocrat
Ahsan manzil	A beautiful building
Apni	The term of respect for a senior or relatively unknown person in conversation
Baidya	Name of a caste associated with the medical profession
Bargadar	Share-cropper
Bhadralok	Gentleman
Caliph	Ruler of Turkey and religious leader
Chhilim	Cone-shaped earthen container of tobacco for smoking placed on the perpendicular cylinder of a **hooka**
Dhyana	Meditation
Farash	Knee-high platform covered with **sataranj** or sheets
Grihastha bhadralok	Those having income from land and a profession
Hartal	Strike
Hooka	Smoking pipe
hookum	Order
jehad	Holy war or effort to establish the supremacy of Islam
jotedar	Large landowner, holding rights of either intermediate tenure or mere tenancy, sometimes having tenants under him and often engaging in money-lending or grain trading.
Kanchhari	Zamindar's administrative block
Kayastha	Writer caste
Khoraki	A maintenance grant to workers while not working
Kisan	Peasant
Krishak samitis	Peasant organizations

GLOSSARY

Madhyabitta sreni	Middle class
Madrassah	A school of Islamic learning
Mahajan	Money lender
Maulana	A title given to a person respected for learning in Islamic theology
Maulvi	A learned man in Islam
Panchayats	Village administration
Piri	Low wooden stool
Praja	Tenant
Pranayama	Breathing exercise
Raiyat or ryot	Cultivator who held lands from landlords subject to certain conditions
Samiti	Organization
Sampanna praja	Well-off cultivators
Samya	Equality
Samyabada	Egalitarianism
Samyabadi	One who believes in equality
Sataranji	A carpet made of cotton
Sikshitya madhyabitta sreni	Educated middle class
Tui	A pronoun used either to show disrespect or to express familiarity and love
Ulema	Expert in Islamic training
Vishayi bhadralok	Those having income from a profession

BIBLIOGRAPHICAL ESSAY

The 1947 Great Divide of the subcontinent of India continues to generate interest among historian, regardless of their ideological persuasion. This was a dramatic event that registered the role of the British rulers, the Congress and Muslim League leadership, and the people who overnight became alien in an area that was declared 'foreign' following the formal articulation of the division of the subcontinent. A political decision, taken at the level of 'high' politics, radically altered the identity of those located in areas which changed their nomenclature after the 1947 vivisection. For those who left their homes, the bifurcation suddenly changed a geographical space into memory. Home became a distant object for those who underwent the trauma apart from the actual brutality that accompanied partition.

Thus partition is not merely an event; it is also the completion of a process that had become manifest in the ever-changing socio-economic and political environment of India under the Raj. The available literature is a pointer to that. Careful reading of the official sources (in the India Office Library, and Archives in India) clearly shows the shift in perceiving the Indian 'problem'. As long as Linlithgow was presiding over the empire, the idea of a separate Muslim state remained conceptual construction, especially in the aftermath of the 1940 Lahore resolution. The official documents of this phase, cited in the bibliography, are illustrative here. Wavell's arrival on the scene was certainly a break with the past because the perception that the empire was no longer viable gained ground. The Wavell Papers clearly identify the changed the direction of the British policy. Mountbatten's tenure as the (last) Viceroy demonstrates how the bifurcation was finally accomplished, taking into account the role of major political parties largely under his stewardship. As Mountbatten recorded everything about his role in this momentous event, his private papers are very useful in grasping (1) the British perception in quickly dismantling the Raj so assiduously maintained for the last 200 years and (2) the role of the Indian political actors representing the Congress, League and other major political parties in what virtually became a counter to bargain as much as possible for their communities. The disagreements among those involved in the division of Bengal, Punjab and Sylhet in Assam allowed the rulers virtually to divide these British Indian provinces according to what appeared to be most appropriate to them.

Apart from the private papers of the British officials and of Congress and League leaders, two compilations that are most useful are *The Transfer of Power* volumes[46] and a series entitled *Towards Freedom*.[47] While the former provides an authentic version of the last historic months of British rule in India and 'an arresting chronicle of great events which culminated in transfer of power and partition',[48] the latter is a combination of both British documents and those available from exclusive Indian sources, to simply underlining the importance of sources other than those identified as 'official'.

Autobiographies of those involved in the events of this tumultuous phase of India's socio-political history constitute an important source for the studies of partition. For instance, the memoirs of Tamijuddin Khan[49] and of Abul Mansur Ahmad[50] are interesting and useful chronicles of the evolution of Muslim identity, underlining the subtle process of clearly segregating the Hindus and Muslims both in the quotidian life as well on the institutional plane. Similarly, Suhrawardy's half-finished autobiography[51] is illuminative of those issues that cropped up, especially during his reign as the Bengal Chief Minister, when the province was clearly divided along religious lines. These tracts are very useful in conceptualising the religiously informed communal identity that appears to have become overblown as the freedom struggle in India came to an end. However, care must be taken because the autobiographical sources may not always be authentic simply because any version is distilled in the light of the probable repercussions following its publication. The way to utilise these sources in the best possible manner is read them in consonance with other materials, available in the writers' correspondence both with the government and with those involved in the political process, their press briefings, and also the newspaper reports. A combination of these two different, yet significant, types of sources will provide a fairly authentic description of a particular historical reality.

As the autobiographical writings of those Indian leaders opposed to Jinnah's two-nation theory are scanty, it is difficult to reproduce their memory. Maulana Azad's *India Wins Freedom*[52] is useful to grasp the role of the Congress and League High Command in 'high' politics, as is Khaliquzzaman's *Pathway to Pakistan*[53] which is a very well-argued position on the rise of Pakistan but not so exciting in illuminating the process at the grassroots in Bengal and Assam that finally led to the vivisection of the provinces. Shyama Prasad Mookherjee left an unfinished autobiography,[54] which is more a commentary on the Hindu–Muslim separatism in a historical perspective. B. R. Ambedkar's *Thoughts on Pakistan* provides a new perspective to the primary literature on partition. Instead of rejecting the thesis of two-nation theory altogether, he sought to find out its basis in India's socio-cultural environment because 'it would be neither wise nor possible to reject summarily a scheme if it has behind it the sentiment if not the passionate support of 90 percent of Muslims in India'.[55]

There is, however, no dearth of materials because of the access to the *All India Congress Committee Papers*, *Hindu Mahashabha Papers*, *Shyama Prasad Mookherjee Papers* and the *B. S. Moonjee Papers* (available at the Nehru Memorial Museum and Library, New Delhi), to name a few – which are most useful and immensely significant in building the stories of partition. A careful reading of these sources reveals the gradual consolidation of movements defending the Bengal partition on the basis of arguments drawing, *inter alia*, on the well-entrenched communal cleavage in the province. For a critical understanding of the historical processes, it is appropriate to juxtapose these sources with the published autobiographies since they may not always be authentic, for the reasons already stated.

Nirad Chaudhuri's *Thy Hand Great Anarch*[56] is an interesting intellectual account of the historical processes on the basis of a personal encounter with the reality he confronted. An admirer of Gandhi and Nehru, Chaudhuri's narrative of the 1946 riots in Calcutta and Noakhali shows the extent to which Hindus and Muslims were polarised in Bengal just before the communal outbreak. Similarly, N. K. Bose's *My Days with Gandhi*[57] is another memoir dealing with post-Noakhali carnage, especially after Gandhi's arrival.

The Great Divide was also the end result of political mobilisation in which the religiously-fed communal identity of Hindus and Muslims played havoc. Rooted in the contemporary socio-economic and political contexts, Hindu–Muslim separate identities created competing, if not antagonistic, blocs in the early 1930s following the recognition of the demographic strength of Muslims in Bengal as a source of power with the introduction of the 1935 Government of India Act. To grasp this development a thorough probing into the provincial political history is of utmost importance, and Bengal has been served well by the historians. There is a large number of well-researched monographs on Bengal stretching over the entire nineteenth and twentieth centuries. As this work is on partition, I have drawn upon those addressing the communal issue in the context of a search for identity of the Bengali Muslims in an organised way. Rafiuddin Ahmed's *The Bengal Muslims: A Quest for Identity*[58] is probably one of the best-written works on the identity formation in the colonial context. For well-documented analysis of Bengal's political history, Rajat Ray's *Social and Political Unrest in Bengal*[59] is a well-argued monograph on Bengal politics, highlighting the gradual consolidation of the Hindu and Muslim communal identity. Sugata Bose has further elaborated the process in his *Agrarian Bengal*[60] by linking the political manifestation of separate identity with Bengal's socio-economic milieu that underwent dramatic changes following the Great Depression of the 1930s. My book entitled *Subhas Chandra Bose and Middle Class Radicalism*[61] is useful in explaining the predicament of the Bengali nationalist leaders in the context of the expanding of boundaries of the freedom struggle involving the peasantry and labour and their ideological agenda. This was the dilemma of the Bengali, particularly Hindu, middle class that gradually lost its significance in provincial political arithmetic due (1) the rise of Gandhi and the growing strength of 'non-violence' as an ideology, and (2) the emergence of the Muslims as a contender for power following the introduction of separate electorates for Muslims. Tazeem Murshid's account provides a well-documented description of the role of Muslims in Bengal since the late nineteenth century.[62] The major theme of this book overlaps with that of Shila Sen's *Muslim politics in Bengal*. Her argument is grounded on both official and non-official sources, though she appears to have taken the responsibility for setting history right by absolving Suhrawardy, the Bengal Premier, of his role in the 1946 Great Calcutta Killings.

Jaya Chatterji's *Bengal Divided*[63] is the latest and probably most discussed monograph on the partition of Bengal. Selectively documented, the book appears to have been written with a bias against those who upheld the demand for partition in 1947. Attributing the movement for partition to Hindu communalism, the author has underplayed the role of both the imperial government and Muslim communalism for reasons unexplained. The account is about the exclusive role of the Hindu communal forces which demanded partition to protect their 'vested' interests. There is no denying that the Hindu communalists had no role. What is historically inaccurate is probably the description highlighting the role of Hindu Mahasabha organising the Hindus along communal lines, ignoring, to a large extent, the part played by the Muslim counterparts in the Great Divide.

In recent times, by seeking to identify 'the face of the crowd' involved in partition violence historians have introduced a new dimension to our understanding of the phenomenon. What is puzzling is the devastating nature of the violence in Punjab compared to its relative absence in Bengal. Gyanendra Pandey's *Remembering Partition*[64] and Urvashi Butalia's *The Other Side of Silence*[65] are two important interventions that highlight the subtext of hatred and violence between Hindus and Muslims accompanying the 1947 partition. Butalia's account is important in another way. By mapping out the facets of experience of women who faced the trauma in Punjab, the book provides 'a gendered narrative of displacement and dispossession, of large scale and widespread communal violence, and of the realignment of family, community and national identities'.[46]

This bibliographical essay is not a book-by-book account of the monographs consulted; instead, it has sought to highlight the basic trends in

BIBLIOGRAPHICAL ESSAY

contemporary writings on India's partition. By underlining the principal argument pursued in these selected books, this essay seeks to acquaint the readers with the current researches on the Great Divide in particular, and India's recent socio-political history in general.

Notes

1 Kumar 2000: 2732.
2 Mahajan 2000: 388.
3 Defending this position, Joya Chatterji thus argues, '[t]he Hindu communal discourse of the bhadralok articulated the deeply conservative world view of an embattled elite, determined to pay whatever price it had to in order to cling to power and privilege. It was a discourse that was deeply communal in intention' (Chatterji 1995: 267).
4 Thus W. Norman Brown argues, 'the immediate responsibility for ... partition must be laid to Hindu–Muslim communal antipathy, fomented by the Muslim League, Hindu Mahasabha and many individuals not belonging to either organisation. But the Indian National Congress short-sightedness and Muslim League intransigence had set the stage, while the British, by the political policies, had augmented the communal mistrust'. See Brown 1962: 103.
5 Ayesha Jalal thus argues, '[c]ontinued recourse to the colonial privileging of religious distinctions thwarted many well-meaning attempts at accommodating differences within a broad framework of Indian nationalism' (Jalal 1998: 2183).
6 In defending Muslims as a completely separate community, Ispahani, one of the most powerful League members, with massive business interests in Bengal, thus argues '[t]he Hindus are in the habit of ascribing the differences to the presence of the third party (the British), and consider that they will disappear when the British quit the country. This is only an attempt at creating confusion by suggesting that all existing differences are of British creation. The differences are permanent and eternal. The British have, like all imperialists, turned them to their advantage' (see IOR, L/I/1/882, M. A. H. Ispahani, The case of Muslim India (pamphlet), November 1946). In his study of the Bengal Muslims, Rafiuddin Ahmed has also shown the role of the elites in sustaining, if not, strengthening the Hindu Muslim schism (see Ahmed 1981: 183–90).
7 In his novel *Neel Kantha Pakhir Khoje* (Bengali), Atin Bandyopadhyay provides an interesting and detailed account of the League election campaign in the 1946 election. See *Neel Kantha Pakhir Khoje*, Vol. 2, pp. 9–11.
8 IOR, Tyson Papers, Eur E 341/41, John Tyson's note, 5 July 1947.
9 Sugata Bose argues that the rupture in the credit relations in rural Bengal seriously damaged, if not completely ruled out, the symbiotic network between the Muslims peasantry and Hindu *mahajans* and *talukdars*. Since they no longer performed any useful social functions, they caused irritation to the Muslim peasants (see Bose 1986: 231–2).
10 Alavi 2002a: 4523.
11 Alavi 2002b: 5124. Due to Abul Hashim's successful campaign, the Bengal Muslim League secured 114 seats in the provincial assembly out of a total of 121 Muslim seats. Religious ideology played, as Alavi claims, no part in this election, not even by way of rhetoric.
12 This indicates a clear polarisation among the businessmen along religious lines. The Calcutta-based Hindu business houses lent their powerful support to the mass mobilisation which the S. P. Mookherjee-led Hindu Mahasabha had

undertaken following the formation of the Bengal Partition League in 1946 in the aftermath of the Great Calcutta Killings. See NMML, S. P. Mookherjee Papers, Subject File 154 (instalment I–IV).

13 The Muslim intellectuals, both in Calcutta and Dhaka, supported the Krishak Praja–League coalition government and later the League government in their efforts to provide opportunities to the hitherto underprivileged Muslim community (Ahmad 1968: 128–31). Maniruzzaman Islamabadi, Akram Khan, and Habibullah Bahar, among others, regularly published their views in the *Saptahik Mohammadi, Saogat* and also *The Morning News*, supporting the activities of the Government as most appropriate to strike a balance between the growth and development of Hindus and Muslims in Bengal.

14 As Haq himself admitted that since 'the League is passing through the most critical period of her history [i]t is, thereofre, essential that Muslims outside the League should immediately come within the fold of the Muslim League which is the only representative institution of the Muslims in India' (see IOR, L/PJ/8/655, Haq's press statement quoted in the Report by the Information Department, 6 September 1946).

15 Das 1991: 210.

16 *The Times*, London, 1 September 1946.

17 IOR, Wavell Papers, Mss. Eur. D/714/72, Wavell's appreciation of the political situation in India, 1946.

18 IOR, Wavell papers, Mss. Eur. D 714/72, Wavell's appreciation of the political situation in India, May, 1946. The Viceroy however failed to gauge the Bengal situation because he apprehended serious troubles in Uttar Pradesh and Bihar, described as 'Mutiny Provinces', where the trouble was 'greatest' both in 1857 and 1942.

19 IOR, Tyson Papers, Mss. Eur E 341/41, John Tyson's note, 23 August 1946.

20 Tuker 1950: 519.

21 IOR, Wavell paper, Mss. Eur. D 714/72, Wavell's appreciation of the political situation in India, November, 1946. He further added, 'unless the His Majesty's Government change their policy and announce that they propose to stay for 15 or 20 years and unless they make it clear that they would use all their resources to put down disorder, the Services can never be revived and reinforced'.

22 IOR, Wavell Paper, Mss. Eur. D714/72, Wavell to the Secretary of State, 22 November 1946.

23 IOR, Wavell Paper, Mss. Eur. D714/72, Auchinleck to Wavell, 22 December 1945.

24 Mansergh 1999: 232–3. In fact, Mansergh further argues that the Congress leaders were not willing to wait was 'a source of strength for Jinnah [who] was prepared to let independence wait upon division, while his opponents for the most part were not prepared to let it wait upon unity'. Endorsing the views of Nicholas Mansergh, Penderel Moon argues that the All India Congress Committee accepted 'the partition plan on the ground that it was the recommendation of the old and tired leaders who could not be replaced' (Moon 1989: 1172). In his autobiography, Maulana Azad also mentioned that 'Patel was convinced that the new state of Pakistan was not viable and could not last. Pakistan would collapse in a short time and the Provinces, which had seceded from India, would have to face untold difficulty and hardship. Perhaps Sardar Patel hoped that they would be forced to return to India' (Azad 1989: 225).

25 IOR, L/I/1/777, Confidential Appreciation of the political situation in India, 22 October 1946.

26 Tuker 1950: 179.

27 NMML, AICC Papers, CL21/1946–47, Ashrafuddin Ahmad Chowdhuri to the Congress President while tendering his resignation from the AICC membership, 10 August 1947.
28 Characterising the 1946 Calcutta riot as 'worst orgy of slaying that Police had ever experienced in India', P. E. S. Finney of the Indian Police argued that 'it began by hordes of Moslem sallying forth from every lane and alleyway in Calcutta and attacking any Hindu they could find. No one was safe, as Hindus and Sikhs were quick to retaliate. ... Hundreds of corpses were seen floating up and down the Hooghly River with the tide; other bodies were stuffed down the manholes of the sewers' (Finney 2000: 262).
29 By glossing over this important aspect of Bengal's political history that unfolded under first the KPP-League and secondly the League ministries, Joya Chatterji actually underplayed, if not trivialised, the role of Muslim communalism in the second partition of Bengal (Chatterji 1995: 266–8).
30 IOR, L/PJ/8/576, *The Times*, London, 19 October 1946.
31 For details, see Chakrabarty 1990: 1–20.
32 For details of the 1928 and 1938 Bengal Tenancy (Amendment) Acts, see Chatterjee 1982.
33 Sanjib Baruah attributed the success of the Muslims to 'Muslim nationalism ... and the appeal of the idea of singular nationhood ... produced a unity among the Muslims despite being divided internally on various counts' (Baruah 1999: 42).
34 Amalendu Guha expalined this in terms of his famous conceptualisation of two inter-twined tracks of Great Nationalism and Little Nationalism. Hence, the Muslim demand for separation from Assam is both indicative of a desire to amalgamate with Pakistan as well as a design to form a regional–linguistic unity. Similarly, the Assam Hindus appeared to have accepted the verdict since it also provided them with an opportunity to align with the Hindu-preponderant India by maintaining simultaneously their distinctive identity (Guha 1977: 334–7).
35 What disturbed the Hindu Assamese was the conception of Assam as an extension of Bengal. This was possible due to the overwhelming dominance of the Bengalis from Sylhet in the colonial bureaucracy. As Baruah informs us, 'in Sylhet, ... there was an English-educated class who took advantage of the opportunities opened in the new frontier. As they came to occupy the bulk of the positions in Assam's colonial bureaucracy, their dominance was resented, especially after an Assamese western-educated class began to emerge' (Baruah 1999: 40).
36 C. R. Das was probably the first Bengali politician to have realised the growing alienation of Muslims from the Congress-led nationalist movement. In order to strengthen the unity between the two communities, Das seems to have drawn on the Swadeshi ideological tradition of 'composite patriotism'. The Bengal Pact of 1923 for which he was responsible incorporated the educated Muslims in the world of bhadralok. Muslims, according to the Pact, were to be given 55 per cent of government jobs and 60 per cent of membership of local bodies in Muslim majority districts. Furthermore, to ascertain the secular credential of the Congress, men like Abdulhahel Baqui of Dinajpur, Maniruzzaman Islamabadi of Chittagong, Akram Khan of 24 Parganas, Shamsuddin Ahmad of Kusthia and Ashrafuddin Ahmad Chowdhury of Tippera were recruited to the provincial Congress hierarchy when he was at the helm of affairs. Das's liberal attitude toward the Muslims was commendable, but, given the depth of communal animosity in rural areas, it is by no means certain that had he lived

longer the history of the subcontinent would have taken a different course. Even his Muslim colleagues apprehended that this would give Muslims a free rein to do whatever they pleased because Das, as Abdullah Suhrawardy, an influential Muslim leader warned, 'was playing into the hands of religious fanatics'. See NMML, Suren Ghosh (oral transcript), p. 182.

37 The shifting political attitudes of the Namasudras in Bengal are, as Sekhar Bandyopadhyay has shown, contingent on how they perceived the situation. While seeking to explain the shift, Bandyoypadhyay argues, 'the mentality of defiance and an urge for social revolution are thus often accompanied by preparedness to accept and accommodate. It is this tendency which indicates the all possibilities of conflict or disjunction, or in fact disintegration of the community cannot be eliminated, even though at a particular conjuncture the community may appear as a real entity (Bandyopadhyay 1997: 245). What was evident in colonial Bengal was also seen in Uttar Pradesh. As Ramnarayan Rawat has demonstrated, the *Dalits* kept changing their political allies in accordance with what they construed as 'best' from their point of view. Thus it was not politically inappropriate to establish 'an alliance with the Muslim League to justify their demand for a separate identity [by underlining] the outcaste status of their community. The Dalits articulated achhut identity forcefully enough to prevent it submerging into Congress or national consensus'. See Ramnarayn Rawat 2001: 115.

38 The novelist Atin Bandyopadhyay articulated this feeling in his novel *Neel Kantha Pakhir Khoje* (Bengali). 'After all you'll be able to perform my last rites on the bank of the Ganges', an old man told his sons while explaining the reasons for migrating to West Bengal. East Bengal for him now stood for 'an unholy land' and West Bengal, the aspired place to protect the dignity and self respect of the Hindus. For details of this argument, see Sandip Bandyopadhyay in Samaddar 1997: 67.

39 In his analysis of the Bengali tract *Chhere Asha Gram*, Dipesh Chakrabarty argues that despite having been the victims of Muslim communalism, in the Bengali Hindu home, the non-Muslim League Muslim – who did not demand Pakistan – was always 'a valued guest' (Chakrabarty 1996: 2150). A review of the contemporary literature shows, as Sisir Das informs, that the Hindu-Muslim bitterness was often underplayed, presumably not to aggravate the situation further (interview with Sisir Das of the University of Delhi, 11 January 2001).

40 The east Bengal refugees looked upon themselves as 'the victims of partition', and as Bengalis, regarded it as their basic right to seek refuge in that part of Bengal which now lay in India. Having faced persecution and intolerance in east Bengal, they believed that 'it was their legitimate claim to seek rehabilitation within West Bengal, which they now felt was their natural habitat' (Tai Yung Tan and Kudaisya 2000: 146). Attributing the continuous flow of refugees in West Bengal even after fifty years of independence to this 'feeling', Joya Chatterji argues that 'unlike those from the west, refugees from the east did not flood into India in one huge wave; they came sometimes in surges but often in barely perceptible trickles over the five decades of independence' (Chatterji, in Kaul 2001: 74.

41 Ismat Chughtai, 'Roots', in Bhalla 1994: 16. As is evident in *Palanka*, Rajmohan's decision not to migrate to Calcutta was due to his reluctance to leave his *desh* (homeland) even when he was left behind by his son who happily settled in Calcutta.

42 Qureshi, in Hasan 1995: 89–90.

43 Pandey 2001: 132.
44 Mushirul Hasan thus argues that no statistical data are required to establish the multi-dimensional Muslim identity in India. 'Their histories, along with social habits, cultural traits and occupational patterns, vary from class to class, from place to place, and from region to region. They speak numerous dialects and languages and observe wide-ranging regional customs and local rites despite the intervention of [theologians and publicists]. Caste exists as a basis of social relations, although it differs from the Hindu caste system in details. In several domains Muslims make up an integral part of the larger socio-cultural complex dominated by values and ideologies of the Hindu caste tradition' (Hasan 1997: 7–8).
45 For a detailed exposition of the 'enumerated' and 'fuzzy' community, see Kaviraj in Chatterjee and Pandey 1992: 20–33.
46 Mansergh *et al.*, Vol. I–XII, 1970–83.
47 Gupta 1996–97.
48 Mansergh 1982–83: 14.
49 Tamijuddin Khan, Memoirs (unpublished) available by courtesy of Dr. M. N. Huda of the University of Dhaka.
50 Ahmad 1968.
51 Ikramullah 1987.
52 Azad 1989.
53 Choudhury 1961.
54 Mookherjee 1993.
55 B. R. Ambedkar's introduction to *Thoughts on Pakistan* (published a year after the 1940 Lahore resolution), cited in Hasan 2000: 2.
56 Chaudhuri 1989.
57 Bose 1974.
58 Ahmed 1981; Oberoi 1999 is another good account of the construction and consolidation of identity under colonialism.
59 Ray 1984.
60 Bose 1986.
61 Chakrabarty 1990.
62 Murshid 1995.
63 Chatterji 1995.
64 Pandey 2001. For a brief discussion of violence during the partition riots, see Pandey 1999.
65 Butalia 1998.
66 Menon and Bhasin, 'Recovery, rupture, resistance: the Indian state and the abduction of women during partition' in Hasan 2000: 210.

BIBLIOGRAPHY

Private papers

India Office Library, London

Anderson (Bengal Governor, 1932–37), Papers, Mss Eur F 207 and Mss Eur D 806
Brabourne (Bengal Governor, 1937–39), Papers, Mss Eur F 97
Linlithgow (Viceroy of India, 1936–43), Papers, Mss Eur F 125
Pethick Lawrence (Secretary of State), Papers, Mss. Eur F 540
Reid (Acting Bengal Governor, 1938–39), Papers, Mss Eur E 278
Templewood (Secretary of State for India, 1931–35), Papers, Mss Eur E 240
Tyson (Private Secretary to the Bengal Governor, 1946–47), Papers, Mss. Eur D 341
Wavell (Viceroy of India, 1943–47), Papers, Mss Eur. D 977
Willingdon (Governor-General of India, 1931–36), Papers, Mss. Eur F 93
Zetland (Secretary of State for India, 1935–40), Papers, Mss Eur D 609

Nehru Memorial Museum and Library, New Delhi

All India Congress Committee Papers, 1931–47
All India Hindu Mahasabha Papers, 1930–47
S. P. Mookherjee Papers
B. S. Moonjee Papers
Jawaharlal Nehru Papers
B. C. Roy Papers
M. N. Roy Papers
N. R. Sarkar Papers
Sahajanand Saraswati Papers
J. B. Kripalani Papers
Purushottamdas Thakurdas Papers

Centre of South Asian Studies, Cambridge

Baker Papers
Bell Papers

BIBLIOGRAPHY

Benthall Papers
Carter Papers
Dash Papers
Taylor Papers
Tegart Papers
Tottenham Papers

National Archives of India, New Delhi

V. J. Patel Papers
Rajendra Prasad Papers
Bholanath Roy Papers
Wood Collection
Sampuranand Papers
P. D. Tandon Papers

Dhaka

Tamijuddin Khan Memoirs (typescript), available by courtesy of Mrs. M. N. Huda of Dhaka University

Government records

India Office Library

File of Bengal Governor's Secretariat, 1938–47, R/3/1 and R/3/2
Records of the Information Department, L/I/1
Records of the Public and Judicial Department, L/PJ
Records of the War Staff Department, L/WS/1

National Archives of India

Record of the Home-Political Department, 1945–47

West Bengal State Archives, Calcutta

Record of the Home-Political (Confidential) Department, 1941–47

Bangladesh Secretariat Record Room, Dhaka

Police Department 'B' Proceedings, 1938–47
Home Political Department 'B' Proceedings, 1938–47
Revenue Department 'B' Proceedings, 1938–47

BIBLIOGRAPHY

Oral Transcripts

Nehru Memorial Museum and Library

Satis Dasgupta, S. M. Ghosh, Bhupati Majumdar, Anil Baran Roy, Promode Sengupta

Published Records

Proceedings of the Bengal Legislative Assembly, 1938–47
Indian Franchise (Lothian) Committee, 1931–32
Bengal Provincial Banking Enquiry (De) Committee, 1929–30
Bengal Jute Enquiry (Finlow) Committee, 1933
Bengal Jute Enquiry (Fawcus) Committee, 1938–39
Bengal Land Revenue (Floud) Commission, 1938–40
Famine Enquiry (Woodhead) Commission, 1944–45
Census of India, 1901, 1911, 1921, 1931 and 1941
Census of Bengal, 1901, 1911, 1921, 1931 and 1941
Census of Assam, 1931 and 1941

Newspapers

Amrita Bazar Patrika (English), Calcutta
Ananda Bazar Patrika (Bengali), Calcutta
Azad (Bengali), Calcutta,
Bangiya Mussalman Sahitya Patriaka (Bengali), Calcutta
Barshik Mohammadi (English), Calcutta
Dawn (English), Lahore
Harijan (English), Pune
Islam Darshan (Bengali), Dhaka
Islam Pracharak (Bengali), Dhaka
Manchester Guardian (English), Birmingham
Sahitya (Bengal), Calcutta
Sanibarer Chhithi (Bengali), Calcutta
The Hindustan Times (English), Delhi
The Morning News (English), Calcutta
The Mussalman (English), Calcutta
The Star of India (English), Calcutta
The Statesman (English), Calcutta
The Times (English), London

Books and articles

Aditya, R. N. *From the Corridors of Memory*, Book Depot, Karimganj, 1970.
Ahmad, A. *Jinnah, Pakistan and the Islamic Identity: The Search for Saladin*, Oxford University Press, Karachi, 1997.

Ahmad, A. M. *Amar Dekha Rajnitir Panchhas Bachhar*, Srijan Prakashani, Dhaka, 1968.
Ahmad, A. M. *Atmakatha*, Khosroj Kitabmahal, Dhaka, 1978.
Ahmad, A. M. *Fifty Years of Politics as I Saw*, Srijan Prakashani, Dhaka, 1988.
Ahmed, M. *Prabandha Sankalan* (Bengali), National Book Agency, Calcutta, 1970.
Ahmed, R. *The Bengal Muslims, 1871–1906: A Quest for Identity*, Oxford University Press, Delhi, 1981.
Ahmed, R. (ed.). *Understanding the Bengal Muslims: Interpretative Essays*, Oxford University Press, Delhi, 2001.
Alavi, H. 'Misreading partition road signs', *Economic and Political Weekly*, November 2–9, 2002a.
Alavi, H. 'Social forces and ideology in the making of Pakistan', *Economic and Political Weekly*, October 21, 2002b.
Ali Chaudhuri Muhammad. *The Emergence of Pakistan*, Columbia University Press, New York, 1967.
Allen, B. C. *District Gazetteers*, Vol. II (Sylhet). Caledonian Steam Printing Networks, Calcutta, 1905.
Ambedkar, B. R. *Pakistan or the Partition of India*, Bombay, 1945.
Anisuzzaman. *Muslim Banglar Samayak Patra*, Bangladesh Asiatic Society, Dacca, 1969.
Azad, M. *India Wins Freedom*, Sangam, London, 1989.
Bagchi Amiya. *Private Investment in India, 1900–39*, Cambridge University Press, Cambridge, 1972.
Bandyapadhyay, A. *Neel Kantha Pakhir Khoje* (Bengali), Karuna Prakashnee, Calcutta, 1976.
Bandyapadhyay Bhavanicharan. *Kalikata Kamalalaya* (Bengali), Calcutta 1343 (Bengali Shakabda).
Bandyopadhyay, Sekhar. *Caste, Protest and Identity in Colonial India: the Namasudras of Bengal, 1872–1947*, Curzon Press, Surrey, 1997.
Bandyopadhyay, Sekhar. (ed.). *Bengal. Rethinking History. Essays in Historiography*, Manohar, New Delhi, 2001.
Baruah, S. *India Against Itself: Assam and the Politics of Nationality*, University of Pennsylvania Press, Philadelphia, 1999.
Basu, Swaraj, *Dynamics of a Caste Movement: the Rajbanshis of North Bengal, 1910–47*, Manohar, New Delhi, 2003.
Bhalla Alok (ed.). *Stories about the Partition of India*, Penguin, New Delhi, 1994.
Bhuyan, A. C. *Political History of Assam*, Vol. 3 (1940–47), Government of Assam, Gauhati, 1980.
Birla, G. D. *In the Shadow of Mahatma: A Personal Memoir*, Orient Longman, Calcutta, 1964.
Bose, N. K. *My Days with Gandhi*, Orient Longman, Calcutta, 1974.
Bose, Sarat C. *Whither Two Bengals*, Netaji Research Bureau, Calcutta, 1970.
Bose, S. K. (ed.). *Crossroads*, Netaji Research Bureau, Calcutta, 1983.
Bose, S. K. (ed.). *The Voice of Sarat Bose*, Oxford University Press, Calcutta, 1979.
Bose, Subhas C. *Indian Struggle, 1920–42*, Asia Publishing House, London, 1964.
Bose, Sugata. *Agrarian Bengal, Economy, Social Structure and Politics, 1919–1947*, Cambridge University Press, Cambridge, 1986.

BIBLIOGRAPHY

Bose, Sugata. 'Nation, reason and religion: India's independence in international perspective', *Economic and Political Weekly*, August 1, 1998.

Bose, Sugata and Ayesha Jalal (eds). *Nationalism, Democracy and Development: State and Politics in India*, Oxford University Press, Delhi, 1997.

Bose, Sugata and Ayesha Jalal (eds). *Modern South Asia, History, Culture, Political Economy*, Oxford University Press, Delhi, 1998.

Brass, P. R. *Language, Religion and Politics in North India*, Cambridge University Press, Cambridge, 1974.

Brass, P. R. *Ethnicity and Nationalism: Theory and Comparison*, Sage, New Delhi, 1991.

Brown, W. N. 'Nationalism, communalism and partition', in M. D. Lewis (ed.), *The British in India: Imperialism and Trusteeship*, D.C. Heath & Co., Boston, 1962.

Butalia, U. *The Other Side of Silence: Voices from the Partition of India*, Viking, New Delhi, 1998.

Campbell-Johnson, Alan. *Mission with Mountbatten*, Robert Hale, London, 1951.

Chakrabarty, Bidyut. 'Peasants and the Bengal Congress, 1928–38', *South Asia Research*, 5(1), 1985.

Chakrabarty, Bidyut. *Subhas Chandra Bose and Middle Class Radicalism: A Study in Indian Nationalism, 1928–40*, Oxford University Press, Delhi, 1990.

Chakrabarty, Bidyut. *Local Politics and Indian Nationalism: Midnapur, 1919–1944*, Manohar, New Delhi, 1997.

Chakrabarty, Bidyut. *Biplabi: A Journal of the 1942 Open Rebellion*, K. P. Bagchi, Calcutta, 2002a.

Chakrabarty, Bidyut. 'Religion, colonialism and modernity: relocating "self" and "collectivity",' *Gandhi Marg*, 23(3) 2002b.

Chakrabarty, Bidyut. (ed.) *Communal Identity in India: Its Construction and Articulation in Twentieth Century India*, Oxford University Press, Delhi, 2003.

Chakrabarty, Dipesh 'Remembered villages: representation of Hindu-Bengali memoirs in the aftermouth of the partition', *Economic and Political Weekly*, August 10, 1996.

Chakrabarty, Dipesh. 'Nation and imagination', *Studies in History*, 15(2), New Series, 1999.

Chatterjee, P. 'Bengal politics and Muslim masses, 1920–47', *Journal of Commonwealth and Comparative Politics*, 20(1), 1982a.

Chatterjee, P. 'Agrarian relations and communalism in Bengal, 1926–1935', in R. Guha (ed.). *Subaltern Studies*, Vol. 1, Oxford University Press, Delhi, 1982b.

Chatterjee, P. 'Agrarian structure in pre-partition Bengal', in A. Sen (ed.), *Three Studies on Bengal Agrarian Structure*, Oxford University Press, Delhi 1982c.

Chatterjee, P. *The Present History of West Bengal: Essays in Political Criticism*, Oxford University Press, Delhi, 1997.

Chatterjee, P. 'The nation in heterogeneous time', *Indian Economic and Social History Review*, 38(4), 2001.

Chatterjee, P. *A Princely Impostor? The Kumar of Bhawal and the Secret History of Indian Nationalism*, Permanent Black, New Delhi, 2002.

Chatterjee, P. and Pandey, G. (eds). *Subaltern Studies: Writings on South Asian History and Society*, Oxford University Press, Delhi, 1992.

Chatterji, J. *Bengal Divided: Hindu Communalism and Partition, 1932–1947*, Cambridge University Press, Cambridge, 1995.

BIBLIOGRAPHY

Chatterji, J. 'The fashioning of a frontier:the Radcliffe line and Bengal's border landscape', *Modern Asian Studies*, 33(1), 1999.

Chaudhuri, B. B. 'Agrarian economy and agrarian relations in Bengal, 1859–85', in N. K. Sinha (ed.), *The History of Bengal*, Firma KLM Publisher, Calcutta, 1967.

Chaudhuri, B. B. 'Eastern India', in D. Kumar (ed.), *The Cambridge Economic History of India, C 1751–1970*, Vol. 2, Orient Longman, New Delhi, 1984.

Chaudhuri Nirad C. *The Autobiography of an Unknown Indian*, University of California Press, Berkeley, 1968.

Chaudhuri Nirad C. *Thy Hand Great Anarch: India, 1921–52*, Chatto and Windus, London, 1987.

Chaudhuri, S. (ed.). *Calcutta: The Living City*, Vol. II, Oxford University Press, Calcutta, 1990.

Choudhury Khaliquzzaman. *Pathway to Pakistan*, Longmans, Lahore, 1961.

Chowdhury Hamidul Haq. *Atmajibani* (Memoirs), Kitabistan, Dhaka, 1989.

Cohn, B. *Colonialism and its Forms of Knowledge: the British in India*, Princeton University Press, Princeton, 1996.

Coswasjee, S. and Duggal, K. S. (eds). *When the British Left: Stories on the Partitioning of India, 1947*, Arnold-Heinemann, New Delhi, 1987.

Damodaran Vinita. 'Bihar in the 1940s: communities, riots and the state', *South Asia*, XVII, 1995.

Darling, Malcolm Lyall. *At Freedom's Dawn*, Oxford University Press, London, 1949.

Das, Durga (ed.). *Vallabhbhai Patel Correspondence, 1945–50*, Vol. IV, Patel Memorial Fund, Ahmedabad, 1972.

Das, Suranjan. 'The politics of agitation: Calcutta, 1912–1947', in S. Chaudhuri (ed.), *Calcutta: The Living City*, Vol. II, *The Present and the Future*, Oxford University Press, Calcutta, 1990.

Das, Suranjan. *Communal Riots in Bengal, 1905–1947*, Oxford University Press, Delhi, 1991.

Datta, N. *Forming an Identity: A Social History of the Jats*, Oxford University Press, Delhi, 1999.

Datta, P. K. *Carving Blocs: Communal Ideology in Early Twentieth Century Bengal*, Oxford University Press, Delhi, 1999.

Datta, V. N. 'Iqbal, Jinnah and India's partition: an intimate relationship', *Economic and Political Weekly*, December, 14–20, 2002.

De Amalendu. 'Fazlul Haq and his reaction to two-nation theory, 1940–47, *Bengal Past and Present*, 13(2), 1974.

De Dhurjati Prasad. *Bengal Muslims in Search of Identity, 1905–1947*, The University Press Limited, Dhaka, 1998.

Dutta, P. K. *Carving Blocs: Communal Ideology in Early Twentieth Century Bengal*, Oxford University Press, Delhi, 1999.

Eaton, R. M. *The Rise of Islam and Bengal Frontier*, 1204–1760, Oxford University Press, Delhi, 1994.

Finney, P. E. S. *Just My Luck: Memories of a Police Officer of the Raj*, University Press Ltd, Dhaka, 2000.

Freitag, Sandria B. *Collective Action and Community: Public Arenas and the Emergence of Communalism in North India*, Oxford University Press, Delhi, 1990.

BIBLIOGRAPHY

French, P. *Liberty or Death: India's Journey to Independence and Division*, HarperCollins, London, 1997.

Gallagher, J. 'Congress in decline, Bengal 1900–39', *Modern Asian Studies*, 7(3), 1973.

Gellner, E. *Saints of the Atlas*, Chicago University Press, Chicago, 1969.

Gilmartin, D. *Empire and Islam: Punjab and the Making of Pakistan*, I. B. Tauris, London, 1988.

Gopal, S. (ed.). *Selected Works of Jawaharlal Nehru*, Jawaharlal Nehru Fund, New Delhi, 1985.

Gordon, L. 'Divided Bengal: problems of nationalism and identity in the 1947 partition', *Journal of Comparative and Commonwealth Politics*, 16(2), 1978.

Griffiths, Percival. *To Guard My People: The History of the Indian Police*, Ernest Benn, London, 1971.

Guha, A. *Planter Raj to Swaraj*, People's Publishing House, New Delhi, 1977.

Guha, A. *Medieval and Early Assam: Society, Polity and Economy*, K. P. Bagchi & Co., Calcutta, 1990.

Guha, Ranajit. *Dominance without Hegemony: History and Power in Colonial India*, Oxford University Press, Delhi, 1998.

Gupta, D. *The Context of Ethnicity: Sikh Identity in a Comparative Perspective*, Oxford University Press, Delhi, 1996.

Gupta, P. S. (ed.). *Towards Freedom: Documents on the Movement for Independence in India*, Oxford University Press, New Delhi, 1996–97.

Haque, Azizul. *A Plea for Separate Electorate in Bengal*, Pamphlet, Calcutta, 1931.

Hardy, P. *The Muslims of British India*, Cambridge University Press, Cambridge, 1972.

Hasan Mushirul (ed.). *India Partitioned: The Other Face of Freedom*, Vol. 1, Roli Books, New Delhi, 1995.

Hasan Mushirul *Legacy of a Divided Nation: India's Muslims since Independence*, Oxford University Press, Delhi, 1997.

Hasan Mushirul (ed.). *Inventing Boundaries: Gender, Politics and the Partition of India*, Oxford University Press, New Delhi, 2000.

Hasan, M. (ed.). *India's Partition: Process, Strategy and Mobilization*, Oxford University Press, Delhi, 1993.

Hasan, M. (ed.). *The Partition Omnibus*, Oxford University Press, Delhi, 2001a.

Hasan, M. *Partition Narratives*, Presidential address, Indian History Congress, 2001b.

Hasan, M. and Asaduddin, M. (eds). *Image and Representation: Stories of Muslim Lives in India*, Oxford University Press, Delhi, 2000.

Hasan, M. and Nakazato, N. (eds) *The Unfinished Agenda: Nation-building in South Asia*, Manohar, New Delhi, 2001.

Hashim Abul. *In Retrospection*, Mowla Brothers, Dhaka, 1974.

Hodson, H. V. *The Great Divide: Britain–India–Pakistan*, Hutchinson, London, 1969.

Ikramullah Begam Shaista Suhrawardy. *Huseyn Shaheed Suhrawardy*, Oxford University Press, Karachi, 1991.

Jalal, Ayesha. *The Sole Spokesman: Jinnah, the Muslim League and the Demand for Pakistan*, Cambridge University Press, Cambridge, 1985.

Jalal, Ayesha. 'Secularists, subalterns and the stigma of "communalism": partition

historiography revisited', *Indian Economic and Social History Review*, 33(1), 1996.
Jalel, Ayesha. 'Nation, reason and religion: Punjab's role in the partition of India', *Economic and Political Weekly*, August 8, 1998.
Jalel, Ayesha. *Self and Sovereignty: Individual and Community in South Asian Islam Since 1850*, Oxford University Press, Delhi, 2001.
Jinnah Muhammad Ali. *Speeches,* Pakistan Publications, Karachi, 1963.
Kamtekar Indivar. 'A different war dance: state and class in India', *Past & Present*, 176, 2002.
Kar, M. *Muslims in Assam Politics*, Vikas, New Delhi, 1997.
Kaul, S. (ed.). *The Partition of Memory: The Afterlife of Division of India*, Permanent Black, New Delhi, 2001.
Kaviraj Sudipta. 'Modernity and politics in India', *Daedalus*, 129(1), 2000.
Khilnani, S. *The Idea of India*, Hamish Hamilton, London, 1997.
Khosla, G. D. *Stern Reckoning: A Survey of the Events Leading up to and Following the Partition of India*, Oxford University Press, Delhi, 1989 (reprint).
Kohli, A. *The State and Poverty in India: The Politics of Reform*, Cambridge University Press, Cambridge, 1987.
Kripalani Sucheta. *An Unfinished Biography*, Navjivan Publishing House, Ahmedabad, 1978.
Krisnan, Y. 'Mountbatten and the partition of India', *History*, 68, 1983.
Kumar, A. 'Partition, Congress secularism and Hindu communalism', *Economic and Political Weekly*, July 29, 2000.
Low, D. A. (ed.). *The Indian National Congress: Contemporary Hindsights*, Oxford University Press, Delhi, 1988.
Low, D. A. (ed.). *The Political Inheritance of Pakistan*, Macmillan, London, 1991.
Low, D. A. and Brasted, H. *Freedom, Trauma and Continuities: Northern India and Independence*, Sage, New Delhi, 1998.
Ludden, David (ed.). *Making India Hindu: Religion, Community and the Politics of Democracy in India*, Oxford University Press, Delhi, 1996.
Mahajan, Sucheta, *Independence and Partition: The Erosion of Colonial Power*, Sage, New Delhi, 2000.
Mansergh, Diana (ed.). *Independence Years: The Selected Indian and Commonwealth Papers of Nicholas Mansergh*, Oxford University Press, Delhi, 1999.
Mansergh, N. (ed.). 'The transfer of power in India: editorial problems and perspectives', *Indian Office Library and Record Report*, January 1982–March 1983.
Mansergh, N., Lumby, E. W. R. and Moon, E. P. (eds). *The Transfer of Power, 1940–47*, Vols I–XII, HMSO, London, 1970–1983.
Menon, Dilip. 'Religion and colonial modernity: rethinking belief and identity', *Economic and Political Weekly*, April 27, 2002.
Menon, M. U. (ed.). *An Epic Unwritten: Penguin Book of Partition Stories in Urdu*, Penguin, New Delhi, 1998.
Menon, R. and Bhasin, K. *Borders and Boundaries: Women in India's Partition*, Kali for Women, Delhi, 1998.
Menon, V. P. *The Transfer of Power in India*, Orient Longman, Hyderabad, 1993 (reprint).
Mitra Ashok. *The New India, 1948–1955: Memoirs of an Indian Civil Servant*, Popular Prakashan, Bombay, 1991.

BIBLIOGRAPHY

Momen, Humaira. *Muslim Politics in Bengal: A Study of the KPP and the Elections of 1937*, Prakashan, Dhaka, 1972.
Mookherjee, S. P. *Leaves from a Diary*, Oxford University Press, Calcutta, 1993.
Moon, P. *Divide and Quit*, Oxford University Press, Delhi, 1998.
Moon, Penderel (ed.). *Wavell: the Viceroy's Journal*, Oxford University Press, Delhi, 1977.
Moon, Penderel *The British Conquest: Dominion of India*, Duckworth, London, 1989.
Moore, R. J. 'Jinnah and the Pakistan demand', *Modern Asian Studies*, 17(4), 1983.
Morris Jones W. H. 'The transfer of power, 1947: a view from the sidelines', *Modern Asian Studies*, 16(1), 1982.
Moseley, Leonard. *The Last Days of the British Raj*, Weidenfield and Nicolson, London, 1961.
Mujeev, M. 'The partition of India in retrospect', in C. H. Philips and M. D. Wainwright (eds), *The Partition of India: Policies and Perspectives*, George Allen and Unwin, London, 1970.
Mukherjee, Karunamoy. *The Problem of Land Transfer*, Viswabharati, Shantiniketan, 1957.
Mukherjee, Radhakamal. *Land Problems of India*, London, 1933; cited in A. Sen (ed.), *Three Studies on Bengal Agrarian Structure*, Oxford University Press, Calcutta, 1981.
Mukherji, Saugata. 'Some aspects of commercialisation of agriculture in eastern India, 1891–1938', in Ashok Sen et al., *Three Studies on Agrarian Structure in Bengal*, Oxford University Press, Calcutta, 1982.
Munir, M. *From Jinnah to Zia*, Vanguard Books Limited, Lahore, 1979.
Murshid, Tazeen M. *The Sacred and the Secular: Bengal Muslim Discourses, 1871–1977*, Oxford University Press, Delhi, 1995.
Nawaz Mumtaz Shah. 'The heart divide', in M. Hasan (ed.), *India Partitioned: The Other Face of Freedom*, Vol. 2, Roli Books, Delhi, 1995.
Nehru, J. *An Autobiography*, John Lane and Bodley Head, London, 1941.
Oberoi, H. *The Construction of Religious Boundaries: Culture, Identity and Diversity*, Oxford University Press, Delhi, 1994.
Omar Badruddin. *Bangladesher Madhyabitta O Sanskritik Paristhithi* (Bengali), Pallav Publishers, Dhaka, 1988.
Page, David. *The Prelude to Partition: The Indian Muslims and the Imperial System of Control, 1920–1932*, Oxford University Press, Delhi, 1982.
Pandey, G. 'The prose of otherness', *Subaltern Studies*, Vol. VIII, Oxford University Press, Delhi, 1994.
Pandey, G. *Hindus and Others: The Question of Identity in India Today*, Viking, New Delhi, 1997.
Pandey, G. *Memory, History and the Question of Violence: Reflections on the Reconstruction of Partition*, K. P. Bagchi, Calcutta, 1999.
Pandey, G. *Remembering Partition: Violence, Nationalism and History in India*, Cambridge University Press, Cambridge, 2001.
Parel, Anthony J. (ed.). *Gandhi, Freedom and Self Rule*, Vistaar, New Delhi, 2000.
Peabody, Norbert. 'Cents, sense, census: human inventories in late pre-colonial and early colonial India', *Comparative Studies in Society and History*, 43(4), 2001.

Pirzada, S. S. (ed.). *Foundations of Pakistan: All India Muslim League Documents*, Vol. II, National Publishing House, Karachi (undated).

Pouchepadass, Jacques. *Champaran and Gandhi; Planters, Peasants and Gandhian Politics*, Oxford University Press, Delhi, 1999.

Prakash, B. 'Nation and identity in the narratives of partition', in V. Damoderan and M. Unnithan (eds), *Post Colonial India: History, Politics and Culture*, Manohar, New Delhi, 2001.

Prasad, Bimal. *Pathway to India's Partition: The Foundations of Muslim Nationalism*, Vol. I, Manohar, Delhi, 1996.

Prasad, Bimal. *Pathway to India's Partition: A Nation within a Nation, 1877–1937* Vol. II, Manohar, New Delhi, 2000.

Prasad, R. *Autobiography*, Popular Press, Bombay, 1957.

Puri, B. 'Iqbal and idea of Pakistan', *European and Political Weekly*, 38(5), 2003.

Rashid Harun-or. *The Foreshadowing of Bangladesh: Bengal Muslim League and Muslim Politics, 1936–1947*, Asiatic Society of Bangladesh, Dhaka, 1987.

Ray Rajat K. (ed.). *Mind, Body and Society: Life and Mentality in Colonial Bengal*, Oxford University Press, Calcutta, 1995.

Ray Rajat K. *Exploring Emotional History: Gender, Mentality and Literature in the Indian Awakening*, Oxford University Press, Delhi, 2001.

Reza, R. M. *The Feuding Families of Village Gangauli* (trans. G. Wright), Viking, Delhi, 1994.

Robinson, Francis. *Separatism among Indian Muslims: The Politics of the United Provinces, 1860–1923*, Cambridge University Press, Cambridge, 1974.

Roy, A. 'The social factors in the making of Bengali Islam', *South Asia* 3(1), 1973.

Roy, A. 'Bengali Muslims and the problem of identity', *Journal of the Asiatic Society of Bangladesh*, 22(3), 1977.

Roy, A. *The Islamic Syncretistic Tradition in Bengal*, Princeton University Press, Princeton, 1983.

Roy, Asim. 'The high politics of India's partition: the revisionist perspective', *Modern Asian Studies*, 24(2), 1990.

Roy, R. K. *Social Conflict and Political Unrest in Bengal, 1875–1927*, Oxford University Press, Delhi, 1984.

Rushd, A. *Nongor*, Boi Ghar, Chittagong, 1967.

Samaddar, R. *Reflections on Partition in the East*, Vikas, New Delhi, 1997.

Samaddar, R. *The Marginal Nation: Transborder Migration from Bangladesh to West Bengal*, Sage, New Delhi, 1999.

Samaddar R. 'Leaders and public: stories in the time of transition', *The Indian Economic and Social History Review*, 37(4), 2000.

Sarkar Chandiprasad. *The Bengali Muslims: A Study of their Politicisation (1912–1929)*, K. P. Bagchi, Calcutta, 1991.

Sarkar Sumit, *The Swadeshi Movement in Bengal, 1903–1908*, People's Publishing House, New Delhi, 1973.

Saul, S. B. *Studies in British Overseas Trade, 1870–1914*, Hamilton Press, Liverpool, 1966.

Seal, A. 'Imperialism and nationalism in India', *Modern Asian Studies*, 7(3), 1973.

Sen, Mrinal. 'Chhabi Karar Ager Dinguli', in Pralay Sur (ed.), *Mrinal Sen*, Katha Shilpa, Calcutta, 1987.

Sen, Shila. *Muslim Politics in Bengal 1937–47*, Impex India, New Delhi, 1976.

BIBLIOGRAPHY

Sengupta Amalendu. *Uttal Challis: Asampta Biplab* (Bengali), Pearl Publishers, Calcutta, 1989.

Sengupta Debjani (ed.). *Mapmaking: Partition Stories from 2 Bengals*, Srishti, New Delhi, 2003.

Settar, S. and Indira, B. Gupta (eds). *Pangs of Partition: The Parting of Ways*, Vol. I, Vol. II, Manohar, New Delhi, 2002.

Shaikh Farzana. 'Muslims and political representation in colonial India: the making of Pakistan', *Modern Asian Studies*, 20(3), 1986.

Shamsuddin, Abul Kalam. 'Sahitye Sampradayikata', *Islam Darshan*, 3(1), Aswin, 1329.

Sharma, M. V. *The Right Man in the Right Place: Subhas Chandra Bose*, Kitabistan, Lahore, 1938.

Sherwani, L. A. *The Partition of India and Mountbatten*, Kitab Mahal, Karachi, 1986.

Singh, Anita Inder. *The origins of the Partition of India, 1936–47*, Oxford University Press, Delhi, 1987.

Sission, R. and Wolpert, S. (eds). *Congress and Indian Nationalism: The Pre-independence Phase*, University of California Press, Berkeley, 1988.

Sitaramayya, B. Pattabhi. *History of the Indian National Congress*, Vol. II (1935–47), S. Chand & Co, Delhi, 1969.

Spear, Percival. *The Oxford History of Modern India, 1740–1947*, Clarendon Press, Oxford, 1965.

Suhrawardy, H. *Memoirs of Huseyn Suhrawardy*, University Press Ltd, Dhaka, 1987

Tai Yong Tan and Gynesh Kudaisya. *The Aftermath of Partition in South Asia*, Routledge, London, 2000.

Talbot, I. *Punjab and the Raj, 1849–1947*, Manohar, New Delhi, 1988.

Talbot, I. and Singh, G. (eds). *Region and Partition: Bengal, Punjab and the Partition of the Subcontinent*, Oxford University Press, Karachi, 1999.

Tarchek, Ronald J. *Gandhi: Struggling for Autonomy*, Vistaar, New Delhi, 1998.

Tazul-Hashmi. *Pakistan as a Peasant Utopia: The Communalisation of Class Politics in East Bengal, 1920–1947*, Westview Press, Boulder, 1989.

Tirmizi S. A. I. (ed.). *The Paradoxes of Partition, 1937–47*, Vol. 1 (1937–39), Centre for Federal Studies, Jamia Hamdard, New Delhi, 1998.

Tuker, F. *While Memory Serves*, Cassell, London, 1950.

van der Veer, Peter. *Religious Nationalism: Hindus and Muslims in India*, Oxford University Press, Delhi 1996.

Zaidi, A. M. and Zaidi, S. G. (eds). *The Encyclopaedia of the Indian National Congress*, Vol. 12, S. Chand & Co, New Delhi, 1981.

Zamon, N. *A Divided Legacy: The Partition in Selected Novels of India, Pakistan and Bangladesh*, Manohar, New Delhi, 2000.

INDEX

A Plea For Separate Electorates in Bengal 58
Abdul Karim 47
Abdul Majid 47
abolition of zamindari and KPP 48
absence of a class-based ideology 85
Abul Hashim 14
Adab 214–15
Adarsha Krishak 11
Adim Ripu 226
Advance 70
agrarian relations in Bengal 36
Ahl-e-Hadis 45
Ahmad, R. (President of the Bengal Presidency Muslim League) 63
AICC 134, 147; Parliamentary Committee 76
Akhand Muslim state 136
Akram Khan 45, 98
All India Communal Award Conference (1935) 73
All India Congress Committee 22, 23, 67, 72–3; and Communal Award 69; and partition 243
All India Muslim League 49
All Parties conference (1928) 57
Alla Ho Akbar 191
Allah 46
Ambedkar, B. R. 5–6
American intelligence report on riot 101
Amrita Bazar Patrika 70, 112, 146
Anderson, John (Bengal governor) 61, 63
announcement of the partition plan (3 June 1947) 147
anti-Communal Award campaign 71
Anti-Communal Award Conference in Delhi 69
anti-national and anti-democratic character of the 1939 Municipal Act 94
anti-partition campaign (1905) 139
anti-partition movement in the swadeshi days 106

anti-Subhas faction in the Bengal Congress 134
anti-White paper campaign 67
Arab imperialism 7
Arabic and Persian influence in Bengali 45, 46
armed police force, role of in riots 109
army and referendum 190
Assam Muslim League and referendum 184
Assam: profile of 176; changing profile of 245–7; civil disobedience movement in 185; divided 195; split 196; topography disturbed 196
Assamese Hindu leadership and separation of Sylhet 247
Attlee, Clement: commitment to political withdrawal 154; 20 February announcement 133
Atul Chandra Gupta and boundary commission 159–60
Auchinleck, Claude 156
August killings 145
August riot (1946) 15
Azad 72
Azadi 10

Baluchistan 4
Bande Mataram 17
Bangiya Mussalman Sahitya Samity (1904) 44
Bangladesh, creation of (1971) 150
Bangladeshiya Kayastha Sabha 109
Bankimchandra Chatterjee 19
Batwara 10
believers and non-believers 11
Bengal: agrarian economy 38; award 164; as a distinct political entity 244; identity 18; and language 42; ministry under Haq; into a separate province 107
Bengal Agricultural Debtors Act (1939) 90

INDEX

Bengal Assembly 92
Bengal Chamber of commerce 77, 133
Bengal Congress 73, 77, 79, 86; Communal Award 68–70; and united Bengal 140
Bengal Legislative Assembly 77, 97; and partition of Bengal 191; votes for partition 111
Bengal Money Lenders Act (1940) 90
Bengal Pact (1923) 79
Bengal Partition (1905) 88
Bengal Partition League 85
Bengal Provincial Muslim League (BPML) 86, 133
Bengal Secondary Education bill (1940) 91
Bengal Tenancy (Amendment) Act (1928) 40
Bengal Tenancy Amendment Act (1938) 50
Bengali *bhadralok* 21
Bengali Hindus 64; and partition 143
Bengali Muslims 23, 46, 48, 49; and regional identity 150
Benthal, Edward 3, 62
Bhadralok 71
Bhasani's *char* 246
Bhisham Sahni 165
Bihar riot (1946) 6
binary opposition 26
Birla, G. D. 133, 134
Bisher Dhonya 226
Bombay resolution (1946) 97
boundaries of two states 1
Boundary Commission 155; meeting at Belvedere Palace, Calcutta 157; memorandum and representations from the leading parties 158
Boundary confusion 218
BPCC (Bengal Provincial Congress Committee) 75, 77, 147
BPML 142
British India Association 77
British: divide and rule strategy 116; rule 2

Cabinet Mission Plan 168
Calcutta: and Noakhali riots 97; *bhardaloks* and Communal Award 66; as the heart of Bengal 138; as a Hindu-majority district 161; massacre 102
Calcutta Municipal (Amendment) Act (1939) 93
Calcutta press (1939), role of 93
Calcutta riot (1946) 21
Calcutta University 145
campaign: for a greater Pakistan 149; for *Musalmani Bangla* 47
carnage in Calcutta and Noakhali (1946) 113, 116

Carter, M. O. (Chittagong Divisional Commissioner) 103
Casey (Bengal governor) 3
census data (1941), importance of 170
Census of India (1931) 57
certificate procedure 40
Champion of the people 219–21
Chaudhury Lhaliq-uz-Zaman: and sylhet referendum 185
Chhilims 41
Childishness (Manik Bandyopadhyay) 224–6
citizenship 10
colonialism 1; and religion 16
Communal Award 20, 21, 25, 43, 50, 55, 60, 74, 75, 78, 85, 88, 115; and European dissatisfaction 62
communal chord, disrupted because of riots 111
communal differences, of Muslims with Hindus 51
communal identity of Bengalis 86
Communal League ministry 96
communal riots in Calcutta and Noakhali 112
communal settlement between the Hindus and Muslims 72
communalism, role of 37
communal-minded Muslim majority 144
complicity of the administration with the rioters 103
composition of the Boundary Commission 155
conflict between Khwaja group and Nazimuddin faction 149
Congress: as anti-peasant 40; complaint and referendum 188; influence of in Gurkha League 109; and KPP 48; memorandum and the 1941 census 160; and Muslim League as key players in the demarcation of boundaries 158; plan on the boundary of Bengal 160
Congress High Command 59, 74, 148; and Communal Award 68, 70
Congress Nationalist Party 72; and Communal Award 65, 68–9
Congress Parliamentary Board Election Manifesto 65
Congress Working Committee resolution of the Communal Award 65
constitution of communities 10
construction of a Muslim bloc 11
creation of two sovereign nation-states (1947) 89
creative literature and partition 234–6
cultural segregation between the Hindus and Muslims 42
Curzon 87

INDEX

Dainik Basumati 91
Darling, Malcom (Punjab governor) 165
Das, C. R. 22, 79; and anti-British platform 244
Dawn 98, 165
Debt Settlement Board (1939) 95
demand for Pakistan 85
Depressed Classes 60
Devaprasad Sarvadhikari (Vice Chancellor of Calcutta University) 64
Dhaka Nawab 136; group and partition 241
difficulty of the Muslim leadership 181
Direct Action 3, 9, 132
Direct Action Day 97, 100, 101, 116, 144
discontented servicemen, role of in riot 104
disjunction between local and national Congress leadership
District Board election (1927–8) 57, 71
divide et impera 2, 74, 85
division: between Hindus and Scheduled Castes 114; of Sylhet 195
Dressing Table, The 215–16
Dui Dik 226

Eastern Command in Calcutta riot, importance of 99
educated high caste bhadralok 48
Elections: (1937) 4, 23; (1946) 4, 13

Farash 41
Faridpur 42
Fazlul Haq 23, 48, 73, 94, 114
feudal forces, role of in partition 241
fragmentation of Bengal (1947) 86
Franchise Committee (1932) 56
Free State of Bengal 142

Gandhian Congress 2
Ghulam Sarwar 102–4, 107
Ghuznavi, A. H. 63, 72–3
Ghuznavi, A. K. 63
Gopinath Bordoloi 184
Government of India Act (1935) 55, 140
Great Calcutta Killing, The 8
Great Depression (1930s) 14, 30
Great Divide 5, 24, 26
Great Slump 40
Greater Pakistan, creation of 139

Hashim–Suhrawardy combination 136
high politics 2
Hindu: bhadralok 21, 71; communal forces 89; communalism 6; dominance in Bengal 245; domination 2, 14; landlord 36, 85; majority 3; moneylenders 36

Hindu Debattor Estates 90
Hindu mahajans, role of as money-lending institutions 91
Hindu Mahasabha 6, 15, 60, 68, 85, 91, 92, 106, 133, 148, 159, 197, 243; and Boundary Commission 163; as communal 6; and Communal Award 70; in municipal administration 95
Hindu Mahasabha High Command 107
Hindu Muslim identities as malleable, fuzzy and contextual 250
Hindu Raj 5, 17
Hindu-centric nation 88
Hindu-majority districts 24
Hindu–Muslim: animosity 218; differences 36; discord 42; division 87; guarantee for joint effort 67; identities and partition 249; quotidian life 211–13; relations 36; relationship 15; representation in Bengal 61; schism 19; unity 87
Hindus: in Bengal 19; of a truncated Bengal 111
history of partition as partition of communities 249
Homeland for the Hindus of Bengal 107
Hooghly River, importance of as a dividing line 146
Hookas 41
Hukumat 96

idea of separatism 79
In Search of Ismail Sheikh 216–17
independent and sovereign Bengal 149
Indian Chamber of commerce 133, 135
Indian Franchise Committee Report 63
Indian National Army as true patriots 242
inherent weaknesses of united Bengal movement 149
inheritance system, importance of 39
institutional level of politics 87
Interim Cabinet 162
intervention by the British administration 148
Iqbal 7
Ishapahani, M. A.: and referendum in Sylhet 186
Ishwar [God] 46
Islam Darshan 44
Islamic: *punthi* 23; revivalism 43; *Tamaddun* 96; words in Bengali 46
Ismat Chugtai's *Root* 249

Jalpaihati 221–3
Janmajanmantar or *mangolghat* 46
Jasimuddin 42

275

INDEX

Jehad 99
Jibananda Das 221–23
Jinnah 2, 9, 12, 27, 43, 49, 67, 97, 112, 132; complaint of Assam ministry interference during referendum 188; on the composition of the Boundary Commission 156; *14 points* 57; and Radcliffe Award 164; and referendum 186; two-nation theory 89
Joint Congress Corporation Election Board 95
joint electorate 59
June plan, the 154
jute-growing areas in Bengal 40

Kafir 17, 47, 99, 189
Kaiser-I-Hind, The 77
Kalmas from *Koran* 192
Khaliquzzaman 3
Khilafat merger 11
Khulafa-i-Rashidin 18
Khwaja group 136
Krishak movement 23
Krishak Praja Party (KPP) 23, 40, 48, 115, 133; alliance with Muslim League (1937) 38, 43, 245; and Bengal 245; formation 50

Lahore resolution (1940) 5, 49, 79, 135, 176
Laiquat Ali Khan 105, 137, 181
Language Movement in east Pakistan (1951–2) 150
League High Command and partition 191
League ministry, role of in the riot 101
League session (1940) 17
League's brutal majority of votes 145
League's communal design 115
Liberty 70
line system 184–5
literature and partition 249
Lord Willingdon (Viceroy) 61
Lothian (Chairman of the Franchise Committee) 69
Lucknow Pact (1916) 11, 57

Macdonald, Ramsay 56
Madhyabitta sreni (middle class) 39
Mahajans 37
Mahatma 104
Mahesh 212–3
maktabs, importance of 91
Mandal, J. N. 112–13
Maniruzzaman Islamabadi 43
Mansergh, Nicholas 8
Marwari Business interests 133

Maulvi nausher ali 58
Menon, V. P.: and Boundary Commission 164
Minto 87
Mitter, P. C. 64
mobilisation for an exclusive Hindu constituency 88
Modern Review 64, 116
Money Lenders Act (1939) 50
Montague–Chelmsford Reform (1919) 56–7, 59
Morley–Minto Reform (1909) 60, 78
Morning News 98, 105, 116
Mother of Dhirednu Mazumdar 232–3
Mountbatten 8, 24, 148, 162, 176; the last Viceroy 154; settling the Indian question 154; as a true Machiavellian 8
movement for Pakistan 13
Mrinal Sen 42
Mullahs 23, 102
mullahs and *moulvis* 18
multi-faceted public faces(s) 224–6
Muslim: anti-zamindari movement 37; homeland 14; identity as complex and bewildering 250; intellectuals 11; majoritarian politics 22; majority districts 147; majority in Bengal 64, 67; ministry in Bengal 114; minorities in the provinces 74; nationalism 45; as a separate community 89
Muslim Chamber of Commerce 135
Muslim leadership (KPP and the Muslim League) 90
Muslim leadership in Bengal 72;
Muslim League 3, 5, 12, 13, 26, 43, 48, 85; and Boundary Commission 161; High Command 86, 110; and partition 240; preparation for 186–9; and Sylhet 192
Muslim middle class: emergence of 244; English-educated 49
Muslim National Guard 99, 102–3, 108; and referendum 187, 189, 190, 193
Muslim peasantry 18; and Islam 240
Muslim state, creation of 13
Muslim-dominated small peasant economy 37
Muslim-majority areas 24
Muslim-majority provinces 3
Muslim-preponderant areas and Pakistan 163
Muslims: in Assam 27; in Bengal 27; in Bengal 64, 95; of Calcutta 9
Mussalmani Bangla 43, 45, 51; as a political majority 4

INDEX

nation formation 247
national bond and Pakistan 240
national constitution, importance of 74
national identity 10
nationalism 2, 15
nationalist agenda 10
Nationalist Party 76
Nausher Ali 94
Nawab Habibullah of Dhaka 48
Nawab's ahsan manzil 48
Nazrul Islam 46
New Bengal Association 159
New Council Bill 56
New Muslim Mazlis 48
newly elected Labour government, role of in India's independence 154
Nikhil Banga Praja Samiti 40
Nirad Chaudhuri 42, 43
no rent mentality 40
Noakhali-Tippera riot 104
non-Bengali character of the Khwaja group 136
Nongor 233
North West Frontier province 4
Nurul Amin, speaker of the Bengal legislative assembly 155
Nutun Ehudi 223

'official' voice, importance of 210
opposition to the Congress High Command 142
organised and unorganised worlds of politics 50
'other factors' in demarcation of boundaries 157

Pakistan 1, 3, 7; constituent assembly 155; formation 13; formula 14; as a nation 5; proposal 98; resolution (1940)14; as a service to Islam and Muslim fraternity 246
Pakistan or Partition of India 6
Pakistani press and Radcliffe Award 165
Palanka 213–14
participation of voters in referendum 193
partition 1; and arbitrary boundaries 235; and British 209; as a challenge to Hindu–Muslim organic unity 250; and communities 200–3; contradictory nature of 239–41; and creative writings 235; and 'multiple voices' 209; and Muslim businessmen 241; and 'nation' 202; and redefining of Hindus and Muslims 233–5; and 'self' 210; and a sense of home for Hindus 248; as a story of displacement and dispossession 230; as a story of re-negotiation or re-ordering 209
partition of Bengal and Punjab 192
Partition Council 162
partition riots (1946) 217
Pattavi Sitaramayya 105
Pendulum 217–18
Pirs 23, 44
plight of the scheduled castes in Bengal 138
Poigambor (saviour) 246
Police Headquarters in riots, role of 100
political economy of Bengal 36
Poona Pact (1932) 60, 66
possibility of greater Pakistan 149
Praja movement 41
Prasad–Jinnah dialogue and Communal Award 67
principle of balance and demarcation of boundary 168
Provincial election (1937) 74
public and private domains 16
Punjab Boundary Commission 156
Punjabi Muslim Guard, role of 109
Punthi 47
Punthi literature 248

Quaid-i-Azam 2, 135
Quarn 96

Rabindranath Tagore 19
Radcliffe Award 85, 163–5; and Algot Bagge 166; and confusion of boundaries 169; and Hindus 164; and mass protests 168; and Muslims 164; and referendum 198
Radcliffe Commission 26
Radcliffe, Cyril 26, 156
Rajendra Prasad, the Congress President 185
Rakter Daag 226
Ramananda Chatterjee, *Modern Review* editor 66
Ramrajya 17
referendum: conduct of administrative staff 194; declaration of results 195; and inclement weather 193; and Moulana Bhasani 198–9; preparation for 180; results 187–8; role of the Assam regiment 184; role of British army 184; role of Urdu-speaking Muslim National Guards 187; serious complaints 182–3; tendered and challenged votes 195
Reid, R. N. (Bengal Governor) 93
religion, importance of 16
religious: communalism 26; communities 55
renowned places in the history of Islam 47

INDEX

rent-receiving class 40
riots: in east and north Bengal 13; and failure of administration 242
rise of a Hindu bloc 88
rise of a *rentier* class 38
roots of the paradox of partition 239–40
rural Muslim 18

Saadullah and referendum 198–9
Sadat hasan Manto 234
Saogat 47
Sarat Chatterjee (writer) 71
Satinath Bhaduri 219–21
Satish Chandra Mishra, a Congress dissident 66
Scheduled Castes 77; of Bengal 112; population in the city 162
second partition of Bengal 89
Second World War (1939–45) 154
Secondary Education Bill 96
Secondary School, role of 92
sectarianism 2
secular communalism 26
secular ideology 11
segregated Hindu–Muslim identities 85
sense of ideological legitimation 14
separate electorate 58–9, 78, 93, 94; for Muslims 64
separate Muslim homeland 170
separatist politics 14
Shariat 7
Shimla Conference (1946) 5
Shyama Pradad Mookherjee 6, 15, 85, 92, 106, 197
Sind 4
socio-economic segregation of the Hindus and Muslims 41
sovereign independent Muslim state 4
Spear, Parcival 9
Star of India, The 5, 116, 134
Statesman, The 100
Stork, I. (Referendum Commissioner) 180
Story of the Tulsi Plant 232–3
subdivision of Sylhet 177
Subhas Chandra Bose 94; and Communal Award 70
Sucheta Kripalani 104
Sufi 13

Suhrawardy 9, 15, 100, 105, 108, 109, 112, 132, 161, 185
surgical operation 2
Swadeshi Movement (1905–8) 87, 147
Swadhinata 10
Sylhet 26; community formation in Assam 247; demographic composition of 178; physical features of 178; referendum 176–99
Syncretistic tradition 2, 23

Tale of a Muslim Woman 211–12
Talukdar-mahajans 14
Tamijuddin Khan 41
Tarakeswar Conference (1947) 106

terror in the Hindu *mohallas* 108
third-dominion movement 146
Trader-*mahajans* 14
Transfer of India, The 132
transfer of power (1947) 20, 24
two-nation theory 2, 17, 43, 49, 147

Udvastus (refugees) 232
ulemas 25
undivided and sovereign Bengal 132
un-fractured Bengali sensibilities 231–3
Unionist Party in Punjab 12
united Bengal: as an example of 'provincialism' 140; movement 147; proposal 139; scheme 142, 160; terms of agreement for 141–2
United Muslim Party 73
upper caste patrons (*kartas*) 248

Vibhajan 10
Vidyasagar 19
village *hats* and partition, importance of 246
violence during the referendum 193
vivisection of Bengal 86

Wajid Ali, S. 45
Wakf Board 90
Wavel 3
wealthy caste Hindus of east Bengal 113
White Horse 218

Zamindari domination in Bengal 41

For Product Safety Concerns and Information please contact our EU representative GPSR@taylorandfrancis.com
Taylor & Francis Verlag GmbH, Kaufingerstraße 24, 80331 München, Germany

www.ingramcontent.com/pod-product-compliance
Lightning Source LLC
Chambersburg PA
CBHW052216300426
44115CB00011B/1713